# MANAGING TIME IN RELATIONAL DATABASES

# Companion Web site

Ancillary materials are available online at:
www.elsevierdirect.com/companions/9780123750419

# MANAGING TIME IN RELATIONAL DATABASES

## How to Design, Update and Query Temporal Data

TOM JOHNSTON
RANDALL WEIS

AMSTERDAM • BOSTON • HEIDELBERG • LONDON
NEW YORK • OXFORD • PARIS • SAN DIEGO
SAN FRANCISCO • SINGAPORE • SYDNEY • TOKYO

Morgan Kaufmann Publishers is an imprint of Elsevier

MORGAN
KAUFMANN

Morgan Kaufmann Publishers is an imprint of Elsevier.
30 Corporate Drive, Suite 400, Burlington, MA 01803, USA

This book is printed on acid-free paper.

**Notices**
Knowledge and best practice in this field are constantly changing. As new research and experience broaden our understanding, changes in research methods, professional practices, or medical treatment may become necessary.

Practitioners and researchers must always rely on their own experience and knowledge in evaluating and using any information, methods, compounds, or experiments described herein. In using such information or methods they should be mindful of their own safety and the safety of others, including parties for whom they have a professional responsibility.

To the fullest extent of the law, neither the Publisher nor the authors, contributors, or editors, assume any liability for any injury and/or damage to persons or property as a matter of products liability, negligence or otherwise, or from any use or operation of any methods, products, instructions, or ideas contained in the material herein.

**Library of Congress Cataloging-in-Publication Data**
Application submitted

**British Library Cataloguing-in-Publication Data**
A catalogue record for this book is available from the British Library.

ISBN: 978-0-12-375041-9

For information on all Morgan Kaufmann publications,
visit our Web site at www.mkp.com or www.elsevierdirect.com

Printed in the United States of America
10  11  12  13  14    5  4  3  2  1

# CONTENTS

# ABOUT THE AUTHORS

## Tom Johnston

Tom Johnston is an independent consultant specializing in the design and management of data at the enterprise level. He has a doctorate in Philosophy, with an academic concentration in ontology, logic and semantics. He has spent his entire working career in business IT, in such roles as programmer, systems programmer, analyst, systems designer, data modeler and enterprise data architect. He has designed and implemented systems in over a dozen industries, including healthcare, telecommunications, banking, manufacturing, transportation and retailing. His current research interests are (i) the management of bi-temporal data with today's DBMS technology; (ii) overcoming this newest generation of information stovepipes—for example, in medical records and national security databases—by more cleanly separating the semantics of data from the syntax of its representation; and (iii) providing additional semantics for the relational model of data by supplementing its first-order predicate logic statements with modalities such as time and person.

## Randall J. Weis

Randall J Weis, founder and CEO of InBase, Inc., has more than 24 years of experience in IT, specializing in enterprise data architecture, including the logical and physical modeling of very large database (VLDB) systems in the financial, insurance and health care industries.

He has been implementing systems with stringent temporal and performance requirements for over 15 years. The bi-temporal pattern he developed for modeling history, retro activity and future dating was used for the implementation of IBM's Insurance Application Architecture (IAA) model. This pattern allows the multidimensional temporal view of data as of any given effective and assertion points in time.

InBase, Inc. has developed software used by many of the nation's largest companies, and is known for creating the first popular mainframe spellchecker, Lingo, early in Randy's career. Weis has been a senior consultant at InBase and other companies, such as PricewaterhouseCoopers LLP, Solving IT International

Inc., Visual Highway and Beyond If Informatics. Randy has been a presenter at various user groups, including Guide, Share, Midwest Database Users Group and Camp IT Expo, and has developed computer courses used in colleges and corporate training programs.

Randy had been married to his wife Marina for over 30 years, and has 3 children, Matt, Michelle and Nicolle. He plays guitar and sings; he enjoys running, and has run several marathons. He also creates web sites and produces commercial videos.

He may be reached via email at randyw@inbaseinc.com.

# PREFACE

Over time, things change—things like customers, products, accounts, and so forth. But most of the data we keep about things describes what they are like currently, not what they used to be like. When things change, we update the data that describes them so that the description remains current. But all these things have a history, and many of them have a future as well, and often data about their past or about their future is also important.

It is usually possible to restore and then to retrieve historical data, given enough time and effort. But businesses are finding it increasingly important to access historical data, as well as data about the future, without those associated delays and costs. More and more, business value attaches to the ability to directly and immediately access non-current data as easily as current data, and to do so with equivalent response times.

*Conventional* tables contain data describing what things are currently like. But to provide comparable access to data describing what things used to be like, and to what they may be like in the future, we believe it is necessary to combine data about the past, the present and the future in the same tables. Tables which do this, which contain data about what the objects they represent used to be like and also data about what they may be like later on, together with data about what those objects are like now, are *versioned* tables.

Versioned tables are one of two kinds of *uni-temporal* tables. In this book, we will show how the use of versioned tables lowers the cost and increases the value of *temporal data*, data that describes what things used to be like as well as what they are like now, and sometimes what they will be like as well. Costs, as we will see, are lowered by simplifying the design, maintenance and querying of temporal data. Value, as we will see, is increased by providing faster and more accurate answers to queries that access temporal data.

Another important thing about data is that, from time to time, we occasionally get it wrong. We might record the wrong data about a particular customer's status, indicating, for example, that a VIP customer is really a deadbeat. If we do, then as soon as we find out about the mistake, we will hasten to fix it by updating the customer's record with the correct data.

But that doesn't just correct the mistake. It also covers it up. Auditors are often able to reconstruct erroneous data from backups and logfiles. But for the ordinary query author, no trace remains in the database that the mistake ever occurred, let alone what the mistake was, or when it happened, or for how long it went undetected.

Fortunately, we can do better than that. Instead of overwriting the mistake, we can keep both the original customer record and its corrected copy in the same table, along with information about when and for how long the original was thought to be correct, and when we finally realized it wasn't and then did something about it. Moreover, while continuing to provide undisturbed, directly queryable, immediate access to the data that we currently believe is correct, we can also provide that same level of access to data that we once believed was correct but now realize is not correct.

There is no generally accepted term for this kind of table. We will call it an *assertion* table. Assertion tables, as we will see, are essential for recreating reports and queries, at a later time, when the objective is to retrieve the data as it was originally entered, warts and all. *Assertion tables* are the second of the two kinds of uni-temporal tables. The same data management methods which lower the cost and increase the value of versioned data also lower the cost and increase the value of asserted data.

There are also tables which combine versions and assertions, and combine them in the sense that every row in these tables is both a version and an assertion. These tables contain data about what we currently believe the objects they represent were/are/will be like, data about what we once believed but no longer believe those objects were/are/will be like, and also data about what we may in the future come to believe those objects were/are/will be like. Tables like these, tables whose rows contain data about both the past, the present and the future of things, and also about the past, the present and the future of our beliefs about those things, are *bi-temporal* tables.

In spite of several decades of work on temporal data, and a growing awareness of the value of real-time access to it, little has been done to help IT professionals manage temporal data in real-world databases. One reason is that a temporal extension to the SQL language has yet to be approved, even though a proposal to add temporal features to the language was submitted over fifteen years ago. Lacking approved standards to guide them, DBMS vendors have been slow to build temporal support into their products.

In the meantime, IT professionals have developed home-grown support for versioning, but have paid almost no attention to bi-temporality. In many cases, they don't know what bi-temporality is. In most cases, their business users, unaware of the benefits of bi-temporal data, don't know to ask for such functionality. And among those who have at least heard of bi-temporality, or to whom we have tried to explain it, we have found two common responses. One is that Ralph Kimball solved this problem a long time ago with his three kinds of slowly changing dimensions. Another is that we can get all the temporal functionality we need by simply versioning the tables to which we wish to add temporal data.

But both responses are mistaken. Slowly changing dimensions do not support bi-temporal data management at all. Nor does versioning. Both are methods of managing versions; but both also fall, as we shall see, far short of the extensive support for versioning that Asserted Versioning provides.

# Objectives of this Book

## Seamless Access to Temporal Data

One objective of this book is to describe how to manage uni-temporal and bi-temporal data in relational databases in such a way that they can be seamlessly accessed together with current data.[1] By "seamlessly" we mean (i) maintained with transactions simple enough that anyone who writes transactions against conventional tables could write them; (ii) accessed with queries simple enough that anyone who writes queries against conventional tables could write them; and (iii) executed with performance similar to that for transactions and queries that target conventional data only.

## Encapsulation of Temporal Data Structures and Processes

A second objective is to describe how to encapsulate the complexities of uni-temporal and bi-temporal data management. These complexities are nowhere better illustrated than in a book published ten years ago by Dr. Richard Snodgrass, the

---

[1]Both forms of temporal data can be implemented in non-relational databases also. For that matter, they can be implemented with a set of flat files. We use the language of relational technology simply because the ubiquity of relational database technology makes that terminology a lingua franca within business IT departments.

leading computer scientist in the field. In this book, *Developing Time-Oriented Database Applications in SQL* (Morgan-Kaufmann, San Francisco, 2000), Dr. Snodgrass provides extensive examples of temporal schemas and also of the SQL, for several different relational DBMSs, that is required to make uni- and bi-temporality work, and especially to enforce the constraints that must be satisfied as temporal data is created and maintained. Many of these SQL examples are dozens of lines long, and quite complex.

This is not the kind of code that should be written over and over again, each time a new database application is developed. It is code that insures the integrity of the database regardless of the applications that use that database. And so until that code is written by vendors into their DBMS products, it is code that should exist as an interface between applications and the DBMS that manages the database—a single codebase used by multiple applications, developed and maintained independently of the applications that will use it. A codebase which plays this role is sometimes called a *data access layer* or a *persistence and query service framework*.

So we have concluded that the best way to provide temporal functionality for databases managed with today's DBMSs, and accessed with today's SQL, is to encapsulate that complexity. Asserted Versioning does this. In doing so, it also provides an enterprise solution to the problem of managing temporal data, thus supporting both the semantic and physical interoperability of temporal data across all the databases in the enterprise.

Asserted Versioning encapsulates the design, maintenance and querying of both uni-temporal and bi-temporal data. *Design encapsulation* means that data modelers do not have to design temporal data structures. Instead, declarative specifications replace that design work. These declarations specify, among other things, which entities in a logical data model are to become bi-temporal tables when physically generated, which column or columns constitute business keys unique to the object represented, and between which pairs of tables there will exist a temporal form of referential integrity.

Maintenance encapsulation and query encapsulation mean, as we indicated earlier, that inserts, updates and deletes to bi-temporal tables, and queries against them, are simple enough that anyone who could write them against non-temporal tables could also write them against Asserted Versioning's temporal tables. *Maintenance encapsulation*, in the Asserted Versioning Framework (AVF) we are developing, is provided by an API, Calls to which may be replaced by native SQL issued directly to a

DBMS once temporal extensions to SQL are approved by standards committees and implemented by vendors.[2] Functioning in this way as a *persistence framework*, what the AVF persists is not simply data in relational tables. It persists both assertions and versions, and it enforces the semantic constraints between and among these rows which are the temporal analogues of entity integrity and referential integrity.

Functioning as a *query service framework*, Asserted Versioning provides query encapsulation for access to *current* data by means of a set of views which allow all queries against current data to continue to work, without modification. Query encapsulation is also provided for queries which need seamless access to any combination and range of past, present and future data, along either or both of two temporal dimensions. With asserted version tables guaranteed to contain only semantically well-formed bi-temporal data, queries against those tables can be remarkably simple, requiring only the addition of one or two point or period of time predicates to an otherwise identical query against current data.

## Enterprise Contextualization

A third objective of this book is to explain how to implement temporal data management as an enterprise solution. The alternative, of course, is to implement it piecemeal, as a series of tactical solutions. With tactical solutions, developed project by project for different applications and different databases, some will support temporal semantics that others will not support. Where the same semantics are supported, the schemas and the code that support them will usually be different and, in some cases, radically different. In most cases, the code that supports temporal semantics will be embedded in the same programs that support the application-specific semantics that have nothing to do with temporality. Federated queries, attempting to join temporal data across databases temporalized in different ways by different tactical solutions, will inevitably fail. In fixing them, those queries will often become several times more complex than they would have been if they had been joining across a unified enterprise solution.

---

[2]As we go to press, we are attempting to support "Instead Of" triggers in release 1 of the AVF. With these triggers, single-statement SQL inserts, updates and deletes can be translated by the AVF into the SQL statements that physically modify the database. Often, this translation generates several SQL statements from the single statement submitted to it.

Asserted Versioning is that enterprise solution. Every table, in every database, that is created as an asserted version table, or that is converted into an asserted version table, will support the full range of bi-temporal semantics. A single unit of code—our Asserted Versioning Framework (AVF), or your own implementation of these concepts—will support every asserted version table in every database.

This code will be physically separate from application code. All logic to maintain temporal data, consequently, will be removed from application programs and replaced, at every point, by an API Call to the AVF. Federated queries against temporal data will not need to contain ad hoc manipulations whose sole purpose is to resolve differences between different implementations of the same temporal semantics, or to scale a more robust implementation for one table down to a less expressive one for another table.

As an enterprise solution, Asserted Versioning is also a bridge to the future. That future is one in which temporal functionality will be provided by commercial DBMSs and directly invoked by SQL transactions and queries.[3] But Asserted Versioning can be implemented now, at a pace and with the priorities chosen by each enterprise. It is a way for businesses to begin to prepare for that future by removing procedural support for temporal data from their applications and replacing it with declarative Call statements which invoke the AVF. Hidden behind API Calls and views, the eventual conversion from Asserted Versioning to commercially implemented solutions, if the business chooses to make that conversion, will be nearly transparent to the enterprise. Most of the work of conversion will already have been done.

But other migration strategies are also possible. One is to leave the AVF in place, and let future versions of the AVF retire its own code and instead invoke the temporal support provided by these future DBMSs, as vendors make that support available. As we will see, in particular in Chapters 12, 13 and 16, there is important bi-temporal functionality provided by Asserted Versioning that is not yet even a topic of discussion within the computer science community. With the Asserted Versioning Framework remaining in place, a business can continue to

---

[3]Although the SQL standard does not yet include temporal extensions to accommodate bi-temporal data, Oracle Corporation has provided support for several aspects of bi-temporality in its 11 g Workspace Manager. We review Workspace Manager, and compare it to Asserted Versioning, in a separate document available on our Elsevier webpage and also at AssertedVersioning.com.

support that important functionality while migrating to commercial implementations of specific temporal features as those implementations become available, and it can do this without needing to modify application code.

## Internalization of Pipeline Datasets

The final objective of this book is to describe how to bring pending transactions into the production tables that are their targets, and how to retain posted transactions in those same tables. *Pending transactions* are insert, update and delete statements that have been written but not yet submitted to the applications that maintain the production database. Sometimes they are collected outside the target database, in batch transaction files. More commonly, they are collected inside the target database, in batch transaction tables. *Posted transactions*, as we use the term, are copies of data about to be inserted, and before-images of data about to be updated or deleted.

Borrowing a metaphor common to many logistics applications, we think of pending transactions as existing at various places along *inflow pipelines*, and posted transactions as data destined for some kind of logfile, and as moving towards that destination along *outflow pipelines*. So if we can bring pending transactions into their target tables, and retain posted transactions in those same tables, we will, in terms of this metaphor, have *internalized* pipeline datasets.[4]

Besides production tables, the batch transaction files which update them, and the logfiles which retain the history of those updates, production data exists in other datasets as well. Some production tables have history tables paired with them, in which all past versions of the data in those production tables is kept. Sometimes a group of rows in one or more production tables is locked and then copied to another physical location. After being worked on in these *staging areas*, the data is moved back to its points of origin, overlaying the original locked copies of that data.

In today's world of IT data management, a great deal of the Operations budget is consumed in managing these multiple physical datasets across which production data is spread. In one

---

[4]"Dataset" is a term with a long history, and not as much in use as it once was. It refers to a named collection of data that the operating system, or the DBMS, can recognize and manage as a single object. For example, anything that shows up in Windows Explorer, including folders, is a dataset. In later chapters, we will need to use the term in a slightly different way, but for now, this is what we mean by it.

sense, that's the *entire* job of IT Operations. The IT Operations schedule, and various workflow management systems, then attempt to coordinate updates to these scattered datasets so those updates happen in the right sequence and produce the right results. Other tools used to insure a consistent, sequenced and coordinated set of production data across the entire system of datasets and pipelines, include DBMS triggers associated with various pre-conditions or post-conditions, asynchronous trans-action managers, and manually coordinated asynchronous feeds from one database to another.

These processes and environments are both expensive to maintain and conducive to error. For example, with history tables, and work-in-progress in external staging areas, and a series of pending transaction datasets, a change to a single semantic unit of information, e.g. to the policy type of an insurance policy, may need to be applied to many physical copies of that information. Even with triggers and other automated processes to help, some of those datasets may be overlooked, especially the external staging areas that are not always there, and so are not part of regularly scheduled maintenance activity. If the coordination is asynchronous, i.e. not part of a single atomic and isolated unit of work, then latency is involved, a period of time in which the database, or set of databases, is in an inconsistent state. Also, error recovery must take these interdependencies into consideration; and while the propagation of updates across multiple datasets may be partially or completely automated, recovery from errors in those processes usually is not, and often requires manual intervention.

This scattering of production data also affects those who write queries. To get the information they are looking for, query authors must know about these scattered datasets because they cannot assume that all the data that might be qualified by their queries is contained in one place. Across these datasets, there are differences in the life cycle stage of the various datasets (e.g. pending transactions, posted transactions, past, present or current versions, etc.). Across these datasets, there will inevitably be some level of redundancy. Frequently, no one table will contain all the instances of a given type (e.g. all policies) that are needed to satisfy a query.

Think of a world of corporate data in which none of that is necessary, a world in which all pipeline datasets are contained in the single table that is their destination or their point of origin. In this world, maintaining data is a "submit it and forget it" activity, not one in which maintenance transactions are initially created, and then must be shepherded through a series of intermediate rest and recuperation points until they are eventually applied to their target tables. In this world, a query is never compromised because some source of relevant data was overlooked. In this world, production tables contain *all* the data about their objects.

## Asserted Versioning as Methodology and as Software

This book presents the concepts on the basis of which a business could choose to build its own framework for managing temporal data. But it also describes software which we ourselves are building as we write this book. A prototype of this software is available at our website, AssertedVersioning.com, where interested users can submit both maintenance transactions and queries against a small bi-temporal database. Our software—the Asserted Versioning Framework, or AVF—generates bi-temporal tables from conventional logical data models, ones which are identical to models that would generate non-temporal database schemas. The data modeler has only to indicate which entities in the logical model should be generated as bi-temporal tables, and to supply as metadata some additional parameters telling the AVF how to manage those tables. There is no specific temporal design work to do.

In its current manifestation, this software generates both its schemas, and the code which implements the rules enforcing temporal data semantics, from ERwin data models only, and relies heavily on ERwin's user-defined properties and its macro scripting language. Computer Associates provided technical resources during the development of this software, and we expect to work closely with them as we market it.

Additional information about Asserted Versioning, as well as a working prototype of this product, can be found on our website, AssertedVersioning.com. We have also recorded several seminars explaining these concepts and demonstrating their implementation in our software. These seminars are available at our website, AssertedVersioning.com, and from Morgan-Kaufmann at www.elsevierdirect.com/companions/9780123750419.

The authors have filed a provisional patent application for Asserted Versioning, and are in the process of converting it to a patent application as this book goes to press. The authors will freely grant any non-software-vendor company the right to develop its own temporal data management software based on the concepts presented in this book and protected by their forthcoming patent, as long as that software is for use by that company only, and is not sold, leased, licensed or given away to any other company or individual.

# Acknowledgements

This book began as a bi-monthly series in *DM /Review* magazine (now *Information Management*) in May of 2006, and the series continued in an on-line companion publication for nearly three years. We want to thank the two senior editors, Mary Jo Nott and, succeeding her, Julie Langenkamp, for their encouragement and for the opportunity they gave us to develop our ideas in that forum.

Our editors at Morgan-Kaufmann were Rick Adams and Heather Scherer. They provided guidance when we needed it, but also stood back when we needed that. Their encouragement, and their trust that we would meet our deadlines even when we fell behind, are very much appreciated.

Our reviewers for this book were Joe Celko, Theo Gantos, Andy Hessey, Jim McCrory, Stan Muse and Mark Winters. They have provided valuable help, suggesting how the organization of the material could be improved, pointing out topics that required more (or less) explanation, and challenging conclusions that they did not agree with. Bi-temporality is a difficult topic, and it is easy to write unclearly about it. Our reviewers have helped us eliminate the most egregious un-clarities, and to sharpen our ideas. But less than perfectly pellucid language certainly remains, and ideas can always be improved. For these and any other shortcomings, we are solely responsible.

We would also like to thank Dr. Rick Snodgrass who, in the summer of 2008, took a couple of unknown writers seriously enough to engage in a lengthy email exchange with them. It is he who identified, and indeed gave the name to, the idea of deferred transactions as a new and possibly useful contribution to the field of data management. After several dozen substantive email exchanges, Rick concluded that our approach contained interesting ideas worth exploring; and it was in good part because of this that my co-author and I were encouraged to write this book.

# Tom Johnston's Acknowledgements

Needless to say, I could not have written this book, nor indeed developed these ideas, without the contributions of my co-author, Randy Weis. Randy and I have often described our relationship as one in which we come up with an idea, and then I think through it in English while he thinks through it in code. And this is pretty much how things work with us.

As this book and our software co-evolved, there was a lot of backtracking and trying out different ways of accomplishing the same thing. If we had not been able to foresee the implementation consequences of many of our theoretical decisions, we could have ended up with a completed design that served very poorly as the blueprint for functioning software. Instead, we have both: a blueprint, and the functioning software which it describes. This book is that blueprint. Our Asserted Versioning Framework is that software.

I have had only two experiences in my career in which that think/design/build iterative cycle was as successful as I could ever have wished for; and my work with Randy has been one of them. Developing software isn't just constructing the schemas and writing the code that implements a set of ideas. Building software is a process which both winnows out bad ideas and suggests—to designers who remain close to the development process, as well as to developers who are already deeply involved in the design process—both better ideas and how the original design might be altered to make use of them. In this iterative creative process, while Randy did most of the software development, the ideas and the design are ours together. Randy has been an ideal collaborative partner, and I hope I have been a good one.

I would also like to thank Jean Ann Brown for her insightful comments and questions raised in several conversations we had while the articles on which this book is based were being written. She was especially helpful in providing perspective for the material in Chapter 1. Her friendship and encouragement over the course of a professional relationship of nearly twenty years is deeply appreciated. I also want to thank Debbie Dean, Cindi Morrison, and Ian Rushton, who were both supportive and helpful when, nearly five years ago, I was making my first attempt to apply bi-temporal concepts to real-world databases.

My deepest values and patterns of thought have evolved in the close partnership and understanding I have shared for over forty years with my wife, Trish. I would not be the person I am without her, and I would not think the way I do but for her.

My two sons are a source of inspiration and pride for me. My older son, Adrian, has already achieved recognition as a professional philosopher. My younger son Ian's accomplishments are less publically visible, but are every bit as substantive.

## Randy Weis' Acknowledgements

Mark Winters and I worked closely together in the mid-90's designing and implementing a bi-temporal data model and a corresponding application based on IBM's Insurance Application Architecture (IAA) conceptual model. The bi-temporal pattern was developed to support the business requirement to be able to view the data and recreate any report exactly as it appeared when originally created, and also as of any other given point in time.

Mark was one of the key architects on this project, and is currently an Enterprise Data Architect at one of the country's leading health insurers. He has continued to be a strong proponent of using bi-temporality, and has developed a series of scenarios to communicate the business value of bi-temporality and to validate the integrity of the application we built. Mark's contribution to this work has been invaluable.

There have also been other Data Architects who have helped me develop the skills necessary to think through and solve these complex problems. Four of these excellent Data Architects are Kim Kraemer, Dave Breymeyer, Paul Dwyer and Morgan Bulman. Two other people I would like to thank are Scott Chisholm and Addison McGuffin, who provided valuable ideas and fervent support in this venture. There are others, too many to mention by name, who have helped me and taught me throughout the years. I would like to thank all of them, too.

This book would have never come to fruition without my coauthor, Tom Johnston. I wanted to write a book on this topic for several years because I saw the significant value that bi-temporality brings to business IT organizations and to the systems they design. Tom had the skills, experience and in-depth knowledge about this topic to make this dream a reality. Not only is Tom an excellent writer, he also knows how to take scattered thoughts and organize them so they can be effectively communicated.

Moreover, Tom is a theoretician. He recognizes patterns, and always tries to make them more useful by integrating them into larger patterns. But he has worked in the world of business IT for his entire career. And in that world, theory is fine, but it must ultimately justify itself in practice. Tom's commitment to theory that works is just as strong as his attraction to patterns that fit together in a beautiful harmony.

Besides Mark Winters, Tom is the only person I ever met who really understands bi-temporal data management. Tom's understanding, writing abilities and contributions to this work are priceless. His patience and willingness to compromise and work with me on various points are very much appreciated, and contributed to the success of this book. It has been great working with Tom on this project. Not only has Tom been an excellent coauthor, but he has also become a wonderful and trusted friend.

I also want to thank my wife, Marina. She has believed in me and supported me for over thirty years. Her faith in me helped me to believe in myself: that my dreams, our dreams, with God's blessings, were attainable. She was also very patient with my working late into the night. She understood me when she was trying to talk with me, and I was fixated on my laptop. She would serve me like I was a king, even when I felt like the court jester. Her encouragement helped me accomplish so much, and I couldn't have done any of it without her. My children, Matt, Michelle and Nicolle were also very supportive while I chased my dreams. I thank God for the opportunities I have been given and for my wonderful family and friends.

Finally, we would both like to thank you, our readers, the current and next generation of business analysts, information architects, systems designers, data modelers, DBAs and application developers. You are the ones who will introduce these methods of temporal data management to your organizations, and explain the value of seamless real-time access to temporal data to your business users. Successful implementation of seamless access to all data, and not just to data about the present, will result in better customer service, more accurate accounting, improved forecasting, and better tracking of data used in research. The methods of managing temporal data introduced in this book will enhance systems used in education, finance, health care, insurance, manufacturing, retailing and transportation—all industries in which the authors have had consulting experience.

In using these methods, you will play your own role in their evolution. If DBMS vendors are wise, your experiences will influence their implementation of server-side temporal functionality and of your interfaces to that functionality. If standards committees are wise, your experiences will influence the evolution of the SQL language itself, as it is extended to support uni- and bi-temporal constructs and transformations. If IT and business management in your own organizations are wise, and if your initial implementations are successful, then your organizations will be positioned on the leading edge of a revolution in the management of data, a position from which business advantage over trailing edge adopters will continue to be enjoyed for many years.

Theory is practical, as we hope this book will demonstrate. But the relationship of theory and practice is a two-way street. Computer scientists are theoreticians, working from theory down to practice, from mathematical abstractions to their best understandings of how those abstractions might be put to work. IT professionals are practitioners, working from specific problems up to best practice approaches to classes of similar problems.

Common ground can sometimes be reached, ground where the "best understandings" of computer scientists meet the "best practices" of IT professionals. Here, theoreticians may glimpse the true complexities of the problems to which their theories are intended to be relevant. Here, practitioners may glimpse the potential of powerful abstractions to make their best practices even better.

We conclude with an example and a maxim about the interplay of theory and practice.

The example: Leonard Euler, one of history's greatest mathematicians, created the field of mathematical graph theory while thinking about various paths he had taken crossing the bridges of Konigsberg, Germany during Sunday afternoon walks.

The maxim: to paraphrase Immanuel Kant, one of history's greatest philosophers: "theory without practice is empty; practice without theory is blind".

## Glossary References

Glossary entries whose definitions form strong interdependencies are grouped together in the following list. The same glossary entries may be grouped together in different ways at the end of different chapters, each grouping reflecting the semantic perspective of each chapter. There will usually be several other, and often many other, glossary entries that are not included in the list, and we recommend that the Glossary be consulted whenever an unfamiliar term is encountered.

Allen relationships
Asserted Versioning
Asserted Versioning Framework (AVF)

assertion table
bi-temporal table
conventional table
non-temporal table
uni-temporal table
version table
deferred transaction
design encapsulation
maintenance encapsulation
query encapsulation
event
object
thing
seamless access
temporal data

# AN INTRODUCTION TO TEMPORAL DATA MANAGEMENT

## Chapter Contents

Historical data first manifested itself as the backups and logfiles we kept and hoped to ignore. We hoped to ignore those datasets because if we had to use them, it meant that something had gone wrong, and we had to recover a state of the database prior to when that happened. Later, as data storage and access technology made it possible to manage massively larger volumes of data than ever before, we brought much of that historical data on-line and organized it in two different ways. On the one hand, backups were stacked on top of one another and turned into data warehouses. On the other hand, logfiles were supplemented with foreign keys and turned into data marts.

We don't mean to say that this is how the IT or computer science communities thought of the development and evolution of warehouses and marts, as it was happening over the last two decades. Nor is it how they think of warehouses and marts

Managing Time in Relational Databases. Doi: 10.1016/B978-0-12-375041-9.00023-6

today. Rather, this is more like what philosophers call a *rational reconstruction* of what happened. It seems to us that, in fact, warehouses *are* the form that backup files took when brought on-line and assembled into a single database instance, and data marts *are* the form that transaction logs took when brought on-line and assembled into their database instances. The former is history as a series of states that things go through as they change over time. The latter is history as a series of those changes themselves.

But warehouses and data marts are *macro* structures. They are structures of temporal data at the level of databases and their instances. In this book, we are concerned with more *micro*-level structures, specifically structures at the level of tables and their instances. And at this level, temporal data is still a second-class citizen. To manage it, developers have to build temporal structures and the code to manage them, by hand. In order to fully appreciate both the costs and the benefits of managing temporal data at this level, we need to see it in the context of methods of temporal data management as a whole. In Chapter 1, the context will be historical. In the next chapter, the context will be taxonomic.

In this book, we will not be discussing hardware, operating systems, local and distributed storage networks, or other advances in the platforms on which we construct the places where we keep our data and the pipelines through which we move it from one place to another. Of course, without significant progress in all of these areas, it would not be possible to support the on-line management of temporal data. The reason is that, since the total amount of non-current data we might want to manage on-line is far greater than the total amount of current data that we already do manage on-line, the technologies for managing on-line data could easily be overwhelmed were those technologies not rapidly advancing themselves.

We have already mentioned, in the Preface, the differences between non-temporal and temporal data and, in the latter category, the two ways that time and data are interwoven. However it is not until Part 2 that we will begin to discuss the complexities of bi-temporal data, and how Asserted Versioning renders that complexity manageable. But since there are any number of things we could be talking about under the joint heading of *time* and *data*, and since it would be helpful to narrow our focus a little before we get to those chapters, we would like to introduce a simple mental model of this key set of distinctions.

# Non-Temporal, Uni-Temporal and Bi-Temporal Data

Figure Part 1.1 is an illustration of a row of data in three different kinds of relational table.[1] *id* is our abbreviation for "unique identifier", PK for "primary key", $bd_1$ and $ed_1$ for one pair of columns, one containing the begin date of a time period and the other containing the end date of that time period, and $bd_2$ and $ed_2$ for columns defining a second time period.[2] For the sake of simplicity, we will use tables that have single-column unique identifiers.

The first illustration in Figure Part 1.1 is of a non-temporal table. This is the common, garden-variety kind of table that we usually deal with. We will also call it a *conventional* table. In this non-temporal table, *id* is the primary key. For our illustrative purposes, all the other data in the table, no matter how many columns it consists of, is represented by the single block labeled "data".

In a non-temporal table, each row stands for a particular instance of what the table is about. So in a Customer table, for example, each row stands for a particular customer and each customer has a unique value for the customer identifier. As long as the business has the discipline to use a unique identifier value for each customer, the DBMS will faithfully guarantee that the Customer table will never concurrently contain two or more rows for the same customer.

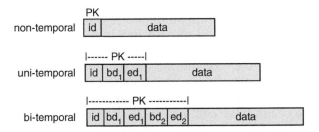

**Figure Part 1.1** Non-Temporal, Uni-Temporal and Bi-Temporal Data.

---

[1]Here, and throughout this book, we use the terminology of relational technology, a terminology understood by data management professionals, rather than the less well-understood terminology of relational theory. Thus, we talk about tables rather than relations, and about rows in those tables rather than tuples.

[2]This book illustrates the management of temporal data with time periods delimited by dates, although we believe it will be far more common for developers to use timestamps instead. Our use of dates is motivated primarily by the need to display rows of temporal data on a single printed line.

The second illustration in Figure Part 1.1 is of a uni-temporal Customer table. In this kind of table, we may have multiple rows for the same customer. Each such row contains data describing that customer during a specified period of time, the period of time delimited by $bd_1$ and $ed_1$.

In order to keep this example as straightforward as possible, let's agree to refrain from a discussion of whether we should or could add just the period begin date, or just the period end date, to the primary key, or whether we should add both dates. So in the second illustration in Figure Part 1.1, we show both $bd_1$ and $ed_1$ added to the primary key, and in Figure Part 1.2 we show a sample uni-temporal table.

Following a standard convention we used in the articles leading up to this book, primary key column headings are underlined. For convenience, dates are represented as a month and a year. The two rows for customer id-1 show a history of that customer over the period May 2012 to January 2013. From May to August, the customer's data was 123; from August to January, it was 456.

Now we can have multiple rows for the same customer in our Customer table, and we (and the DBMS) can keep them distinct. Each of these rows is a *version* of the customer, and the table is now a versioned Customer table. We use this terminology in this book, but generally prefer to add the term "uni-temporal" because the term "uni-temporal" suggests the idea of a single temporal dimension to the data, a single kind of time associated with the data, and this notion of one (or two) temporal dimensions is a useful one to keep in mind. In fact, it may be useful to think of these two temporal dimensions as the X and Y axes of a Cartesian graph, and of each row in a bi-temporal table as represented by a rectangle on that graph.

Now we come to the last of the three illustrations in Figure Part 1.1. Pretty clearly, we can transform the second table into this third table exactly the same way we transformed the first into the second: we can add another pair of dates to the primary key. And just as clearly, we achieve the same effect. Just as the first two date columns allow us to keep multiple rows all having the same identifier, $bd_2$ and $ed_2$ allow us to keep

| id | $bd_1$ | $ed_1$ | data |
|---|---|---|---|
| id-1 | May12 | Aug12 | 123 |
| id-1 | Aug12 | Jan13 | 456 |
| id-2 | Jul12 | Nov12 | 345 |

**Figure Part 1.2** A Uni-Temporal Table.

multiple rows all having the same identifier *and* the same first two dates.

At least, that's the idea. In fact, as we all know, a five-column primary key allows us to keep any number of rows in the table as long as the value in just one column distinguishes that primary key from all others. So, for example, the DBMS would allow us to have multiple rows with the same identifier and with all four dates the same except for, say, the first begin date.

This first example of bi-temporal data shows us several important things. However, it also has the potential to mislead us if we are not careful. So let's try to draw the valid conclusions we can from it, and remind ourselves of what conclusions we should not draw.

First of all, the third illustration in Figure Part 1.1 does show us a valid bi-temporal schema. It is a table whose primary key contains three logical components. The first is a unique identifier of the object which the row represents. In this case, it is a specific customer. The second is a unique identifier of a period of time. That is the period of time during which the object existed with the characteristics which the row ascribes to it, e.g. the period of time during which that particular customer had that specific name and address, that specific customer status, and so on.

The third logical component of the primary key is the pair of dates which define a second time period. This is the period of time during which we believe that the row is correct, that what it says its object is like during that first time period is indeed true. The main reason for introducing this second time period, then, is to handle the occasions on which the data is in fact wrong. For if it is wrong, we now have a way to both retain the error (for auditing or other regulatory purposes, for example) and also replace it with its correction.

Now we can have two rows that have exactly the same identifier, and exactly the same first time period. And our convention will be that, of those two rows, the one whose second time period begins later will be the row providing the correction, and the one with the earlier second time period will be the row being corrected. Figure Part 1.3 shows a sample bi-temporal table containing versions and a correction to one of those versions.

In the column $ed_2$, the value 9999 represents the highest date the DBMS can represent. For example, with SQL Server, that date is 12/31/9999. As we will explain later, when used in end-date columns, that value represents an unknown end date, and the time period it delimits is interpreted as still current.

The last row in Figure Part 1.3 is a correction to the second row. Because of the date values used, the example assumes that

| id | $bd_1$ | $ed_1$ | $bd_2$ | $ed_2$ | data |
|------|--------|--------|--------|--------|------|
| id-1 | May12 | Aug12 | May12 | 9999 | 123 |
| id-1 | Aug12 | Jan13 | Aug12 | Mar13 | 456 |
| id-2 | Jul12 | Nov12 | Jul12 | 9999 | 345 |
| id-1 | Aug12 | Jan13 | Mar13 | 9999 | 457 |

**Figure Part 1.3** A Bi-Temporal Table.

it is currently some time later than March 2013. Until March 2013, this table said that customer id-1 had data 456 from August 2013 to the following January. But beginning on March 2013, the table says that customer id-1 had data 457 during exactly that same period of time.

We can now recreate a report (or run a query) about customers during that period of time that is either an *as-was* report or an *as-is* report. The report specifies a date that is between $bd_2$ and $ed_2$. If the specified date is any date from August 2012 to March 2013, it will produce an as-was report. It will show only the first three rows because the specified date does not fall within the second time period for the fourth row in the table. But if the specified date is any date from March 2013 onwards, it will produce an as-is report. That report will show all rows but the second row because it falls within the second time period for those rows, but does not fall within the second time period for the second row.

Both reports will show the continuous history of customer id-1 from May 2012 to January 2013. The first will report that customer id-1 had data 123 and 456 during that period of time. The second will report that customer id-1 had data 123 and 457 during that same period of time. So $bd_1$ and $ed_1$ delimit the time period out in the world during which things were as the data describes them, whereas $bd_2$ and $ed_2$ delimit a time period in the table, the time period during which we claimed that things were as each row of data says they were.

Clearly, with both rows in the table, any query looking for a version of that customer, i.e. a row representing that customer as she was at a particular point or period in time, will have to distinguish the two rows. Any query will have to specify which one is the correct one (or the incorrect one, if that is the intent). And, not to anticipate too much, we may notice that if the end date of the second time period on the incorrect row is set to the same value as the begin date of the second time period on its correcting row, then simply by querying for rows whose second time period contains the current date, we will always be sure to get the correct row for our specific version of our specific customer.

That's a lot of information to derive from Figures Part 1.1, Part 1.2 and Part 1.3. But many experienced data modelers and their managers will have constructed and managed structures somewhat like that third row shown in Figure Part 1.1. Also, most computer scientists who have worked on issues connected with bi-temporal data will recognize that row as an example of a bi-temporal data structure.

This illustrates, we think, the simple fact that when good minds think about similar problems, they often come up with similar solutions. Similar solutions, yes; but not identical ones. And here is where we need to be careful not to be misled.

## Not to Be Misled

Given the bi-temporal structure shown here, any good IT development team could transform a conventional table into a bi-temporal table of that same general structure. But there is a significant amount of complexity which must then be managed. For example, consider the fact mentioned just above that, with a table like this, the DBMS will permit us to insert a new row which is identical to a row already on the table except for the begin date of the first time period or, for that matter, except for the end date of the first time period. But that would be a mistake, a mistake that would allow "overlapping versions" into the table.

Once again, experienced data management professionals may be one step ahead of us. They may already have recognized the potential for this kind of mistake in the kind of primary key that the third table illustrates, and so what we have just pointed out will not be news to them.

But that mistake, the "overlapping versions" mistake, is just one thing a development group will have to write code to prevent. There is an entire web of constraints, beyond those the DBMS can enforce for us, which determine when inserts, updates and deletes to uni-temporal or bi-temporal tables are and are not valid. For example, think of the possibilities of getting it wrong when it comes to a delete cascade that begins with, or comes to as it cascades, a row in a temporal table; or with referential integrity dependencies in which the related rows are temporal. Or the possibilities of writing queries that have to correctly specify three logical components to select the one row the query author is interested in, two of those components being time periods that may or may not intersect in various ways. Continuing on, consider the possibilities involved in joining bi-temporal tables to one another, or to uni-temporal tables, or to non-temporal tables!

This is where computer science gets put to good use. By now, after more than a quarter-century of research, academics are likely to have identified most of the complex issues involved in managing temporal data, even if they haven't come to an agreement on how to deal with all of them. And given the way they think and write, they are likely to have described these issues, albeit in their own mathematical dialects, at a level of detail from which we IT professionals can both design and code with confidence that further bi-temporal complexities probably do not lie hidden in the bushes.

So one reason IT practitioners should not look at Figures Part 1.1, Part 1.2 and Part 1.3 and conclude that there is nothing new here is that there is a great deal more to managing temporal data than just writing the DDL for temporal schemas. And if many practitioners remain ignorant of these complexities, it is probably because they have never made full use of the entire range of uni-temporal functionality, let alone of bi-temporal functionality. In fact, in our experience, which between us amounts to over a half-century of IT consulting, for dozens of clients, we have seen little in the way of temporal data management beyond a limited use of the capabilities of uni-temporal versioned tables.

So for most of us, there is a good deal more to learn about managing temporal data. Most of the code that many of us have written to make sure that uni- or bi-temporal updates are done correctly addresses only the tip of the iceberg of temporal data management complexities.

To summarize our prospectus of Part 1, Chapter 1 will be a history of how the business IT world has managed the intersection of time and data. Chapter 2 will be a taxonomy of those methods, whose purpose is to highlight the similarities and differences among them.

## Glossary References

Glossary entries whose definitions form strong interdependencies are grouped together in the following list. The same Glossary entries may be grouped together in different ways at the end of different chapters, each grouping reflecting the semantic perspective of each chapter. There will usually be several other, and often many other, Glossary entries that are not included in the list, and we recommend that the Glossary be consulted whenever an unfamiliar term is encountered.

---

9999
time period

historical data
non-temporal data
uni-temporal data

object
version

---

# A BRIEF HISTORY OF TEMPORAL DATA MANAGEMENT

## CONTENTS

Temporal data management is not a new development. From the earliest days of business data processing (as it was called back then), transactions were captured in a transaction log and the files and tables those transactions were applied to were periodically backed up. With those backups and logfiles, we could usually re-create what the data looked like at any point in time along either of the temporal dimensions we will be discussing. Indeed, together they contain all the "raw material" needed to support fully bi-temporal data management. As we will see in this chapter, what has changed about temporal data management, over the decades, is *accessibility* to temporal data. These days, it takes less effort to get to temporal data than it used to, and it takes less time as well. But significant additional progress is possible, and computer scientists are working on it. We are, too. Our work has led to this book, and to the software we are developing to implement its concepts.

Managing Time in Relational Databases. Doi: 10.1016/B978-0-12-375041-9.00001-7

We emphasize that the following history is not a history in any strict sense. It is more like our reflections on changes in methods of managing data which we have observed, as IT consultants, over the last quarter-century. It is our attempt to look back on those changes, and impose some order and structure on them. It does not fall short of history, in a strict sense, in attempting to impose order and structure. All historical narrative does that, no matter how purely descriptive it claims to be. Rather, it falls short in its reliance solely on personal reminiscence.

## Excluding Time from Databases: A Ubiquitous Paradigm

In one sense, temporal data has been accorded only second-class status since the advent of computers and their use in managing business data. Neither database management systems (DBMSs) and the tables they manage, nor access methods and the files they manage, provide explicit mechanisms and structures to distinguish data about the past, present or future of the things we keep track of. Instead, unless *developer-designed data structures* and *developer-written code* is deployed, every object is represented by one and only one row in a table. If the row is there, the corresponding object is represented in our databases; otherwise it is not. If something about a represented object changes, the row is retrieved, updated and rewritten to reflect that change.

This focus on current data is reflected in a basic paradigm that has been used since we began managing data with computers. The paradigm is that of one data structure to represent a type of object or event, containing multiple other data structures, each representing an instance of an object or event of that type. Contained within the latter data structures are additional structures, each representing a property of the instance in question, or a relationship it has to another instance of the same type or (more usually) a different type.

This paradigm has manifested itself in such terminologies as (i) files, records, fields and pointers; (ii) tables, rows, columns and foreign keys; and (iii) classes, objects, slots and links. For the remainder of this book, we will use the table, row, column and foreign key terminology, although the concepts of uni-temporal and bi-temporal data management apply equally well to data managed by directly invoking access methods, to data managed with proprietary software, and to data managed with object-oriented structures and transformations.

# The 1980s

## Historical Databases

In the 80s, as disk storage costs plummeted, it was inevitable that someone would think to put the most recent backup files onto disk where it would be possible to access them without first restoring them from off-line storage media. After that, the next step was to realize that there was value, not just in having a particular set of backup data remain on-line, but also in having the ability to compare multiple backups of the same data, made at different points in time.

Each backup is a snapshot of a set of data of interest, and just as a movie film makes motion apparent while being itself a series of still images, so too a series of database snapshots can make change apparent while being itself a series of still images. Thus was born the concept of a data warehouse, whose originators were Barry Devlin and Paul Murphy.[1] This concept introduced temporal data management at the database level (as opposed to the table, row or column levels), since data warehouses are entire databases devoted to historical data.

## History Tables

On an architecturally smaller scale, IT developers were also beginning to design and implement several other ways of managing temporal data. One of them was the use of history tables, and another the use of version tables. In the former case, temporal data management is implemented at the table level in the sense that individual tables are the objects devoted to historical data, usually populated by triggers based on updates to the corresponding current tables. In the latter case, temporal data management is also implemented at the table level, but in this case historical and current data reside in the same table. In some cases, intrepid developers have even attempted to introduce temporal data management at the level of individual columns.

In addition, developers were also beginning to create on-line transaction tables by bringing collections of transactions back from off-line storage media, transactions that originally had been moved onto that media as soon as their current accounting periods were over. The difference between history tables and version tables, on the one hand, and transaction tables on the

---

[1] See [1988, Devlin & Murphy]. The full citation may be found in the appendix *Bibliographical Essay.* The year is the year of publication, and entries in that appendix are organized by year of publication.

other hand, is that history and version tables record the state of *objects* at different times, whereas transaction tables record the *events* that change the states of those objects and, in particular, the relationships among them.

## The 1990s

### Temporal Extensions to SQL

By the early 90s, significant computer science research on bi-temporality had been completed. To the extent that word of these developments made its way into the business IT community, bi-temporality was understood as a distinction between logical time and physical time. Logical time, corresponding to what computer scientists called *valid time*, was generally referred to by IT professionals as *effective time*. It was understood to be that period of time, denoted by either a single date or by a pair of dates, during which the object represented by a row conformed to the description that row provided. The term "effective time" derives from the fact that for specific and non-overlapping periods of time, each of these rows is *in effect* as the representative of an object—as the authorized description of what the object is like during that specific period of time. As for physical time, it was understood to be a single date, the physical date on which the bi-temporal data is created.

This view was, in fact, either a misunderstanding of what the computer scientists were saying, or else an independently developed understanding of two kinds of time that were relevant to data. Either way, it fell short of full bi-temporality. For while it acknowledged that one kind of time is a period of time, it believed that the other kind of time is a point in time. With only one temporal *extent* represented, this was at best a *quasi*-bi-temporal model of data.

This misunderstanding aside, the computer science work on bi-temporality resulted in a proposal for bi-temporal extensions to the SQL language. The extensions were formulated originally as TSQL, later superceded by TSQL2. This proposal was submitted to the SQL Standards Committee in 1994 by Dr. Rick Snodgrass, but to this date has still not been ratified. Nonetheless, there is much that can be done to support bi-temporal functionality using today's technology, and much to be gained from doing so.

### Data Warehouses and Data Marts Come of Age

The second major development in the 90s was that the concept of a data warehouse was proselytized and extended by Bill

Inmon [1996, Inmon].[2] As a result of this work, the IT industry began to take note of data warehousing. In its purest form, a data warehouse records history as a series of snapshots of the non-transactional tables in legacy system databases.

This reflects the fact that, from the point of view of data warehousing, what is important are persistent objects and what they are like at different points in time, i.e. what *states* they are in as they pass through time. If we are interested in the changes rather than the states themselves, we can reconstruct the history of those changes by extracting the deltas between successive states.

At about the same time, Ralph Kimball [1996, Kimball] took a complementary approach, describing a method of recording history by means of a collection of transactions. With transactions, the focus changes from objects to the relationships among them, for example from a company and its customers to the account balances which track the relationship between that company and each of those customers. Starting with a base state of a relationship, such as account balances on the first of each year, the metrics of those relationships can be recreated, at any subsequent point in time, by applying statistical functions to the base states and the subsequent transactions, e.g. by adding a chronological series of all purchases, payments and returns by a customer to the beginning balance of her account, until any desired point in time is reached.

As the 90s progressed, a religious war developed between those IT professionals who followed Inmon's data warehouse method of managing history, and those who followed Kimball's data mart method. These disputes generated more heat than light, and they did so because the complementary nature of the warehouse vs. mart approaches was never clearly recognized.

Because this was the major focus of discussions by IT professionals, during the 90s, about how historical data should be recorded and managed, it is worth trying to describe both what the two camps thought was at stake, as well as what was really at stake. We will describe what was really at stake in the next chapter. Here, we will describe what the two camps thought was at stake.

---

[2]The first edition of Inmon's first book was apparently published in 1991, but we can find no reliable references to it. It seems to us that it was only with the second edition, published in 1996, that the IT community began to take notice of data warehousing.

## The Inmon/Kimball Religious Wars

### The Kimball Perspective

What the Kimball advocates thought was at stake, in the middle to late 90s, was the difference between a cumbersome and a nimble way of providing access to historical data. They thought the issue was an either/or issue, a choice to be made between data warehouses and data marts, with the correct choice being obvious.

It is true that "nimbleness" was a major concern during those years. Data warehouse projects were nearly always long-term, big-budget projects. Like most such projects, they tended to fail at a high rate. Most failures were probably due to the fact that, in general, big complex projects produce big, complex products, and that with increasing complexity comes increasing odds of mistakes which, over time, often result in failure.

But some failures were also due to senior management losing faith in data warehouse projects. As these large projects fell increasingly behind schedule and rose increasingly over budget—something large projects tend to do—the pressure increased to produce results that had recognizable business value. Patience wore thin, and many data warehouse projects that might have been completed successfully were terminated prematurely.

Against the background of failed data warehouse projects, data mart projects promised results, and promised to deliver them quickly. The typical difference in length of project was about three-to-one: something like two to three years for the typical data warehouse project, but only 8 to 12 months for the typical data mart project.

And in fact, the success rate for data mart projects was significantly higher than the success rate for data warehouse projects. For the most part, this was due to more modest objectives: one-room schoolhouses vs. multi-story skyscrapers. It was part of Kimball's brilliance to find one-room schoolhouses that were worth building.

### The Inmon Perspective

What the Inmon advocates thought was at stake was a "one size fits all" approach vs. an approach that provided different solutions for different requirements. Instead of Kimball's either/or, they took a both/and stance, and advocated the use of operational data stores (ODSs), historical data warehouses *and* dimensional data marts, with each one serving different needs.

Indeed, the Inmon approach eventually resulted in an architecture with four components, in which (i) OLTP legacy systems feed an updatable consolidated Operational Data Store (ODS), which in turn (ii) feeds a data warehouse of historical snapshots, which in turn (iii) supplies the dimensions for data marts. At the same time, transactions generated/received by the OLTP systems are consolidated into the fact tables of those data marts.

This was an "if you can't beat them, join them" response to the challenge posed by Kimball and his data marts. And it was coupled with a criticism of Kimball. How, Inmon advocates asked, can the data mart approach guarantee consistency across dimensions which are used by multiple fact tables? And if that approach could not guarantee consistency, they pointed out, then the consequences could be as devastating as you care to imagine.

For example, suppose costs summarized in a data mart using a sales organization dimension are compared with revenues summarized in a different data mart using purportedly the same sales organization dimension, but a dimension which was actually created a few days later, and which contained several salesperson assignments not present in the first mart's dimension. In that case, the cost and revenue comparisons for any number of given sales organizations will be comparisons of slightly different organizational units, albeit ones with the same names and unique identifiers.

Once problems like these surface, how can management ever have faith in what either data mart tells them? Doesn't Kimball's data mart approach, Inmon's supporters asked, in effect recreate the data *stovepipes* of legacy systems, stovepipes which everyone recognized need to be eliminated?

Inmon's supporters had their own answer to this question. They pointed out that if the dimensions for all data marts were extracted from a single source, that source being the enterprise data warehouse, then it would be easy to guarantee that the different dimensions were either identical in content or else conformable in content, i.e. mappable one into the other.

### Inmon and Kimball: Going Forward

Acknowledging the force of this criticism, Kimball and his supporters developed an approach called *conformed dimensions*. They agreed that data, in physically distinct dimensions of data marts, needs to be the same when that data is about the same things. That data, they said, needs to be *conformed*. It needs to be either instance for instance identical, or derivable one from the other as, for example, when one set of data is a summarization of the other.

A straightforward way to conform data is to derive it from the same source, at the same time. If transformations are applied to the data as that data is being copied, then semantically like transformations, e.g. summaries or averages, should be based on the same mathematical formulas being applied to the same data. If identical data is subjected to different transformations, but those transformations are mathematically mappable one onto the other, then information derived from those two different sets of derived data will be in agreement.

## The 2000s

In the first decade of the new millennium, several major developments took place related to the management of temporal data. They were:
  **i.** On-line analytical processing (OLAP) data cubes;
  **ii.** Slowly changing dimensions (SCDs); and
**iii.** Real-time data warehousing.

Data cubes are a software structure, manipulated by business intelligence software, that provides rapid and easy access to very large collections of dimensional data, based on often terabyte-sized fact tables. Slowly changing dimensions are a family of uni-temporal structures which provide limited support for historical data in data mart dimension tables. Real-time data warehousing is an evolution from monthly, weekly and then nightly batch updating of warehouses, to real-time transactional updating.

## Data Cubes

The first of these three developments is of minimal interest because it is pure technology, involving no advance in the semantics of temporal concepts. We briefly discuss it because it is a convenient way to focus attention on the "cube explosion problem", the fact that even with terabyte-sized fact tables, a full materialization of sums, counts, and other statistical summarizations of all the instances of all the permutations and combinations of all of the hierarchical levels of all of the dimensions of the typical data mart would dwarf, by many orders of magnitude, the amount of data contained in those terabyte-sized fact tables themselves. Since including uni-temporal or bi-temporal data in the dimensions of a data mart would increase the number of summarization instances by any number of orders of magnitude, any discussion about introducing temporality into data mart dimensions will have to pay close attention to this potentially overwhelming issue.

## Slowly Changing Dimensions

The second development, slowly changing dimensions (SCDs), provides a limited solution to part of the problem that bi-temporality addresses, but it is a solution that we believe has confused and continues to confuse the majority of IT practitioners about what bi-temporal data management really is. All too often, when we begin to present bi-temporal concepts, we hear "But Ralph Kimball solved all that with his slowly changing dimensions."

A new idea is unlikely to attract much attention if its audience believes it addresses a problem that has already been solved. Some clarification is needed, and we hope that, by the end of this book, we will have provided enough clarification to disabuse most IT professionals of that mistaken notion.

But here, we can make two brief points. First of all, SCDs are uni-temporal, not bi-temporal. They do not distinguish changes from corrections.

Moreover, SCDs put much of the semantic burden of accessing temporal data directly on the end user. She is the one who has to know where to look for a specific temporal version of an instance of a dimension. Is it in a different row in the dimension table? If so, which one? If a date column distinguishes them, which date column is it? Or perhaps the temporally distinct instances are to be found in different columns in the same row. If there are several of them, which column is the one she wants?

Of course, there may exist developer-written code which translates the user's request into physical access to physical rows and columns within the dimension. Perhaps, as should be the case, all the user has to specify, for example, is that she wants, in the product dimension, a specific sku and, for that sku, the description in effect on a specific date.

This is an improvement. But all it really does is move the semantic burden from the end user to the developer and her hand-written code. It is like the days long ago when assembler programmers, about to update a set of records in memory, had to load a starting address in one register, the row length of the records in another register, the number of records in the set in a third register, and then code a loop through the set of records by updating each record, adding the record length to the current memory location and thus moving on to the next record.

Whenever we can specify the semantics of what we need, without having to specify the steps required to fulfill our requests, those requests are satisfied at lower cost, in less time, and more reliably. SCDs stand on the wrong side of that what vs. how divide.

Some IT professionals refer to a type 1.5 SCD. Others describe types 0, 4, 5 and 6. Suffice it to say that none of these variations overcome these two fundamental limitations of SCDs. SCDs do have their place, of course. They are one tool in the data manager's toolkit. Our point here is, first of all, that they are not bi-temporal. In addition, even for accessing uni-temporal data, SCDs are cumbersome and costly. They can, and should, be replaced by a declarative way of requesting what data is needed without having to provide explicit directions to that data.

### Real-Time Data Warehouses

As for the third of these developments, it muddles the data warehousing paradigm by blurring the line between regular, periodic snapshots of tables or entire databases, and irregular as-needed before-images of rows about to be changed. There is value in the regularity of periodic snapshots, just as there is value in the regular mileposts along interstate highways. Before-images of individual rows, taken just before they are updated, violate this regular snapshot paradigm, and while not destroying, certainly erode the milepost value of regular snapshots.

On the other hand, periodic snapshots fail to capture changes that are overwritten by later changes, and also fail to capture inserts that are cancelled by deletes, and vice versa, when these actions all take place between one snapshot and the next. As-needed row-level warehousing (real-time warehousing) will capture all of these database modifications.

Both kinds of historical data have value when collected and managed properly. But what we actually have, in all too many historical data warehouses today, is an ill-understood and thus poorly managed mish-mash of the two kinds of historical data. As result, these warehouses provide the best of neither world.

## The Future of Databases: Seamless Access to Temporal Data

Let's say that this brief history has shown a progression in making temporal data "readily available". But what does "readily available" really mean, with respect to temporal data?

One thing it might mean is "more available than by using backups and logfiles". And the most salient feature of the advance from backups and logfiles to these other methods of managing historical data is that backups and logfiles require the intervention of IT Operations to restore desired data from off-line media, while history tables, warehouses and data marts do not. When IT Operations has to get involved, emails and phone calls fly back and forth. The Operations manager complains that his personnel are already overloaded with the work of keeping production systems running, and don't have time for these one-off requests, especially as those requests are being made more and more frequently.

What is going on is that the job of Operations, as its management sees it, is to run the IT production schedule and to complete that scheduled work on time. Anything else is extra. Anything else is outside what their annual reviews, salary increases and bonuses are based on.

And so it is frequently necessary to bump the issue up a level, and for Directors or even VPs within IT to talk to one another. Finally, when Operations at last agrees to restore a backup and apply a logfile (and do the clean-up work afterwards, the manager is sure to point out), it is often a few days or a few weeks after the business use for that data led to the request being made in the first place. Soon enough, data consumers learn what a headache it is to get access to backed-up historical data. They learn how long it takes to get the data, and so learn to do a quick mental calculation to figure out whether or not the answer they need is likely to be available quickly enough to check out a hunch about next year's optimum product mix before production schedules are finalized, or support a position they took in a meeting which someone else has challenged. They learn, in short, to do without a lot of the data they need, to not even bother asking for it.

But instead of the comparative objective of making temporal data "more available" than it is, given some other way of managing it, let's formulate the absolute objective for availability of temporal data. It is, simply, for temporal data to be as quickly and easily accessible as it needs to be. We will call this the requirement to have *seamless, real-time access* to what we once believed, currently believe, or may come to believe is true about what things of interest to us were like, are like, or may come to be like in the future.

This requirement has two parts. First, it means access to non-current states of persistent objects which is just as available to the data consumer as is access to current states. The temporal data must be available on-line, just as current data is. Transactions to maintain temporal data must be as easy to write as are transactions to maintain current data. Queries to retrieve temporal data, or a combination of temporal and current data, must be as easy to write as are queries to retrieve current data only. This is the *usability aspect* of seamless access.

Second, it means that queries which return temporal data, or a mix of temporal and current data, must return equivalent-sized results in an equivalent amount of elapsed time. This is the *performance aspect* of seamless access.

## Closing In on Seamless Access

Throughout the history of computerized data management, file access methods (e.g. VSAM) and database management systems (DBMSs) have been designed and deployed to manage current data. All of them have a structure for representing types of objects, a structure for representing instances of those types, and a structure for representing properties and relationships of those instances. But none of them have structures for representing objects as they exist within periods of time, let alone structures for representing objects as they exist within two periods of time.

The earliest DBMSs supported sequential (one-to-one) and hierarchical (one-to-many) relationships among types and instances, and the main example was IBM's IMS. Later systems more directly supported network (many-to-many) relationships than did IMS. Important examples were Cincom's TOTAL, ADR's DataCom, and Cullinet's IDMS (the latter two now Computer Associates' products).

Later, beginning with IBM's System R, and Dr. Michael Stonebreaker's Ingres, Dr. Ted Codd's relational paradigm for data management began to be deployed. Relational DBMSs could do everything that network DBMSs could do, but less well understood is the fact that they could also do nothing more than network DBMSs could do. Relational DBMSs prevailed over CODASYL network DBMSs because they simplified the work required to maintain and access data by supporting declaratively specified set-at-a-time operations rather than procedurally specified record-at-a-time operations.

Those record-at-a-time operations work like this. Network DBMSs require us to retrieve or update multiple rows in tables by coding a *loop*. In doing so, we are writing a procedure; we are telling the computer *how* to retrieve the rows we are interested in. So we wrote these loops, and retrieved (or updated) one row at a time. Sometimes we wrote code that produced infinite loops when confronted with unanticipated combinations of data. Sometimes we wrote code that contained "off by one" errors. But SQL, issued against relational databases, allows us to simply specify what results we want, e.g. to say that we want all rows where the customer status is XYZ. Using SQL, there are no infinite loops, and there are no off-by-one errors.

For the most part, today's databases are still specialized for managing current data, data that tells us what we currently believe things are currently like. Everything else is an exception. Nonetheless, we can make historical data accessible to queries by organizing it into specialized databases, or into specialized tables within databases, or even into specialized rows within tables that also contain current data.

But each of these ways of accommodating historical data requires extra work on the part of IT personnel. Each of these ways of accommodating historical data goes beyond the basic paradigm of one table for every type of object, and one row for every instance of a type. And so DBMSs don't come with built-in support for these structures that contain historical data. We developers have to design, deploy and manage these structures ourselves. In addition, we must design, deploy and manage the code that maintains historical data, because this code goes beyond the basic paradigm of inserting a row for a new object, retrieving, updating and rewriting a row for an object that has changed, and deleting a row for an object no longer of interest to us.

We developers must also design, deploy and maintain code to simplify the retrieval of instances of historical data. SQL, and the various reporting and querying tools that generate it, supports the basic paradigm used to access current data. This is the paradigm of choosing one or more rows from a target table by specifying selection criteria, projecting one or more columns by listing the columns to be included in the query's result set, and joining from one table to another by specifying match or other qualifying criteria from selected rows to other rows.

When different rows represent objects at different periods of time, transactions to insert, update and delete data must specify not just the object, but also the period of time of interest. When different rows represent different statements about what was true about the same object at a specified period of time, those transactions must specify *two* periods of time in addition to the object.

Queries also become more complex. When different rows represent objects at different points in time, queries must specify not just the object, but also the point in time of interest. When different rows represent different statements about what was true about the same object at the same point in time, queries must specify two points in time in addition to the criteria which designate the object or objects of interest.

We believe that the relational model, with its supporting theory and technology, is now in much the same position that the CODASYL network model, with its supporting theory and technology, was three decades ago. It is in the same position, in the following sense.

Relational DBMSs were never able to do anything with data that network DBMSs could not do. Both supported sequential, hierarchical and network relationships among instances of types of data. The difference was in how much work was required on the part of IT personnel and end users to maintain and access the managed data.

And now we have the relational model, a model invented by Dr. E. F. Codd. An underlying assumption of the relational model is that it deals with current data only. But temporal data can be managed with relational technology. Dr. Snodgrass's book describes how current relational technology can be adapted to handle temporal data, and indeed to handle data along two orthogonal temporal dimensions. But in the process of doing so, it also shows how difficult it is to do.

In today's world, the assumption is that DBMSs manage current data. But we are moving into a world in which DBMSs will be called on to manage data which describes the past, present or future states of objects, and the past, present or future assertions made about those states. Of this two-dimensional temporalization of data describing what we believe about how things are in the world, currently true and currently asserted data will always be the default state of data managed in a database and retrieved from it. But overrides to those defaults should be specifiable declaratively, simply by specifying points in time other than right now for versions of objects and also for assertions about those versions.

Asserted Versioning provides seamless, real-time access to bi-temporal data, and provides mechanisms which support the declarative specification of bi-temporal parameters on both maintenance transactions and on queries against bi-temporal data.

## Glossary References

Glossary entries whose definitions form strong interdependencies are grouped together in the following list. The same glossary entries may be grouped together in different ways at the end of different chapters, each grouping reflecting the semantic perspective of each chapter. There will usually be several other, and often many other, glossary entries that are not included in the list, and we recommend that the Glossary be consulted whenever an unfamiliar term is encountered.

---

effective time
valid time

event
state

external pipeline dataset, history table
transaction table
version table

instance
type

object
persistent object
thing

seamless access
seamless access, performance aspect
seamless access, usability aspect

---

# A TAXONOMY OF BI-TEMPORAL DATA MANAGEMENT METHODS

**CONTENTS**

In Chapter 1, we presented an historical account of various ways that temporal data has been managed with computers. In this chapter, we will develop a *taxonomy*, and situate those methods described in Chapter 1, as well as several variations on them, in this taxonomy.

A taxonomy is a special kind of hierarchy. It is a hierarchy which is a partitioning of the instances of its highest-level node into different kinds, types or classes of things. While an historical approach tells us how things came to be, and how they evolved over time, a taxonomic approach tells us what kinds of things we have come up with, and what their similarities and differences are. In both cases, i.e. in the previous chapter and in this one, the purpose is to provide the background for our later discussions of temporal data management and, in particular, of how Asserted Versioning supports non-temporal, uni-temporal and bi-temporal data by means of physical bi-temporal tables.[1]

---

[1]Because Asserted Versioning directly manages bi-temporal tables, and supports uni-temporal tables as views on bi-temporal tables, we sometimes refer to it as a method of bi-temporal data management and at other times refer to it as a method of temporal data management. The difference in terminology, then, reflects simply a difference in emphasis which may vary depending on context.

**Managing Time in Relational Databases. Doi: 10.1016/B978-0-12-375041-9.00002-9**

# Taxonomies

Originally, the word "taxonomy" referred to a method of classification used in biology, and introduced into that science in the 18th century by Carl Linnaeus. Taxonomy in biology began as a system of classification based on morphological similarities and differences among groups of living things. But with the modern synthesis of Darwinian evolutionary theory, Mendelian genetics, and the Watson–Crick discovery of the molecular basis of life and its foundations in the chemistry of DNA, biological taxonomy has, for the most part, become a system of classification based on common genetic ancestry.

## Partitioned Semantic Trees

As borrowed by computer scientists, the term "taxonomy" refers to a partitioned semantic tree. A tree structure is a hierarchy, which is a set of non-looping (*acyclic*) one-to-many relationships. In each relationship, the item on the "one" side is called the *parent* item in the relationship, and the one or more items on the "many" side are called the *child* items. The items that are related are often called *nodes* of the hierarchy. Continuing the arboreal metaphor, a tree consists of one root node (usually shown at the top of the structure, and not, as the metaphor would lead one to expect, at the bottom), zero or more branch nodes, and zero or more leaf nodes on each branch. This terminology is illustrated in Figure 2.1.

*Tree structure.* Each taxonomy is a hierarchy. Therefore, except for the root node, every node has exactly one parent node. Except for the leaf nodes, unless the hierarchy consists of

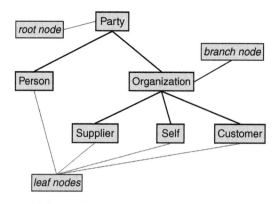

**Figure 2.1** An Illustrative Taxonomy.

the root node only, every node has at least one child node. Each node except the root node has as ancestors all the nodes from its direct parent node, in linear ascent from child to parent, up to and including the root node. No node can be a parent to any of its ancestors.

*Partitioned.* The set of child nodes under a given parent node are jointly exhaustive and mutually exclusive. Being jointly exhaustive means that every instance of a parent node is also an instance of one of its child nodes. Being mutually exclusive means that no instance of a parent node is an instance of more than one of its child nodes. A corollary is that every instance of the root node is also an instance of one and only one leaf node.

*Semantic.* The relationships between nodes are often called links. The links between nodes, and between instances and nodes, are based on the meaning of those nodes. Conventionally, node-to-node relationships are called KIND-OF links, because each child node can be said to be a kind of its parent node. In our illustrative taxonomy, shown in Figure 2.1, for example, Supplier is a kind of Organization.

A leaf node, and only a leaf node, can be the direct parent of an instance. Instances are individual things of the type indicated by that node. The relationship between individuals and the (leaf and non-leaf) nodes they are instances of is called an IS-A relationship, because each instance is an instance of its node. Our company may have a supplier, let us suppose, called the Acme Company. In our illustrative taxonomy shown in Figure 2.1, therefore, Acme is a direct instance of a Supplier, and indirectly an instance of an Organization and of a Party. In ordinary conversation, we usually drop the "instance of" phrase, and would say simply that Acme is a supplier, an organization and a party.

Among IT professionals, taxonomies have been used in data models for many years. They are the exclusive subtype hierarchies defined in logical data models, and in the (single-inheritance) class hierarchies defined in object-oriented models. An example familiar to most data modelers is the entity Party. Under it are the two entities Person and Organization. The business rule for this two-level hierarchy is: every party is either a person or an organization (but not both). This hierarchy could be extended for as many levels as are useful for a specific modeling requirement. For example, Organization might be partitioned into Supplier, Self and Customer. This particular taxonomy is shown in Figure 2.1.

We note that most data modelers, on the assumption that this taxonomy would be implemented as a subtype hierarchy in a logical data model, will recognize right away that it is not a very good taxonomy. For one thing, it says that persons are not customers. But many companies do sell their goods or services to people; so for them, this is a bad taxonomy. Either the label "customer" is being used in a specialized (and misleading) way, or else the taxonomy is simply wrong.

A related mistake is that, for most companies, Supplier, Self and Customer are not mutually exclusive. For example, many companies sell their goods or services to other companies who are also suppliers to them. If this is the case, then this hierarchy is not a taxonomy, because an instance—a company that is both a supplier and a customer—belongs to more than one leaf node. As a data modeling subtype hierarchy, it is a non-exclusive hierarchy, not an exclusive one.

This specific taxonomy has nothing to do with temporal data management; but it does give us an opportunity to make an important point that most data modelers will understand. That point is that even very bad data models can be and often are, put into production. And when that happens, the price that is paid is confusion: confusion about what the entities of the model really represent and thus where data about something of interest can be found within the database, what sums and averages over a given entity really mean, and so on.

In this case, for example, some organizations may be represented by a row in only one of these three tables, but other organizations may be represented by rows in two or even in all three of them. Queries which extract statistics from this hierarchy must now be written very carefully, to avoid the possibility of double- or triple-counting organizational metrics.

As well as all this, the company may quite reasonably want to keep a row in the Customer table for every customer, whether it be an organization or a person. This requires an even more confusing use of the taxonomy, because while an organization might be represented multiple times in this taxonomy, at least it is still possible to find additional information about organizational customers in the parent node. But this is not possible when those customers are persons.

So the data modeler will want to modify the hierarchy so that persons can be included as customers. There are various ways to do this, but if the hierarchy is already populated and in use, none of them are likely to be implemented. The cost is just too high. Queries and code, and the result sets and reports based on them, have already been written, and are already in production. If the hierarchy is modified, all those queries and all that code will have to be modified. The path of least resistance is an unfortunate one. It is to leave the whole mess alone, and to rely on the end users to understand that mess as they interpret their reports and query results, and as they write their own queries.

Experienced data modelers may recognize that what is wrong with this taxonomy is that it mixes types and roles. This distinction is often called the distinction between exclusive and non-exclusive subtypes, but data modelers are also familiar with roles, and non-exclusive subtypes are how roles are implemented in a data model. In a hierarchy of roles, things can play multiple roles concurrently; but in a hierarchy of types, each thing is one type of thing, not several types.

## Jointly Exhaustive

It is important that the child nodes directly under a parent node are *jointly exhaustive*. If they aren't, then there can be instances of a node in the hierarchy that are not also instances of any of its immediate child nodes, for example an organization, in Figure 2.1, that is neither a supplier, nor the company itself, nor a customer. This makes that particular node a confusing object. Some of its instances can be found as instances of a node directly underneath it, but others of its instances cannot.

So suppose we have an instance of the latter type. Is it really such an instance? Or is it a mistake? Is an organization without any subtypes really a supplier, for example, and we simply forgot to add a row for it in the Supplier table? Or is it some kind of organization that simply doesn't fit any of the three subtypes of Organization? If we don't have and enforce the jointly exhaustive rule, we don't know. And it will take time and effort to find out. But if we had that rule, then we would know right away that any such situations are errors, and we could move immediately to correct them (and the code that let them through).

For example, consider again our taxonomy containing the three leaf nodes of Supplier, Self and Customer. This set of organization subtypes is based on the mental image of work as transforming material of less value, obtained from suppliers, into products of greater value, which are then sold to customers. The price paid by the customer, less the cost of materials, overhead and labor, is the profit made by the company.

Is this set of three leaf nodes exhaustive? It depends on how we choose to interpret that set of nodes. For example, what about a regulatory agency that monitors volatile organic compounds which manufacturing plants emit into the atmosphere? Is this monitoring agency a supplier or a customer? The most likely way to "shoe-horn" regulatory agencies into this three-part breakdown of Organization is to treat them as suppliers of regulatory services. But it is somewhat unintuitive, and therefore potentially misleading, to call a regulatory agency a supplier. Business users who rely on a weekly report which counts suppliers for them and computes various per-supplier averages may eventually be surprised to learn that regulatory agencies have been counted as suppliers in those reports for as long as those reports have been run.

Perhaps we should we represent regulatory agencies as direct instances of Organization, and not of any of Organization's child nodes. But in that case we have transformed a branch node into a confusing hybrid—a node which is both a branch and a leaf. In either case, the result is unsatisfactory. Business users of the data organized under this hierarchy will very likely misinterpret at least some of their report and query results, especially those less experienced users who haven't yet fully realized how messy this data really is.

Good taxonomies aren't like this. Good taxonomies don't push the problems created by messy data onto the users of that data. Good taxonomies are partitioned semantic trees.

## Mutually Exclusive

It is also important for the child nodes directly under a parent node to be *mutually exclusive*. If they aren't mutually exclusive, then there can be instances of a node in the hierarchy that are also instances of two or more of its immediate child nodes. For example, consider a manufacturing company made up of several dozen plants, these plants being organizations, of course. There might be a plant which receives semi-finished product from another plant and, after working on it, sends it on to a third plant to be finished, packaged and shipped. Is this plant a supplier, a *self* organization, or a customer? It seems that it is all three. Correctly accounting for costs and revenues, in a situation like this, may prove to be quite complex.

Needless to say, this makes that organizational hierarchy difficult to manage, and its data difficult to understand. Some of its instances can be found as instances of just one node directly under a parent node, but others of its instances can be found as instances of more than one such node.

So suppose we have an instance of the latter type, such as the plant just described. Is it really such an instance? Or is it a mistake, a failure on our part to realize that we inadvertently created multiple child rows to correspond to the one parent row? It will take time and effort to find out, and until we do, we simply aren't sure. Confidence in our data is lessened, and business decisions made on the basis of that data are made knowing that such anomalies exist in the data.

But if we knew that the taxonomy was intended to be a full partitioning, then we would know right away that any such situations are errors. We could monitor the hierarchy of tables and prevent those errors from happening in the first place. We could restore the reliability of the data, and the confidence our users have in it. We could help our company make better business decisions.

Consider another example of violating the mutually exclusive rule. Perhaps when our hierarchy was originally set up, there were no examples of organizations that were instances of more than one of these three categories. But over time, such instances might very well occur, the most common being organizations which begin as suppliers, and then later become customers as well. So when our taxonomy was first created, these three nodes were, at that time, mutually exclusive. The reason we ended up with a taxonomy which violated this rule is that over time, business policy changed. One of our major suppliers wanted to start purchasing products from us; and they were likely to become a major customer. So executive management told IT to accommodate that company as a customer.

By far the easiest way to do this is to relax the mutually exclusive rule for this node of the taxonomy. But to relax the mutually exclusive rule is to change a hierarchy of types into a hierarchy of roles. And since other parts of the hierarchy, supposedly, still reflect the decision to represent types, the result is to mix types and roles in the same hierarchy. It is to make what these nodes of the hierarchy stand for inherently unclear. It is to introduce semantic ambiguity into the basic structures of the database. In this way, over time, as business policy changes, the semantic clarity of data structures such as true taxonomies is lost, and the burden of sorting out the resulting confusion is left to the user.

But after all, what is the alternative? Is it to split off the roles into a separate non-taxonomic hierarchy, and rewrite the taxonomy to preserve the mutually exclusive rule? And then to unload, transform and reload some of the data that originally belonged with the old taxonomy? And then to redirect some queries to the new taxonomy, leave some queries pointed at the original structure which has now become a non-exclusive hierarchy, and duplicate some queries so that one of each pair points at the new non-exclusive hierarchy and the other of the pair points at the new taxonomy, in each case depending on the selection criteria they use? And to train the user community to properly use both the new taxonomy and also the new non-taxonomic hierarchy of non-exclusive child nodes? Any experienced data management professional knows that nothing of the sort is going to happen.

As long as the cost of pushing semantic burdens onto end users is never measured, and seldom even noticed, putting the burden on the user will continue to be the easy way out. "Old hand" users, familiar with the quirks of semantically rococo databases like these, may still be able to extract high-quality information from them. They know which numbers to trust, on which reports, and which numbers to be suspicious of. They know which screens have the most accurate demographic data, and which the most accurate current balances. Less experienced users, on the other hand, inevitably obtain lower-quality information from those same databases. They don't know where the semantic skeletons are hidden. They can tell good data from not so good data about as well as a Florida orange grower can tell a healthy reindeer from one with brucellosis.

And so the gap between the quality of information obtained when an experienced user queries a database, and the quality of information obtained when an average or novice user poses what is supposedly the same question to the database, increases over time. Eventually, the experienced user retires. The understanding of the database which she has acquired over the years retires with her. The same reports are run. The same SQL populates the same screens. But the understanding of the business formed on the basis of the data on those reports and screens is sadly diminished.

The taxonomy we will develop in this chapter is a partitioned semantic hierarchy. In general, any reasonably rich subject matter admits of any number of taxonomies. So the taxonomy described here is not the only taxonomy possible for comparing and contrasting different ways of managing temporal data. It is a taxonomy designed to lead us through a range of possible ways of managing temporal data, and to end up with Asserted Versioning as a leaf node. The contrasts that are drawn at each level of the taxonomy are not the only possible contrasts that would lead to Asserted Versioning. They are just the contrasts which we think best bring out what is both unique and valuable about Asserted Versioning.

# A Taxonomy of Methods for Managing Temporal Data

In terms of granularity, temporal data can be managed at the level of databases, or tables within databases, or rows within tables, or even columns within rows. And at each of these levels, we could be managing non-temporal, uni-temporal or bi-temporal data. Of course, with two organizing principles—four levels of granularity, and the non/uni/bi distinction—the result would be a matrix rather than a hierarchy. In this case, it would be a matrix of 12 cells. Indeed, in places in Chapter 1, this alternative organization of temporal data management methods seems to peek out from between the lines. However, we believe that the taxonomy we are about to develop will bring out the similarities and differences among various methods of managing temporal data better than that matrix; and so, from this point forward, we will focus on the taxonomy.

## The Root Node of the Taxonomy

The root node of a taxonomy defines the scope and limits of what the taxonomy is about. Our root node says that our taxonomy is about methods for managing temporal data. Temporal data is data about, not just how things are right now, but also about how things used to be and how things will become or might become, and also about what we said things were like and when we said it. Our full taxonomy for temporal data management is shown in Figure 2.2.

The two nodes which partition temporal data management are reconstructable data and queryable data. Reconstructable data is the node under which we classify all methods of managing temporal data that require manipulation of the data before it can be queried. Queryable data is the opposite.

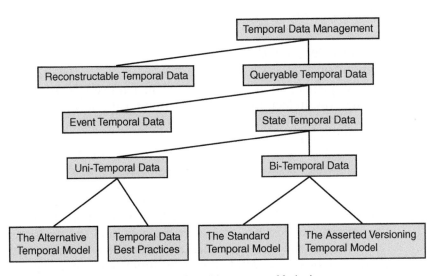

**Figure 2.2** A Taxonomy of Temporal Data Management Methods.

### Reconstructable Temporal Data

In Chapter 1, we said that the combination of backup files and logfiles permits us to reconstruct the state of a database as of any point in time. That is the only reconstructable method of managing temporal data that we discussed in that chapter. With that method, we retrieve data about the past by restoring a backup copy of that data and, if necessary, applying logfile transactions from that point in time forward to the point in time we are interested in.

But the defining feature of reconstructable methods is not the movement of data from off-line to on-line storage. The defining feature is the inability of users to access the data until it has been manipulated and transformed in some way. For this reason, among all these temporal data management methods, reconstructable temporal data takes the longest to get to, and has the highest cost of access.

Besides the time and effort involved in preparing the data for querying—either through direct queries or via various tools which generate queries from graphical or other user directives—many queries or reports against reconstructed data are modified from production queries or reports. Production queries or reports point to production databases and production tables; and so before they are used to access reconstructed data, they must be rewritten to point to that reconstructed data. This rewrite of production queries and reports may involve changing database names, and sometimes tables names and even column names. Sometimes, a query that accessed a single table in the production database must be modified to join, or even to union, multiple tables when pointed at reconstructed data.

### Queryable Temporal Data

Queryable temporal data, in contrast, is data which can be directly queried, without the need to first transform that data in some way. In fact, the principal reason for the success of data warehousing is that it transformed reconstructable historical data into queryable historical data.

Queryable data is obviously less costly to access than reconstructable data, in terms of several different kinds of costs. The most obvious one, as indicated previously, is the cost of the man-hours of time on the part of IT Operations personnel, and perhaps software developers and DBAs as well. Another cost is the opportunity cost of waiting for the data, and the decisions delayed until the data becomes available. In an increasingly fast-paced business world, the opportunity cost of delays in accessing data is increasingly significant.

But in our experience, which combines several decades of work in business IT, the greatest cost is the cost of the business community learning to do without the data they need. In many cases, it simply never crosses their minds to ask for temporal data that isn't already directly queryable. The core of the problem is that satisfying these requests is not the part of the work of computer operators, DBAs and developers that they get evaluated on. If performance reviews, raises, bonuses and promotions depend on meeting other criteria, then it is those other criteria that will be met. Doing a favor for a business user you like, which is what satisfying this kind of one-off request often amounts to, takes a decidedly second place. To paraphrase Samuel Johnson, "The imminent prospect of being passed over for a promotion wonderfully focuses the mind".[2]

## Queryable Temporal Data: Events and States

Having distinguished queryable data from reconstructable data, we move on to a partitioning of the former. We think that the most important distinction among methods of managing queryable data is the distinction between data about things and data about events. Things are what *exist;* events are what *happen.* Things are what change; events are the occasions on which they change.

The issue here is change, and the best way to keep track of it. One way is to keep a history of things, of the states that objects take on. As an object changes from one state to the next, we store the before-image of the current state and update a copy of that state, not the original. The update represents the new current state.

Another way to keep track of change is to record the initial state of an object and then keep a history of the events in which the object changed. For example, with insurance policies, we could keep an event-based history of changes to policies by adding a row to the Policy table each time a new policy is created, and after that maintaining a transaction table in which each transaction is an update or delete to the policy. The relevance of transactions to event-based temporal data management

---

[2]The form in which we knew this quotation is exactly as it is written above, with the word "death" substituted for "being passed over for a promotion". But in fact, as reported in Boswell's *Life of Johnson,* what Johnson actually said was: "Depend upon it, sir, when a man knows he is to be hanged in a fortnight, it concentrates his mind wonderfully." The criteria for annual bonuses do the same thing.

is this: transactions are the records of events, the footprints which events leave on the sands of time.[3]

### Event Temporal Data

Methods for managing event data are most appropriately used to manage changes to metric values of relationships among persistent objects, values such as counts, quantities and amounts. Persistent objects are the things that change, things like policies, clients, organizational structures, and so on. As persistent objects, they have three important features: (i) they exist over time; (ii) they can change over time; and (iii) each is distinguishable from other objects of the same type. In addition, they should be recognizable as the same object when we encounter them at different times (although sometimes the quality of our data is not good enough to guarantee this).

Events are the occasions on which changes happen to persistent objects. As events, they have two important features: (i) they occur at a point in time, or sometimes last for a limited period of time; and (ii) in either case, they do not change. An event happens, and then it's over. Once it's over, that's it; it is frozen in time.

For example, the receipt of a shipment of product alters the on-hand balance of that product at a store. The completion of an MBA degree alters the level of education of an employee. The assignment of an employee to the position of store manager alters the relationship between the employee and the company. Of course, the transactions which record these events may have been written up incorrectly. In that case, adjustments to the data must be made. But those adjustments do not reflect changes in the original events; they just correct mistakes made in recording them.

### A Special Relationship: Balance Tables

The event transactions that most businesses are interested in are those that affect relationships that have quantitative measures. A payment is received. This is an event, and a transaction records it. It alters the relationship between the payer and payee by the

---

[3]In this book, and in IT in general, *transaction* has two uses. The first designates a row of data that represents an event. For example, a customer purchase is an event, represented by a row in a sales table; the receipt of a shipment is an event, represented by a row in a receipts table. In this sense, transactions are what are collected in the fact tables of fact-dimension data marts. The second designates any insert, update or delete applied to a database. For example, it is an insert transaction that creates a new customer record, an update transaction that changes a customer's name, and a delete transaction that removes a customer from the database. In general, context will make it clear which sense of the word "transaction" is being used.

amount of the payment. That relationship is recorded, for example, in a revolving credit balance, or perhaps in a traditional accounts receivable balance. The payment is recorded as a credit, and the balance due is decreased by that amount.

These records are called balance records because they reflect the changing state of the relationship between the two parties, as if purchases and payments are added to opposite trays of an old-fashioned scale which then tilts back and forth. Each change is triggered by an event and recorded as a transaction, and the net effect of all the transactions, applied to a beginning balance, gives the current balance of the relationship.

But it isn't just the current balance that is valuable information. The transactions themselves are important because they tell us how the current balance got to be what it is. They tell us about the events that account for the balance. In doing so, they support the ability to drill down into the foundations of those balances, to understand how the current state of the relationship came about. They also support the ability to re-create the balance as of any point in time between the starting balance and the current balance by going back to the starting balance and applying transactions, in chronological sequence, up to the desired point.

We no longer need to go back to archives and logfiles, and write one-off code to get to the point in time we are interested in—as we once needed to do quite frequently. Conceptually, starting balances, and the collections of transactions against them, are like single-table backups and their logfiles, respectively, brought on-line. Organized into the structures discovered by Dr. Ralph Kimball, they are fact/dimension data marts.

Of course, balances aren't the only kind of relationship. For example, a Customer to Salesperson cross-reference table—an associative table, in relational terms—represents a relationship between customers and salespersons. This table, among other things, tells us which salespersons a business has assigned to which customers. This table is updated with transactions, but those transactions themselves are not important enough to keep on-line. If we want to keep track of changes to this kind of relationship, we will likely choose to keep a chronological history of states, not of events. A history table of that associative relationship is one way we might keep that chronological history of states.

To summarize: businesses are all about ongoing relationships. Those relationships are affected by events, which are recorded as transactions. Financial account tables are balance tables; each account number uniquely identifies a particular relationship, and the metrical properties of that account tell us the current state of the relationship.

The standard implementation of event time, as we mentioned earlier, is the data mart and the fact/dimension, star or snowflake structures that it uses.

### State Temporal Data

Event data, as we have seen, is not the best way of tracking changes to non-metric relationships. It is also not ideal for managing changes to non-metric properties of persistent objects, such as customer names or bill of material hierarchies. Who ever heard of a data mart with customers or bill of material hierarchies as the *fact* tables? For such relationships and such objects, state-based history is the preferred option. One reason is that, for persistent objects, we are usually more interested in what state they are in at a given point in time than in what changes they have undergone. If we want to know about changes to the status of an insurance policy, for example, we can always reconstruct a history of those changes from the series of states of the policy. With balances, and their rapidly changing metrics, on the other hand, we generally are at least as interested in how they changed over time as we are in what state they are currently in.

So we conclude that, except for keeping track of metric properties of relationships, the best queryable method of managing temporal data about persistent objects is to keep track of the succession of states through which the objects pass. When managing time using state data, what we record are not transactions, but rather the *results* of transactions, the rows resulting from inserts and (logical) deletes, and the rows representing both a before- and an after-image of every update.

State data describes those things that can have states, which means those things that can change over time. An event, like a withdrawal from a bank account, as we have already pointed out, can't change. Events don't do that. But the customer who owns that account can change. The branch the account is with can change. Balances can also change over time, but as we have just pointed out, it is usually more efficient to keep track of balances by means of periodic snapshots of beginning balances, and then an accumulation of all the transactions from that point forward.

But from a logical point of view, event data and state data are interchangeable. No temporal information is preserved with one method that cannot be preserved with the other. We have these two methods simply because an event data approach is preferable for describing metric-based relationships, while a state data approach is better at tracking changes to persistent objects and to relationships other than metric balances.

## State Temporal Data: Uni-Temporal and Bi-Temporal Data

At this point in our discussion, we are concerned with state data rather than with event data, and with state data that is queryable rather than state data that needs to be reconstructed. What then are the various options for managing temporal queryable state data?

First of all, we need to recognize that there are two kinds of states to manage. One is the state of the things we are interested in, the states those things pass through as they change over time. But there is another kind of state, that being the state of the data itself. Data, such as rows in tables, can be in one of two states: correct or incorrect. (As we will see in Chapter 12, it can also be in a third state, one in which it is neither correct nor incorrect.) Version tables and assertion tables record, respectively, the state of objects and the state of our data about those objects.

### Uni-Temporal State Data

In a conventional Customer table, each row represents the current state of a customer. Each time the state of a customer changes, i.e. each time a row is updated, the old data is overwritten with the new data. By adding one (or sometimes two) date(s) or timestamp(s) to the primary key of the table, it becomes a uni-temporal table. But since we already know that there are two different temporal dimensions that can be associated with data, we know to ask "What kind of uni-temporal table?"

As we saw in the Preface, there are uni-temporal version tables and uni-temporal assertion tables. Version tables keep track of changes that happen in the real world, changes to the objects represented in those tables. Each change is recorded as a new version of an object. Assertion tables keep track of corrections we have made to data we later discovered to be in error. Each correction is recorded as a new assertion about the object. The versions make up a true history of what happened to those objects. The assertions make up a virtual logfile of corrections to the data in the table.

Usually, when table-level temporal data is discussed, the tables turn out to be version tables, not assertion tables. In their book describing the alternative temporal model [2002, Date, Darwen, Lorentzos], the authors focus on uni-temporal versioned data. Bi-temporality is not even alluded to until the penultimate chapter, at which point it is suggested that "logged time history" tables be used to manage the other temporal dimension. Since bi-temporality receives only a passing mention in that book, we choose to classify the alternative temporal model as a uni-temporal model.

In IT best practices for managing temporal data—which we will discuss in detail in Chapter 4—once again the temporal tables are version tables, and error correction is an issue that is mostly left to take care of itself.[4] For the most part, it does so by overwriting incorrect data.[5] This is why we classify IT best practices as uni-temporal models.

### The Alternative Temporal Model

What we call *the alternative temporal model* was developed by Chris Date, Hugh Darwen and Dr. Nikos Lorentzos in their book *Temporal Data and the Relational Model* (Morgan-Kaufmann, 2002).[6] This model is based in large part on techniques developed by Dr. Lorentzos to manage temporal data by breaking temporal durations down into temporally atomic components, applying various transformations to those components, and then re-assembling the components back into those temporal durations—a technique, as the authors note, whose applicability is not restricted to temporal data.

As we said, except for the penultimate chapter in that book, the entire book is a discussion of uni-temporal versioned tables. In that chapter, the authors recommend that if there is a requirement to keep track of the assertion time history of a table (which they call "logged-time history"), it be implemented by means of an auxiliary table which is maintained by the DBMS.

---

[4]Lacking criteria to distinguish the best from the rest, the term "best practices" has come to mean little more than "standard practices". What we call "best practices", and which we discuss in Chapter 4, are standard practices we have seen used by many of our clients.

[5]An even worse solution is to mix up versions and assertions by creating a new row, with a begin date of Now(), both every time there is a real change, and also every time there is an error in the data to correct. When that happens, we no longer have a history of the changes things went through, because we cannot distinguish versions from corrections. And we no longer have a "virtual logfile" of corrections because we don't know how far back the corrections should actually have taken effect.

[6]The word "model", as used here and also in the phrases "alternative model" and "Asserted Versioning model" obviously doesn't refer to a data model of specific subject matter. It means something like *theory*, but with an emphasis on its applicability to real-world problems. So "the relational model", as we use the term, for example, means something like "relational theory as implemented in current relational technology".

In addition, these authors do not attempt, in their book, to explain how this method of managing temporal data would work with current relational technology. Like much of the computer science research on temporal data, they allude to SQL operators and other constructs that do not yet exist, and so their book is in large part a recommendation to the standards committees to adopt the changes to the SQL language which they describe.

Because our own concern is with how to implement temporal concepts with today's technologies, and also with how to support both kinds of uni-temporal data, as well as fully bi-temporal data, we will have little more to say about the alternative temporal model in this book.

Best Practices

Over several decades, a best practice has emerged in managing temporal queryable state data. It is to manage this kind of data by *versioning* otherwise conventional tables. The result is *versioned tables* which, logically speaking, are tables which combine the history tables and current tables described previously. Past, present and future states of customers, for example, are kept in one and the same Customer table. Corrections may or may not be flagged; but if they are not, it will be impossible to distinguish versions created because something about a customer changed from versions created because past customer data was entered incorrectly. On the other hand, if they are flagged, the management and use of these flags will quickly become difficult and confusing.

There are many variations on the theme of versioning, which we have grouped into four major categories. We will discuss them in Chapter 4.

The IT community has always used the term "version" for this kind of uni-temporal data. And this terminology seems to reflect an awareness of an important concept that, as we shall see, is central to the Asserted Versioning approach to temporal data. For the term "version" naturally raises the question "A version of what?", to which our answer is "A version of anything that can persist and change over time". This is the concept of a persistent object, and it is, most fundamentally, what Asserted Versioning is about.

### Bi-Temporal State Data

We now come to our second option, which is to manage both versions and assertions and, most importantly, their interdependencies. This is bi-temporal data management, the subject of both Dr. Rick Snodgrass's book [2000, Snodgrass] and of our book.

### The Standard Temporal Model

What we call *the standard temporal model* was developed by Dr. Rick Snodgrass in his book *Developing Time-Oriented Database Applications in SQL* (Morgan-Kaufmann, 2000). Based on the computer science work current at that time, and especially on the work Dr. Snodgrass and others had done on the TSQL (temporal SQL) proposal to the SQL standards committees, it shows how to implement both uni-temporal and bi-temporal data management using then-current DBMSs and then-current SQL.

We emphasize that, as we are writing, Dr. Snodgrass's book is a decade old. We use it as our baseline view of computer science work on bi-temporal data because most of the computer science literature exists in the form of articles in scientific journals that are not readily accessible to many IT professionals. We also emphasize that Dr. Snodgrass did not write that book as a compendium of computer science research for an IT audience. Instead, he wrote it as a description of how some of that research could be adapted to provide a means of managing bi-temporal data with the SQL and the DBMSs available at that time.

One of the greatest strengths of the standard model is that it discusses and illustrates both the maintenance and the querying of temporal data at the level of SQL statements. For example, it shows us the kind of code that is needed to apply the temporal analogues of entity integrity and referential integrity to temporal data. And for any readers who might think that temporal data management is just a small step beyond the versioning they are already familiar with, many of the constraint-checking SQL statements shown in Dr. Snodgrass's book should suffice to disabuse them of that notion.

### The Asserted Versioning Temporal Model

What we call *the Asserted Versioning temporal model* is our own approach to managing temporal data. Like the standard model, it attempts to manage temporal data with current technology and current SQL.

The Asserted Versioning model of uni-temporal and bi-temporal data management supports all of the functionality of the standard model. In addition, it extends the standard model's notion of transaction time by permitting data to be physically added to a table *prior* to the time when that data will appear in the table as production data, available for use. This is done by means of *deferred transactions*, which result in *deferred assertions*, those being the inserted, updated or logically deleted rows resulting from those transactions.[7] Deferred assertions, although physically co-located in the same tables as other data, will not be immediately available to normal queries. But once time in the real world reaches the beginning of their assertion periods, they will, by that very fact, become currently asserted data, part of the production data that makes up the database as it is perceived by its users.

We emphasize that deferred assertions are not the same thing as rows describing what things will be like at some time in the future. Those latter rows are current claims about what things will be like in the future. They are *ontologically* post-dated. Deferred assertions are rows describing what things were, are, or will be like, but rows which we are not yet willing to claim make true statements. They are *epistemologically* post-dated.

Another way that Asserted Versioning differs from the standard temporal model is in the encapsulation and simplification of integrity constraints. The *encapsulation* of integrity constraints is made possible by distinguishing temporal transactions from physical transactions. Temporal transactions are the ones that users write. The corresponding physical transactions are what the DBMS applies to asserted version tables. The Asserted Versioning Framework (AVF) uses an API to accept temporal transactions. Once it validates them, the AVF translates each temporal transaction into one or more physical transactions. By means of triggers generated from a combination of a logical data model together with supplementary metadata, the AVF enforces temporal semantic constraints as it submits physical transactions to the DBMS.

The *simplification* of these integrity constraints is made possible by introducing the concept of an *episode*. With non-temporal tables, a row representing an object can be inserted into that table at some point in time, and later deleted from the table. After it is deleted, of course, that table no longer contains the information that the row was ever present. Corresponding to the period of time during which that row existed in that non-temporal table, there would be an episode in an asserted version table, consisting of one or more temporally contiguous rows for the same object. So an episode of an object in an asserted version table is in effect during exactly the period of time that a row for that object would exist in a non-temporal table. And just as a deletion in a conventional table can sometime later be followed by the insertion of a new row with the same primary key, the termination of an

---

[7]The term "deferred transaction" was suggested by Dr. Snodgrass during a series of email exchanges which the authors had with him in the summer of 2008.

episode in an assertion version table can sometime later be followed by the insertion of a new episode for the same object.

In a non-temporal table, each row must conform to entity integrity and referential integrity constraints. In an asserted version table, each version must conform to temporal entity integrity and temporal referential integrity constraints. As we will see, the parallels are in more than name only. Temporal entity integrity really is entity integrity applied to temporal data. Temporal referential integrity really is referential integrity applied to temporal data.

## Glossary References

Glossary entries whose definitions form strong interdependencies are grouped together in the following list. The same glossary entries may be grouped together in different ways at the end of different chapters, each grouping reflecting the semantic perspective of each chapter. There will usually be several other, and often many other, glossary entries that are not included in the list, and we recommend that the Glossary be consulted whenever an unfamiliar term is encountered.

---

as-is
as-was

Asserted Versioning
Asserted Versioning Framework (AVF)

episode
persistent object
state
thing

physical transaction
temporal transaction

temporal entity integrity (TEI)
temporal referential integrity (TRI)

the alternative temporal model
the Asserted Versioning temporal model
the standard temporal model

---

# AN INTRODUCTION TO ASSERTED VERSIONING

## Chapter Contents

Part 1 provided the context for Asserted Versioning, a history and a taxonomy of various ways in which temporal data has been managed over the last several decades. Here in Part 2, we introduce Asserted Versioning itself and prepare the way for the detailed discussion in Part 3 of how Asserted Versioning actually works.

In Chapter 3, we discuss the origins of Asserted Versioning in computer science research. Based on the work of computer scientists, we introduce the concepts of a *clock tick* and an *atomic clock tick*, the latter of which, in their terminology, is called a *chronon*. We go on to discuss the various ways in which *time periods* are represented by pairs of dates or of timestamps, since SQL does not directly support the concept of a time period.

There are only a finite number of ways that two time periods can be situated, with respect to one another, along a common

Managing Time in Relational Databases. Doi: 10.1016/B978-0-12-375041-9.00024-8

timeline. For example, one time period may entirely precede or entirely follow another, they may partially overlap or be identical, they may start at different times but end at the same time, and so on. These different relationships among pairs of time periods have been identified and catalogued, and are called the *Allen relationships*. They will play an important role in our discussions of Asserted Versioning because there are various ways in which we will want to compare time periods. With the Allen relationships as a completeness check, we can make sure that we have considered all the possibilities.

Another important section of this chapter discusses the difference between the computer science notion of transaction time, and our own notion of assertion time. This difference is based on our development of the concepts of *deferred transactions* and *deferred assertions*, and for their subsumption under the more general concept of a *pipeline dataset*.

In Chapter 4, we discuss the origins of Asserted Versioning in IT best practices, specifically those related to versioning. We believe that these practices are variations on four basic methods of versioning data. In this chapter, we present each of these methods by means of examples which include sample tables and a running commentary on how inserts, updates and deletes affect the data in those tables.

In Chapter 5, we present the conceptual foundations of Asserted Versioning. The core concepts of *objects, episodes, versions* and *assertions* are defined, a discussion which leads us to the fundamental statement of Asserted Versioning, that every row in an asserted version table is the assertion of a version of an episode of an object. We continue on to discuss how time periods are represented in asserted version tables, how *temporal entity integrity* and *temporal referential integrity* enforce the core semantics of Asserted Versioning, and finally how Asserted Versioning internalizes the complexities of temporal data management.

In Chapter 6, we introduce the schema common to all asserted version tables, as well as various diagrams and notations that will be used in the rest of the book. We also introduce the topic of how Asserted Versioning supports the dynamic views that hide the complexities of that schema from query authors who would otherwise likely be confused by that complexity.

When an object is represented by a row in a non-temporal table, the sequence of events begins with the insertion of that row, continues with zero or more updates, and either continues on with no further activity, or ends when the row is eventually deleted. When an object is represented in an asserted version table, the result includes one row corresponding to the insert in the non-temporal table, additional rows corresponding to the updates to the original row in the non-temporal table, and an additional row if a delete eventually takes place. This sequence of events constitutes what we call the *basic scenario* of activity against both conventional and asserted version tables. In Chapter 7, we describe how the basic scenario works when the target of that activity is an asserted version table.

## Glossary References

Glossary entries whose definitions form strong interdependencies are grouped together in the following list. The same Glossary entries may be grouped together in different ways at the end of different chapters, each grouping reflecting the semantic perspective of each chapter. There will usually be several other, and often many other, Glossary entries that are not included in the list, and we recommend that the Glossary be consulted whenever an unfamiliar term is encountered.

Allen relationships
time period

assertion
version
episode
object

assertion time
transaction time

atomic clock tick
chronon
clock tick

deferred assertion
deferred transaction
pipeline dataset

temporal entity integrity
temporal referential integrity

# THE ORIGINS OF ASSERTED VERSIONING: COMPUTER SCIENCE RESEARCH

We begin this chapter with an overview of the three sources of Asserted Versioning: computer science work on temporal data; best practices in the IT profession related to versioning; and original work by the authors themselves. We then spend the rest of this chapter discussing computer science contributions to temporal data management, and the relevance of some of these concepts to Asserted Versioning.

## The Roots of Asserted Versioning

Over the last three decades, the computer science community has done extensive work on temporal data, and especially on bi-temporal data. During that same period of time, the IT community has developed various forms of versioning, all of which are methods of managing one of the two kinds of uni-temporal data.

Asserted Versioning may be thought of as a method of managing both uni- and bi-temporal data which, unlike the standard model of temporal data management, recognizes that rows in bi-temporal tables represent versions of things and that,

Managing Time in Relational Databases. Doi: 10.1016/B978-0-12-375041-9.00003-0

consequently, these rows do not stand alone as semantic objects. Versions that are versions of the same thing are related to one another by that very fact. Versions that are versions of the same thing, and also that together represent an unbroken period of time in the life of that thing, are even more closely related to one another. Groups of temporally contiguous versions of the same thing are semantic objects that must be managed as single temporal objects, even though they may consist of any number of physical rows. These single semantic objects are what we call *episodes*.

Asserted Versioning may also be thought of as a form of *versioning*, a technique for managing historical data that has evolved in the IT industry over the last quarter-century. But unlike existing best practice variations on that theme, Asserted Versioning supports the *full* semantics of versions, i.e. everything that it is conceptually possible to do with versions. In addition, Asserted Versioning also integrates the management of versions with the management of assertions and with the management of bi-temporal data. As we pointed out earlier, it directly manages bi-temporal physical tables, and manages both forms of uni-temporal tables, as well as conventional tables, as views over those bi-temporal tables.

Besides embracing contributions from computer science research and from business IT best practices, we believe that Asserted Versioning introduces three new concepts to the field of temporal data management. The first concept is that of an *episode*. In making episodes central to its management of temporal data, Asserted Versioning breaks with a basic component of the relational model, which is that integrity constraints apply only to individual rows. For example, referential integrity, in the relational model, requires that every foreign key in one row expresses a valid relationship which that row has to one other row. In Asserted Versioning, a temporalized foreign key expresses a relationship which one row, called a version, has to an episode, not to any single row which is part of that episode.

The second concept is that of the *internalization of pipeline datasets*. We define a *pipeline dataset* as any collection of business data that is not a production table, but that contains data whose destination or origin is such a table.[1] Pipeline datasets

---

[1]The term "production" indicates that these tables contain "real" data. Regularly scheduled processes are being carried out to maintain these tables, and to keep their contents as accurate, secure and current as possible. Regularly scheduled processes, as well as non-scheduled ones, are being carried out to access this data to obtain needed information. So production tables are the tables that the business tries to keep accurate, current and secure, and from which it draws the information it needs to carry out its mission and meet its objectives.

which contains data destined for production tables are *inflow pipeline datasets*. Pipeline datasets which contain data derived from production tables are *outflow pipeline datasets*.

History tables are one example of a pipeline dataset. Sets of transactions, accumulated in files or tables and waiting to be applied to their target tables, are another example. While the use of versions eliminates history tables by internalizing them within the tables whose history they track, the use of *deferred transactions* and *deferred assertions* eliminates batch files of transactions waiting to be applied to a database by also internalizing them within their target tables. In this book, we will show how the use of these internalized managed objects reduces the costs of maintaining databases by replacing external files or tables such as history tables, transaction files and logfiles, with structures internalized within production tables rather than being external to them.

The third concept is that of *encapsulation*, as it applies to the management of temporal data. Asserted Versioning fully encapsulates the complexities of maintaining temporal tables by distinguishing between *temporal transactions* and *physical transactions*. Temporal transactions are inserts, updates and deletes, as written by their authors, whose targets are asserted version tables. They are submitted to the Asserted Versioning Framework (AVF), not directly to the DBMS. The AVF translates them into physical insert and update transactions which it submits to the DBMS. These physical transactions implement the intentions expressed in those temporal transactions, and we note that, except for temporal insert transactions, one temporal transaction will always be translated into multiple physical transactions. In Part 3, we discuss several temporal transactions, and show both the physical transactions the AVF creates to implement these temporal transactions, and also how the AVF knows how to map between the two.

The practical orientation of Asserted Versioning is manifest in its encapsulation of the complexities of temporal data structures and the processes that manage them. Asserted Versioning is an integrated method of managing temporal data which relieves *data modelers* of the burden of designing and maintaining data models that must explicitly define temporal data structures and integrity constraints on them. It also relieves *developers* of the burden of designing, writing and maintaining code that enforces the rules which provide the semantics of temporal data. And it relieves *query authors*, whether developers or end users, of the burden of writing complex queries that must explicitly check for temporal gaps or overlaps, along one or two temporal dimensions, among a set of rows accessed by the query.

The origins of Asserted Versioning in computer science research, in IT best practices, and in contributions from the authors, are illustrated in Figure 3.1. Although deferred transactions and deferred assertions are the mechanisms for the internalization of several pipeline datasets, they are shown as a separate item in Figure 3.1 because of their particular importance.

## Computer Science Research

In 2000, Dr. Rick Snodgrass stated that academics had published, at that time, over 1500 articles on temporal data management [2000, Snodgrass, xviii]. And over the last decade, much additional work has been done. For our purposes, this work falls into two categories: (i) research relevant to our task of designing and building a method of temporal data management that works with today's technology; and (ii) research on future directions for the implementation of temporal functions in commercial DBMSs, and for the specification of these functions in extensions to the current SQL standard.

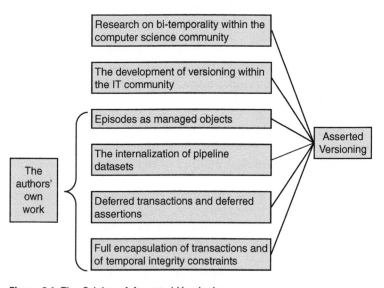

**Figure 3.1** The Origins of Asserted Versioning.

## Clocks and Clock Ticks

An *atomic clock tick* is the smallest interval of time recognized by the DBMS that can elapse between any two physical modifications to a database.[2] We note that the standard computer science term for an atomic clock tick is a *chronon*. A *clock tick* is an interval of time defined on the basis of atomic clock ticks, and that is used in an Asserted Versioning database to delimit the two time periods of rows in asserted version tables, and also to indicate several important points in time. In asserted version tables, clock ticks are used for effective time begin and end dates and for episode begin dates; and atomic clock ticks are used for assertion time begin and end dates, and for row create dates.

Clock ticks may be defined at any level of granularity supported by the underlying DBMS. A timestamp is a typical clock tick. A date represents a daily clock tick. A 1-month clock tick represents a situation in which a database is updated from a collection of transactions at most once a month.

When time periods measured in clock ticks of different granularities are compared, the technical issues involved in the comparison are complex, even if the conceptual issues are not. In our own implementation of Asserted Versioning, we finesse these issues by requiring that all asserted version tables in the same database use clock ticks of the same granularity. In this book, we assume, albeit somewhat unrealistically, that all asserted version tables use a clock that ticks once a month (except where otherwise noted), and we will use the first day of each month to represent those clock ticks. This means that changes to these asserted version tables happen on the first of each month and, by the same token, that the state of the database after each monthly update will remain unaltered for the rest of the month.

But no matter what granularity we choose for our clock ticks, there is the issue of how clock ticks of one level of granularity are mapped onto those of another level. For example, if we choose a clock tick of one day, when does that day start? Does June 1st, 2012 begin at 2012-06-01-12:00:00.000, or perhaps at 2012-06-01-12:00:00.001, or perhaps even at 2012-05-31-11:59:59.999? The simplest solution is to let the DBMS determine the mapping for us; and in most cases this is perfectly adequate. But IT data management professionals should at least be aware that issues like these do exist.

---

[2]We are not referring here to the cesium-based atomic clock on which standard time is based. An atomic clock tick, in the sense being defined here, is a logical concept, not a physical one.

They should also be aware that another issue exists, that of how SQL timestamps map to when things happen in the real world. SQL uses Universal Coordinated Time (UTC), which is based on cesium clocks, which might lead us to conclude that SQL timestamps are extremely accurate. *Precise* they may be; but issues of *accuracy* involved in their use do exist.

For example, suppose we know that an astronomical event which has just happened will happen again in exactly 725 days, 5 hours and 23 seconds. If we know the SQL timestamp when the event occurred, can we calculate exactly what the SQL timestamp will be when the event happens again? We can, of course, calculate the number of seconds that will have elapsed between the two events, that number being 62,658,023.

But it is a mistake to conclude that from knowing the timestamp of the first event and also knowing the number of seconds until the second event, we can calculate the timestamp of the second event. In fact, we cannot reliably do that. The reason is that from the moment the first timestamp is current to the moment that the second timestamp is current, one or more leap seconds may have been added to or subtracted from the count of cesium clock ticks between those two timestamps, and for the same reason that a leap day is added to the Gregorian calendar once every four years. But unlike the leap year adjustment, which is regular enough to count on, we do not know, in advance, how many leap seconds might be added or subtracted between now and the next occurrence of that astronomical event, or when those adjustments may occur.

The unpredictable adjustment of UTC and its SQL timestamps by means of leap seconds is seldom an issue in business IT. The reason is that for business purposes, we all tag our data with SQL timestamps, and we all regard those timestamps as an accurate record of when business events happen in the real world. In addition, for most business purposes, we assume that a SQL timestamp plus a defined interval of time will result in a second timestamp that represents when some second event will occur.[3]

## Time Periods and Date Pairs

SQL does not recognize a period of time as a managed object. Instead, we have to use a pair of dates. There are four ways we can use a pair of dates to do this. Either the beginning date, or

---

[3]A more detailed discussion of how SQL timestamps relate to real-world events is contained in Chapter 3 of Dr. Snodgrass's book.

the ending date, or both, may or may not be included in the time period they delimit. If a date is not included, the time period is said to be open on that end; otherwise it is said to be closed.

A discussion of all four ways of representing time periods with begin and end dates can be found in the book presenting the standard temporal model [2000, Snodgrass] and also in the book presenting the alternative temporal model [2002, Date, Darwen, Lorentzos]. Here, we discuss just two of the four combinations: closed-open and closed-closed. This is because the closed-open representation is actually the best way of representing time periods, whereas the closed-closed representation *appears* to be the best way of doing that.

Consider two versions of the same object, $V_1$ and $V_2$. In both cases, in this example, the first time period for the object starts on 2/19/2011 and ends on 5/22/2011, and the second starts on 5/23/2011 and ends on 10/14/2012.[4] Consequently there is no gap in time between these two time periods. 5/22/2011 and 5/23/2011 are contiguous clock ticks.

How are we to represent this? Two of the possibilities are shown in Figures 3.2 and 3.3.

Given that the first time period starts on 2/19/2011 and ends on 5/22/2011, and that the second time period starts on 5/23/2011 and ends on 10/14/2012, it might seem that the closed-closed representation is obviously the correct one, and that the closed-open representation is obviously wrong. But that is not the case.

If we wanted to argue in support of the closed-closed representation, we could try to show that the closed-open representation

|       | $D_1$     | $D_2$      |
|-------|-----------|------------|
| $V_1$ | 2/19/2011 | 5/23/2011  |
| $V_2$ | 5/23/2011 | 10/15/2012 |

**Figure 3.2** A Closed-Open Representation of Two Time Periods.

|       | $D_1$     | $D_2$      |
|-------|-----------|------------|
| $V_1$ | 2/19/2011 | 5/22/2011  |
| $V_2$ | 5/23/2011 | 10/14/2012 |

**Figure 3.3** A Closed-Closed Representation of Two Time Periods.

[4]In this section, we will assume that our clock ticks once a day.

should not be used by querying for the time period that contains the date 5/23/2011. On the closed-open representation, it might seem that we can't tell to which version 5/23/2011 belongs. But in fact, we can. We just need the following WHERE clause predicate in our SQL query:

```
WHERE D₁ <= '05/23/2011' AND '05/23/2011' < D₂
```

With this predicate, the query will correctly pick out $V_2$ from Figure 3.2.

So one reason we might have thought that the closed-closed representation is right is that its begin and end dates are the same dates we used to set up the example when we said that one period begins and ends on one set of dates and the other period begins and ends on the other set of dates. Another reason we might have thought that the closed-closed representation is right is that we are looking for a pair of dates that a third date is *between*.

*Between*, in one sense, is on display in the statement "Pick a number between 1 and 10". We all know that 1 and 10 are both numbers that we can pick. And the SQL BETWEEN operator corresponds to this sense of the word. So if we use the closed-closed representation, we can write:

```
WHERE '05/23/2011' BETWEEN D₁ AND D₂
```

In other words, when a closed-closed representation is used, we can rely on SQL's BETWEEN to express what we ordinarily mean by "between", which is what we might call the *inclusive sense* of "between".

But there is another sense of *between*, which is on display in the statement "The abandoned car is somewhere between mileposts 6 and 10, along I-65N, heading out of Pensacola". We all know that to find the car, we should start at milepost 6 and continue up to milepost 10. In particular, we know that we don't need to search past milepost 10, i.e. past the start of the tenth mile heading out of Pensacola.

This is the sense of *between* used in the closed-open convention. The closest English equivalent would be "from . . . . . up to", in the sense of "from" and then "up to but not including". But since each SQL predicate returns the correct result, provided each is used with its corresponding method of representing periods of time, each method is correct.

What, then, is the advantage of using the closed-open representation? Well, look again at the two ways of representing $V_1$ and $V_2$. In both cases, $V_1$ and $V_2$ are contiguous. We know this because we have set up the example that way. And with the closed-open representation, we can immediately *see* that there is no gap between $V_1$ and $V_2$. But with the closed-closed representation, we don't know whether there is a gap or not. To make that determination, we also need to know at what rate the clock ticks. Assuming for this particular example that the clock ticks once a day, then only when given this additional information can we determine, from a closed-closed representation, that $V_1$ and $V_2$ have no gap between them.

This difficulty of determining whether or not two consecutive versions of the same object are contiguous is not just a problem for the human beings trying to understand the data. It is also a problem for the code which will often be called upon to determine, of two consecutive versions, whether or not they are contiguous, i.e. whether or not there is a clock tick between them. With a closed-open representation, the code only has to compare two values to see whether or not they are EQUAL.

Making matters worse, the granularity of DBMS timestamp datatypes has changed over time. Originally, these timestamps were seconds. Later, they were expressed as milliseconds, then partial microseconds, then microseconds, and now we are almost at the point where timestamps will be expressed in nanoseconds. With this sliding scale, across DBMSs and DBMS upgrades, we might not even know the granularity at which to try to determine if two versions are or are not contiguous. With a closed-open representation, the code to make this determination is trivial. With a closed-open representation, it may actually be impossible.

Once the SQL standards groups can agree on temporal extensions to the SQL standard, part of that agreement will certainly be a way of representing time periods directly, without relying on the confusing circumlocutions of various ways of using pairs of dates to represent time periods. But our concern, in this book, is with today's SQL, and so we must choose a date-pair method of representation.[5] Therefore, from this point forward, we will use the closed-open representation for time periods.

### 9999 and 12/31/9999

We will use the notation *9999* in our illustrations, to represent the latest date that the DBMS can recognize and manipulate.

---

[5]Support for a PERIOD datatype has been introduced by such vendors as Oracle and Teradata. But what that support means may differ from vendor to vendor. Can a unique index be defined on a PERIOD datatype? Which of the Allen relationship comparisons are also supported? So, lacking a standard for the PERIOD datatype, we will continue the practice of defining periods of time in terms of their begin and end points in time.

That latest date cannot be used in effective or assertion *begin* dates. If it is used as business data, then it has whatever meaning its users assign to it, which will probably be as the designation of a day which is still a long way off. But if it is used in effective or assertion *end* dates, it is treated as a date by the DBMS but is not interpreted as a date by the users of the system. Instead, to those users, it means "later than now". Equivalently, we can say that it means "end of the time period not known, but assumed to not have happened yet". We will generally use the phrase *until further notice* to represent this semantics—in effect until further notice, or asserted as true until further notice.

When we specify an insert or an update against a conventional table, we normally do not know when, if ever, the target row will be next updated or deleted. By the same token, when we specify a temporal insert or a temporal update against a bi-temporal table, we normally do not know when, if ever, the effective time period of the new version will end, because we don't know when, if ever, a subsequent update or deletion will occur.

Some data modelers will argue that NULL should be used for unknown data. While logically, this is true, the performance of the physical model will benefit from this non-null datatype, as will be explained in Chapter 15. Moreover, we do know one thing about this unknown date. For as long as it is unknown, we choose to assume that it has not happened yet. In other words, for as long as it is unknown, we want the DBMS to tell us that it is greater than the value of Now(), whenever we ask that question. If we used NULL instead of a data value, the DBMS would *not* give us that answer to that question.

If an effective end date is unknown, then, instead of using NULL, we will set it to *12/31/9999*, or to whatever value represents the future-most date that the particular DBMS can manage. So the semantics is *date unknown* (but still in the future), but the implementation is a real date, one in this case that is nearly 8000 years from now. How does a date like that represent semantics like that?

First, we assume that the date 12/31/9999 will not be required to represent that far-off New Year's Eve. So it is available to use for a special purpose. In the case of an effective end date, we often insert or update versions without knowing when the effective time period of the new version may end. So in this case, 12/31/9999 means that the end of the effective time period of the version thus marked is unknown, and that the time period will remain in effect until further notice. For example, when a customer's address is added to the database, we usually will not know when that customer will move from that address.

So the status of that address is that it will remain in effect until that customer moves, at some unknown date in the future.

In the case of an assertion end date, that date is always set to 12/31/9999 when a row is created. This reflects the assumption that we would never want to assert that a version is true, while also knowing that, at some later point in time, we will change our minds and no longer be willing to make that assertion. While we adopt this assumption in this book, and in the software which is our implementation of these concepts, we note that a more robust semantics might not include this assumption and that, consequently, later releases of our Asserted Versioning Framework may permit non-12/31/9999 assertion end dates to be specified on temporal transactions.[6]

An effective end date may be changed, i.e. the time period it ends may be shortened or lengthened, as long as the change does not violate temporal integrity constraints, which we will discuss in Part 3. As for an assertion end date, it may be changed for one of four reasons.

First, an assertion end date may be changed because we realize that the assertion is incorrect, and we have the correction for that error. In that case, the incorrect assertion will cease to be asserted, i.e. it will be *withdrawn*, as part of the same atomic unit of work that inserts the correcting assertion, and the same date will be used both for the assertion end date of the incorrect assertion and the assertion begin date of the correcting assertion.

Second, an assertion end date may be changed because we realize that an assertion is incorrect even though we do not know what the correct data is, or else just because, for some reason, we do not wish to make that assertion any longer. Third, we may conclude that an assertion about the future is no longer actionable, probably because both we and our competitors have more recent and presumably more accurate forecasts. In either case,

---

[6]As we briefly allude to, later on, what we assert by means of a row in a table is not so much that the statement made by the row is true. It is, rather, that the statement is actionable. An actionable statement, roughly, is one which is good enough to base a business decision on. Presumably, statements about the past or the present must be true in order to be actionable. But statements about the future, such as financial forecasts, lack a known truth value until the future time about which they are forecasting comes to pass, at which point those statements become either true or false. Such statements may be actionable when first made, and thus be actionable without being true. Moreover, they may be actionable when first made but, over time, become outdated, even prior to becoming true or false. (See, later in this chapter, the section The Very Concept of Bi-Temporality. See also Chapter 13, the section *Posted Projections: Past Claims About the Future*.)

the row representing that assertion will cease to be asserted on that date even if no correcting assertion is supplied to replace it.

The last reason an assertion end date may be changed is to *lock* an assertion which has been updated or deleted by a deferred transaction, until the resulting deferred assertion becomes current. We will have more to say about deferred transactions, deferred assertions and locking in Chapter 13.

### Now() and UTC

Keeping our notation DBMS agnostic, and keeping the clock tick granularity generic, we will refer to the current moment, to right now, as *Now()*.[7] SQL Server may use *getdate()*, and DB2 may use *Current Timestamp* or *Current Date*. Depending on our clock tick duration, we might need to use a date formatting function to set the current granularity. In our examples, we generally use one month as our clock tick granularity. However for our purposes, *Now()* can take on values at whatever level of granularity we choose to use, including day, second or microsecond.

Now() is usually assumed to represent the current moment by using local time. But local time may change because of entering or leaving Daylight Savings Time. And another issue is time zone. At any one time, data about to update a database may exist in a different time zone than the database itself. Users about to retrieve data from a database may exist in a different time zone than the database itself. And, of course, federated queries may attempt to join data from databases located in different time zones.

So the data values returned by Now() can change for reasons other than the passage of time. Daylight Savings Time can change those values. At any one point in time, those values can differ because of time zones. Clearly, we need a reference framework, and a set of values, that will not change for any reason other than the passage of time, and that will be the same value, at any point in time, the world over and year around.

This reference framework is Universal Coordinated Time (UTC).[8] To make use of UTC, our Asserted Versioning Framework will convert local time to UTC on maintenance and queries, and

---

[7]Now() is a function that returns the current date. It is not a value. However, we will often use it to designate a specific point in time. For example, we may say that a time period starts at Now() and continues on until 12/31/9999. This is a shorthand way of emphasizing that, whenever that time period was created, it was given as its begin date the value returned by Now() at that moment.

[8]However, even in UTC, some variations in time values do not reflect the passage of time. We are referring here to the periodic adjustments in UTC made by adding or removing leap seconds, as we described in an earlier section of this chapter.

will store Asserted Versioning temporal parameters, such as begin and end dates, in UTC. For example, with Policy_AV being an asserted version table of insurance policies, we would insert a policy like this:

```
INSERT INTO Policy_AV (oid, asr_beg_dt . . . . .)
VALUES (55, CURRENT TIMESTAMP - CURRENT TIMEZONE . . . . .)
```

For queries, they will perform better if we do the time conversion before using the value as a selection predicate in the SQL itself. This is because most optimizers treat functions that appear in predicates as non-indexable. For example, in DB2, we should write:

```
SET :my-cut = TIMESTAMP(:my-local-time-value) - CURRENT
TIMEZONE
SELECT . . . . . FROM . . . . .
      WHERE oid = 55
      AND asr_beg_dt <= :my-cut
      AND asr_end_dt > :my-cut
```

rather than

```
SELECT . . . . . FROM . . . . .
      WHERE oid = 55
      AND asr_beg_dt <=
      TIMESTAMP(:my-local-time-value) - CURRENT TIMEZONE
      AND . . . . .
```

However, if these functions are used for display purposes, then there is no reason to exclude them from the queries. For example:

```
SELECT asr_beg_dt + CURRENT TIMEZONE AS my_local_asr_beg_dt . .
. . . FROM . . . . .
```

It would also be useful to add alternate columns for the temporal dates in our views that have the translation to local time performed already.

## The Very Concept of Bi-Temporality

Business IT professionals were using tables with both an effective date and a physical row create date by the early 90s.[9] But they were doing so with apparently no knowledge of

---

[9]Or timestamps, or other datatypes. We remind the reader that, throughout this book, we use the date datatype for all temporal columns, and a first of the month value for all our dates. This simplifies the presentation without affecting any of the semantics. In real business applications, of course, these columns would often be timestamps.

academic work on bi-temporality. At that time, these version tables which also contained a row create date were state of the art in best practice methods for managing temporal data. We will discuss them in the next chapter.

With a row creation date, of course, any query can be restricted to the rows present in a table as of any specific date by including a WHERE clause predicate that qualifies only those rows whose create date is less than or equal to the specified date. With two effective dates, tables like these are also able to specify one of the two temporal dimensions that make up full bi-temporality.

The standard temporal model uses the term "valid time" where we use the term "effective time". But the difference is purely verbal. We have found no differences between how valid time works in the standard model, and how effective time works in Asserted Versioning. We use "effective time" because it is the preferred term among business IT professionals, and also because it readily adapts itself to other grammatical forms such as "becoming effective" and "in effect".

The standard model states that "(v)alid time . . . captur(es) the history of a changing reality, and transaction time . . . . . captur(es) the sequence of states of a changing table . . . . . A table supporting both is termed a "bi-temporal table" [2000, Snodgrass, p. 20]. But as we will see later, Asserted Versioning does not define bi-temporality in exactly the same way. The difference lies primarily in the second of the two temporal dimensions, what computer scientists call "transaction time" and what we call "assertion time". While a transaction begin date always indicates when a row is physically inserted into a table, an assertion begin date indicates when we are first willing to assert, or claim, that a row is a true statement about the object it represents, during that row's effective (valid) time period, and also that the quality of the row's data is good enough to base business decisions on.

In the standard temporal model, the beginning of a transaction time period is the date on which the row is created. Obviously, once the row is created, that date cannot be changed. But in the Asserted Versioning temporal model, an assertion time period begins *either* on the date a row is created, *or* on a later date.

Because an assertion begin date is not necessarily the same as the date on which its row is physically created, Asserted Versioning needs, in addition to the pair of dates that define this time period, an additional date which is the physical creation date of each row. That date serves as an audit trail, and as a means of reconstructing a table as it physically existed at any past point in time.

What are these rows with future assertion begin dates? To take a single example, they might be rows for which we have some of the business data, but not all of it, rows which are in the process of being made ready "for prime time". These rows—which may be assertions about past, present or future versions—are not yet ready, we will say, to become part of the *production data* in the table, not yet ready to become rows that we are willing to present to the world and of which we are willing to say "We stand behind the statements these rows make. We claim that the statements they make are (or are likely to become) true, and that the information these rows provide meets the standards of reliability understood (or explicitly stated) to apply to all rows in this table".

So the semantics of the standard temporal model are fully supported by Asserted Versioning. But Asserted Versioning adds the semantics of what we call *deferred assertions*, and which we have just briefly described. As we will see in later chapters, deferred assertions are just one kind of internalized pipeline dataset, and the internalization of pipeline datasets can eliminate a large part of the IT maintenance budget by eliminating the need to manage pipeline datasets as distinct physical objects.

## Allen Relationships

Allen relationships describe all possible positional relationships between two time periods along a common timeline. This includes the special case of one or both time periods being a point in time, i.e. being exactly one clock tick in length.

There are 13 Allen relationships in total. Six have a corresponding inverse relationship, and one does not. Standard treatments of the Allen relationships may be found in both [2000, Snodgrass] and [2002, Date, Darwen, Lorentzos]. We have found it useful to reconstruct the Allen relationships as a binary taxonomy. Our taxonomy is shown in Figure 3.4.

In this diagram, the leaf nodes include a graphic in which there are two timelines, each represented by a dashed line. All the leaf nodes but one have an inverse, and that one is italicized; when two time periods are identical, they do not have a distinct inverse. Thus, this taxonomy specifies 13 leaf-node relationships which are, in fact, precisely the 13 Allen relationships.

The names of the Allen relationships are standard, and have been since Allen wrote his seminal article in 1983. But those names, and the names of the higher-level nodes in our own taxonomy of the Allen relationships, are also expressions in

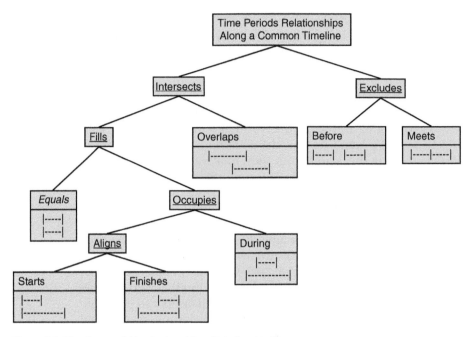

**Figure 3.4** The Asserted Versioning Allen Relationship Taxonomy.

ordinary language. In order to distinguish between the ordinary language and the technical uses of these terms, we will include the names of Allen relationships and our other taxonomy nodes in brackets when we are discussing them. We will also underline the non-leaf node relationships in the taxonomy, to emphasize that they are relationships we have defined, and are not one of the Allen relationships.

In the following discussion, the first time period in a pair of them is the one that is either earlier than the other, or not longer than the other.

Given two time periods on a common timeline, either they have at least one clock tick in common or they do not. If they do, we will say that they [intersect] one another. If they do not, we will say that they [exclude] one another.

If there is an [intersects] relationship between two time periods, then either one [fills] the other or each [overlaps] the other. If one time period [fills] another, then all its clock ticks are also in the time period it [fills], but not necessarily vice versa. If one time period [overlaps] another, then the latter also overlaps the former; but, being the later of the two time periods, we say that the latter time period has the inverse relationship, [overlaps$^{-1}$]. In the overlaps cases, each has at least one clock tick that the other does not have, as well as having at least one clock tick that the other does have.

If two time periods [exclude] one another, then they do not share any clock ticks, and they are either non-contiguous or contiguous. If there is at least one clock tick between them, they are non-contiguous and we say that one is [before] the other. Otherwise they are contiguous and we say that one [meets] the other.

If one time period [fills] the other, then either they are [*equal*], or one [occupies] the other. If they are [*equal*], then neither has a clock tick that the other does not have. If one [occupies] the other, then all the clock ticks in the occupying time period are also in the occupied time period, but not vice versa.

If one time period [occupies] the other, then either they share an [aligns] relationship, or one occurs [during] the other. If they are aligned, then they either start on the same clock tick or end on the same clock tick, and we say that one either [starts] or [finishes] the other. Otherwise, one occurs [during] the other, beginning after the other and ending before it. Note that if two time periods are aligned, one cannot both [start] and [finish] the other because if it did, it would be [*equal*] to the other.

If one time period [starts] another, they both begin on the same clock tick. If one [finishes] the other, they both end on the same clock tick. If one time period [occupies] another, but they are not aligned, then one occurs [during] the other.

Now let's consider the special case in which one of the two time periods is a point in time, i.e. is exactly one clock tick in length, and the other one contains two or more clock ticks. This point in time may either [intersect] or [exclude] the time period. If the point in time [intersects] the time period, it also [fills] and [occupies] that time period. If it [aligns] with the time period, then it either [starts] the time period or [finishes] it. Otherwise, the point in time occurs [during] the time period. If the point in time [excludes] the time period, then either may be [before] the other, or they may [meet].

Finally, let's consider one more special case, that in which both the time periods are points in time. Those two points in time may be [*equal*], or one may be [before] the other, or they may [meet]. There are no other Allen relationships possible for them.

As we will see later, four of these Allen relationship categories are especially important. They will be discussed in later chapters, but we choose to mention them here.

(i) The [intersects] relationship is important because for a temporal insert transaction to be valid, its effective time period cannot intersect that of any episode for the same object which is already in the target table. By the same token, for a temporal update or delete transaction to be valid, the target table must already contain at least one episode for the same object whose effective time period does [intersect] the time period designated by the transaction.

**(ii)** The [fills] relationship is important because violations of the temporal analog of referential integrity always involve the failure of a child time period to [fill] a parent time period. We will be frequently discussing this relationship from the parent side, and we would like to avoid having to say things like ". . . . . failure of a parent time period to be filled by a child time period". So we will use the term "includes" as a synonym for "is filled by", i.e. as a synonym for [fills$^{-1}$]. Now we can say ". . . . . failure of a parent time period to include a child time period".

**(iii)** The [before] relationship is important because it distinguishes episodes from one another. Every episode of an object is non-contiguous with every other episode of the same object, and so for each pair of them, one of them must be [before] the other.

**(iv)** The [meets] relationship is important because it groups versions for the same object into episodes. A series of versions for the same object that are all contiguous, i.e. that all [meet], fall within the same episode of that object.

## Advanced Indexing Strategies

Indexes are one way to improve performance. And it should be clear that it would be a serious performance handicap if we could not define indexes over either or both of the two time periods of a bi-temporal table. But this proves to be more complex than it might at first sight appear to be.

The issue is that traditional indexes contain pointers to rows, pointers which are based on discrete values, while the two time periods of rows in bi-temporal tables are not discrete values, but rather an unbroken and non-overlapping sequence of such values. Such rows occupy points in effective (valid) time or in assertion (transaction) time only as a limit case. What they really occupy are *intervals* along those two timelines. That's the reason we need two dates to describe each of them. Traditional balanced-tree indexes work well with discrete values, including such discrete values as dates. But they don't work well with intervals of time, i.e. with time periods.

But indexing methods which manage intervals are being developed. Specifically, some bi-temporal indexing methods manage the two intervals for a bi-temporal object as a single unit, which would appear as a rectangle on a Cartesian graph in which one temporal dimension is represented by the X-axis and the other by the Y-axis.

Another approach is to manage each of the two temporal dimensions separately. One reason for taking this approach is that, for the standard temporal model, the two temporal dimensions behave differently. Specifically, for the standard model, transaction time always moves forwards, whereas valid time can move forwards or backwards. This means that a bi-temporal row can be inserted into a table proactively in valid time, but can never be inserted into a table proactively in transaction time.

Asserted Versioning, as we have already pointed out, supports both forwards and backwards movement in both temporal dimensions. So for Asserted Versioning, there is no difference in behavior which would justify separating the two temporal dimensions for indexing purposes. Specifically, Asserted Versioning supports both proactive (future-dated) versions and proactive assertions (i.e. deferred assertions) and also both retroactive versions and an *approval* transaction which can move deferred assertions backwards in time, but not prior to Now(). In Chapter 15, we will describe certain indexing strategies that will improve performance using today's DBMS index designs.

## Temporal Extensions to SQL

Following [2000, Snodgrass], we will refer to a future release of the SQL language that will contain temporal extensions as SQL3. A more detailed discussion may be found in that book, although we should note that the book is, at the time of publication of this book, 10 years old.

### Temporal Upward Compatibility

One issue related to changes in the SQL standard is temporal upward compatibility. In describing SQL3, Snodgrass states that "(t)emporal upward compatibility at its core says this: 'Take an application that doesn't involve time, that concerns only the current reality. . . . . Alter one or more of the tables so that they now have temporal support . . . . . The application should run as before, *without changing a single line of code*'" [2000, Snodgrass, p. 449].

This cannot be an objective for Asserted Versioning, because we are limited to current SQL, not to a future release of SQL that builds temporal extensions into the language itself. But we can come close. We can achieve this objective for queries by using a view which filters out all but current data, and by redirecting existing queries to that view. We can achieve this objective for temporal inserts, updates and deletes by defining default effective and assertion dates for these transactions. These will be default dates that cause these transactions, as written by their authors, and as parsed and submitted to the DBMS by the AVF, to physically insert and update current assertions of the current versions of the objects they reference.

### The PERIOD Datatype

A second issue related to changes in the SQL standard is the need for a PERIOD datatype. This new datatype will not change the semantics of temporal data management, but it will simplify the expression of those semantics. For one thing, a single column will replace a pair of dates. This will simplify the way that Allen relationships are specified in SQL statements. For example, it will change the expression with which we ask whether a point in time is or is not contained in a period of time. Where P and T are, respectively, a point in time and a period of time, and $T_1$ and $T_2$ are dates delimiting T using the closed-open representation, we currently must ask whether P is a clock tick within T like this:

```
WHERE T₁ <= P AND P < T₂
```

With the PERIOD datatype, and the new Allen relationship operators that will accompany it (including such derivative operators as those used in our taxonomy), we will be able to ask the same question like this:

```
WHERE T OCCUPIES P
```

A PERIOD datatype will also make it easier to enforce constraints on time periods, such as insuring that two time periods do not intersect. When representing time periods by means of begin and end dates, this is impossible to do with only an index. Here's why.

Consider the time period represented by the closed-open pair [4/23/2012 – 8/04/2014]. Suppose that we want to define an exclusive index on time periods. The problem is that there is no way, by means of any standards-compliant indexing method available with today's technology, to exclude [3/12/2011 – 4/24/2012], or [10/15/2012 – 9/30/2013], or [6/1/2014 – 12/31/2014], or any other time period that in fact [intersects] the time period designated by [4/23/2012 – 8/04/2014]. The index sees two columns of values, and knows that the combination of values must be unique in each instance. That's all it sees, that's all it knows, and that's all it can enforce.

But if we had a PERIOD datatype, and SQL extensions and indexing methods that could recognize and manage that datatype, then all the Allen relationships among time periods could be easily expressed, and the very important [excludes] relationship could be enforced by means of a unique index. Lacking that future technology, and the standards needed to insure interoperability across different vendor implementations, the AVF contains its own code that effectively turns pairs of dates into a user-defined PERIOD datatype.

### Temporal Primary Keys

A third issue related to changes in the SQL standard is support for temporal primary keys. With those temporal extensions, we will be able to declare a temporal primary key to the DBMS and, by the same token, declare temporal foreign keys as well. But what is it we will be declaring? Temporal tags added to physically unique identifiers of rows of otherwise non-temporal tables? Or something more?

If a SQL standard for bi-temporality, when we eventually have one, is a standard for adding two temporal tags to rows in otherwise non-temporal tables, and providing a PERIOD data type and Allen relationship operators to manage the data thus tagged, then most of the semantics of bi-temporality will have been left out of that standard, and left up to developers. The managed objects of temporal data management are *not* physical rows in physical tables. They are collections of one or more rows which represent temporally delimited claims about temporally delimited statements about what real-world persistent objects were like, are like, or will be like.

As long as every database table contains one and only one row for each instance of the type indicated by the table, it is easy to forget about the semantics and concentrate on the mechanics. Primary key uniqueness is mechanics; its role in eliminating row-level synonyms—and its failure to address the problem of row-level homonyms—is the semantics that are easily and almost always overlooked. Foreign key referential integrity is mechanics; its role in expressing existence dependencies among the objects represented by those rows is the semantics that are easily and almost always overlooked.

It has been this one-to-one correlation between rows and the objects they represent that has made it easy to give short shrift to semantics, and to then get right down to what really fascinates engineering types—the mechanics of making things work. But once we attempt to manage both the epistemological and the ontological temporal dimensions of data, i.e. both assertion time and effective time, we must give up this comfortable one-to-one correlation. We must recognize that rows are no longer an adequate representation of the semantic objects that the bi-temporality of data reveals to us.

From the point of view of the conceptual foundations of Asserted Versioning, the declaration of a bi-temporal primary key must specify (i) a unique identifier for an *object*, (ii) an assertion time period, and (iii) an effective time period. In particular, that declaration must *not* specify simply (i) a unique identifier for an otherwise non-temporal *row*, (ii) a valid time period, and (iii) a transaction time period, one whose begin date is always the date on which the row was physically created.

### Temporal Logic

A fourth issue related to changes in the SQL standard is temporal logic. SQL implements a subset of propositional and first-order predicate logic (FOPL). Temporal extensions to SQL are not a matter of simply adding temporal features to SQL until we're pleased with the result. The logical foundations of those temporal extensions must be explored so that, as SQL is extended, we can remain confident that it is logically sound. Examples of work in temporal logic include first-order temporal logic (FOTL). Just as FOPL uses the quantifiers *for all X* and *for some X*, FOTL adds the quantifiers *at some time in the past, at every time in the past, at some time in the future* and *at every time in the future*, and also adds the binary predicates *SINCE* and *UNTIL*.

## Glossary References

Glossary entries whose definitions form strong interdependencies are grouped together in the following list. The same glossary entries may be grouped together in different ways at the end of different chapters, each grouping reflecting the semantic perspective of each chapter. There will usually be several other, and often many other, glossary entries that are not included in the list, and we recommend that the Glossary be consulted whenever an unfamiliar term is encountered.

We note, in particular, that none of the nodes in our Allen relationships taxonomy are included in this list. In general, we leave taxonomy nodes out of these lists, but recommend that the reader look them up in the Glossary.

clock tick
granularity
PERIOD datatype
point in time
time period

episode
managed object
object

pipeline dataset
inflow pipeline dataset
internalization of pipeline datasets
outflow pipeline dataset

replace
supercede
withdraw

statement

# THE ORIGINS OF ASSERTED VERSIONING: IT BEST PRACTICES

Lots of things are important to us. That's why we keep data about them in our databases. In a non-temporal table, each one of them, i.e. each object, is represented by one and only one row. In a *version table*, however, each row represents a period of time in the life of an object, and is a description of what that object is like during that time. And so, in a version table, there can be any number of rows representing the same object, each describing what the object is like during a different period of time.

In an *assertion table*, on the other hand, each row represents an assertion about an object, and represents what we said, during a specific period of time, that object is like. And so, in an assertion table, there also can be any number of rows representing the same object, each describing what we said, at a different period of time, the object is like.

Managing Time in Relational Databases. Doi: 10.1016/B978-0-12-375041-9.00004-2

Bi-temporal tables contain both kinds of information. Their rows tell us what we once asserted as true, currently assert as true, or may at some future time assert as true, a statement about what an object used to be like, is like right now, or may be like at some time in the future.

Because each object is represented by exactly one row in a non-temporal table, when updates are applied, those updates overwrite the data that was there before the update. Such updates are called "updates in place". But one problem with updates in place, of course, is that they lose information. They lose the information about what the object used to be like, about what it was like before the update. They lose historical information because they overwrite data.

Historical data can usually be found somewhere, of course, in archives and transaction logs if nowhere else. But if it is important to be able to quickly and easily access data about what objects used to be like, either by itself or together with data about what those objects are like now, then keeping that data in the same table that also contains data about the current state of those objects makes a lot of sense.

If we don't keep historical and current data in the same table, then query authors who need that data will need to be aware of the multiple table and column names, and the multiple different locations, where different subsets of historical data are kept; and, as we know, they often are not. Even if aware of all the places from which they will have to assemble the historical data they are interested in, they will also have to know which of possibly redundant copies of that data is the most current, and which the most reliable and complete; and, as we also know, they often don't.

They may need to rewrite queries, changing table and column names prior to pointing them to whichever copy of that data is chosen as the target for those queries; and in doing so, as we all know, they often make mistakes. And when tables of historical data are not kept column for column union-ably parallel with the corresponding tables containing current data, which is often the case, then the job of query authors becomes even more difficult and error-prone. They won't be able to simply copy production queries and change names. They will have to write new queries, perhaps joining data that the production queries did not have to join, perhaps assembling intermediate results and then combining those intermediate results in various complicated ways. In short, they may very quickly be taken into the realm of SQL queries that all but the most experienced query authors have no business writing.

Versioning is the IT community's way of providing queryable access to historical, current and future data. However, there are far too many variations of versioning to make an exhaustive review of them possible. So in this chapter, we will distinguish four main types of versioning, and will discuss one representative method of each type. Those four types are:

**(i)** Basic versioning;
**(ii)** Logical delete versioning;
**(iii)** Temporal gap versioning; and
**(iv)** Effective time versioning.

In this chapter, we will use several variations of a version table, and a corresponding non-temporal table, to present the basic mental model which we believe is essential to understanding how to manage versioned data. That mental model is that conventional and version tables of the same persistent objects (customers, policies, etc.) are related as follows.

An object is represented in a non-temporal table by a row which is put into that table at a certain point in time, may be updated during its tenure on the table, and may eventually be removed from that table. These three stages in the life history of an object as represented in a non-temporal table are inaugurated by, respectively, an insert transaction, zero or more update transactions, and zero or one delete transaction.

That same object is represented in a version table by a series of one or more temporally tagged rows. The object that is identified by a primary key in the non-temporal table is, in the corresponding basic version table, represented by that primary key plus a clock tick. So the primary key for the first row for an object to appear in a basic version table contains the object's unique identifier and the date the row was inserted. For each update to that object, a new row is inserted into the version table. That row has the same unique identifier for the object, but its date is different than the date of other rows for that object already on the table because its date is the date it is inserted into the table. As for a delete, some approaches to versioning carry it out as a physical delete, and others as a logical delete.

# A Non-Temporal Table and a Basic Version Table

Figure 4.1 introduces the diagram we will use to compare a non-temporal table with various types of version tables.

Two tables are shown. The one on top represents a non-temporal table of insurance policies. The one below it represents

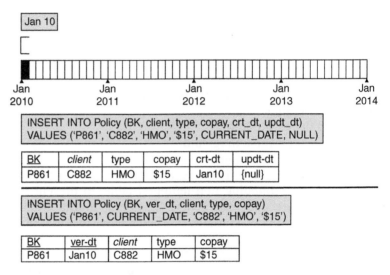

**Figure 4.1** Conventional and Basic Version Tables: An Insert Transaction.

a basic version table of those same policies. Above each table is the SQL statement that inserted or most recently altered the data in that table.

In each table, primary key columns are indicated by underlining their column headings. In each table, the italicized column is a foreign key to a table which will make its first appearance in Chapter 11. Type and copay are the two business data columns in both tables. Create date and update date in the non-temporal table are, respectively, the date the row was inserted into the table, and the date the row was last updated.

In all sample tables, dates are shown in the format "mmmyy". Thus, "Jan10" is short for January 1st, 2010, which is the start of the January 2010 clock tick. Since the clock used in most of these examples ticks once a month, the notation is unambiguous. The reason for the "mmmyy" representation is that it takes up minimal horizontal space on the page, which is important for the sample transactions, rows and tables used in illustrations throughout the book.

In the version table, there is no update date because rows are not physically updated. Instead, each logical update is carried out by copying the most current version, applying the update to the copy and inserting the result as the new most current version. As for a physical create date, that is the same thing as the version date in basic versioning.

The upper components of the diagram read as follows:

(i) The box in the upper left-hand corner of the diagram indicates what time it is now, in the example.

(ii) The row of vertical bars represents a timeline. Each vertical bar on that timeline represents one month. The month which is current, in the context of each example, is marked by filling in its vertical bar. This is a graphical representation of the same information provided in the clock tick box.

(iii) The open-ended rectangle located below the clock tick box and directly above the January 2010 bar indicates the effective time period of the single version of the policy object, P861. Rectangles which are open-ended will be used to represent versions with unknown end dates. As we will see in later diagrams, as soon as the end date for a version is known, the rectangle will be closed.

# Basic Versioning

IT professionals have been using version tables for at least a quarter-century, when they want to keep track of changes that would otherwise be lost because of updating by overwriting data. The simplest versioning method is to add a date to the primary key of the table to be versioned, thus transforming it from a non-temporal into a uni-temporal table, i.e. into a table with one temporal dimension. This is the method we call *basic versioning*.

## An Insert Transaction

Figure 4.1 shows the results of applying the same insert transaction to each table. In both cases, that result is a single row, as shown. An open-ended rectangle is situated directly above January 2010. This marks the start of the time period during which policy P861 is represented in the basic version table.

After the insert, the rectangle extends through to the end of the current month even though, on the date of the insert, we are at the beginning of that month, not at its end. This is because we are using a clock that ticks once a month and so that transaction, once applied, will remain in the database for at least that one month. Thus, our concept of a clock tick is a logical concept, not a physical one.

There is no upper limit to the length of a clock tick. The lower limit is the granularity of a full machine timestamp, as accessible by the DBMS. It is what we called, in the previous chapter, an *atomic* clock tick. Although it is possible to compare points in time and periods of time that use different size clock ticks, it is far simpler when all temporal tables use the same size clock ticks. In this book, as we said, we will manage temporal data with a clock that ticks once a month. Management of different size clock ticks can be left to the eventual implementation of temporal data management by vendors because it is a discrete technical issue whose absence from this discussion does not affect the discussion in any other way.

## An Update Transaction

Figure 4.2 shows the results of applying the same update transaction to each table. In the case of the version table, the update is carried out as an insert, resulting in a new row which is a new version of the policy. In the case of the non-temporal table, the update is carried out as a simple update in place.

That transaction changes the copay amount on the policy from $15 to $20. The update was applied in May, so the rectangle for this update extends through the end of that month. Note also that the transaction closes the first rectangle, and closes it as of the same clock tick that begins the new version.

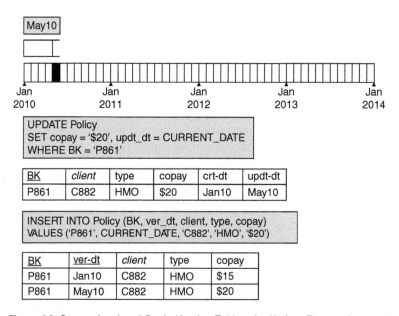

**Figure 4.2** Conventional and Basic Version Tables: An Update Transaction.

Now the information content of the two tables begins to diverge. The version table tells us that P861 had a copay of $15 from January to May, and a copay of $20 thereafter. The non-temporal table does tell us that an update was made in May, and that the copay for P861 is now $20, but it doesn't tell us what data the update changed, or how many updates have already been applied to the policy.

But the version table tells us all these things. We can determine what was changed by the update by comparing each non-initial version of the object with its immediate predecessor. We can tell what the policy was like before the change by looking at the previous version. We can tell how many updates have been applied to the policy by counting the versions, and we can tell when each one took place.

## A Second Update Transaction

Figure 4.3 shows a second update transaction. This transaction updates the policy type from HMO (Health Maintenance Organization) to PPO (Preferred Provider Organization).

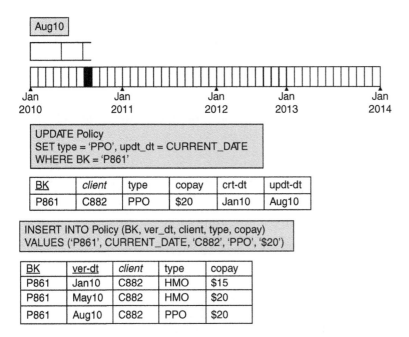

**Figure 4.3** Conventional and Basic Version Tables: A Second Update Transaction.

After the transaction is applied to the version table, a third version is created. So we now know when the second version ended. It ended when the third version began. This is shown graphically, in Figure 4.3, by starting a third rectangle to show that the transaction has resulted in a third version of the object. Of course we don't know, at this point, if or when that third version will ever end.

The non-temporal table records the fact that an August 2010 update was applied. But it cannot tell us whether or not any previous updates were applied or, if any were, how many of them there were. Nor can it tell us what the August update changed, or what the prior state of the policy was at any time between January and August. The version table, on the other hand, can tell us all of these things.

## A Delete Transaction

As shown in Figure 4.4, the result of applying the indicated delete transaction is that the row representing the policy is removed from the non-temporal table on December 2010, and that all the rows representing that policy are removed from the basic version table on that date. There remains no evidence, in either table, that policy P861 ever existed.

For a modest set of business requirements, basic versioning may be all that is needed. And by beginning with basic versioning, we have been able to present an uncluttered comparison of a non-temporal table and a version table. An object is represented by a single row in a non-temporal table. The equivalent representation of that object, in a version table, is a temporally contiguous set of one or more rows, all of them

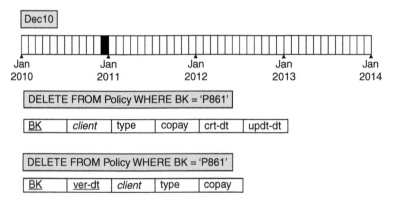

**Figure 4.4** Conventional and Basic Version Tables: A Delete Transaction.

representing that object during some period of its existence. The one non-temporal row, and the set of version rows, cover exactly the same period of time.

But basic versioning is the least frequently used kind of versioning in real-world databases. The reason is that it preserves a history of changes to an object for only as long as the object exists in the database. When a delete transaction for the object is applied, all the information about that object is removed.

One type of versioning that *is* frequently seen in real-world databases is *logical delete versioning*. It is similar to basic versioning, but it uses logical deletes instead of physical deletes. As a result, the history of an object remains in the table even after a delete transaction is applied.

## Logical Delete Versioning

In this variation on versioning, a logical delete flag is included in the version table. It has two values, one marking the row as not being a delete, and the other marking the row as being a delete. We will use the values "Y" and "N".

After the same insert and the same update transactions, our non-temporal and logical delete version tables look as shown in Figure 4.5.

We are now at one clock tick before December 2010, i.e. at November 2010. Although we have chosen to use a one-month clock in our examples primarily because a full timestamp or even a full date would take up too much space across the width

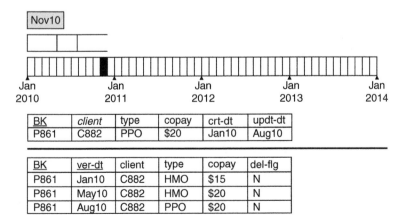

| BK | client | type | copay | crt-dt | updt-dt |
|----|--------|------|-------|--------|---------|
| P861 | C882 | PPO | $20 | Jan10 | Aug10 |

| BK | ver-dt | client | type | copay | del-flg |
|----|--------|--------|------|-------|---------|
| P861 | Jan10 | C882 | HMO | $15 | N |
| P861 | May10 | C882 | HMO | $20 | N |
| P861 | Aug10 | C882 | PPO | $20 | N |

**Figure 4.5** A Logical Delete Version Table: Before the Delete Transaction.

of the page, a 1-month clock is not completely unrealistic. It corresponds to a database that is updated only in batch mode, and only at one-month intervals. Nonetheless, the reader should be aware that all these examples, and all these discussions, would remain valid if any other granularity, such as a full timestamp, were used instead.

Let us assume that it is now December 2010, and time to apply the logical delete transaction. The result is shown in Figure 4.6. However, the non-temporal table is not shown in Figure 4.6, or in any of the remaining diagrams in this chapter, because our comparison of non-temporal tables and version tables is now complete.

Note that none of policy P861's rows have been physically removed from the table. The logical deletion has been carried out by physically inserting a row whose delete flag is set to "Y". The version date indicates when the deletion took place, and because this is not an update transaction, all the other data remains unchanged. The logical deletion is graphically represented by closing the open-ended rectangle.

At this point, the difference in information content between the two tables is at its most extreme. The non-temporal table has lost all information about policy P861, including the information that it ever existed. The version table, on the other hand, can tell us the state of policy P861 at any point in time between its initial creation on January 2010 and its deletion on December 2010.

These differences in the expressive power of non-temporal and logical delete version tables are well known to experienced

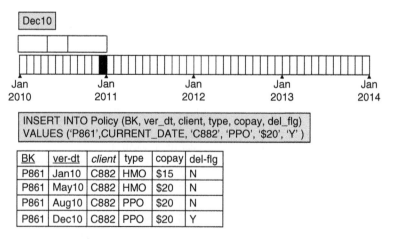

**Figure 4.6** A Logical Delete Version Table: After the Delete Transaction.

IT professionals. They are the reason we turn to such version tables in the first place.

But version tables are often required to do one more thing, which is to manage temporal gaps between versions of objects. In a non-temporal table, these gaps correspond to the period of time between when a row representing an object was deleted, and when another row representing that same object was later inserted.

When only one version date is used, each version for an object other than the latest version is current from its version date up to the date of the next later version; and the latest version for an object is current from its version date until it is logically deleted or until a new current version for the same object is added to the table. But by inferring the end dates for versions in this way, it becomes impossible to record two consecutive versions for the same object which do not [meet]. It becomes impossible to record a temporal gap between versions.

To handle temporal gaps, IT professionals often use two version dates, a begin and an end date. Of course, if business requirements guarantee that every version of an object will begin precisely when the previous version ends, then only a single version date is needed. But this guarantee can seldom be made; and even if it can be made, it is not a guarantee we should rely on. The reason is that it is equivalent to guaranteeing that the business will never want to use the same identifier for an object which was once represented in the database, then later on was not, and which after some amount of time had elapsed, was represented again. It is equivalent to the guarantee that the business will never want to identify an object as the reappearance of an object the business has encountered before.

Let's look a little more closely at this important point. As difficult as it often is, given the ubiquity of unreliable data, to support the concept of *same object*, there is often much to be gained. Consider customers, for example. If someone was a customer of ours, and then for some reason was deleted from our Customer table, will we assign that person a new customer number, a new identifier, when she decides to become a customer once again? If we do so, we lose valuable information about her, namely the information we have about her past behavior as a customer. If instead we reassign her the same customer number she had before, then all of that historical information can be brought to bear on the challenge of anticipating what she is likely to be interested in purchasing in the near future. This is the motivation for moving beyond logical delete versioning to the next versioning best practice—*temporal gap versioning*.

# Temporal Gap Versioning

Let's begin by looking at the state of a temporal gap version table that would have resulted from applying all our transactions to this kind of version table. We begin with the state of the table on November 2010, just before the delete transaction is applied, as shown in Figure 4.7.

We notice, first of all, that a logical delete flag is not present on the table. We will see later why it isn't needed. Next, we see that except for the last version, each version's end date is the same as the next version's begin date. As we explained in Chapter 3, the interpretation of these pair of dates is that each version begins on the clock tick represented by its begin date, and ends one clock tick before its end date.

In the last row, we use the value 9999 to represent the highest date the DBMS is capable of recording. In the text, we usually use the value 12/31/9999, which is that date for SQL Server, the DBMS we have used for our initial implementation of the Asserted Versioning Framework. Notice that, with this value in *ver_end*, at any time from August 2010 forward the following WHERE clause predicate will pick out the last row:

```
WHERE ver_dt <= Now() AND Now() < ver_end¹
```

Or, at any time from May to August, the same predicate will pick out the middle row. In other words, this WHERE clause predicate will always pick out the row current at the time the query containing it is issued, no matter when that is.

Figure 4.8 shows how logical deletions are handled in temporal gap version tables.

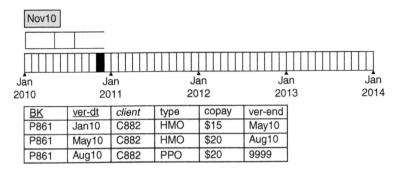

| BK | ver-dt | client | type | copay | ver-end |
|------|--------|--------|------|-------|---------|
| P861 | Jan10 | C882 | HMO | $15 | May10 |
| P861 | May10 | C882 | HMO | $20 | Aug10 |
| P861 | Aug10 | C882 | PPO | $20 | 9999 |

**Figure 4.7** A Temporal Gap Version Table: Before the Delete Transaction.

---

¹We use hyphens in column names in the illustrations, because underscores are more difficult to see inside the outline of the cell that contains them. In sample SQL, we replace those hyphens with underscores.

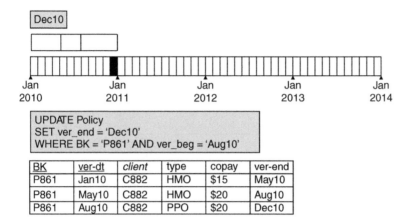

**Figure 4.8** A Temporal Gap Version Table: After the Delete Transaction.

As we have seen, when an insert or update is made, the version created is given an end date of 12/31/9999. Since most of the time, we do not know how long a version will remain current, this isn't an unreasonable thing to do. So each of the first two rows was originally entered with a 12/31/9999 end date. Then, when the next version was created, its end date was given the same value as the begin date of that next version.

So when applying a delete to a temporal gap version table, all we need to do is set the end date of the latest version of the object to the deletion date, as shown in Figure 4.8. In fact, although the delete in this example takes effect as soon as the transaction is processed, there is no reason why we can't do "proactive deletes", processing a delete transaction but specifying a date later than the current date as the value to use in place of 12/31/9999.

## Effective Time Versioning

The most advanced best practice for managing versioned data which we have encountered in the IT world, other than our own early implementations of the standard temporal model, is *effective time versioning*. Figure 4.9 shows the schema for effective time versioning, and the results of applying a proactive insert, one which specifies that the new version being created will not take effect until two months after it is physically inserted.

Effective time versioning actually supports a limited kind of bi-temporality. As we will see, the ways in which it falls short of full bi-temporality are due to two features. First, instead of adding a second a pair of dates to delimit a second time period

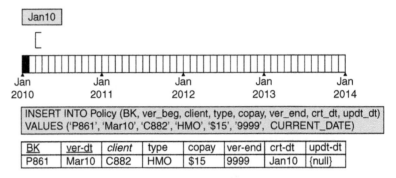

**Figure 4.9** Effective Time Versioning: After a Proactive Insert Transaction.

for version tables—a time period which we call *assertion time*, and computer scientists call *transaction time*—effective time versioning adds a single date. Next, instead of adding this date to the primary key of the table, as was done with the version begin date, this new date is included as a non-key column.

With effective time versioning, the version begin and end dates indicate when versions are "in effect" from a business point of view. So if we used the same schema for effective time versioning as we used for temporal gap versioning, we would be unable to tell when each version physically appeared in the table because the versioning dates would no longer be physical dates.

That information is often very useful, however. For example, suppose that we want to recreate the exact state of a set of tables as they were on March 17th, 2010. If there is a physical date of insertion for every row in each of those tables, then it is an easy matter to do so. However, if there is not, then it will be necessary to restore those tables as of their most recent backup prior to that date, and then apply transactions from the DBMS logfile forward through March 17th. For this reason, IT professionals usually include a physical insertion date on their effective time version tables.

Once the proactive insert transaction shown in Figure 4.9 has completed, then at any time from January 1st to the day before March 1st, the following filter will exclude this not yet effective row from query result sets:

```
WHERE ver_dt <= Now() AND Now()< ver_end
```

But beginning on March 1st, this filter will allow the row into result sets. So the use of this filter on queries, perhaps to create a dynamic view which contains only currently effective data, makes it possible to proactively insert a row which will then

| BK | ver-dt | client | type | copay | ver-end | crt-dt | updt-dt |
|---|---|---|---|---|---|---|---|
| P861 | Mar10 | C882 | HMO | $15 | May10 | Jan10 | Apr10 |
| P861 | May10 | C882 | HMO | $20 | Aug10 | Apr10 | Jul10 |

**Figure 4.10** Effective Time Versioning: After Three Proactive Transactions.

appear in the current view exactly when it is due to go into effect, and not a moment before or a moment after. The time at which physical maintenance is done is then completely independent of the time at which its results become eligible for retrieval as current data.

Proactive updates or deletes are just as straightforward. For example, suppose we had processed a proactive update and then a proactive delete in, respectively, April and July. In that case, our Policy table would be as shown in Figure 4.10.

To see how three transactions resulted in these two versions, let's read the history of P861 as recorded here. In January, we created a version of P861 which would not take effect until March. Not knowing the version end date, at the time of the transaction, that column was given a value of 12/31/9999. In April, we created a second version which would not take effect until May. In order to avoid any gap in coverage, we also updated the version end date of the previous version to May. Not knowing the version end date of this new version, we gave it a value of 12/31/9999.

Finally, in July, we were told by the business that the policy would terminate in August. Only then did we know the end date for the current version of the policy. Therefore, in July, we updated the version end date on the then-current version of the policy, changing its value from 12/31/9999 to August.

## Effective Time Versioning and Retroactive Updates

We might ask what kind of an update was applied to the first row in April, and to the second row in July. This is a version table, and so aren't updates supposed to result in new versions added to the table? But as we can see, no new versions were created on either of those dates. So those two updates must have *overwritten* data on the two versions that are in the table.

There are a couple of reasons for overwriting data on versions. One is that there is a business rule that some columns should be updated in place whereas other columns should be versioned. In our Policy table, we can see that copay amount is one of those columns that will cause a new version to be created whenever a change happens to it. But we may suppose that there are other columns on the Policy table, columns not shown in the example, and that the changes made on the update dates of those rows are changes to one or more of those other columns, which have been designated as columns for which updates will be done as overwrites.

The other reason is that the data, as originally entered, was in error, and the updates are corrections. Any "real change", we may assume, will cause a new version to be created. But suppose we aren't dealing with a "real change"; suppose we have discovered a mistake that has to be corrected. For example, let's assume that when it was first created, that first row had PPO as its policy type and that, after checking our documents, we realized that the correct type, all along, was HMO. It is now April. How do we correct the mistake?

We could update the policy and create a new row. But what version date would that new row have? It can't have March as its version date because that would create a primary key conflict with the incorrect row already in the table. But if it is given April as its version date, then the result is a pair of rows that together tell us that P861 was a PPO policy in March, and then became an HMO policy in April. But that's still wrong. The policy was an HMO policy in March, too.

We need one row that says that, for both March and April, P861 was an HMO policy. And the only way to do that is to overwrite the policy type on the first row. We can't do that by creating a new row, because its primary key would conflict with the primary key of the original row.

## Effective Time Versioning and Retroactive Inserts and Deletions

Corrections are changes to what we said. And we have just seen that effective time versioning, which is the most advanced of the versioning best practices that we are aware of, cannot keep track of corrections to data that was originally entered in error. It does not prevent us from making those corrections. But it does prevent us from seeing that they are corrections, and distinguishing them from genuine updates.

Next, let us consider mistakes made, not in the data entered, but in when it is entered. For example, consider the situation in which there are no versions for policy P861 in our version table, and in which we are late in performing an insert for that policy. Let's suppose it is now May, but that P861 was supposed to take

| BK | ver-dt | client | type | copay | ver-end | crt-dt | updt-dt |
|------|--------|--------|------|-------|---------|--------|---------|
| P861 | Mar10 | C882 | HMO | $15 | 9999 | May10 | {null} |

**Figure 4.11** Effective Time Versioning: A Retroactive Insert Transaction.

effect in March. What should we do? Well, by analogy with a pro-active insert, we might do a retroactive insert, as shown in Figure 4.11.

So suppose that it is now June, and we are asked to run a report on all policies that were in effect on April 10th. The WHERE clause of the query underlying that report would be something like this:

```
WHERE ver_dt <= '04/10/2010' AND '04/10/2010' < ver_end
```

Based on a query using this filter, run on June 1st, the report would include the version shown. But suppose now that we had already run the very same report, and that we did so back on April 25th, and the business intent is to rerun that report, getting exactly the same results. So it uses the same query, with the same WHERE clause. Clearly, however, the report run back on April 25th did not include P861, which didn't make its way into the table until May 1st.

If there is any chance that retroactive inserts may have been applied to a version table, the WHERE clause predicate we have been using is inadequate, because it only allows us to pick out a "when in effect" point in time. We also need to pick out a "when in the life of the data in the table" point in time. And for that purpose, we can use the create date.

With this new WHERE clause, we can do this. The filter

```
WHERE ver_dt <= '04/10/2010' AND '04/01/2010' < ver_end
AND crt_dt <= '04/25/2010'
```

will return all versions in effect on 4/10/2010, provided those physical rows were in the table no later than 4/25/2010. And the filter

```
WHERE ver_dt <= '04/10/2010' AND '04/10/2010' < ver_end
AND crt_dt > '05/01/2010'
```

will return all versions in effect on 4/10/2010, provided those physical rows were in the table no earlier than 5/01/2010. Clearly, by using version dates along with create dates, effective time versioning can keep track of both changes to policies and other persistent objects, and also the creation and logical deletion of versions that were not done on time.

# The Scope and Limits of Best Practice Versioning

Versioning maintains a history of the changes that have happened to policies and other persistent objects. It also permits us to anticipate changes, by means of proactively creating new versions, creating them in advance of when they will go into effect. All four of the basic types of versioning which we have reviewed in this chapter provide this functionality.

*Basic versioning* is hardly ever used, however, because its deletions are physical deletions. But when a business user says that a policy should be deleted, she is (or should be) making a business statement. She is saying that as of a given point in time, the policy is no longer in effect. In a conventional table, our only option for carrying out this business directive is to physically delete the row representing that policy. But in a version table, whose primary purpose is to retain a history of what has happened to the things we are interested in, we can carry out that business directive by logically deleting the then-current version of the policy.

*Logical delete versioning*, however, is not very elegant. And the cost of that lack of elegance is extra work for the query author. Logical delete versioning adds a delete flag to the schema for basic versioning. But this turns its version date into a homonym. If the flag is set to "N", the version date is the date on which that version became effective. But if the flag is set to "Y", that date is the date on which that policy ceased to be effective. So users must understand the dual meaning of the version date, and must include a flag on all their queries to explicitly draw that distinction.

*Temporal gap versioning* is an improvement on logical delete versioning in two ways. First of all, it eliminates the ambiguity in the version date. With temporal gap versioning, that date is always the date on which that version went into effect. When the business says to delete a policy as of a certain date, the action taken is to set the version end date on the currently effective version for that policy to that date. No history is lost. The version date is always the date the version became effective. There is no flag that must be included on all the queries against that table.

Secondly, temporal gap versioning can record a situation in which instead of beginning exactly when a prior version ended, a version of a policy begins some time after the prior version of that policy ended. Expressed in business terms, this is the ability of the database to let us reinstate a policy after a period of time during which it was not in effect. In more general terms, it allows us to record the reappearance of an object after a period of non-effectivity.

*Effective time versioning* builds on temporal gap versioning. And it does so by providing limited support for bi-temporality. With temporal gap versioning, the two dates—the version begin and end dates—are what they say they are; they are version dates. They say when the version became effective and if and when it stopped being in effect. But effective time versioning has no way to make corrections to existing versions other than by overwriting the erroneous data on those versions. And this is a shortcoming common to all best practice forms of versioning.

When temporal gaps between adjacent versions of the same object must be supported, data designers usually use effective time versioning, not merely temporal gap versioning. One reason is that effective time versioning only requires one more column on the table, a row create date. And the maintenance of that column is trivial; whenever a row is physically created, the current date is put into its row create date column.

Both temporal gap versioning and effective time versioning also allow us to recognize the reappearance of an object as the same object we once kept track of, but one for which we no longer have a currently effective version.

In this chapter, we are not yet concerned with bi-temporality. But any form of versioning which supports the as-was vs. as-is distinction is bi-temporal. Effective time versioning starts us on the road to bi-temporality because it includes both (i) dates which designate a period of time that applies to the object itself, and also (ii) one date which describes a point in time that applies to the data about that object, i.e. to the row itself. But there is a lot more to bi-temporality than we have seen so far, and a lot of bi-temporal support which is lacking in effective time versioning. We need to move beyond existing best practices.

## Glossary References

Glossary entries whose definitions form strong inter-dependencies are grouped together in the following list. The same glossary entries may be grouped together in different ways at the end of different chapters, each grouping reflecting the semantic perspective of each chapter. There will usually be several other, and often many other, glossary entries that are not included in the list, and we recommend that the Glossary be consulted whenever an unfamiliar term is encountered.

---

assertion table
assertion time
transaction time

atomic clock tick
clock tick

bi-temporal table
non-temporal table

object
persistent object

version data
version table

---

# THE CORE CONCEPTS OF ASSERTED VERSIONING

**CONTENTS**

Managed objects are data which transformations and constraints treat as a single unit. In the relational model, individual rows of data are the managed objects to which integrity constraints are applied, and these individual rows of data each represent a different object. One object: one row. The relational model is built on this fundamental correlation.

The managed objects of Asserted Versioning are episodes, versions and assertions, all of which exist within tables. Tables represent *kinds* of things—policies, customers, products, and so on. In a conventional table, each row represents one *instance* of its kind—a specific policy, a specific customer, a specific product, and so on. But in temporal tables, *multiple* rows can represent the same instance of a kind, i.e. the same object, during some time period of its existence. Each of these rows is a *version* of the object it represents.

Managing Time in Relational Databases. Doi: 10.1016/B978-0-12-375041-9.00005-4

In temporal tables, then, where the one-to-one correspondence between objects and rows no longer holds, we claim that the most *semantically* fundamental managed object in such temporal tables is not a row. Nor is it the collection of all the rows that are versions of the same object. Rather, it is a group of temporally contiguous rows, a group that we call an *episode* of that object. The implications for relational theory are significant, we believe, because relational theory does not recognize the need for a semantic object whose instances are contained in tables, but which may be physically made up of many rows.

In addition to objects, episodes and versions, Asserted Versioning introduces the concept of an *assertion*. An assertion is a claim that a row in an asserted version table makes a true statement about what the object it represents is like during the time period designated by the version. Significantly, bi-temporal tables may contain rows that represent assertions we are no longer willing to make, rows that make statements that we no longer believe are correct. Just as significantly, bi-temporal tables which are asserted version tables may also contain rows that we are not yet ready to assert, rows to which we are not yet willing to assign a truth value.

After discussing objects, episodes, versions and assertions, we go on to discuss the temporal constraints which are the temporal analogs of entity integrity and referential integrity. *Temporal entity integrity* is entity integrity applied to temporal tables. But we need to understand what "entity integrity applied to temporal tables" means. *Temporal referential integrity* is referential integrity in which the parent table is a temporal table, and the parent object is an episode. But again, we need to understand what this means.

Our next topic in this chapter is how query encapsulation is provided for two types of queries written against asserted version tables. One type of query is what we call an *ad hoc query*. These queries are usually written by business researchers and analysts, and are often run only a few times before they are discarded. Thus the cost of writing them is amortized over only a few occasions on which they are run, and so it is important to keep the query-writing costs as low as possible. For these queries, and these query authors, we believe that a set of basic views on asserted version tables will prove to be very helpful.

The other type of query is what we call a *production query*. These queries are usually written by developers and DBAs, and usually are embedded in application programs. Generally, they are run over and over again. Since the cost of writing them is amortized over hundreds or often thousands of executions, it is a negligible cost.

To provide seamless access to bi-temporal data, developers will usually write these production queries directly against asserted version tables, primarily to avoid the inflexibility which exists when views are used. For these queries, and these query authors, we believe that by imposing bi-temporal semantic constraints on bi-temporal data as that data is maintained, Asserted Versioning makes queries against its tables nearly as easy to write as queries against conventional tables.

In the final section of this chapter, we discuss the use of surrogate keys. Asserted Versioning uses a surrogate key as a unique identifier of each represented object. When surrogate keys are used with non-temporal tables, the logic for adding them to transactions which do not already have them is simple: an insert transaction gets assigned a surrogate key if and only if its business key does not match a row already in the database; an update or delete transaction that lacks a surrogate key gets assigned the surrogate key of a row already in the database that has a matching business key, and is otherwise rejected. But with temporal tables, surrogate key assignment logic is more complex than this. We conclude this chapter by noting the differences and introducing the topic of how surrogate keys are assigned to asserted version tables.

# Objects, Episodes, Versions and Assertions

The basic statement of Asserted Versioning is this:

*Every row in an asserted version table is the assertion of a version of an episode of an object.*

Asserted Versioning is a special kind of temporal data management. One thing that makes it special is these core concepts.

## Objects

Asserted Versioning recognizes *persistent objects* as the fundamental things its rows are about. Every row is about some particular thing, and that thing is an object that persists over time. Every row contains business data which describes that object.

Objects are what, in Chapter 2, we called *things*. These things may be abstract or concrete, real or imagined. The term "persistent object", borrowed from the language of object oriented theory, is meant to emphasize the fact that these things last over time.

Objects should be distinguished from events. Events are the occasions on which objects are created or destroyed, or on which objects change their properties or their relationships. Objects change by means of their involvement in events. A client changes her name. This event alters a property of the client. A customer charges a purchase at a store. This event alters the financial relationship between that customer and that store.

Some objects are relatively static. Documents, like purchase orders or invoices, are usually created once and then not modified. Code sets are often represented as tables, and are usually updated periodically and all at once. Other objects are relatively dynamic. A good example is objects monitored by instruments, such as atomic nuclei or automobile engines. The objects that businesses are interested in generally fall in the mid-range in terms of being static or dynamic.

Both objects and events can be represented in tables. An event is represented by a transaction, and so a transaction table is a record of events of the same type, e.g. sales, inventory resupply, or claims against policies.

Objects are represented by descriptions of their relevant properties and relationships, both of which appear in databases as columns of tables. Each row represents an object, and each column instance represents either a property of an object, or a relationship it has to another object or perhaps to an event. In the case of a many-to-many relationship in which an object is involved, each instance of the relationship is a row in a separate table, one that relational theory calls an associative table. These rows also represent persistent objects, those objects being relationships which may have their own properties and relationships that can change over time.

## Episodes

Each row in an asserted version table is part of one and only one *episode*. An episode is a set of one or more rows representing the same object. Each row represents that object during a specified period of time; it is a version of that object, and that period of time is a period of effective time. If these rows occur one after the other, i.e. if there are no temporal gaps between them (and no temporal overlaps either), then these rows belong to the same episode of that object. But because asserted version tables are bi-temporal, these rows are also assertions. Episodes are a series of versions of the same object that are contiguous in effective time *within* a period of shared assertion time.[1] They represent what we believe, during that period of assertion time, the life history of that object was/is/will be like, across those contiguous periods of effective time.

Consider a row representing an object that is inserted into a non-temporal table at some point in time, say $T_1$. Updates take place at $T_2$, $T_3$ and $T_4$. These updates modify the contents of the row, but do not create new rows. Eventually, the row may be deleted from that table at, let's say, $T_5$. After it's deleted, of course, the table contains no indication that the row was ever present.

If this same object, over this same period of time, is represented in a version table, it is represented by an effective-time contiguous series of rows, starting with a row representing that object in the time period $T_1 - T_2$ and continuing with rows representing the object in time periods $T_2 - T_3$, $T_3 - T_4$, and $T_4 - T_5$. This contiguous set of rows is an *episode* of the object. Notice that the deletion did not remove any data from the table; it merely set $T_5$ as the end date for the last row in the series.

Now suppose that at $T_{10}$, a row representing that same object is inserted into the same table, goes through a series of three modifications at $T_{11}$, $T_{12}$ and $T_{13}$, and is eventually deleted at $T_{14}$. If this same object, over this same period of time, is represented in a version table (and again, we emphasize that "version table" refers to a view over an asserted version bi-temporal table), it is represented by an effective-time contiguous series of rows, starting with a row representing that object in the time period $T_{10} - T_{11}$ and continuing with rows representing the object in time periods $T_{11} - T_{12}$, $T_{12} - T_{13}$, and $T_{13} - T_{14}$. This contiguous set of rows is another episode of the same object.

In this way, episodes mirror the existence of rows in non-temporal tables. They start and end at the same points in time. But whereas updates to a row in a non-temporal table simply overwrite the old data, the corresponding updates in an asserted version table copy the latest row in the episode, apply the update to that copy, and insert the copy back into the table as the new latest row in that episode. In the process, the same point in time

---

[1]*All* effective time relationships exist within shared assertion time. Because this is so important to keep in mind, we will often add the qualifier "within shared assertion time" to statements about effective time relationships. At other times, including the qualifying phrase seems to interfere with clarity. But whether or not the phrase is included, the qualification is always there.

is assigned as the end of the time period of the former row and the beginning of the time period of the latter row.[2]

## Versions

Each row in an asserted version table represents one *version* of an object. Each version represents the state of an object during a specified period of time. In an asserted version table, that period of time extends from each version's effective begin date to its effective end date. In Asserted Versioning, the begin and end dates associated with versions are called effective time dates. In the standard temporal model, they are called valid time dates.

In version tables, every time a change happens to an object, the version representing the current state of that object is copied. The copy is updated, and is then inserted to become the new current version of that object. The original copied-from version ends its effective time period at this point in time, just as the updated copy of that version begins its effective time period at this same point in time. When this happens, we say that the new version *supercedes* the old one.

### Row-Level vs. Column-Level Versioning

We might think that some changes to certain columns of data in versioned tables are not important enough to keep track of. In those cases, we could *overwrite* an old value with a new value instead of creating a new version. In the early stages of the development of Asserted Versioning, we supported this distinction between what we then called *versionable* changes and *non-versionable* changes, the latter being the ones that were handled by overwriting data.

But Asserted Versioning no longer supports this distinction. On the one hand, the only value we are able to find for it is that non-versionable updates save disk space by not creating new versions every time an update takes place. In a table of 100 columns, for example, in which we are only interested in keeping track of changes to a handful of those columns, and in which many of the other columns change frequently, we would indeed consume a lot more disk space than we would if we

---

[2]This, in fact, is a description of what we call a basic temporal update. Basic transactions will be discussed in Chapter 7, but we point out that many temporal insert, update and delete transactions are *not* basic, and are far more complex than this.

versioned only those handful of columns. On the other hand, non-versionable changes make it impossible for a table to support the as-was vs. as-is distinction. And we believe that this is too great a cost to incur in order to save, for example, a few gigabytes of disk space. Here's why.

No matter how sure we are that we don't need a history of changes to specific columns in a table, how sure can we be that we will never need to see exactly the data that appeared on a report or query run at some point in the past? Suppose we ask for a report that duplicates a report run last year, and later on discover that what we got wasn't "exactly" a duplicate. When we point this out to the person or department who provided the report, we are told that someone else, maybe several years ago, had determined that changes to those columns of data where the discrepancies appeared weren't worth keeping track of. But all the "important" data on the rerun report, we are assured, *is* exactly the same as when the report was first run.

How confident is that going to make us feel? Will we make the same, "no hedging our bets" business decision we would have made if the report had contained *no* discrepancies, and if experience had shown us that our IT department could reliably rerun reports and queries and get them exactly right? And suppose the party requesting the exact duplicate report is not someone within our own company, but rather an outside party, for example a regulatory agency? Is the savings in disk space going to seem worth the cost of explaining that *almost* identical reports are in fact *exactly* identical in what someone in our company once determined was "all relevant respects"?

To exactly reproduce a report or query requires the ability to rerun reports or queries in an *as-was* mode. If changes to even a single column of a single table are not versioned, the database cannot guarantee to exactly reproduce any original report or query that contains that column or that uses it as a selection criterion.[3]

---

[3]Considerations like these motivate attempts to do column-level versioning. We have not attempted to support column-level versioning because (i) it is considerably more complex than row-level versioning; (ii) it saves less disk space than might be imagined, because each primary key must be repeated for every versioned column and ideally for every column versioned or not; and (iii) because disk space is no longer so expensive that we need to consider such extreme measures. Certainly much more could be said about row-level vs. column-level versioning, but it would all be in the nature of an aside. Column-level versioning might have its place as an internals-only mechanism in some future DBMS. But Asserted Versioning is not a DBMS; it does row-level versioning, and that is what this book is about.

Objections to versioning every change to every column because of storage considerations also overlook the fact that on-line *transaction* tables take far more space in nearly every organization than tables of persistent objects ever will, no matter how frequently versions are created. In our experience, half a petabyte of disk space to extend our transaction histories back another few years is an easier sell to the CIO than a few dozen gigabytes of disk space to support versioning the most important persistent objects the enterprise engages with.

We also believe that objections to versioning every column of every table of persistent objects overlook the orders of magnitude increases in available on-line storage volume, and the orders of magnitude reduction in per unit cost for that storage. In addition, these objections often overlook the fact that versioning all changes to persistent object tables removes the need to take periodic snapshots of those tables because any snapshot of those tables, as of *any* point in past time, can be created from those versions.

Another issue with mixing updates in place with versioning is that updates in place create a potential inconsistency with other versions of that same data. If there are 10 versions of an object, let us suppose, and we do an update in place to one of those versions, what should we do about the other versions? An update in place is a non-temporal update, so perhaps we should replicate that update onto all versions, earlier ones as well as later ones. As an update in place column, our interpretation of its data should be that it is always current. Whether or not we do replicate the update onto past versions, we should probably replicate it onto all future versions. And whatever replication strategy we decide on, the performance cost of the replication process could easily outweigh any savings in storage costs that might result from avoiding one extra version.

## Assertions

Creating a version of an episode of an object is, usually, to *assert* that version. (Later on, we will discuss *deferred assertions*, in which a row is asserted some time after it is created.) Just as a version has an associated time period, an assertion does too. The former time period is the effective time period of the version. The latter time period is the assertion time period of the assertion. Since both the version and its assertion are represented by the same physical row, both time periods are associated with that row.

As we might imagine from this description, assertions are handled with begin and end dates, just as versions are. The result is that asserted version bi-temporal tables have two pairs of dates, representing two different time periods. They are the effective time period and the assertion time period of the rows in those tables.

To assert a version is to claim that it is true. With any tables other than bi-temporal tables, if something happens that makes a row no longer true, that row is either updated or deleted. But with asserted version tables, that isn't how we handle a row that we discover is not true. We handle it by assigning it an assertion end date (or a transaction end date, in the case of the standard temporal model) representing the date on which we acknowledge that it is not true. Then we add another row to the table. This new row is a new *assertion* about the same version, a new assertion about what the object is like during the same period of time. The multiple rows representing the same version are multiple assertions of that version.

In a series of assertions about the same object during the same effective time period, the later one (in assertion time) of every consecutive pair is a correction to the earlier one, and the latest one of all is our current assertion about what is true. We may also note here that corrections and the versions they correct do not necessarily line up one to one. An error may span only part of a version, or may span multiple versions, or may span both. The ability to include in a table both corrections to versions, as well as the original versions themselves, is precisely what is lost when we remain with uni-temporal versions. This ability is precisely what we gain when we manage data bi-temporally.

For example, suppose that a row in a table states that policy P861 had a copay amount of $25 during the first six months of 2010. But on July $1^{st}$ of that year, we realized that the copay amount was actually $20 for that policy over that time period. If we were to overwrite that copay amount, we would lose the information that prior to July $1^{st}$, all reports and queries would have shown a copay of $25. To avoid losing that information, we instead end the assertion time period for the row showing a $25 copay, and insert another row. This new row is also for policy P861, during the same six months of 2010, but it shows the correct copay of $20. Its assertion begin date is the same as the assertion end date of the row showing the $25 copay—July $1^{st}$. We no longer assert that P861 had a $25 copay during that period of time. Instead, we now assert that it had a $20 copay during that period of time. We have corrected a mistake without losing track of what the mistake was, when it occurred, and for how long it was mistakenly treated as the truth.

## Temporal Integrity Constraints

The three integrity constraints in relational theory are entity integrity, referential integrity and domain integrity. Entity integrity insures that the object represented by a row in a non-temporal table is represented by that row only, and no other. But as we have seen, with temporal tables, an object may be represented by any number of rows. For these tables, then, the entity integrity constraint must be modified. That modification results in what we call *temporal entity integrity.*

As for domain integrity, it is obviously possible for a domain to change over time. But such changes are not changes to data. They are changes to types of data, indeed to datatypes. Domain changes are one form of what computer scientists call *schema evolution.* Adding or removing tables, altering primary or foreign keys, and adding or removing non-key columns, are other ways in which database schemas evolve. Both the standard temporal model and Asserted Versioning are formalizations of temporal data management within a snapshot of the evolution of a database schema. Both temporal models, along with the IT industry's best versioning practices, assume unchanging, stable database schemas.

What, then, of referential integrity? Well, suppose we have two conventional tables, X and Y, with Y having a referential integrity dependency on X. Typically we would say that X is the *parent* table, and Y the *child* table. Now suppose that both tables are bi-temporal tables. In this case, any number of rows in X may represent the same object. So for any row in Y, which of the multiple rows in X, all representing the same object, is that row in Y dependent on? Which row in X does the foreign key in Y point to?

The answer is that the foreign key in Y does not point to *any* specific row in X. For these tables, then, the referential integrity constraint must be modified. That modification results in what we call *temporal referential integrity* (TRI). The foreign key in Y becomes what we call a *temporal foreign key* (TFK).

### Temporal Entity Integrity

Breaking the one-to-one correspondence between objects and rows is no small thing. Its implications are significant. One of them is that the relational rule of entity integrity must be understood in a new way.

With a non-temporal table, entity integrity is usually enforced by a primary key uniqueness constraint on the table. It may also be enforced by defining a unique index on an alternate key. When a surrogate key is used as the primary key of a table, primary key uniqueness will guarantee only that rows are physically distinguishable from one another. To guarantee entity integrity, which is a semantic constraint, a unique index must also be defined on an alternate key, none of whose component columns are surrogate-valued.

For temporal tables, the corresponding constraint is *temporal entity integrity*. Basically, it works like this. In a non-temporal table, DBMS-enforced entity integrity blocks any insertion that would result in a pair of rows both of which represent the same object. But when the target table is an asserted version table, temporal entity integrity (TEI) blocks any insertion that would result in a pair of rows that represent the same object *and* that have one or more effective time clock ticks in common within one or more assertion time clock ticks that they also have in common.

In enforcing the rule that no two versions of the same object may conflict, TEI is obviously analogous to conventional entity integrity. For having one or more effective time clock ticks in common means that there are two rows which both purport to describe the same object during the same period of time. So both entity integrity and temporal entity integrity play the same semantic role; they both prevent conflicting truth claims.

However, TEI has additional work to do, work that is not required of entity integrity. First of all, TEI must insure that adjacent versions within the same episode [meet], i.e. that there are no temporal gaps between them. In addition, TEI must also insure that there *are* temporal gaps between adjacent episodes, i.e. that one episode is always [before] the other. And it's important to understand why there must be at least one clock tick between any pair of adjacent episodes. It has to do with understanding and enforcing the user's intentions when she submits a temporal transaction.

First, let's consider insert transactions. With an insert to a conventional table, the user tacitly agrees that if a row with the same unique identifier already exists in the target table, the DBMS will reject the transaction. The user is telling the DBMS "I believe that this table does not contain a row for this object. So if I'm wrong, I don't want the transaction to proceed. I want you to kick out the transaction, and notify me."

By the same token, then, with an insert to an asserted version table, the user is telling the DBMS to create a new episode of the indicated object, or to extend an existing episode into effective time clock ticks that it does not yet occupy. And analogously to entity integrity in non-temporal tables, the user is tacitly agreeing that if an episode of the same object already exists in the target table *and* if its effective and assertion time periods have any clock ticks in common with the time periods targeted by the transaction, the transaction should be rejected. The user is telling the Asserted Versioning Framework "I believe that this table does not contain any row or rows for this object that already represent the object in even a single clock tick that is specified on the transaction. So if I'm wrong, I don't want the transaction to proceed. I want you to kick out the transaction, and notify me."

Next, let's consider update and delete transactions. By a similar process of reasoning, we can see that in submitting either type of transaction, the user is telling the Asserted Versioning Framework "I believe that the table does contain one or more rows for this object with one or more clock ticks that [intersect] the clock ticks specified on this transaction. So if I'm wrong, I don't want the transaction to proceed. I want you to kick out the transaction, and notify me."

### One Clock Tick: Convention or Constraint?

Given two rows representing the same object, there are three temporal relationships between them that are distinguishable by means of a single clock tick. First, if there is even a single clock tick between the end of one and the start of the next, then they are non-contiguous. In Allen relationship terms, one is [before] the other. Next, if there is even a single clock tick that is contained in both their time periods, then they [intersect]. Finally, if neither is the case, then they are contiguous. In Allen relationship terms, they [meet].

Two versions of the same object that are non-contiguous may exist in the same target table at the same time. But if they do, they necessarily belong to different episodes. And if one of those versions is the only version of that object already in the target table and the other is a transaction, that transaction cannot be an update. If it were an update transaction, it would be equivalent to attempting a conventional update when there was no row for that object already in the target table. By the same token, if one of those versions is in the target table and the other is a transaction, that transaction cannot be a deletion.

Two versions of the same object that [intersect], in both effective and assertion time, cannot exist in the same target table at the same time. If they did, they would violate temporal entity integrity. They would be two concurrently asserted statements about what the same object is like at the same time. By the same token, if one of those versions is in the target table and the other is a transaction, that transaction cannot be an insert transaction. If it were an insert transaction, it would be equivalent to attempting a conventional insert when a row for that object is already in the target table.

But what about the third case, when the two versions are contiguous? As we have already seen, two contiguous versions of the same object can exist in the same table at the same time, and that, in doing so, they belong to the same episode. But when one is a transaction and the other a row already in the target table, which is the correct transaction to use—an insert or an update?

As far as the results of the transaction are concerned, it doesn't matter. Whether an insert or an update is used, the effect will be to expand an existing episode either forwards or backwards in time. Of course, if the episode is being expanded forwards in time, it must be an episode which, prior to the transaction, ended in a non-12/31/9999 date. Otherwise, the transaction's begin date could not be contiguous with the end date of the episode, but instead would be included within the time period of the episode. But the principle is still the same. We have chosen to use an insert transaction in cases of contiguous time periods, but we could have chosen to use an update transaction instead. It is entirely a matter of convention, of deciding on a convention that will make a user's background assumptions clear.

We chose to use temporal insert transactions, in fact, to preserve a pleasing symmetry. For we now have a set of transactions in which all increases in clock tick representation are done with inserts, all reductions in clock tick representation are done with deletes, and updates do neither. Of course, pleasing symmetries often turn out to have practical as well as aesthetic benefits. In this case, for example, the AVF will never have to be concerned with temporal entity integrity or temporal referential integrity on update transactions, except for an update which changes the parent object referenced by a version. Making that determination on nothing more than transaction type is certainly more efficient than making it on the basis of some more complex set of criteria.

With our convention in place, we have a clear and intuitive model of how time and transaction types pair up with one another. For a given object, if the effective and assertion time periods specified on a temporal transaction do not [intersect] the time periods on any rows already in the target table, then the transaction is valid if it is an insert, and invalid otherwise. Conversely, for a given object, if the effective and assertion time periods specified on a temporal transaction do [intersect] the time periods on one or more rows already in the target table, then the transaction is valid if it is an update or delete, and invalid otherwise.

What we could *not* have chosen to do is to permit *either* inserts or updates to be used in the case of contiguous time periods. The reason is that we must preserve a core element in the semantics of conventional insert and update transactions, which is that the user knows whether or not the target table already contains a row which matches the transaction. By using a conventional insert, the user is telling us to reject the transaction if a matching representation of that object already exists in the table. The same must be true of temporal inserts against temporal tables. By using a conventional update, the user is telling us to reject the transaction unless a matching representation of that object already exists in the table. Again, the same must be true of temporal updates. The difference is that a "matching representation", in a conventional table, is simply a row representing the same object. A "matching representation", in an asserted version table, is a row representing the same object at the same time, i.e. in a set of one or more identical clock ticks.

## Temporal Referential Integrity

Another consequence of breaking the one-to-one correspondence between objects and rows is that the relational rule of referential integrity breaks down when the parent table in a referential integrity relationship is an asserted version table. In that case, the parent in any instance of that relationship is not a row; rather, it is an episode, and it may consist of any number of rows.

Referential integrity (RI) reflects an *existence dependency*. If a child row is RI-dependent on a parent row, this is based on the fact that the object represented by the child row is existence-dependent on the object represented by the parent row. Therefore, a child row cannot be inserted into the database unless its referenced parent row is already present, and that parent row cannot be deleted from the database as long as any child row referencing it is present.

The same logic is at work in the case of temporal referential integrity. If there is an existence dependency between a parent object and a child object—between a client and a policy, for example—then we cannot assert that the policy is ever in effect when the client is not. It follows that no change which *reduces* the total number of clock ticks in which a child policy is in effect, and no change which *increases* the total number of clock ticks in which a parent client is in effect, can create a TRI violation. And so the AVF never has to enforce TRI on a child-side temporal delete or a parent side-temporal insert. As for temporal updates, they never alter the number of clock ticks in which an object is represented. And so, unless they change the parent object for a version, there is no TRI enforcement needed.

By the same token, any change which *increases* the total number of clock ticks in which a child policy is in effect, and any change which *decreases* the total number of clock ticks in which a parent client is in effect, *can* create a TRI violation. And so the AVF must enforce temporal referential integrity on parent-side temporal delete transactions, and also on child-side temporal inserts.

### Child-Side Temporal Referential Integrity

The foreign key in a row in a child asserted version table is a temporal foreign key (TFK). It contains the object identifier (the *oid*) of the object that its object is existence-dependent on. But this object identifier isn't sufficient to identify a specific row in the parent table. There may be many rows in the parent table with that object identifier. And that one row in the child table may be TRI-dependent on any number of those rows in the parent table. That one row in the child table is TRI-dependent on an *episode* in the parent table, an episode of the object designated by the object identifier in its TFK. The episode it is dependent on is the one episode of the object designated by that *oid* that, within shared assertion time, includes the effective time period of that version.

Although the parent managed object in a TRI relationship is an episode, the child managed object is a version. Just as the foreign key value in a row in a conventional table may change over time, so too the temporal foreign key value in a version in a temporal table may change over time from one version of an object to the next version of that same object. It does not have to be the same as the TFK value in any other version of the same object. Even within the same episode, a TFK value may change from one version in that episode to the next version in that same episode. TRI child objects are versions, not episodes, because among versions of the same object, what is referenced by a temporal foreign key may change over time and, consequently, over versions.

*Parent-Side Temporal Referential Integrity*

Of course, TRI, like RI, can be violated from the parent side as well. In the case of TRI, a violation cannot occur unless the temporal extent of the parent episode is reduced. This can happen in one of three ways, First of all, the effective-time start of the episode can be moved forwards. Second, the effective-time end of the episode can be moved back. This will happen when either the effective-time end of an episode is changed from 12/31/9999 to any other date, or is changed from a non-12/31/9999 date to an earlier date. Finally, the episode can be split into two episodes, leaving a gap where previously there had been none.

But shortening the effective time extent of a parent episode will not always result in a TRI violation. It will do so only if the reduction removes the representation of the parent object from one or more clock ticks that are occupied by a child version whose TFK matches the *oid* of the versions in that parent episode. For example, suppose a parent episode's effective time is all of 2009, and a delete transaction splits that episode and creates in its place one January to April episode and another October to December episode. If none of the child versions has an effective time period that includes any of the six months from April to October, then TRI has not been violated.

Conceptually, reducing the time period of an episode with dependent versions (versions which may be in the same table but, more commonly, are in other tables) so that the parent episode no longer fully includes the time period of one or more of those child versions, is like a deletion in a conventional parent table in that there are three options for handling it. First, we may want to simply restrict the transaction and prevent the reduction from taking place. Second, we may want to permit the transaction to proceed, but find all the dependent child rows and set their temporal foreign keys to the parent object to NULL. Or, finally, we may want to reduce the temporal extent of all affected child rows so that the TRI constraint is re-established. For example, if a client is deleted effective September 2010, then any policy owned by that client must be deleted as of that same date. In asserted version tables, this means that if the most recent episode of that client is given an effective end date of September 2010, then the most recent episode of the policy she owns must have an effective end date no later than September 2010.[4]

---

[4]To be completely accurate, this description would have to be modified a little to include situations in which there are future versions or episodes of that client or that policy. But we will leave those details for later.

The mechanisms by which we check for and enforce temporal referential integrity constraints are proprietary to Asserted Versioning, LLC. But one thing is obvious. At some point in the design process, the data modeler is going to have to declare TRI relationships; and from a record of those declarations, a mechanism will have the metadata needed to enforce both sides of the relationship.

# Bi-Temporal Tables and Non-Bi-Temporal Views

The only physical tables managed by Asserted Versioning are bi-temporal tables. But on the basis of those bi-temporal tables, Asserted Versioning also manages two uni-temporal views, and one non-temporal view. Although we will frequently refer to them as views, sometimes it will be convenient to refer to them as tables instead. This is because we are accustomed to managing the data they contain by means of physical tables.

For example, in the preceding chapter, we reviewed several types of version tables. Asserted Versioning supports all the functionality of all those types of version tables, and important additional functionality as well. But version tables are not a distinct kind of physical table for which Asserted Versioning must define both schemas and the code to manage them. Instead, Asserted Versioning defines one bi-temporal schema, and manages only that one kind of physical table. Those tables support uni-temporal versions and uni-temporal assertions, but it supports them as *views*. And by means of views, those tables also support what appear to be conventional, non-temporal tables.

The rows in uni-temporal *version* tables (views) have a single time period associated with them. This is the period from when the object, as it exists in the world, is as the row describes it to be, extending to 12/31/9999, or to when the object changes so that the description no longer applies to it, or to when the existence of the object is no longer of concern to us.

The rows in uni-temporal *assertion* tables (views) also have a single time period associated with them. This is the period from when they begin to be asserted as true statements, extending to either 12/31/9999 or to when they cease being asserted as true statements about what the objects they represent are currently like. Rows in uni-temporal assertion tables can only describe what the objects they represent are currently like because, by definition, such rows have no effective time. Having no effective time, like rows in conventional tables, the time in the life history of the objects they represent is the eternal Now().

In physical versioned tables, there is only one version for an object during any one period of time. It describes what the object was/is/will be like during that period of time. If we later find that the description is wrong, all we can do is overwrite it. We cannot create a second version about the same object during that same period of time. But when we overwrite it, we destroy the information that we once described that period of time in the life history of that object differently.

In physical assertion tables, there is only one version for an object. It describes what the object is currently like, just as rows in conventional tables do. If something about the object changes, we update that version, just as we update conventional data. We overwrite the old data with the new data, destroying information about what the object used to be like. On the other hand, if we discover, not that the object has changed, but rather that our data is wrong, we do not overwrite the erroneous data. Instead, we create a new assertion about that object and, on the same clock tick that we enter that new, corrected assertion, we stop asserting the row with the erroneous data.[5]

Of course, the rows in the physical tables that Asserted Versioning manages have both time periods. Each row is both a version and an assertion about that version. Assertion tables, as we said, are views on these physical tables. They are, as we will see, views of objects which are never represented by more than one version at a time. And version tables, by the same token, are also views on these physical tables. They are views of objects for which there is only one version in effect during any given period of time, that being the currently asserted description of what that object is like at that time.

A conventional table view can also be defined on an asserted version bi-temporal table. This is a view of all and only those rows which are currently asserted and currently in effect. These rows in conventional table views have neither assertion nor effective time periods associated with them. Updates may either correct mistakes in the data, or reflect changes in the world. As with physical conventional tables, there is no way to look at the data and tell the difference. However, with a conventional table view, versions with future effective begin dates automatically roll into the view when that date arrives. Similarly, versions

---

[5]If this description sounds unfamiliar, it is because IT professionals seldom use assertion tables. It would be like keeping a logfile of corrections inside a conventional table, and it just isn't done.

with future effective end dates automatically roll off the view when that date arrives. This responsiveness to the passage of time is a feature of most Asserted Versioning views, and because of it, these views remain current and do not have to be periodically modified.

A non-temporal view presents a conventional table as a queryable object. The mental image associated with this view is that there is no such thing as assertion time or effective time; there is simply the eternal present, our efforts to update data to keep up with it, and our occasional updates to correct mistakes we have made along the way. This view supports the mental image of a conventional table for the person querying the database.

And the mental image of a conventional table is also supported for those *updating* an asserted version table, not just for those querying one. As long as they do not specify either assertion time or effective time on their insert, update or delete transactions, it will seem to them that they are maintaining data in a conventional table. This maintenance is not done by writing SQL transactions; it is done by making an API Call to our Asserted Versioning Framework.[6] These are insert, update and delete transactions that are submitted via the API to the AVF. We call them temporal transactions, and our first introduction to how they work will be in Chapter 7. Our point here is that in a database all of whose tables are asserted version tables, any table can be made to look like a conventional table to those who query it and to those who maintain it. And by the same means, any table can be made to look like a version table to both sets of users, or like an assertion table.

But as important as views are, we believe that most SQL written against asserted version tables, at least SQL that is written by developers, will *not* make use of views. The reason is that views have limited flexibility, and that the benefits they provide in return are often not that important to developers.

The benefit provided by views is simplification. Views can select a specific set of rows, implement specific joins, and project a specific set of columns from across the joined tables. The larger the number of queries that would otherwise have to do this same work themselves, the more value the view provides. With a view, these specifications are written once, not once in each of the queries that share the criteria.

---

[6]However, as we go to press, we have incorporated *Instead Of* triggers in release 1 of the Asserted Versioning Framework. With these triggers, the person writing these transactions is able to write them as standard SQL transactions, and the AVF will translate them into the physical SQL which will update the database.

Views are particularly useful for supporting an environment in which new queries are frequently written, and in which those queries are often run once or twice, and then discarded. These "what-if" queries are usually written by business researchers and analysts, sometimes with and sometimes without the assistance of query tools. We will call them *ad hoc queries*.

But developer-written queries, most of which exist within application programs, usually do not make use of views. They are *production queries*, the ones which are run over and over again to produce standard reports and data extracts, usually on a standard schedule.

One reason that developers usually write queries directly against physical tables is that simplification is not an important benefit for them. (If it is, perhaps they should consider another line of work!) Another is that the queries which developers write are usually written, tested and put into production where they will be run over and over again. Developers generally don't sit around writing throw-away queries all day long.

But the main reason that developers usually write queries directly against physical tables is that views are restrictive. For the most part, criteria in views are hardcoded, and do not make use of variables. For example, CURRENT_DATE can be used in most views, but a user-defined date or timestamp cannot. Production queries, which are run day after day, for weeks, months or years, often need to include user-defined variables, and especially dates and timestamps. In contexts like application programs, the benefits of views are negligible, while the flexibility of writing queries directly against physical tables is essential.

With Asserted Versioning's bi-temporal tables, the flexibility of writing queries directly against those tables is even more valuable. As we will see in Chapters 12–14, the full range of all possible bi-temporal data is covered by nine categories of that data, those categories being the three-by-three combination of data which is in the past, present or future of either assertion time or effective time. Because the AVF guarantees that all data in asserted version tables is semantically valid (as far as bi-temporality is concerned), queries against that data need nothing more than one or two additional predicates, over and above the predicates needed for the query if it were against a conventional table. These predicates specify a date or a time period (specified as a pair of dates), and one of the Allen relationships or other nodes in our Allen relationship taxonomy, and the query will return only those rows whose assertion and/or effective time periods satisfy those predicates. The ability to write queries that retrieve data from any or all of those nine categories, and that find all of that data in the same tables that, in today's databases, contain only current data, is precisely what we mean by *seamless access* to bi-temporal data.

So Asserted Versioning simplifies the life of the query author in two ways. For those writing *ad hoc queries*, a wide range of views can be provided that express criteria that would otherwise have to be written into each ad hoc query. One such view is a view which makes an asserted version table look like a conventional non-temporal table. Another one is a view which makes an asserted version table look like a uni-temporal versioned table.

For those writing production queries, Asserted Versioning guarantees that the bi-temporal data those queries access will be semantically valid. There will be no temporal gaps in the representation of an object between each temporal insert transaction for that object, and the temporal delete transaction for all but the current episode of that object. There will be no periods of time at which two or more rows will both claim to describe the object as it was/is/will be during a period of time in its life history. There will be no cases in which any representation of an existence-dependent child object will exist in effective time unless a representation of its parent object also exists in that effective time.

# Surrogate Keys and Bi-Temporal Match Logic

In Chapter 7, we will see each of the three temporal transactions used in what we called the *basic scenario*. In those examples, the object identifier we will use will be P861, representing an insurance policy. This object identifier will be used on all three temporal transactions. But if the string "P861" is in fact a surrogate key value, then on the temporal *insert* transaction specifically, where did that value come from?

## Surrogate Keys, Business Keys and Conventional Tables

If we abstract from implementation details, surrogate keys always work the same way. An insert transaction will not have a surrogate key on it, because the presumption is that there is no surrogate key already assigned to the object it represents. So the search for a match between the transaction and the target table must be made on the basis of a *business key* for the object in question. If no match is found, a new surrogate key value is generated, and is used for the new row the transaction is about to create. If a match is found, then a row for the object is already in the target table, and the insert transaction is rejected.

In some implementations, surrogate keys are circulated out of the target database back into the databases that are the sources of the transactions. In that case, update and delete transactions may already have a surrogate key when they show up to be processed. If they do arrive with a surrogate key in hand, then the search for a match is made with that surrogate key, and is conducted with a business key only in the case of an insert transaction. Otherwise, update and delete transactions are matched to their target rows on the basis of business keys, and are rejected if matching rows are not present.

Surrogate keys can be assigned in either a pre-processing step or as part of the same process which submits transactions to the DBMS. Surrogate keys may or may not be supplied on update and delete transactions. But in terms of the semantics that have to be carried out, these distinctions don't matter. Regardless of how we design the process of assigning surrogate keys, the important point is that it is not just a matter of requesting a unique key value for an insert transaction.

## Surrogate Keys, Business Keys and Asserted Version Tables

We can now return to the question of where the P861 surrogate key value on a temporal insert transaction, such as the one shown in the next chapter, came from. Our brief review of surrogate key match logic tells us that there must have been a match process that used a business key. But because we are now considering a temporal table and a temporal transaction, the match process is not identical to the process we just described.

When the target table is a temporal table, in this case an asserted version table, the question is not whether or not that object is already represented in the table. The question is whether or not the object is already represented in the table in the time period specified on the transaction. For example, an insert of policy P861, effective for all of 2010, will not be rejected because the Policy table already shows that policy effective for all of 2009. However, the actual use of surrogate keys with temporal transactions is more complicated than this. It will be discussed in detail in Chapter 9.

# Glossary References

Glossary entries whose definitions form strong inter-dependencies are grouped together in the following list. The same glossary entries may be grouped together in different ways at the end of different chapters, each grouping reflecting the semantic perspective of each chapter. There will usually be several other, and often many other, glossary entries that are not included in the list, and we recommend that the Glossary be consulted whenever an unfamiliar term is encountered.

assert
Asserted Versioning
Asserted Versioning Framework (AVF)

bi-temporal

business key

ad hoc query
production query

clock tick

conventional transaction

deferred assertion

effective begin date
effective end date
effective time period
valid time

episode
episode end date

event

existence dependency

managed object
object
object identifier
oid
persistent object
thing

row-level homonym
row-level synonym

state

supercede

temporal entity integrity (TEI)
temporal foreign key (TFK)
temporal referential integrity (TRI)

temporal transaction

the standard temporal model

transaction
transaction table

# DIAGRAMS AND OTHER NOTATIONS

In the first section of this chapter, we present the schema common to all asserted version tables, using a table of health insurance policies as an example. All of the concepts introduced in the last chapter, such as objects, episodes, versions and assertions, and the two principal semantic constraints of temporal entity integrity and temporal referential integrity, are physically realized as rows in tables which are all based on this schema.

In the next two sections, we present several diagrams which will be used in the rest of this book. The basic diagram consists of a sample table and, above it, graphics which position that data in both effective time and assertion time. As well as additional diagrams which focus more on effective time than assertion time, we also present an in-line notation for single asserted

Managing Time in Relational Databases. Doi: 10.1016/B978-0-12-375041-9.00006-6

version rows so we don't have to use diagrams when the discussion concerns single rows.

The final section contains our initial reflections on how asserted version tables should be accessed, and how the syntactic complexities of our approach to temporal data management may be hidden from those issuing queries to such data.

## The Asserted Version Table

All asserted version tables have the same non-business-data columns. Figure 6.1 shows an asserted version table of health insurance policies which has two business data columns: type and copay. All the other columns are part of the syntax common to all asserted version tables, part of the bi-temporal *machinery* of Asserted Versioning. We will learn how to read these diagrams in the next section. For now, let's examine each column, and the roles that various columns and pairs of columns play.

*Row #. Row number.* This column is not part of the table. Row numbers are tags we place on asserted version rows in these diagrams. We will sometimes use these tags in our discussions to indicate which rows we are talking about. Note that if this column were included as part of the table, it could be used as a single-column surrogate primary key.

*Oid. Object identifier.* A surrogate-valued unique identifier of the persistent object for which the row is a bi-temporally located description, i.e. a description located in both a specific effective time period and also a specific assertion time period. If an asserted version table were a conventional table instead, the *oid* would be the full primary key of that table.

*Eff-beg. Effective begin date.* The date on which the business data in a row goes into effect, i.e. on which it first becomes a

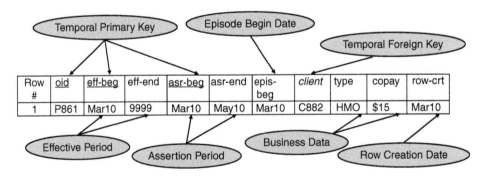

**Figure 6.1** The Asserted Versioning Table.

description of what that object is like, beginning on that date. As we have pointed out before, these columns which implement Asserted Versioning are all shown as date columns in this book, but they could as well be timestamps.

Also note that although this column heading is *eff-beg*, all SQL statements or predicates which reference this column will refer to it as *eff_beg_dt*. We use hyphens in these column headings because underscores do not stand out as well, particularly when a column heading is underlined, as it is for all primary key columns. When these columns names are used in the text, they will be italicized, although usually we will replace them with their full spelling equivalents. For example, when referring, in the text, to the column heading *eff-beg*, we will either use *eff_beg_dt* or the full name, as for example, in saying that the effective begin date is the temporal delimiter of the start of an effective time period.

*Eff-end. Effective end date.* The date on which the business data in a row is no longer in effect. In other words, the date which is one clock tick past the last date on which the business data in a row is in effect.

*Asr-beg. Assertion begin date.* The date on which the business data in a row is first asserted as being a true and/or actionable description of what that object is like, during its effective time period.

*Asr-end. Assertion end date.* The date on which the business data in a row is no longer asserted to be a true and/or actionable statement of what that object is like, during its effective time period. In other words, the date which is one clock tick past the last date on which that assertion is made.

*Epis-beg. Episode begin date.* The date on which the episode which contains the version begins. The begin date of an episode is always the same as the effective begin date of the first version in the episode.

*Temporal Foreign Key: Client.* The object identifier of the client who owns the policy, functioning as a temporal foreign key to an asserted version Client table.

*Business data: Type.* The type of the insurance policy. Types used in these examples are: HMO (Health Maintenance Organization); PPO (Preferred Provider Organization); and POS (point of service).

*Business data: Copay.* The copay amount that the policy holder is obligated to pay for each covered healthcare product or service.

*Row-crt. Row creation date.* The date on which the row is physically inserted into the table.

## The Temporal Primary Key

Together, the object identifier, the effective begin date and the assertion begin date make up the primary key of an asserted version table. Note that in our diagrams we do not show all three primary key columns left-most, although that is the normal convention. Instead, we keep the two effective dates together, followed by the two assertion dates, to emphasize that each pair of dates goes together, each pair delimiting a different period of time.

The object identifier in an asserted version table is a surrogate-valued single-column unique identifier for an object—in this case, for a policy. When unique identifiers based on business data are used as primary keys, those keys can contain any number of columns. This would make it very difficult to build an enterprise framework for implementing Asserted Versioning, a framework that supports the maintenance and querying of any asserted version table, in any database, and that enforces the integrity constraints that give bi-temporal data the semantics that it has. An enterprise implementation of Asserted Versioning therefore requires that all asserted version tables use a single-column identifier, of the same datatype and length, for the persistent objects they represent.

When surrogate keys are used in an asserted version table, the primary key columns for the corresponding entity in the logical data model must be included as non-primary key columns in the asserted version table. These columns make up what we call the *business key* of an asserted version table.

In order to be able to show sample tables across the width of a page, we have not included business keys in our examples. Instead, we have used values for our surrogate keys which suggest that they could be business keys as well. But this convention, forced on us because of page width considerations, should not obscure the fact that business data is never used in surrogate keys, and that Asserted Versioning object identifiers are surrogate-valued.

Semantically, the unique identifier of any bi-temporal table consists of (i) a unique identifier of the object represented; (ii) a unique identifier of the effective time period of the business data on that row; and (iii) a unique identifier of the assertion time period of that version. In the Asserted Versioning implementation of bi-temporality, the effective and assertion begin dates each represent their full time periods in the table's primary key.

But how can each of these dates represent an entire time period? For example, in Figure 6.1, the effective time period extends from March 2010 into the indefinite future. What is to prevent us from inserting another row for policy P861, with an effective begin date of, let's say, April 2010?

The answer is that Asserted Versioning explicitly recognizes and enforces temporal entity integrity, a concept we introduced in the preceding chapter. As we said there, any Asserted Versioning implementation must reject a transaction that would create a version whose effective time period [intersects], within shared assertion time, even a single effective-time clock tick included in another version of that object already in the table.

Most *physical* transactions against bi-temporal tables are inserts. When we distinguish inserts from updates, as we have done here, we are talking about logical transactions against bi-temporal tables, transactions we call *temporal* transactions.

## The Temporal Foreign Key

A temporal foreign key (TFK) is analogous to a normal foreign key, and serves much the same purpose; but it is one which the DBMS does not know how to use. A foreign key, at the schema level, points from one table to a table it is dependent on. At the row level, a foreign key value points from one row in the former table to one row in the latter table.

At the schema level, a TFK also points from one table to a table it is dependent on. But at the row level, it points from one row, which is a version, to a group of one or more rows which make up an episode of the object whose *oid* matches the *oid* in the temporal foreign key.

So a TFK does not point to a specific row in its referenced table. But it also does not point to the episode which the version containing it is dependent on. It points only to an object. In our example, it says only that this version of policy P861 belongs to client C882. But since no row in particular represents a client, i.e. since clients are themselves versioned, and since their versions are also asserted, the TFK points to no row in particular. Since there may be multiple episodes for any object, the TFK points to no episode of that object in particular.

The very existence of a TFK instance does make the claim, however, that there is an episode of the designated object in the referenced table, and that the effective time period of that episode in the referenced table includes, i.e. is filled by ([fills$^{-1}$]), the effective time period of the version which contains the referring TFK. And it is one of the responsibilities of the Asserted Versioning Framework to insure that for every TFK instance in a database, there is exactly one such episode. Although the TFK, by itself, does not designate this parent episode, the TFK together with the assertion and effective time periods on the child row does designate it.

## The Effective Time Period

A pair of dates defines the effective time period for each version. As we explained in Chapter 3, we use the closed-open convention, for both effective dates and assertion dates, in which a time period starts on its begin date, and ends one clock tick prior to its end date. Effective begin and end dates, of course, indicate when the version began and ceased to be effective. They delimit the period of time during which the object was as that row in the table describes it to be.

With non-temporal tables, we create a version of an object by the act of inserting a row into its table. But because there are no dates to delimit the effective time period of the row, the row goes into effect when it is physically created, and remains in effect until it is physically deleted. And while it exists in the table, no other versions of that object may co-exist with it. For if they did, there would be two or more statements each claiming to be the true description of the object during the entire time that all of them co-existed in the table.

## The Episode Begin Date

Just as versions have effective time periods, episodes do too. An episode's begin date is an effective begin date, and it is the same as the effective begin date of its earliest version. An episode's end date, although not explicitly represented in the Asserted Versioning schema, is the same as the effective end date of its latest version.

The episode begin date is repeated on every row so that by looking at an episode's latest version we can determine the entire effective time period for the episode itself. By the same token, we can also look at any version and know that from its episode begin date to its own effective end date, its object was continuously represented in effective time. The ability to do this without retrieving and looking at multiple rows will be important, later on, when we see how temporal referential integrity is enforced.

## The Assertion Time Period

Using the same closed-open convention, this pair of dates indicates when we began to assert a version as true and when, if ever, we stopped asserting that it is true. Even when a version ceases to be in effect, i.e. even when it has an effective end date in the past, we will usually continue to assert that, during its effective time period, it was a true description of what its object was like at that time.

However, and this is a very important point, there are exceptions. With both the Asserted Versioning and the standard temporal models, assertions may end even though the rows that made them remain in the table. We terminate assertions if and when we learn that they are mistaken, that the statement they make is not true. In addition, with Asserted Versioning, but not with the standard temporal model, rows can also be created whose assertion is postponed until some later point in time.

With non-temporal tables, we assert a row to be true by the act of inserting it into its table, and we cease to assert that it is true by deleting it from its table. With non-temporal tables, the assertion time period of a row coincides with the row's physical presence in the table. In these cases, the assertion begin date is the same as the row creation date. Also, in most cases, once we assert a row to be true, we continue to do so "until further notice".

## The Row Creation Date

The row creation date is the date the row is physically inserted into its table. In most cases, the row creation date will be identical with the assertion begin date. In the standard temporal model, it always is, and consequently, in that model, the two dates are not distinguished. However, in our Asserted Versioning implementation of bi-temporal data management, it is valid to create a row with an assertion begin date in the future. Thus, for Asserted Versioning, it is necessary to have a row creation date which is distinct from the assertion begin date.

## The Basic Asserted Versioning Diagram

Figure 6.2 is an example of the basic diagram we will use to illustrate Asserted Versioning. The schema in this diagram was explained in the previous section. Now it's time to explain how to read the diagram itself. Figure 6.2 shows us the state of an asserted version table after a temporal insert transaction which took place on January 2010, and a temporal update transaction which took place on May 2010.

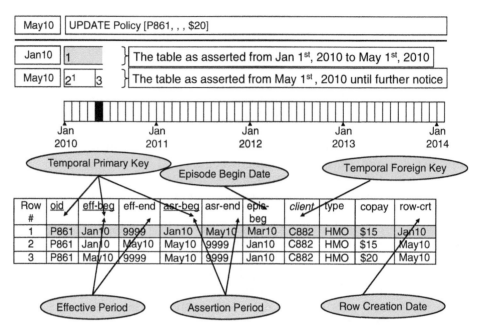

**Figure 6.2** The Basic Asserted Versioning Diagram.

On January 2010, a temporal insert transaction was processed for policy P861.[1] It said that policy P861 was to become effective on that date, and that, as is almost always the case when a temporal transaction is processed, was to be immediately asserted.

Then in May, a temporal update transaction for that policy was processed. The transaction changed the copay amount from $15 to $20, effective immediately. But this invalidated row 1 because row 1 asserted that a copay of $15 would continue to be in effect after May. So as part of carrying out the directives specified by that temporal transaction, we *withdrew* the assertion made by row 1, by overwriting the original assertion end date of 12/31/9999 on row 1 with the date May 2010.

When a row is withdrawn, it is given a non-12/31/9999 assertion end date. Withdrawn rows, in these diagrams, are graphically

---

[1]The format for showing bi-temporal dates, in the text itself, is slightly different from the format used in the sample tables. For example, a date shown as "Jan10" in any of the tables will be written as "January 2010" in the text. Time periods are shown in the text as date pairs with the month still shortened but the century added to the year. Thus "[Feb 2010 – Oct 2012]" designates the time period beginning on February 2010 and ending one clock tick before October 2012, but would be represented in the diagram by "Feb10" and "Oct12".

indicated by shading them. In addition, every row is represented by a numbered rectangular box on a horizontal row of all versions whose assertions begin on the same date. We will call these horizontal rows *assertion time snapshots*. These snapshots are located above the calendar timeline, and when their rectangular boxes represent *withdrawn* rows, those boxes are also shaded. So in Figure 6.2, the box for row 1 is shaded.

After row 1 was withdrawn, the update whose results are reflected in Figure 6.2 was then completed by inserting two rows which together represent our new knowledge about the policy, namely that it had a copay of $15 from January 2010 to May 2010, and had a copay of $20 thereafter.

The clock tick box is located to the left of the transaction, at the top of the diagram. It tells us that it is currently May 2010, in this example. This is graphically indicated by the solid vertical bar representing that month on the calendar timeline above the sample table. In this example, rows 2 and 3 have just been created. We can tell this because their row create date is May 2010.

The first row is no longer asserted. It has been withdrawn. It was first asserted on January 2010, but it stopped being asserted as part of the process of being replaced as a current assertion by row 2, and then superceded by row 3. This is indicated by the May 2010 value in row 1's assertion end date and the May 2010 value in the assertion begin dates of rows 2 and 3. It is graphically indicated by the two assertion time snapshots above and to the left of the timeline. Each snapshot shows the rows of the table that were currently asserted starting on that date. So from January 2010 to May 2010, row 1 is what we asserted about policy P861. From May 2010 forwards, rows 2 and 3 began to be asserted instead.

We say "instead" because rows 2 and 3 together *replace* and *supercede* row 1, in the following sense. First of all, they describe the same object that row 1 describes, that object being policy P861. Second, rows 2 and 3 together [*equal*] the effective time period of row 1, the period [Jan 2010 – 12/31/9999]. Row 2's effective time period is [Jan 2010 – May 2010]. Then, without skipping a clock tick, row 3's effective time period is [May 2010 – 12/31/9999]. Row 2 includes the part of row 1's effective time whose business data is not changed by the update; so we will say that row 2 *replaces* that part of row 1. Row 3 includes the part of row 1's effective time whose business data is changed by the update; so we will say that row 3 *supercedes* that part of row 1.

In our illustrations, 9999 represents the latest date that the DBMS can represent. In the case of SQL Server, for example, that date is 12/31/9999. This date does *not* represent a New Year's Eve some 8000 years hence. But it *is* a date as far as the DBMS is concerned. The importance of this "dual semantics" will become important later on when we explain how Asserted Versioning queries work.

Notice that all three rows in this example have assertion begin dates that are identical to their corresponding row creation dates. In the standard temporal model, a transaction time period is used instead of an assertion time period; and with transaction time periods, the begin date is *always* identical to the row creation date, and so a separate row creation date is not necessary.

But in the Asserted Versioning model, assertion begin dates and row creation dates are not semantically identical, and they do not necessarily have the same value in every row in which they appear. With Asserted Versioning, while no assertion begin date can be earlier than the corresponding row creation date, it can be later. If it is later, the transaction which creates the row is said to be a *deferred transaction*, not a current one. The row it creates in an asserted version table is said to be a *deferred assertion*, not a current one. Such rows are rows that we may eventually claim or assert are true, but that we are not yet willing to.

In this example, both before and after May 2010, the effective end date for policy P861 is not known. But sometimes effective end dates are known. Perhaps in another insurance company, all policies stop being in effect at the end of each calendar year. In that case, instead of an effective end date of 12/31/9999 in rows 1 and 3, the example would show a date of January 2011 (meaning, because of the closed-open convention, that the last date of effectivity for these policies is one clock tick prior to January 2011, that being December 2010).

We turn now to the graphics, the part of Figure 6.2 above the sample table. The purpose of these graphics is to abstract from the business details in the sample table and focus attention exclusively on the temporal features of the example.

Above a calendar which runs from January 2010 to February 2014, there are two horizontal rows of rectangular boxes. These rows are what we have already referred to as assertion time snapshots, with each rectangular box representing one version of the associated table. The lowest snapshot in a series of them contains a representation of the most recently asserted row or rows. These most recently asserted rows are almost always currently asserted and usually will continue to be asserted until further notice.

There are, however, two exceptions. Neither of them is part of the standard temporal model, but both of them support useful semantics. One exception is created by the presence of deferred assertions in the table which are, by definition, assertions whose begin dates, at the time the transaction is processed, lie in the future. The other exception is created when assertions are withdrawn without being replaced or superceded, i.e. when after a certain point in time we no longer wish to claim that those assertions ever were, are or will be a true description of what their object was, is or might be like during some stretch of effective time. But as we said earlier, we will not discuss deferred assertions until several chapters from now, at which time we will also discuss withdrawn assertions that are not replaced and/or superceded by other assertions.

Each of these assertion time snapshots consists of one or more boxes. As we said, each box contains the row number of the row it represents. The vertical line on the left-hand side of each box corresponds to the effective begin date of the row it represents. In this illustration, only one of the boxes is closed, in the sense of having a line on its right-hand side. The other two are open both graphically and, as we will see, semantically.

Let's consider these boxes, one at a time. The box for row 1 is open-ended. This always means that the corresponding row has an effective end date of 12/31/9999. The box directly below the box for row 1 represents row 2. Because that box is closed on its right-hand side, we know that the row it represents has a known effective end date which, in this case, is May 2010.

In these boxes that line up one under the other, the business data in the rows may or may not be identical. If the business data is identical, then the box underneath the other represents a replacement, and we will indicate that it has the same business data as the row it replaces by using the row number of the row it replaces as a superscript. But if the business data in two rows for the same object, during the same effective time period, is not identical, then the row represented by the lower box supercedes the row represented by the upper box, and in that case we will not include a superscript. This convention is illustrated in Figure 6.2, in which the box for row 2 has a superscript designating row 1, whereas the box for row 3 has no superscript.

The box directly to the right of the box for row 2 represents row 3. We can tell that the two rows are temporally adjacent along their effectivity timelines because the same vertical line which ends row 2's effective time period also begins row 3's effective time period. So this diagram shows us that there is an unbroken effective time period for policy P861, which began to be asserted on May 2010, and which extends from row 2's effective begin date of January 2010 to row 3's effective end date of

12/31/9999, this being exactly the same effective time period previously (in assertion time) represented by row 1 alone.

This description of Asserted Versioning's basic diagram has focused on a sample table whose contents reflect one temporal insert transaction, and one temporal update transaction.

## Additional Diagrams and Notations

Before proceeding, we need a more flexible way to supplement English in our discussions of Asserted Versioning. In the last section, we used what we called the "basic diagram" of an asserted version table. That diagram contains five main components. They are:

(i) The current clock tick, which indicates what time it is in the example;

(ii) A temporal insert, update or delete transaction;

(iii) A calendar timeline covering approximately four years, in monthly increments;

(iv) A stacked series of assertion time snapshots of the table used in the example; and

(v) The table itself, including all rows across all effective and assertion times.

We will still need to use this basic diagram to illustrate many points. But for the most part, discussions in the next several chapters will focus on effective time. So we will often use a diagram in which rows in past assertion time are not shown in the sample table, and in which there are no assertion time snapshots either.

So, leaving assertion time snapshots out of the picture, we will often use the kind of diagram shown in Figure 6.3. And sometimes we will simply show a few rows from a sample table, as in Figure 6.4.

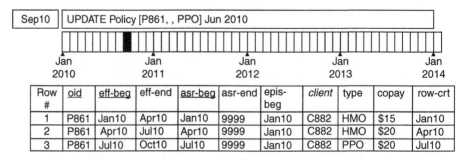

| Row # | oid | eff-beg | eff-end | asr-beg | asr-end | epis-beg | client | type | copay | row-crt |
|-------|-----|---------|---------|---------|---------|----------|--------|------|-------|---------|
| 1 | P861 | Jan10 | Apr10 | Jan10 | 9999 | Jan10 | C882 | HMO | $15 | Jan10 |
| 2 | P861 | Apr10 | Jul10 | Apr10 | 9999 | Jan10 | C882 | HMO | $20 | Apr10 |
| 3 | P861 | Jul10 | Oct10 | Jul10 | 9999 | Jan10 | C882 | PPO | $20 | Jul10 |

**Figure 6.3** The Effective Time Diagram.

| Row # | oid | eff-beg | eff-end | asr-beg | asr-end | epis-beg | client | type | copay | row-crt |
|---|---|---|---|---|---|---|---|---|---|---|
| 1 | P861 | Jan10 | Apr10 | Jan10 | 9999 | Jan10 | C882 | HMO | $15 | Jan10 |
| 2 | P861 | Apr10 | Jul10 | Apr10 | 9999 | Jan10 | C882 | HMO | $20 | Apr10 |
| 3 | P861 | Jul10 | Oct10 | Jul10 | 9999 | Jan10 | C882 | PPO | $20 | Jul10 |

**Figure 6.4** A Sample Asserted Version Table.

While illustrations are essential to understanding the complexities of bi-temporal data management, it will also be useful to have a notation that we can embed in-line with the text. In this notation, we will use capital letters to represent our sample tables. So far we have concentrated on the Policy table, and we will use "P" to represent it.

Almost always, what we will have to say involves rows and transactions that all contain data about the same object. For example, we will often be concerned with whether time periods for rows representing the same policy do or do not [meet]. But for the most part we will not be concerned with whether or not time periods for rows representing different policies [meet]. So the notation "P[X]" will indicate all rows in the Policy table that represent policy X.

In the next several chapters, we will be primarily concerned with the effective time periods of asserted version rows. So for example, the notation P[P861[Jun12-Mar14]] stands for the row (or possibly multiple rows) in the Policy table for the one or more versions of P861 that are in effect from June 2012 to March 2014. With this notation, we could point out that there is exactly one clock tick between P[P861[Jun12-Mar14]] and P[P861 [Apr14-9999]]. If we needed to include assertion time as well, the notation would be, for example, P[P861[Jun12-Mar14] [Jun12-9999]]. If we were concerned with assertion time but not with effective time, we would refer to the row(s) P[P861[] [Jun12-9999]].

An example of the notation describing a complete asserted version row is:

```
P[P861[Jun12-Mar14][Jun12-9999][Jun12][C882, HMO, $15]
[Jun12]]
```

We will use abbreviated forms of the notation wherever possible. For one thing, we will seldom refer to the row creation date, until Chapter 12, because until we discuss deferred assertions, the row creation date will always be the same as the assertion begin date. Also, the episode begin date is always identical to the effective begin date of the first version of an episode, so we will often leave it out of our in-line representation of an asserted version row unless it is relevant to the example at hand.

What is lost with this in-line notation is context. What is gained is focus. Diagrams also present us with a graphical representation of a timeline and a snapshot of effective time periods, grouped by common assertion times along that timeline. With the in-line notation, that context, too, is not represented.

## Viewing the Asserted Version Table

We can already see that asserted version tables are more complex than non-temporal tables. For one thing, they have about half a dozen columns that are not present in non-temporal tables; and the semantics of these columns, the rules governing their correct use and interpretation, are sometimes subtle. For another thing, the fact that there are now multiple rows representing a single object adds another level of complexity to an asserted version table. Some of those rows represent what those objects used to be like, others what they are like right now, and yet others what they may, at some time in the future, be like. In addition, and quite distinctly, some of those rows represent what we used to say those objects were, are, or will be like; others what we currently say they were, are, or will be like; and yet others what we may, at some time in the future, say they were, are, or will be like.

All in all, the sum and interplay of these factors make asserted version tables quite complex. They can be complex to maintain in the sense that they can be easy to update in ways whose results do not reflect what the person writing the updates intended to do. And they can be difficult to interpret, as we just said.

Asserted Versioning attempts to eliminate this maintenance complexity, as far as possible, by making it seem to the user who writes temporal transactions which utilize default values for their temporal parameters that the insert she writes creates a single row, that the updates she writes update that single row, and that the delete she writes removes it. In this way, by providing a set of transactions that conform to the paradigm she is already familiar with, the possibility of misinterpretation, on the maintenance side of things, is minimized.

But what about the query side of things? What about looking at the data in an asserted version table? How can this data be presented so as to hide the mechanisms by which it is managed—those extras columns and extra rows we referred to a moment ago—leaving what looks like a non-temporal or a uni-temporal table?

It is particularly important to hide the complexity of asserted version tables from query authors who are not IT professionals, from query authors who may be business analysts, scientists or researchers. For these query authors, the solution is to query asserted version tables through views. And no matter how much history is contained in an asserted version table, and no matter how much conjecture about or anticipation of the future may be contained in an asserted version table, we are still going to be primarily interested in what we believe, right now, things are like right now. That is, our most frequent view of an asserted version table will be the view that makes it look like a non-temporal table containing current data.

## The Conventional Table View

So let's create that view. Its DDL looks something like this:

```
CREATE VIEW V_Policy_Curr AS
        SELECT oid, client, type, copay
        FROM Policy_AV
        WHERE eff_beg_dt <= Now()
        AND Now() < eff_end_dt
        AND asr_beg_dt <= Now()
        AND Now() < asr_end_dt
```

Now() may be replaced with CURRENT TIMESTAMP, CURRENT_DATE or getdate(), depending on the granularity and the DBMS.

This statement will result in a view that is current whenever it is run. So, for example, run any time prior to January 2010, against a table containing just the three rows shown in Figure 6.4, it would return an empty result set. Run on January 2010, or on any date after that, up to but not including April 2010, it would return the result set shown in Figure 6.5.

And if run on April 2010, or on any date after that, up to but not including July 2010, it would return the result set shown in Figure 6.6.

| Row # | oid | client | type | copay |
|-------|-----|--------|------|-------|
| 1 | P861 | C882 | HMO | $15 |

**Figure 6.5** The Current Non-Temporal View from January to April.

| Row # | oid | client | type | copay |
|-------|------|--------|------|-------|
| 1 | P861 | C882 | HMO | $20 |

**Figure 6.6** The Current Non-Temporal View from April to July.

## The Version Table View

Next, let's create a view which looks like the best of our best practice versioning methods, the one we called effective time versioning, in Chapter 4. As a version table view, it knows nothing about assertions. But because the table the view is based on is a bi-temporal table, there may be multiple assertions about the same set of one or more effective time clock ticks. So in order to filter out any past assertions, those being rows which contain data we no longer think is correct, this view will present only currently asserted versions, versions that we currently believe make true statements about the objects they represent.

```
CREATE VIEW V_Policy_Ver AS
    SELECT oid, eff_beg_dt, eff_end_dt, client, type, copay
    FROM Policy_AV
    WHERE asr_beg_dt <= Now()
    AND Now() < asr_end_dt
```

This statement does not include effective begin or end dates in its WHERE clause because we are selecting all versions, across all effective time. It does include an assertion time WHERE clause predicate to guarantee that all versions in the view represent our current assertions about what those things are like, during those periods of effective time. If any data was originally entered incorrectly, and later corrected by means of a temporal transaction, this predicate guarantees that we will get the correction, not the error.

This statement does include effective begin and end dates in its projection of the table. This is because this view is a view of versions, and the two effective dates are needed to specify the effective time period of each version. Without these two dates, multiple versions of the same object would have the same *oid*, and could have the same business data as well. Without these two dates, multiple versions of the same object could be indistinguishable.

We also point out that without the AVF code to enforce temporal entity integrity, these two dates could not prevent overlapping versions. For example, P[P861[Mar10-Nov10]] and P[P861[Mar10-Sep10]] are different sets of three values each.

A unique index on them would find nothing wrong. But as far as versions are concerned, these two rows should not both be in the table. As far as versions are concerned, there is something very wrong.

Semantically, these are not two pairs of dates. They are the delimiters of a PERIOD datatype, and in this case, there is a 6-month overlap of these two time periods. The AVF enforces temporal entity integrity on the basis of an interpretation of these date pairs as time period delimiters. As far as integrity constraints are concerned, the AVF is code which implements, in a middleware layer located between temporal transactions and the DBMS, a user-defined PERIOD datatype, and which then uses that PERIOD datatype in its enforcement of both temporal entity integrity and temporal referential integrity.

This SQL creates a view that is current whenever it is run. That is, whenever it is run, it will show all currently asserted versions about the past, the present and the future. For example, run any time prior to January 2010, against a table containing just the three rows used in this example, it would return an empty result set. Run on January 2010, or on any date after that, up to but not including April 2010, it would return the result shown in Figure 6.7.

And if run on July 2010 or any date after that and prior to any further changes to the table, it would return the result shown in Figure 6.8.

## The Assertion Table View

While there are several best practices supporting versions, there are none that we know of supporting assertions. Future-dated assertions are something no one other than ourselves appears to have thought of. Past-dated assertions are just errors

| Row # | oid | eff-beg | eff-end | client | type | copay |
|-------|-----|---------|---------|--------|------|-------|
| 1 | P861 | Jan10 | Apr10 | C882 | HMO | $15 |

**Figure 6.7** The Current Version Table View as of April 2010.

| Row # | oid | eff-beg | eff-end | client | type | copay |
|-------|-----|---------|---------|--------|------|-------|
| 1 | P861 | Jan10 | Apr10 | C882 | HMO | $15 |
| 2 | P861 | Apr10 | Jul10 | C882 | HMO | $20 |
| 3 | P861 | Jul10 | Oct10 | C882 | PPO | $20 |

**Figure 6.8** The Current Version Table View from July Forwards.

that we keep around, probably for auditing purposes. And we have logfiles to take care of that.

The value of assertion table views on bi-temporal tables will become clearer as this book progresses. As we will see, assertion table views are of particular interest to auditors.

For now, let's look at the SQL which will provide a view of all assertions in our bi-temporal Policy table that have anything to do with currently effective data. The version table view was a view of all currently asserted versions. This assertion table view is a view of all currently effective assertions.

```
CREATE VIEW V_Policy_Asr AS
     SELECT oid, asr_beg_dt, asr_end_dt, eff_beg_dt,
     eff_end_dt, client, type, copay
     FROM Policy_AV
     WHERE eff_beg_dt <= Now()
     AND Now() < eff_end_dt
```

This view filters out all rows that are not about what things are like currently. It excludes past versions and future versions. But this does not mean that the view is restricted to one row per object. If this table ever contained erroneous data about what things are currently like, that data will no longer be asserted. It will be a past assertion about a current state of affairs, and this view will include it. In addition, as we will see in Chapter 12, an asserted version table may contain anticipated data about what things are currently like. These will be future assertions about a current state of affairs, and this view will include those assertions as well.

Another aspect of the asymmetry between assertion time and effective time is that two or more effective-time [intersecting] versions of the same object, in shared assertion time, would violate temporal entity integrity, making conflicting truth claims wherever they shared an effective-time clock tick. Consequently, the AVF includes code to prevent that from happening. But two or more effective-time [intersecting] versions of the same object, whose assertion time periods [exclude] one another, do not violate temporal entity integrity. In fact, they violate *no* integrity constraints, nor do they make conflicting truth claims. Rows which share no clock ticks in assertion time are semantically and truth-functionally isolated from one another. They are what philosophers call *incommensurable*.

This is why this assertion table view must include both assertion dates and effective dates in its projection.

In general, any asymmetry in what is otherwise a profoundly symmetric set of concepts points to something important.

Understanding why such asymmetries exist almost always deepens one's understanding of the underlying theory. This particular asymmetry is important in this way, and we will have more to say about it in later chapters.

Like the version table view, this assertion table view is also current whenever it is run. Whenever this view is run, it will show all assertions, past, present or future, that reference even a single clock tick in current effective time. Our sample database, shown in Figures 6.3 and 6.4, does not contain data that will illustrate this view which presents a current assertion table. But we will discuss assertion table views in depth in Chapters 12 and 13.

## Views and Mental Images

Assuming (until Chapter 12) that temporal transactions never specify assertion dates, we can have three kinds of temporal transactions against asserted version tables, for example against our Policy table. With the first kind, no effective dates are specified. To authors of these transactions, they appear to be doing normal maintenance to a conventional Policy table, one that looks like the table shown in Figures 6.5 and 6.6. They have, or need have, no idea that the table they are actually maintaining is the table shown in Figures 6.3 and 6.4.

With the second kind of temporal transaction, effective begin and end dates may be specified, but neither of them can be a date which is already past at the time of the transaction. This is the way maintenance is done to version tables. Normally, current versions are created whenever they are needed to reflect a change in the object they represent. The version that was current at the time of the transaction is given an end date, and the transaction creates the new current version.

But Asserted Versioning, and the two most complete best practice forms of versioning, also permit transactions to create future versions. To authors of these transactions, they appear to be doing normal maintenance to a uni-temporal versioned Policy table, one that looks like the table shown in Figures 6.7 and 6.8. They have, or need have, no idea that the table they are actually maintaining is the table shown in Figures 6.3 and 6.4.

With the third kind of temporal transaction, effective begin and end dates may be specified, and either or both of them may be dates which are already past at the time of the transaction. This is the way maintenance is done to tables which support assertions of versions. But to authors whose mandate is to maintain either conventional or uni-temporal versioned tables, this kind of maintenance is impossible. A conventional table has no way of recognizing effective time. And it is semantically illegitimate to create past versions in uni-temporal version tables.

Here's why. If a past version were created in a version table, let's say one with an effective begin date of a week ago, it would be a lie. For all that week, the database would have said that the object represented by that version was not in effect during that week. Then, after the transaction, the database would say that the object *was* in effect during that same week. One or the other of those claims must be false. In fact, the latter one is.

But in a chapter whose purpose is to introduce notation that will be used in the rest of this book, much of what we have just said anticipates more detailed discussions that will occur later, particularly in Part 3.

## Glossary References

Glossary entries whose definitions form strong interdependencies are grouped together in the following list. The same glossary entries may be grouped together in different ways at the end of different chapters, each grouping reflecting the semantic perspective of each chapter. There will usually be several other, and often many other, glossary entries that are not included in the list, and we recommend that the Glossary be consulted whenever an unfamiliar term is encountered.

---

12/31/9999
until further notice

asserted version table
Asserted Versioning Framework (AVF)

assertion begin date
assertion end date
assertion table

assertion time period
transaction time period

bi-temporal data

business data
business key

clock tick
closed-open

conventional table
conventional transaction
non-temporal table

deferred assertion
deferred transaction

episode
episode begin date
episode end date

include

incommensurable

maintenance encapsulation
query encapsulation

object
object identifier
oid
persistent object

PERIOD datatype

physical transaction
temporal transaction

replace
supercede
withdraw

row creation date

statement

temporal foreign key (TFK)
temporal primary key (TPK)
temporal referential integrity (TRI)

version
effective begin date
effective end date
effective time period

# THE BASIC SCENARIO

When representing an object in a non-temporal table, the most basic things we can do are to insert a row representing the object, update the row as changes happen to the object, and delete the row if and when the object ceases to exist, or ceases to be of interest to us. Almost always, we don't know in advance if or when any of these things will happen: if or when a row will be inserted; if or when the next update will occur; if or when the row will be deleted.

These rows represent objects of interest to us. They are not the objects themselves. A row in a Policy table is not a policy; it is data which represents the policy in our database. Through the DBMS, for the most part mediated by application software, we manage these rows. We insert them, update them and sometimes delete them. We put them in result sets in response to queries. We put them on reports. By managing them, we are able to manage the policies which they represent. For this reason, we will call these rows *managed objects*.

Sometimes it is harmless enough to finesse this distinction, and speak of the DBMS, for example, updating policies. But what the DBMS updates, of course, are rows representing policies. It updates managed objects, not the objects they represent. As we enter into a series of chapters which will describe our method of temporal data management in great detail, we will sometimes

Managing Time in Relational Databases. Doi: 10.1016/B978-0-12-375041-9.00007-8

find it useful to emphasize the distinction between objects and managed objects. But if we do occasionally speak of software doing something to an object, that will simply be a non-tendentious shorthand for speaking about software doing something to a managed object which represents that object.

This basic sequence of insert, update and delete transactions accounts for most of the activity against any table, whether non-temporal or bi-temporal. And just as we usually don't know if or when updates to a non-temporal row will occur, and if or when it will be deleted, so too, as each row representing some stage in the life history of an object is inserted into a bi-temporal table, we usually don't know if or when another row for that same object will come along.

In this chapter, we will follow a sequence of basic temporal transactions. Temporal transactions are inserts, updates and deletes whose target is an asserted version table. As we explained in Chapter 5, all asserted version tables are bi-temporal tables. Uni-temporal assertion tables and uni-temporal version tables, as we sometimes call them, are actually *views* on bi-temporal tables. Conventional tables, which we also call non-temporal tables, are the third kind of view which can be defined on Asserted Versioning's physical bi-temporal tables.

*Basic temporal transactions* are temporal transactions that do not specify any bi-temporal parameters. As we will see later, any one or more of three bi-temporal parameters—an assertion begin date, an effective begin date or an effective end date—may be specified on a temporal transaction. On a *basic* temporal transaction, none of them are specified.

By starting out with basic temporal transactions, we can introduce the most common sequence of transactions that occur against asserted version tables, and show how these transactions are processed. In chapters that follow, we will examine temporal transactions which are not basic, and whose processing is considerably more complex, although because of the maintenance encapsulation provided by Asserted Versioning, are just as easy for the user to write as are basic temporal transactions.

## The Representation of Objects in Time Periods

The basic scenario, and by far the most commonly encountered one, is for a series of updates that would overwrite data in a conventional table to result in an effective-time contiguous series of versions in an asserted version table. Just as it is logically impossible to apply an update to a conventional table that takes effect either in the past or in the future, basic temporal updates to asserted version tables also take place in the present. Just as an update to a conventional table remains in effect until further notice, rather than for a predetermined length of time, a basic temporal update to an asserted version table will be to a current episode that is open, i.e. whose latest version has an effective end date of 12/31/9999, and it will always leave that episode open after the transaction is complete.

Basic temporal transactions are the Asserted Versioning equivalent of conventional transactions. No bi-temporal parameters are specified on them, and so their content is identical to that of their corresponding conventional transactions. They contain exactly the same information that is present on conventional transactions— nothing more and nothing less. But if temporal transactions are to take effect some time in the future, or some time in the past, then those non-current effective time periods must be explicitly specified on those transactions. And if we wish to update the database with deferred assertions, the assertion begin date must also be specified. In these cases, the temporal transactions are no longer basic; they explicitly state the bi-temporal parameters they want.

Corresponding to each appearance of a managed object in a conventional table, i.e. to each period of time starting when a row for an object is inserted and ending if and when it is deleted, there would be an episode of that object if that table were instead an asserted version table. It follows that there can be any number of episodes of the same object present at the same time in an asserted version table, although no more than one of them, of course, can be current. Each episode is a managed object, representing an object as it exists over a continuous period of time. Each version of that episode is also a managed object, representing an object as it exists over one continuous period of time that is included within the episode's period of time.

In Figure 7.1, eight versions, grouped into three episodes, are shown along a timeline. The first two episodes are closed, as all but the latest episode of an object must be. The last one is open. All are managed objects representing one object, policy P861.

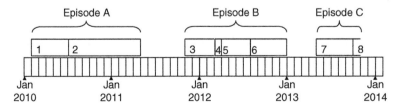

**Figure 7.1** Eight Versions and Three Episodes of Policy P861.

### Occupied and Represented

In subsequent discussions, we will find it convenient to speak of time periods as being *occupied* by an object or, equivalently, of an object being *represented* in a time period by a managed object. In a conventional table, a time period is occupied by an object just in case a row representing that object exists in its table throughout that time period. In an asserted version table, a time period is occupied by an object just in case one or more contiguous versions representing that object span that time period or, as we will also say, occupy every clock tick in that time period. For example, the clock tick of March 2010 is occupied by policy P861 just in case there is a row with the value "P861" as its object identifier and which has an effective begin date less than or equal to March 2010 and an effective end date greater than March 2010. We can equivalently say that policy P861 is represented in the effective time clock tick of March 2010.

Because Asserted Versioning is a method of managing bi-temporal data, the time periods in question may be either effective time periods or assertion time periods. But we will often find it convenient to speak simply about versions and their effective times, presupposing that the rows we are talking about all exist in current assertion time.

# Basic Temporal Transactions:
# The Mental Model

The mental model supported by basic temporal transactions is one which completely hides the temporality of the tables that those transactions maintain. As far as the user is concerned, she submits transactions to a program, which then submits them to the DBMS. It is no concern of hers that the program actually calls the AVF which, after some translation and constraint checking, submits one or more SQL transactions to the DBMS. Rather, it seems to her that she is inserting, updating or deleting rows in conventional tables.

Consequently, the user thinks about what she is doing in the same way whether she is updating a conventional table or an asserted version table. This means that as long as the user writes basic temporal transactions—which will be the vast majority of temporal transactions she will write—maintenance of temporal rather than conventional data places no additional semantic burden on her.

# Maintaining Asserted Version Tables: The Basic Scenario

In response to a temporal transaction, the AVF generates one or more physical transactions and at the same time enforces temporal entity integrity and temporal referential integrity. In this way, it encapsulates bi-temporal complexity, and preserves for the user the image of a single transaction affecting a single physical representation of a single object.

Let's now see how temporal transactions are mapped to physical transactions in this situation we call the basic scenario. To avoid unnecessary complications in this initial look at how asserted version tables are updated, we will ignore temporal referential integrity issues, and leave an explanation of how they work to a later chapter.

## A Temporal Insert Transaction

Figure 7.2 shows the mapping for a temporal insert transaction. In the example shown in Figure 7.3, the transaction specifies no bi-temporal parameters and is therefore a basic transaction.

Assertion begin and end dates delimit the assertion time period for a row in an asserted version table. For the next several chapters, we will assume that all temporal transactions accept the default value for the assertion begin date, that default value being the date current when the version is created. As long as this is the case, our assertion time periods will behave like what the standard temporal model calls transaction time periods. This means that an assertion begin date will function like a row creation date. Not only are both assigned the date current when the physical transaction is applied, but also once created, neither date can be changed.[1]

**Temporal Insert**          **Physical Transaction(s)**

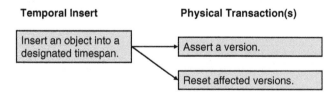

**Figure 7.2** Basic Scenario, Insert Transaction: Temporal to Physical Mapping.

[1]In fact, a future assertion begin date can be changed. But in this basic scenario, we are limiting ourselves to temporal transactions which use the current date as the assertion begin date. And neither past nor current assertion begin dates can be changed because once we begin to claim that something is so, we can't "take it back". If we did, we would lose the information that once upon a time, we did make such claims. And it is an explicit objective of bi-temporal data management to preserve such information.

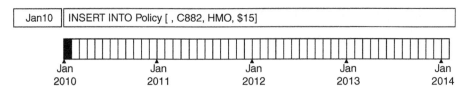

**Figure 7.3** Basic Scenario, Temporal Insert: Before the Physical Transaction.

An insert into a non-temporal table is valid just in case a row for the object does not exist in the target table at the time of the insert. In the same way, a temporal insert into an asserted version table is valid just in case no version for that object exists in the target table, at the time of the insert, anywhere within the effective time period specified on the transaction. If such a version did exist, its time period would [intersect] that of the transaction. Since every version is part of an episode, the intersection of an insert transaction with a version already in the table is a temporal entity integrity conflict. It is equivalent, if only for a single clock tick, to an attempt to insert a row into a non-temporal table which has the same primary key as a row already in that table.

Thus, an insert whose target is an asserted version table is valid if the target table is empty, and is also valid if the target table contains other episodes of the same object, provided that the transaction's effective time period does not [intersect] the effective time period of any of those other episodes. In the non-temporal case, this constraint is known as entity integrity. In the Asserted Versioning case, it is what we call temporal entity integrity (TEI).

The physical transaction is derived from the temporal transaction by the AVF. Before it is applied, the target table is as shown in Figure 7.3. In this example, it is now January 2010.

Figure 7.4 shows the result of applying the physical transaction derived from this temporal transaction to the target

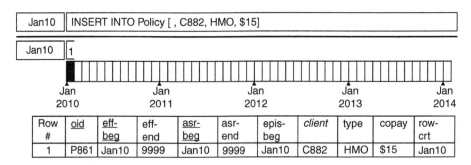

| Row # | oid | eff-beg | eff-end | asr-beg | asr-end | epis-beg | client | type | copay | row-crt |
|---|---|---|---|---|---|---|---|---|---|---|
| 1 | P861 | Jan10 | 9999 | Jan10 | 9999 | Jan10 | C882 | HMO | $15 | Jan10 |

**Figure 7.4** Basic Scenario, Temporal Insert: After the Physical Transaction.

table. The unique identifier of the policy is its object identifier, P861. The AVF supplied this unique identifier, since on an insert transaction, a surrogate key value has not yet been assigned to represent the object. This version is effective beginning in January 2010 because it was applied in January 2010 and no effective begin date was specified on the temporal transaction. It will remain in effect until further notice because no effective end date was specified.

The third component of the primary key of an asserted version table is the assertion begin date. Because no assertion begin date was specified on the temporal transaction, the current date is used. In other words, the default is for a version to be asserted as soon as it is created. The assertion end date is set to 12/31/9999, as it is for all temporal transactions, meaning that we will continue to assert what this row represents until further notice.

A valid temporal insert transaction results in a new episode unless it [meets] or [meets$^{-1}$] an adjacent episode. If it [meets$^{-1}$] an earlier episode, its begin date matches the end date of that earlier episode, and it has the effect of extending that episode forwards in time. If it [meets] a later episode, its end date matches the begin date of that later episode, and it has the effect of extending that episode backwards in time.[2] And if it does both, its begin and end dates match, respectively, the end date of the earlier episode and the begin date of the later episode, and it has the effect of "filling in the gap" between those two episodes, merging them into a single episode. In this chapter, however, we assume that our temporal insert creates a new episode.

An episode begin date is always set to the effective begin date of its earliest version. So in this case, since this transaction creates the initial version of a new episode, the episode begin date is set to January 2010.

## A Temporal Update Transaction

In the scenario shown in Figure 7.5, it is now May 2010, and we are about to change the policy's copay amount to $20.

We can read this diagram as follows. Row 1 represents the only version of this episode of policy P861. The business data on this row became effective on January 2010. It is currently in effect and will remain in effect until further notice. We currently assert that row 1 is correct, i.e. that the statement made by row 1 is true.

Since January 2010, this policy has been owned by client C882, and has been an HMO policy with a $15 copay. The client column

---

[2]We will sometimes use "contiguous with" to mean "either [meets] or [meets$^{-1}$]".

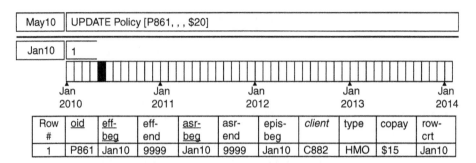

**Figure 7.5** Basic Scenario, Temporal Update: Before the First Physical Transaction.

is a temporal foreign key (TFK), implementing a temporal referential integrity relationship (TRI). It designates an object in a referenced asserted version Client table (not shown), but it does not designate any specific version or episode of that object. The AVF would not have permitted row 1 to be created, however, unless it satisfied the TRI constraint.

This means that, at the time the temporal update took place—which is indicated by the row creation date—the AVF was able to find an episode of client C882 whose effective time period included that of the new policy episode. In other words, there was, at that time, an episode of C882 with an effective begin date on or before January 2010, and an effective end date of 12/31/9999.

This policy row was inserted into the table in January 2010. There are several columns with a January 2010 value in row 1, but the column that records the physical insertion date is the row creation date column. This row was immediately asserted, meaning that we were ready, right away, to claim that the row makes a true statement. Until further notice, this row will be what we return to any query asking about what we currently believe is the case about this policy during this effective time period. At the time this row was created, no row for P861 was current, i.e. it was not the case that there was a row for P861 whose effective time period and assertion time period were both then current.

Updating the data about policy P861 is not the same thing as updating the row we currently have for that policy, as it would be if the Policy table were a non-temporal table. Instead, to update the policy while retaining the data which is about to be replaced and superceded by the new data in the update transaction, three physical transactions have to be applied to the target table. Figure 7.6 shows a temporal update transaction and its mapping into three types of physical transactions, resulting in any number of individual physical transactions.

**Temporal Update**          **Physical Transaction(s)**

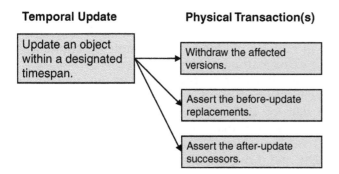

**Figure 7.6** Basic Scenario, Update Transaction: Temporal to Physical Mapping.

## The First Physical Transaction

The result of applying the first of these physical transactions is shown in Figure 7.7. This physical transaction *withdraws* the current assertion. It does so by doing a physical update of row 1, overwriting its assertion end date with the same date on which the two new versions will begin to be asserted. In this case, that is the same date as the date of the transaction itself, i.e. May 2010. In Figure 7.7, we can see that the database now shows that row 1 was asserted from January 2010 to May 2010, but not after that.

Row 1, and its assertion time snapshot, are shaded to indicate that row 1 is no longer asserted. The row number is enclosed within angle brackets as a way of showing that the row is locked. It is locked—from other updates and also, unless dirty reads are allowed, from viewing as well—because it is part of an all-or-nothing isolated unit of work that will not be complete until the third physical transaction is complete.

This row says that from January 2010 to 12/31/9999, policy P861 is as shown. But based on the information supplied by the temporal update transaction, we now know that it is not true

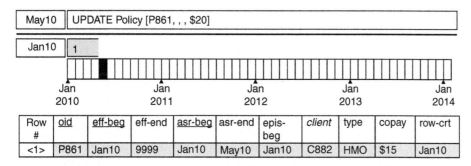

**Figure 7.7** Basic Scenario, First Temporal Update: After the First Physical Transaction.

that the data in row 1 describes the policy throughout the period [Jan 2010 – 12/31/9999]. We now know, starting in May 2010, that the data in row 1 is no longer an accurate description of the object as it exists starting in May 2010.

Updates in place, however, overwrite the data they update. So haven't we now lost the information that row 1 originally had an assertion end date of 12/31/9999? No, we have not lost that information. The reason is that no row can be physically added to an asserted version table with any assertion end date other than 12/31/9999; and if the assertion end date is ever changed, it can be changed only once. The AVF, which translates temporal into physical transactions, guarantees this.

Therefore, the assertion end date in row 1, as it exists in Figure 7.7, tells us two things. It tells us that from January 2010 (the assertion begin date), up to May 2010, this row had an assertion end date of 12/31/9999. It also tells us that, starting in May 2010, it will no longer be asserted. Any asserted version with a non-12/31/9999 assertion end date is one that was (or will be) moved into past assertion time on that assertion end date.

### The Second Physical Transaction

We have now *withdrawn* row 1, "clearing the decks" for *replacing* part of it and *superceding* the rest of it. The temporal update will result, when the final physical transaction is applied, in a new current version of P861 with an effective begin date of May 2010.

But what about the effective time prior to then, the effective time period of [Jan 2010 – May 2010]? The temporal update says nothing about what the policy was like prior to May 2010. Yet by withdrawing row 1, i.e. by moving it into past assertion time, we have placed the database in a state (albeit an atomic transaction isolated state) in which nothing at all is asserted about P861 as it was prior to May 2010. And yet the purpose of the temporal update was certainly not to alter anything about P861 prior to May 2010. So we need to replace the withdrawn assertion with one which is identical to it except that, instead of an unknown effective end date, it has an end date of May 2010. The result is shown in Figure 7.8.

The superscript, in the assertion time snapshot of row 2, tells us that this row has the same business data as row 1. At this moment, row 2 is the only row which exists in current assertion time; it is the only row which we currently assert to be true. However, we are still in the midst of an atomic unit of work, one which isolates all affected rows until the unit of work is completed. So at this point, no one can see that row 1 is withdrawn, and no one can

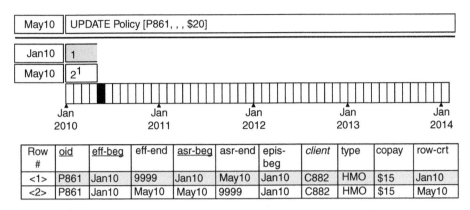

| Row # | oid | eff-beg | eff-end | asr-beg | asr-end | epis-beg | client | type | copay | row-crt |
|-------|-----|---------|---------|---------|---------|----------|--------|------|-------|---------|
| <1> | P861 | Jan10 | 9999 | Jan10 | May10 | Jan10 | C882 | HMO | $15 | Jan10 |
| <2> | P861 | Jan10 | May10 | May10 | 9999 | Jan10 | C882 | HMO | $15 | May10 |

**Figure 7.8** Basic Scenario, First Temporal Update: After the Second Physical Transaction.

see that row 2 has been created. With row 2 we assert, starting in May 2010, that policy P861, with client, type and copay as indicated, was in effect during the period [Jan 2010 – May 2010].

## The Third Physical Transaction

Having withdrawn an assertion, and asserted its replacement, we can now complete the temporal transaction by asserting its successor. As shown in Figure 7.9, this is done by inserting row 3. This now becomes the new current version of this current episode for P861, an episode which began in January 2010. With the physical insertion of row 3, this atomic unit of work is now complete and the rows it has updated and inserted become visible in the database. This is shown by removing the angle brackets from the row numbers.

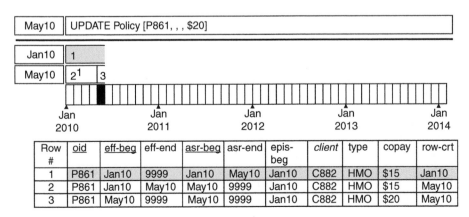

| Row # | oid | eff-beg | eff-end | asr-beg | asr-end | epis-beg | client | type | copay | row-crt |
|-------|-----|---------|---------|---------|---------|----------|--------|------|-------|---------|
| 1 | P861 | Jan10 | 9999 | Jan10 | May10 | Jan10 | C882 | HMO | $15 | Jan10 |
| 2 | P861 | Jan10 | May10 | May10 | 9999 | Jan10 | C882 | HMO | $15 | May10 |
| 3 | P861 | May10 | 9999 | May10 | 9999 | Jan10 | C882 | HMO | $20 | May10 |

**Figure 7.9** Basic Scenario, First Temporal Update: After the Third Physical Transaction.

Because the temporal transaction specified neither an effective end date nor an assertion begin date, the effective end date on row 3 defaults to 12/31/9999 and the assertion begin date to May 2010, the date of the physical insert.

## A Second Temporal Update Transaction

Let's see how a second temporal update affects the asserted version Policy table. Figure 7.10 shows the state of the Policy table before that transaction begins.

### The First Physical Transaction

Figure 7.11 shows the state of the target table after the first of the three physical transactions has been applied. This physical transaction *withdraws* the current assertion. It does so by doing

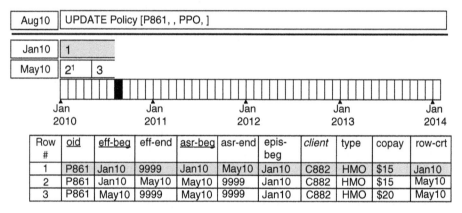

| Row # | oid | eff-beg | eff-end | asr-beg | asr-end | epis-beg | client | type | copay | row-crt |
|---|---|---|---|---|---|---|---|---|---|---|
| 1 | P861 | Jan10 | 9999 | Jan10 | May10 | Jan10 | C882 | HMO | $15 | Jan10 |
| 2 | P861 | Jan10 | May10 | May10 | 9999 | Jan10 | C882 | HMO | $15 | May10 |
| 3 | P861 | May10 | 9999 | May10 | 9999 | Jan10 | C882 | HMO | $20 | May10 |

**Figure 7.10** Basic Scenario, Second Temporal Update: Before the First Physical Transaction.

| Row # | oid | eff-beg | eff-end | asr-beg | asr-end | epis-beg | client | type | copay | row-crt |
|---|---|---|---|---|---|---|---|---|---|---|
| 1 | P861 | Jan10 | 9999 | Jan10 | May10 | Jan10 | C882 | HMO | $15 | Jan10 |
| 2 | P861 | Jan10 | May10 | May10 | 9999 | Jan10 | C882 | HMO | $15 | May10 |
| <3> | P861 | May10 | 9999 | May10 | Aug10 | Jan10 | C882 | HMO | $20 | May10 |

**Figure 7.11** Basic Scenario, Second Temporal Update: After the First Physical Transaction.

a physical update of row 3, overwriting its assertion end date with the date the new transaction will begin to be asserted. In this case, that is the same date as the date of the update itself, i.e. August 2010. In Figure 7.11, we can see that the database now shows that row 3 was asserted from May 2010 to August 2010, at which time it was withdrawn.

### The Second Physical Transaction

The second physical transaction for this update replaces the version that was withdrawn by the first physical transaction. In Figure 7.12, row 4 is that replacement. Its effect is to shorten the effective time period of row 3 to precisely one clock tick before the effective time period of the superceding row will begin. (Recall that, because of the closed-open use of date pairs, this means that those two date values will be identical.)

Notice that row 2 now appears in two assertion time snapshots. It appears in the May 2010 snapshot because that was when it was first asserted. It also appears in the August 2010 snapshot because, at that point in time, it is still currently asserted.

### The Third Physical Transaction

We have withdrawn the version of P861 which was current as this second update transaction began. And we have now replaced it with a newly asserted version that covers all of the effective time of that original version that will not be covered by its superceding version. The final step is to insert the superceding version, which becomes the new current version, and which

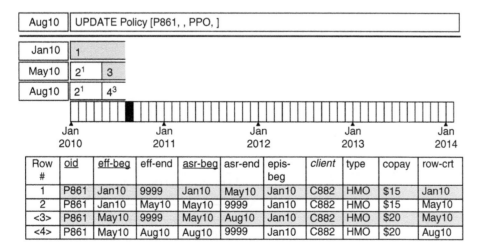

**Figure 7.12** Basic Scenario, Second Temporal Update: After the Second Physical Transaction.

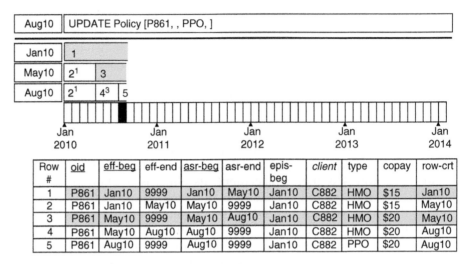

| Row # | oid | eff-beg | eff-end | asr-beg | asr-end | epis-beg | client | type | copay | row-crt |
|---|---|---|---|---|---|---|---|---|---|---|
| 1 | P861 | Jan10 | 9999 | Jan10 | May10 | Jan10 | C882 | HMO | $15 | Jan10 |
| 2 | P861 | Jan10 | May10 | May10 | 9999 | Jan10 | C882 | HMO | $15 | May10 |
| 3 | P861 | May10 | 9999 | May10 | Aug10 | Jan10 | C882 | HMO | $20 | May10 |
| 4 | P861 | May10 | Aug10 | Aug10 | 9999 | Jan10 | C882 | HMO | $20 | Aug10 |
| 5 | P861 | Aug10 | 9999 | Aug10 | 9999 | Jan10 | C882 | PPO | $20 | Aug10 |

**Figure 7.13** Basic Scenario, Second Temporal Update: After the Third Physical Transaction.

contains the changes specified in the temporal update. The result of doing this is shown in Figure 7.13. The transaction is complete, and all locks have been released.

## A Temporal Delete Transaction

Figure 7.13 shows us an asserted version table after a temporal insert and two temporal updates. This time, we will process a temporal delete. As Figure 7.14 shows, a temporal delete is translated into a set of physical update transactions which withdraw the affected versions, followed by either one or two physical insert transactions which delimit the scope of the delete and, if necessary, any number of withdrawals and replacements to adjust episode begin dates that may have been affected.

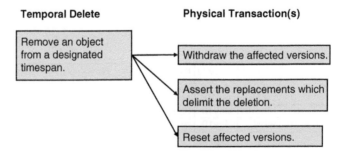

**Figure 7.14** Basic Scenario, Delete Transaction: Temporal to Physical Mapping.

Note that, like all temporal transactions, a temporal delete transaction refers to an object. It says that the policy is to be deleted which, for a temporally managed object, is to remove its representation from a period of time. Physical transactions are the transactions which are submitted to the DBMS, and which insert or update rows in asserted version tables. They are created by the AVF which translates temporal transactions into physical transactions.

The targets of these transactions, however, are not objects; nor are they versions or assertions. The targets of these transactions are episodes of objects. Just as transactions against non-temporal tables insert, update or delete individual rows representing objects, transactions against asserted version tables insert into a period of time, update within a period of time, or remove from a period of time, all or parts of individual episodes representing those objects.

Figure 7.15 shows the state of the target table before the delete transaction begins.

Rows 1 and 2 contain the same business data, the same information about the version of policy P861 which began in January 2010. The difference is that row 1 asserted that P861 would be a type HMO policy, with a $15 copay, from that date until further notice. But in May 2010, we learned that the copay changed to $20, effective on that date. Therefore, at that point in time, the assertion made by row 1 ceased being true. It ceased being the case that P861 would continue to be an HMO policy with a $15 copay until further notice. In May 2010, "further notice" was given, and so the original assertion had to be withdrawn. In its place, we put an assertion identical

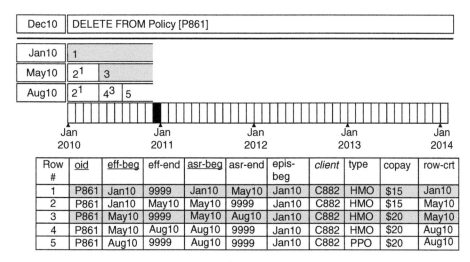

| Row # | oid | eff-beg | eff-end | asr-beg | asr-end | epis-beg | client | type | copay | row-crt |
|---|---|---|---|---|---|---|---|---|---|---|
| 1 | P861 | Jan10 | 9999 | Jan10 | May10 | Jan10 | C882 | HMO | $15 | Jan10 |
| 2 | P861 | Jan10 | May10 | May10 | 9999 | Jan10 | C882 | HMO | $15 | May10 |
| 3 | P861 | May10 | 9999 | May10 | Aug10 | Jan10 | C882 | HMO | $20 | May10 |
| 4 | P861 | May10 | Aug10 | Aug10 | 9999 | Jan10 | C882 | HMO | $20 | Aug10 |
| 5 | P861 | Aug10 | 9999 | Aug10 | 9999 | Jan10 | C882 | PPO | $20 | Aug10 |

**Figure 7.15** Basic Scenario, Temporal Delete: Before the First Physical Transaction.

to it except that it states that the business data it contains ceases to be effective on May 2010. We then follow that with another assertion which records the actual change in business data that does become effective on May 2010.

### The First Physical Transaction

It is now December 2010. Figure 7.15 shows the state of the target table before the first of the two physical transactions for this temporal delete transaction has been applied. Because the temporal transaction does not include any bi-temporal parameters, default values are used. The result is that the transaction tells us to delete P861 as of December 2010. Using the default values, the transaction specifies an assertion and effective time range, in both cases, of [Dec 2010 – 12/31/9999]. It is row 5 which the transaction's two time periods overlap, and so it is row 5 which will be affected by the delete.

Figure 7.16 shows the results of applying the first physical transaction.

As indicated in Figure 7.16, the first of these physical transactions withdraws the currently asserted, currently effective row, row 5. Because a specific assertion end date is not specified, the default of Now() is used, and the assertion end date for row 5 is therefore changed from 12/31/9999 to December 2010. This "clears the decks" because the latest thing we are still currently asserting about P861 is a version covering May 2010 to August 2010, which is row 4.

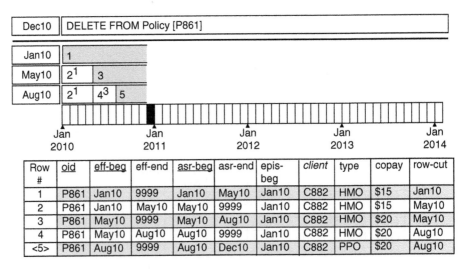

| Row # | oid | eff-beg | eff-end | asr-beg | asr-end | epis-beg | client | type | copay | row-cut |
|-------|------|---------|---------|---------|---------|----------|--------|------|-------|---------|
| 1 | P861 | Jan10 | 9999 | Jan10 | May10 | Jan10 | C882 | HMO | $15 | Jan10 |
| 2 | P861 | Jan10 | May10 | May10 | 9999 | Jan10 | C882 | HMO | $15 | May10 |
| 3 | P861 | May10 | 9999 | May10 | Aug10 | Jan10 | C882 | HMO | $20 | May10 |
| 4 | P861 | May10 | Aug10 | Aug10 | 9999 | Jan10 | C882 | HMO | $20 | Aug10 |
| <5> | P861 | Aug10 | 9999 | Aug10 | Dec10 | Jan10 | C882 | PPO | $20 | Aug10 |

**Figure 7.16** Basic Scenario, Temporal Delete: After the First Physical Transaction.

### The Second Physical Transaction

The result of applying the second physical transaction implementing the temporal delete is shown in Figure 7.17.

Row 5 was the current version before the temporal transaction began. The first physical transaction withdraws it, and this second physical transaction replaces it. It replaces it with a version identical to the withdrawn version, except for having an effective end date of December 2010, which is the default value from the temporal transaction. With this effective end date, we now currently assert a closed episode, and remove all traces of P861, in current assertion time, from the time period of [Dec 2010 – 12/31/9999].

This is what the result of a delete against an asserted version table looks like. It removes the representation of an object from an indicated period of effective time. In this case, doing so results in closing an open episode as of the specific effective end date.

We now have enough detail in our Policy table to illustrate how to read the history of an object from its assertion time snapshots. From the four snapshots in Figure 7.17, and without consulting the table itself, we can follow the assertion time history of this policy.

**(i)** In January 2010, we begin to assert an episode of policy P861, effective on that same date.[3] At this point in time, the episode consists of a single version with an effective time period beginning in January 2010 and extending to 12/31/9999. Because the effective end date is 12/31/9999, this is an open episode, one which will remain in effect "until further notice". Row 1, at this time, is not shaded because it has not yet been withdrawn.

**(ii)** In May 2010, we update P861, effective on that same date. This episode now has two versions, and remains an open episode. Row 1 is now shaded because it is withdrawn as part of this update transaction. Row 3 will not be withdrawn, of course, until August 2010. So from now until August 2010, what we assert about this episode is rows 2 and 3.

**(iii)** On August 2010, we update P861 again, effective on that same date. The episode now has three versions, and remains an open episode. Row 3 is withdrawn at this time. From now until December 2010, what we assert about this episode is rows 2, 4 and 5.

---

[3]Notice that we read the assertion begin date from the left of the snapshot, but read the effective begin date from the vertical alignment of each rectangle with the calendar timeline underneath the snapshots. These are two distinct dates which, because our transactions are using default values, happen in this case to be the same.

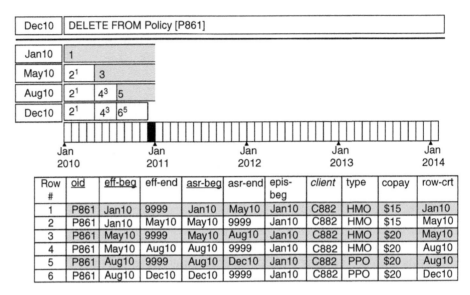

| Row # | oid | eff-beg | eff-end | asr-beg | asr-end | epis-beg | client | type | copay | row-crt |
|---|---|---|---|---|---|---|---|---|---|---|
| 1 | P861 | Jan10 | 9999 | Jan10 | May10 | Jan10 | C882 | HMO | $15 | Jan10 |
| 2 | P861 | Jan10 | May10 | May10 | 9999 | Jan10 | C882 | HMO | $15 | May10 |
| 3 | P861 | May10 | 9999 | May10 | Aug10 | Jan10 | C882 | HMO | $20 | May10 |
| 4 | P861 | May10 | Aug10 | Aug10 | 9999 | Jan10 | C882 | HMO | $20 | Aug10 |
| 5 | P861 | Aug10 | 9999 | Aug10 | Dec10 | Jan10 | C882 | PPO | $20 | Aug10 |
| 6 | P861 | Aug10 | Dec10 | Dec10 | 9999 | Jan10 | C882 | PPO | $20 | Dec10 |

**Figure 7.17** Basic Scenario, Temporal Delete: After the Second Physical Transaction.

(iv) In December 2010, we terminate this episode, effective on that same date. The episode still has three versions, but is now a closed episode. From this point in time, until further notice, what we assert about this episode of P861 is rows 2, 4 and 6.

While updates and deletes are very different actions as applied to a non-temporal table, temporal updates and temporal deletes actually result in very similar actions applied to an asserted version table. As we have seen, the first two physical transactions for a temporal update withdraw the current assertion, and replace it with a new currently asserted version which occupies all the effective time of the withdrawn assertion other than the effective time the superceding version will occupy. In most cases, including this basic scenario, that means that the replacement version will have the same effective begin date as the withdrawn version, and will have the current date as its effective end date. The superceding version picks it up from there. A temporal delete is simply a temporal update for which there is no superceding version, but instead only, if necessary, one or two (but never more than two) replacement versions.

We conclude by pointing out a subtlety of the graphic notation used here. In Figure 7.17, note that the "above the calendar timeline" graphics for row 1, 3 and 5 extend *through* December 2010, while the graphic for row 6 extends *up to* December

2010. The graphics for those three rows extend through December 2010 because, with this temporal transaction complete, the results are guaranteed to remain in the table, unaltered in any way, until the next clock tick. And as we said before, throughout this book we are using a clock that ticks once a month. The graphic for row 6 only extends up to December 2010 because the delete transaction sets the effective end date for that version (and thus for the entire episode) to December 2010.

## Glossary References

Glossary entries whose definitions form strong interdependencies are grouped together in the following list. The same glossary entries may be grouped together in different ways at the end of different chapters, each grouping reflecting the semantic perspective of each chapter. There will usually be several other, and often many other, glossary entries that are not included in the list, and we recommend that the Glossary be consulted whenever an unfamiliar term is encountered.

---

12/31/9999
until further notice
temporal parameter

adjacent
include

asserted version table
Asserted Versioning Framework (AVF)
Asserted Versioning

assertion begin date
assertion end date
assertion time period

Now()
temporal default values

bi-temporal table

business data

clock tick
closed-open

conventional table
conventional transaction

deferred assertion

effective begin date
effective end date
effective time period

episode
closed episode
open episode
current episode
episode begin date
lock

managed object
object
object identifier

non-temporal table
uni-temporal assertion table
uni-temporal version table

occupied
replace
represented

successor
supercede
withdraw

physical transaction
temporal transaction
temporal insert transaction
temporal update transaction
temporal delete transaction

row creation date

statement

target table

temporal entity integrity (TEI)
temporal foreign key (TFK)
temporal referential integrity (TRI)

the standard temporal model

time period
transaction time period

# DESIGNING, MAINTAINING AND QUERYING ASSERTED VERSION DATABASES

## Chapter Contents

In Part 1, we introduced the topic of temporal data management. We presented a brief history of how temporal data has been managed over the last quarter-century, and we also developed a taxonomy of temporal data management methods. Within the distinction between reconstructable and queryable data, we situated Asserted Versioning as, first of all, a method of managing and providing access to queryable data. Next, within the distinction between keeping track of changes over time as a series of events or as a series of states through which objects pass, we situated Asserted Versioning as a method of managing data which describes the states through which persistent objects pass as they change over time. At the third level of the taxonomy, we distinguished between the management of data along a single temporal dimension from the management of data along two temporal dimensions, and situated Asserted Versioning as a method in the latter category. Finally, within the category of the management of queryable bi-temporal data about persistent objects, we distinguished Asserted Versioning from the standard temporal model on the basis of its management of future assertion time and its encapsulation of the mechanisms which enforce temporal semantics.

In Part 2, we introduced the core concepts of Asserted Versioning, reviewed the schema common to all asserted version tables, and developed a scenario which illustrates the use of basic temporal insert, update and delete transactions. The most basic concept of Asserted Versioning is that of a persistent object. Although hardly a novel concept, we believe that the organization of methods of temporal data management on the basis of that concept is novel.

Like the standard temporal model, Asserted Versioning distinguishes two temporal dimensions in which persistent object data is located. The ontological dimension is called *effective time* in Asserted Versioning, and *valid time* in both the standard model and in the computer science community. The epistemological dimension is called *assertion time* in Asserted Versioning, and *transaction time* in the standard model and by computer scientists; and it is here that their accounts and ours differ.

Asserted Versioning manages data located in future assertion time, while the standard model ignores the notion of future transaction time. Asserted Versioning also emphasizes that effective time exists *within* assertion time, while the standard model seems to treat its two temporal dimensions as orthogonal.

With the completion of Parts 1 and 2, all the preliminary work is behind us. Part 3 is an in-depth presentation of Asserted Versioning itself. It begins with Chapter 8, in which we discuss how temporal design requirements are expressed in metadata associated with a conventional logical data model, how this metadata is used to convert non-temporal table schemas into bi-temporal table schemas, and also how it is used to generate the code, such as stored procedures, that enforce both temporal entity integrity and temporal referential integrity on those tables. If ERwin is used as the data modeling tool, then a set of ERwin macros which we have written will do the conversion automatically. Otherwise, the conversion will be a manual process.

In Chapter 9, we discuss the temporal transactions with which asserted version tables are maintained. From the external point of view, that being the point of view of the person writing those transactions, the three temporal parameters that may be specified on these transactions are optional. The most common case is that these transactions are intended to result in production data that is immediately asserted, that becomes effective the moment the transactions are complete, and that remains in effect until a later transaction for the same object is applied. When these are the intentions accompanying transactions against asserted version tables, those transactions will be identical in content to conventional SQL transactions against non-temporal tables, and we will call them *basic* temporal transactions.

But maintenance to asserted version tables doesn't just insert, update or delete single rows. It brings about transformations of those tables from one state to a new state, transformations which may affect any number of physical rows in any number of physical tables. In order to be sure that all valid transformations can be specified with temporal transactions, we once again need a taxonomy. So in Chapter 9, we also develop a taxonomy of what we will call *temporal extent state transformations* to asserted version tables.

In Chapter 10, we focus our discussion on the maintenance of individual asserted version tables. This allows us to exclude considerations of temporal referential integrity (TRI) from the discussion. Then in Chapter 11, we examine scenarios that do modify multiple asserted version tables, and that do involve temporal referential integrity and its enforcement.

In Chapter 12, we discuss the topic of pipeline datasets, in general, and of one kind of pipeline dataset—deferred assertions—in particular. We begin by noting that deferred assertions represent past, present and future versions in future assertion time, but that past, present and future versions also exist in past and present assertion time. This gives us nine categories of temporal data, one of which is currently asserted current versions of things. That category is what we know as *conventional data*, physically located in what we call *production tables*. The other eight categories correspond to what we call *pipeline datasets*, being data that has those production tables as either their destinations or their origins.

Deferred assertions are the result of applying deferred transactions to the database. Instead of holding on to maintenance transactions until it is the right time to apply them, Asserted Versioning applies them right away, but does not immediately assert them. These deferred assertions may themselves be updated or deleted, and the moment on which their assertion periods become current is the moment on which we begin to claim that the world was, is or will be as they describe it.

Just as deferred assertions replace collections of transactions that have not yet been applied to the database, bi-temporal data in any of the other seven categories replaces other physically external datasets. Asserted version tables contain data in all these temporal categories and, in doing so, internalize what would otherwise be physically distinct datasets, ones whose management costs are obviously significant.

In Chapter 13, we look more closely at the entire family of pipeline datasets. We distinguish eight logical categories of pipeline datasets, based on where in a combination of past, present or future assertion and effective time their data is located. Having previously shown how to eliminate these physically distinct datasets by bringing them into the production tables which are their destinations and points of origin, we now discuss each of them and show how queries and views can reassemble, as queryable objects, exactly the data that had existed in those datasets. This demonstrates that while eliminating the management costs associated with this data, we can still make this data available in whatever combinations it is needed.

In Chapter 14, we discuss how to query asserted version tables. As we said before, many queries, especially the ad hoc queries written by non-technical database users, will be directed against non-temporal or uni-temporal views of asserted version tables, not against those bi-temporal tables themselves. But many queries will be written directly against those physical tables, especially those we call production queries. In that case, the effective time period specified on the query, and which qualifies the result set, will have to be compared to the effective time periods of the rows targeted by the query; and as we know from our review of the Allen relationships, there are 13 different ways in which those two time periods may be positioned with respect to one another. And when those queries involve joins across two (or more) asserted version tables, then the Allen relationship issues can become even more difficult.

In Chapter 15, we discuss how to optimize the performance of Asserted Versioning databases. Our focus is on optimizing access to currently asserted current versions, i.e. to the rows that correspond to rows in a conventional table of persistent objects.

In this chapter, we focus on index design, although a wide range of other optimization techniques are also considered.

In Chapter 16, we conclude our presentation of Asserted Versioning. We discuss each of the four objectives we had for Asserted Versioning, and which we described in the Preface, and explain why we think those objectives have been met. We point out that Asserted Versioning has value both as a bridge to a future standards-based and vendor-provided implementation of bi-temporal data, and as a destination, being itself a semantically complete implementation of bi-temporal data which works with today's SQL and today's databases. In the last section, we discuss ongoing research and development at Asserted Versioning LLC, and explain how interested readers can learn more about Asserted Versioning.

## Glossary References

Glossary entries whose definitions form strong inter-dependencies are grouped together in the following list. The same Glossary entries may be grouped together in different ways at the end of different chapters, each grouping reflecting the semantic perspective of each chapter. There will usually be several other, and often many other, Glossary entries that are not included in the list, and we recommend that the Glossary be consulted whenever an unfamiliar term is encountered.

We note, in particular, that none of the nodes in our taxonomy of data management methods, or our state transformation taxonomy, are included in this list. In general, we leave taxonomy nodes out of these lists, but recommend that the reader look them up in the Glossary.

---

Allen relationships

asserted version table
Asserted Versioning Framework (AVF)

assertion time
transaction time

bi-temporal
uni-temporal

deferred assertion
deferred transaction

effective time
valid time

object
persistent object

physical transaction
temporal transaction
temporal parameter

pipeline dataset
production table

temporal entity integrity (TEI)
temporal referential integrity (TRI)

temporal extent state transformation

the standard temporal model

# DESIGNING AND GENERATING ASSERTED VERSIONING DATABASES

An Asserted Versioning database is one that contains at least one asserted version table. An asserted version table is one whose schema is that shown in Chapter 6, and on which the two temporal integrity constraints are enforced.

Figure 8.1 shows how Asserted Versioning databases are generated from the combination of a conventional logical data model and a set of metadata entries. Note that the logical data model has no temporal features. This means that logical data models of conventional databases, developed perhaps years ago, do not have to be changed if a decision is made to convert one or more of the tables in those databases into bi-temporal asserted

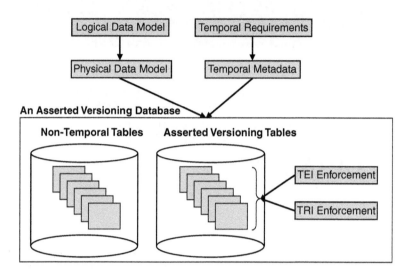

**Figure 8.1** Designing and Generating an Asserted Versioning Database.

version tables. This means that when building new logical data models, or extending old ones, data modelers can ignore temporal requirements and focus on design issues which are often complex enough without introducing temporal considerations. It means that temporal requirements can be expressed declaratively, in metadata associated with a conventional data model, rather than by hardcoding those requirements in the data model itself.

This greatly simplifies the work of the data modeler. Her work, as far as temporality is concerned, is not to translate temporal requirements into data model constructs. Instead, it becomes that of simply expressing business requirements for temporal data as a set of metadata associated with the data model.

As well as developing the logical model, the other task for the data modeler is to translate business requirements for temporal information into metadata. There are metadata entries for each table in the data model which is to be generated as an asserted version table. For these tables, there are entries to specify which business column or columns make up the business key for the table. This metadata also provides the information which the AVF needs to enforce temporal entity integrity and temporal referential integrity.

Once the logical model and its associated metadata are complete, the next step is to generate a physical data model from the logical model. At this point, of course, the physical model that is generated has no temporal features; all of its tables are conventional non-temporal tables.

The final step is a process in which a team consisting of the data modeler and a DBA uses the temporal metadata to modify the physical data model, changing specific tables into asserted version tables. In this process, pairs of date columns are added to implement assertion time and effective time. Surrogate primary keys are created as object identifiers. Physical primary keys are converted into Asserted Versioning business keys, and physical foreign keys into Asserted Versioning temporal foreign keys.

However, for organizations using the ERwin data modeling tool, this manual process is unnecessary. In the first release of the AVF, we provide ERwin user-defined properties (UDPs) to hold all temporal metadata, and ERwin scripting macros which use these UDPs to generate a physical data model in which all the temporal conversion work has already been done.

Note also that the Asserted Versioning database is more than a set of entries in a database catalog—more than the temporal data schemas shown in Figure 8.1. It is also the stored procedures, triggers or other code that enforces temporal integrity constraints on temporal tables.

In the Preface, we stated that Asserted Versioning simplifies the management of temporal databases by providing maintenance encapsulation, query encapsulation and design encapsulation. What we have just described here is how Asserted Versioning provides design encapsulation. In the rest of this chapter, we will see how design encapsulation works.

# Translating a Non-Temporal Logical Data Model into a Temporal Physical Data Model

## The Logical Data Model

Figure 8.2 is the logical data model (LDM) of a sample database we have constructed, and which can be accessed at AssertedVersioning.com. The most important thing to notice about this LDM is that there is nothing special about it. In particular, there is nothing explicitly temporal about it. And yet from this model, supplemented with metadata provided by the data modeler, the AVF will create an Asserted Versioning database in which all of the tables are bi-temporal tables.

There may be other tables in an Asserted Versioning database which are non-temporal tables. But we are not concerned with them. The DBMS enforces entity integrity on them, while the

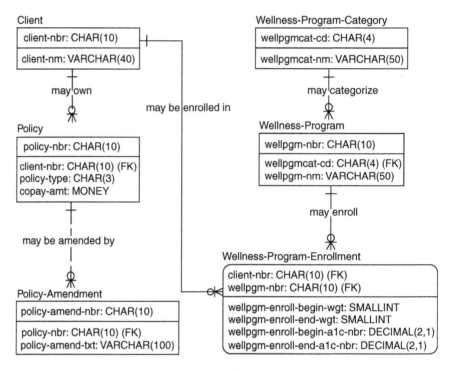

**Figure 8.2** The Sample Database Logical Data Model.

AVF enforces temporal entity integrity on its tables. The DBMS enforces referential integrity on them, while the AVF enforces temporal referential integrity on its tables. Later on, additional non-temporal tables may be converted to asserted version tables, and this can be done without making any changes to the logical data models of those databases. Temporality is introduced "downstream" from the logical data models, by making entries in asserted version metadata tables, and then by modifying DDL in accordance with this metadata before that DDL is submitted to the DBMS.

This particular logical data model is a simple one. In it, a client may own any number of policies, each of which must be owned by exactly one client. Each policy may be amended by any number of policy amendments, each of which amends exactly one policy.[1] A wellness program category categorizes any number of wellness programs, each of which is categorized by exactly one wellness program category. A client may be

---

[1]"Any number of" is our substitute for the less graceful expression "zero, one or more". The two expressions mean the same thing.

enrolled in any number of wellness programs, each of which may enroll any number of clients. Thus, the entity Wellness Program Enrollment is an associative entity, implementing a many-to-many relationship between clients and programs.

The business meaning of the entities, attributes and relationships should need no explanation, with the possible exception of the two attributes with a suffix of "a1c". As all diabetics know, a1c is a blood test that measures what percentage of a person's hemoglobin has glucose attached to it.

As ERwin data modelers will immediately recognize, primary keys are shown above the horizontal line in each entity. Foreign keys, of course, have "(FK)" as a separate suffix. Since all of these entities will be generated as temporal tables, all these FKs will be replaced by temporal foreign keys, by TFKs.

As we said earlier, the current implementation of Asserted Versioning uses ERwin's user-defined properties to capture the metadata needed to generate a bi-temporal database schema from a non-temporal data model. In this chapter, however, we will organize that metadata as a set of five metadata tables.

## Referential Constraints Between Non-Temporal and Bi-Temporal Tables

There is nothing semantically wrong about a bi-temporal table being the child table in a referential integrity relationship. In that case, the bi-temporal table will contain a conventional foreign key which points to a row in a parent non-temporal table. Conversely, there is nothing semantically wrong about a non-temporal table being the child table in a temporal referential integrity relationship. In that case, the non-temporal table will contain a temporal foreign key which points to an episode in a parent bi-temporal table.

In both cases, the referential relationships reflect an *existence dependency* between the objects involved. When both tables are non-temporal, we represent that existence dependency as a referential integrity dependency. When both tables are bi-temporal, we represent it as a temporal referential integrity dependency. When one table is non-temporal and the other bi-temporal, the existence dependency between their objects isn't somehow nullified because of our choice of how to represent it. And so our managed objects should be able to express that dependency even in that "mixed" case.

As bi-temporal theory, Asserted Versioning interprets non-temporal tables as tables whose rows are bi-temporal, but implicitly so. Rows in non-temporal tables exist in an assertion time which is co-temporal with their physical presence, and so too for effective time. In other words, non-temporal rows are asserted for as long as they physically exist, and are versions which describe what their objects are currently like for as long as those rows physically exist. Their assertion time periods and their effective time periods are fixed; both are always [row create date – 12/31/9999].

In an alternative interpretation, non-temporal rows are asserted for as long as they physically exist *in their current form*, and are versions which describe their objects for as long as those rows physically exist *in their current form*. Each time a row is updated, its old form, i.e. an exact image of all of the data in that row, is lost because at least some of it is overwritten. In this interpretation, those rows must have a last update date, in which case their assertion time periods and their effective time periods are not fixed because both are [last update date – 12/31/9999].

In our initial release of the AVF, however, we will *not* support mixed referential relationships. One of these relationships won't work, and the other one is dangerous. The relationship that won't work is the one in which the child table is a non-temporal table, and contains a temporal foreign key. This temporal foreign key is not declared in DDL because current DBMSs cannot recognize it. This temporal foreign key cannot be managed by the DBMS because, unlike normal foreign keys, it does not point to a specific row in the parent table.

The relationship that is dangerous is the one in which the child table is an asserted version table, and contains a conventional foreign key. This foreign key *is* declared in DDL, and the DBMS can recognize it. The danger lies in the fact that the DBMS can then carry out a delete cascade from the parent table to the child table, if it is so directed.

This delete cascade, however, is unaware of the temporal semantics of the child table. It will simply find every physical row in that child table that contains the referenced foreign key value, and will then physically delete that row. This is meat cleaver work where delicate surgery is required. It can destroy past, current and future episodes in the child table, leaving collections of versions which are semantically invalid, and which the AVF will be unable to manage. It will physically remove both version history and assertion history, whereas bi-temporal data management is a promise to preserve both. The conventional *delete set null* rule would be a safer alternative because episode timelines would not be destroyed. Nonetheless, column-level history would still be lost.

Mixed referential relationships should be addressed, but they will not be addressed in the first release of the AVF. And so, in the remainder of this chapter, and in most of the remainder of this book, we will not discuss them.

## Asserted Versioning Metadata

Figures 8.3 through 8.7 show the metadata needed by the AVF to generate an Asserted Versioning database from the LDM shown in Figure 8.2. As with other figures showing tables, we indicate foreign keys by italicizing the column heading, and primary keys by underlining the column heading.

We show these metadata tables as themselves conventional tables, and therefore all relationships as ones implemented with conventional foreign keys. This simplifies the discussions in this chapter, and allows us to concentrate on the metadata without being concerned about keeping a bi-temporal history of changes to that data.

### Table Type Metadata

In a logical data model that will generate an Asserted Versioning database, we need a metadata list of which entities to generate as non-temporal tables and which entities to generate as asserted version tables. This metadata table lists all the tables that will be generated as asserted version tables, as shown in Figure 8.3. For this data model, we will generate all its entities as asserted version tables.

The non-key column in this metadata table is the business key flag. If it is set to 'Y', then the table is considered to have a reliable business key. Otherwise, it is set to 'N', indicating that the business key for the table is not reliable.

**Table-Type**

| tbl-nm | bus-key-rlb-flag |
|--------|------------------|
| Client | Y |
| Policy | Y |
| Policy_Amendment | Y |
| Wellness_Program | Y |
| Wellness_Program_Category | Y |
| Wellness_Program_Enrollment | Y |

**Figure 8.3** The Table Type Metadata Table.

The term *business key* usually refers to a set of one or more columns of data which can be used as unique identifiers for the objects they represent, and which contain business-meaningful data only, and no surrogate-valued columns. Sometimes business keys are used as primary keys. But sometimes, surrogate-valued columns are used as primary keys instead of business keys.

Asserted Versioning uses the term "business key" to refer to the one or more columns of an asserted version table which are the primary key of the corresponding entity in the logical data model, or of the corresponding conventional table which has been converted to an asserted version table. Sometimes these columns contain business-meaningful data, but sometimes they do not. The role of business keys in asserted version tables is to identify the object represented by each row in the same way that object would be identified, or was identified, in a conventional table.

Most of the time, business keys are reliable. In other words, most of the time, each business key value is a unique identifier for one and only one object. So in a non-temporal table, it would be possible to define a unique index on the business key, whether or not it is used as the primary key.

Unfortunately, it is sometimes necessary to manage tables whose business keys are not reliable. If the business keys for a table are not completely reliable, we cannot be sure that each business key value represents one and only one object. We may sometimes have to manage transactions, and rows in tables, that have missing or incomplete business keys.

In Chapter 5, we discussed how business keys are used when matching transactions to non-temporal tables, and how they are used when matching transactions to asserted version tables. But throughout that discussion, we assumed that the business keys for those tables were reliable. When they are not, it is more difficult to match transactions to a target table, especially when that target table is bi-temporal. In the next chapter, we will discuss the match logic that must be used when temporal inserts, updates and deletes are applied both to asserted version tables with reliable business keys, and also to asserted version tables with unreliable business keys.

### Temporal Foreign Key Metadata

The temporal foreign key metadata table contains one entry for every temporal foreign key. Recall that temporal foreign keys, like conventional foreign keys, express an existence dependency, one in which the existence of the child object represented by the

**TFK**

| *src-tbl-nm* | col-nm | *tar-tbl-nm* | req-flg | del-rule-ind |
|---|---|---|---|---|
| Policy | client_oid | Client | Yes | Cascade |
| Policy_ Amendment | policy_oid | Policy | Yes | Cascade |
| Wellness_ Program | wellpgmcat_ oid | Wellness_ Program_ Category | No | Set Null |
| Wellness_ Program_ Enrollment | client_oid | Client | Yes | Cascade |
| Wellness_ Program_ Enrollment | wellpgm_oid | Wellness_ Program | Yes | Restrict |

**Figure 8.4** The Temporal Foreign Key Metadata Table.

child row depends on the existence of the parent object represented by a parent episode. In our model, for example, policies are existence dependent on clients, policy amendments are existence dependent on policies, and so on.

But unlike a conventional foreign key, which picks out a unique row in the parent table, a temporal foreign key designates an object, but does not pick out any one managed object, any specific episode or version of that object. The AVF takes the *oid* and searches for an episode of that object whose assertion and effective time periods include those of the child row. The temporal foreign key itself is always a single column, containing an *oid* value; none of the other columns making up a full Asserted Versioning primary key are part of the TFK.

Both the source table name and the target table name columns are foreign keys back to the Table Type metadata table. For each entry, the source table name column says which table contains the TFK, while the target table name column says which table is referenced by the TFK. Column name provides the name of the TFK column itself. Generally, all TFK columns have the same name as the *oid* they point to, but this obviously will not work when there are two or more TFKs in the same child table that point to the same parent table.

The required flag says whether the TFK is required or not. Like FKs, TFKs may be optional or required. If they are required, the TFK in each row of the table must, at all times, contain an *oid* to an object one of whose episodes has an effective time period that includes ([fills$^{-1}$]) the effective time period of the row that contains the TFK. If the TFK is not required, the TFK in each row must either contain a valid *oid* reference, or be null. In our sample database, we have made the TFK to Wellness

Program Category optional so we can illustrate how the SET NULL option works with temporal foreign keys.

The delete rule indicator has the usual three choices. A delete may be restricted if there are any dependent children; or the foreign key in those children may be set to NULL; or the children may be delete cascaded. These same three choices exist when the dependent children are temporally dependent, i.e. when their dependency is expressed by means of a TFK rather than an FK. The delete indicator for a TFK cannot be set to the null option, of course, unless the TFK required flag is set to "No".

But unlike a conventional delete cascade, a temporal delete cascade does not simply delete a dependent child managed object. Instead, a temporal delete cascade removes the representation of a dependent child managed object from all of the clock ticks from which the managed object it is dependent on is being removed. So, for example, if a delete to a client removes that client's representation from the months of March and April 2015, then the delete cascade down to that client's policies will guarantee that none of those policies are in effect during those two months.

### Business Key Metadata

The business key metadata table, shown in Figure 8.5, lists the business key for every temporal table. This is the business key that uniquely identifies an object. In a non-temporal table, the business key may or may not also function as the primary key. But even if a business key is not used as a primary key, a reliable business key still uniquely identifies a row, since in a non-temporal table each object is represented by only one row. This is usually enforced with a unique index in a conventional database.

**Buskey**

| _tbl-nm_ | bus-key-col-nm |
|---|---|
| Client | client_nbr |
| Policy | policy_nbr |
| Policy_Amendment | policy_amend_nbr |
| Wellness_Program_Category | wellpgmcat_cd |
| Wellness_Program | wellpgm_nbr |
| Wellness_Program_Enrollment | client_oid |
| Wellness_Program_Enrollment | wellpgm_oid |

**Figure 8.5** The Business Key Metadata Table.

But in a temporal table, multiple rows may represent the same object, and so all of those rows will have the same business key. Consequently, we cannot guarantee that each business key points to one and only one object by defining a unique index on it. Nor can we simply extend the scope of the index by defining a unique index on the business key *plus* assertion begin and end dates and effective begin and end dates. On the other hand, once SQL supports a PERIOD datatype, then new index methods already defined by computer scientists could enforce uniqueness on the combination of a business key plus an assertion and effective time period.

A business key can be made up of any number of columns. For example, the business key for the Wellness Program Enrollment table consists of two columns. Each column is a temporal foreign key which points back to an object in a parent table. The Wellness Program Enrollment table is a temporal associative table, expressing a many-to-many relationship between wellness programs and the clients that enroll in them.

Business keys are unique to the objects they designate. But in temporal tables, a business key may appear on multiple rows, and consequently their uniqueness cannot be guaranteed simply by defining a unique index on them. Nonetheless, they have an important role to play. We discuss business keys, how the AVF's enforcement of temporal entity integrity guarantees that no two objects will ever have the same business key, and how business keys help the business user clarify her intentions when submitting transactions to an Asserted Versioning database, in Chapter 9.

### Foreign Key Mapping Metadata

The foreign key mapping metadata table, shown in Figure 8.6, lists the foreign keys used by tables that were originally conventional tables, and that have been converted into asserted version tables. For each foreign key, whether it consists of a single column or multiple columns, the table shows the single-column

**FK-TFK**

| *tbl-nm* | fkey-col-nm | tfk-col-nm |
|----------|-------------|------------|
| Policy | client_nbr | client_oid |
| Policy_Amendment | policy_nbr | policy_oid |
| Wellness_Program | wellpgmcat_cd | wellpgmcat_oid |
| Wellness_Program_Enrollment | client_nbr | client_oid |
| Wellness_Program_Enrollment | wellpgm_nbr | wellpgm_oid |

**Figure 8.6** The Foreign Key to Temporal Foreign Key Metadata Table.

temporal foreign key that replaces it. The TFK must be included in this table to avoid ambiguities in the FK to TFK mapping when the same parent and child tables have more than one referential relationship between them.

The purpose of this metadata table is to assist in reconstructing a view of the asserted version table which is exactly like the original conventional table. This view will have exactly the same name as the original table. And so if it is also column for column and row for row identical with that original table, all queries which worked against the original table will work, unchanged, against this view.

As we can see in Figure 8.8, this foreign key information is lost when the tables are converted. None of the DBMS catalog entries for the tables in Figure 8.8 will contain any foreign key declarations because as far as the DBMS knows, those tables contain no foreign keys. None of the foreign keys shown in Figure 8.2 have made their way into the DBMS catalog for this database.

In place of their original foreign keys (FKs), these tables now contain temporal foreign keys (TFKs). But today's DBMSs cannot recognize temporal foreign keys, and so to them, these non-PK *oid* columns are just non-key columns, not references to objects on which the object represented by their own row is existence-dependent. To these DBMSs, the PK *oid* columns are just primary key columns, and so they are oblivious to the role of these columns as object identifiers. To these DBMSs, the two PK date columns in each table are just two PK date columns. They do not recognize these two dates as each representing a PERIOD of time, which is a concept, i.e. a datatype, that these DBMSs don't have to begin with. All in all, to these DBMSs, there is nothing especially temporal about the database described by Figure 8.8.

### Miscellaneous Metadata

The miscellaneous metadata table, shown in Figure 8.7, contains additional metadata needed by the AVF. In release 1 of the AVF, there are only two such items. One is the granularity

**MiscMetaData**

| type | data |
|---|---|
| assertion time granularity | {microsecond timestamp} |
| effective time granularity | {month, 1} |

**Figure 8.7** The Miscellaneous Metadata Table.

for assertion time, and the other the granularity for effective time. Granularity, of course, is the size of the clock tick.

As we have said, the clock ticks being used in examples in this book are one-month clock ticks, for both assertion time and effective time. But in our consulting experience, companies often use one granularity for versioning, and a different granularity to record row creation dates. Versioning, of course, is the best practice approximation to Asserted Versioning's effective time, and row creation dates are an approximation to Asserted Versioning's assertion time. And in our own prior implementations of bi-temporal data management, we have used dates for effective time and microsecond timestamps for assertion time.

By using the same granularity for all assertion times in the same database, and the same granularity for all effective times, it is easy to determine the Allen relationship between any two time periods. So suppose that the same granularity is *not* used, and that there are two time periods which start at the same time, one of which is delimited by dates and the other by timestamps. The values, each of which designate the same point in time, are not identical. But if the same granularity is used, the EQUALS operator will tell us whether or not those time periods begin at the same time.

Of particular importance is whether or not two time periods have a gap in time between them or not. By using the same granularity for all asserted version tables in the same database, it is easy to spot two versions of the same object that are contiguous in either assertion or in effective time. Because of the closed-open convention, two time periods [meet] (are contiguous) if and only if the end point in time of one has the same value as the begin point in time of the other. This is a very important temporal relationship because two versions of the same object that effective-time [meet] belong to the same episode, whereas two versions that do not [meet] belong to different episodes.

We note that no granularity mismatch issues should arise when assertion time and effective time are based on different granularities. This is because there seem to be no semantically meaningful queries that would compare an assertion time period or point in time to an effective time period or point in time.

One final point. We recommend that assertion time granularity be set to the level of the *atomic* clock tick for the DBMS, i.e. the smallest clock tick that could occur between two successive modifications to the database. The reason is that if a non-atomic clock tick is used for assertion time, then it would be physically possible to place two or more asserted version rows, for the same object and the same or [intersecting] effective time periods, in the same clock tick of assertion time.

For example, let's assume that one row is a policy row that results from a temporal insert, and the other row results from a temporal update, and that the temporal update changes the policy's type from HMO to PPO. Let's also assume that the clock tick granularity chosen for assertion time is one day. Now if both the insert and the update take place on the same day, then we have two truth-functionally conflicting assertions. We assert, with those two rows, that during a shared period of effective time, the policy was an HMO policy, and was also a PPO policy.

We now have all the temporal metadata we need. Together with the logical data model, this is all the information we need to both generate an Asserted Versioning database, and to manage it.

## The Physical Data Model

Figure 8.8 shows the physical data model which the AVF created from (i) the non-temporal physical data model generated by ERwin from the logical data model shown in Figure 8.2, together with (ii) the metadata shown in Figures 8.3 through 8.7.

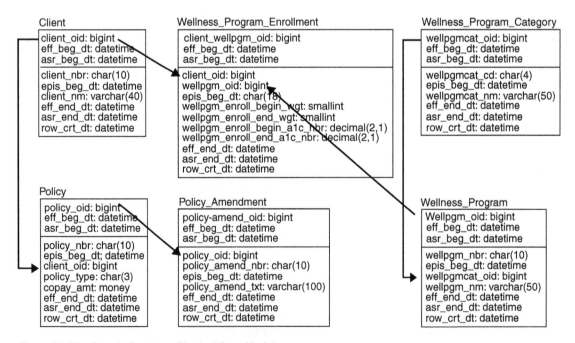

**Figure 8.8** The Sample Database Physical Data Model.

A primary key column with an *oid* suffix is the unique identifier of the object whose type is indicated by that table, and which is represented by one or more managed objects contained in that table. Thus *client_oid*, in the Client table, identifies a particular client which is represented in the Client table by one or more episodes each consisting of one or more versions.

A non-primary key column with an *oid* suffix is a temporal foreign key. Thus *client_oid*, in the Policy and Wellness Program Enrollment tables, is a temporal foreign key. Temporal foreign key relationships are graphically represented, in Figure 8.8, by arrows from the primary key *oid* to the TFK *oid*.

Since we do not append a suffix to business key column names, we have adopted the convention of listing the business key column or columns of a table immediately below the primary key, and immediately followed by the episode begin date. This shows us that Client, Policy, Wellness Program Category and Wellness Program all have single-column business keys, that the business key of Policy Amendment is the policy identifier plus an amendment number, and that the business key of Wellness Program Enrollment is the concatenation of the client and wellness program identifiers.

The process by which this physical data model (PDM) is generated from the non-temporal PDM corresponding to the LDM of Figures 8.1 and 8.2 is straightforward. As illustrated in Figure 8.1, the AVF does this automatically. However, as with all the work the AVF does, this transformation of a non-temporal PDM to a temporal PDM can be done manually. We describe this process in the following section.

# Generating an Asserted Versioning Database from a Physical Data Model and Metadata

An Asserted Versioning database consists of data structures plus constraints on the instances of data that conform to them. The data structures are the table definitions. The constraints are temporal entity integrity and temporal referential integrity, applied to the asserted version tables in the database, and implemented by the AVF as stored procedures.

However, other techniques could also be used to enforce these constraints, including triggers, generalized and reusable application code, and Java object persistence frameworks. The AVF generates this logic based on the metadata associated with each data model, and so it does not need to recreate this code for each table.

## Temporalizing the Physical Data Model

ERwin generates a physical data model from the logical data model shown in Figure 8.2. At that point, the physical data model is a conventional model. The next step is to apply the metadata shown in Figures 8.3 through 8.7. The result of that step is the temporalized physical data model shown in Figure 8.8.

An enterprise which chooses to build its own framework, based on the ideas presented in this book, may choose to use some other data modeling tool, of course. But Asserted Versioning LLC's commercially available AVF stores this metadata in ERwin User-Defined Properties, not in metadata tables like those shown in this chapter; and it automatically applies that metadata as the physical model is generated.

Absent that automated process in which temporal metadata is applied, the temporalization process works like this.

*The Client Table.* According to the Table Type metadata table, the Client table is an asserted version table. Prior to temporalization, the primary key of this table was *client_nbr*. From this column we derive the name *client_oid* for the first column in the bi-temporal primary key by dropping the suffix and replacing it with *oid*. We then add effective begin date and assertion begin date as the other two primary key columns. Client number itself is now treated as the business key of the table, and so it appears in the temporalized table as a non-key column. Client name is left unchanged. Episode begin date, effective end date, assertion end date and row create date are added as non-key columns. Where necessary, unique constraints and indexes defined in the non-temporal model are augmented with temporal date columns, and converted to non-unique indexes. And at this point, the temporalization of the Client table is complete.

*The Policy Table.* According to the Table Type metadata table, the Policy table is an asserted version table. Prior to temporalization, the primary key of this table was *policy_nbr*. From this column we derive the name *policy_oid* for the first column in the bi-temporal primary key. We then add effective begin date and assertion begin date as the other two primary key columns. Policy number itself is designated as the business key of this table, and appears in it as a non-key column. Policy type and copay amount are left unchanged. Episode begin date, effective end date, assertion end date and row create date are added as non-key columns. As before, unique constraints and indexes are augmented and modified, as required.

*Client_nbr* appears in the logical data model as a foreign key to the Client table, and so the AVF must convert it into a temporal foreign key. So the foreign key declaration is dropped from the DDL, the client number column is also dropped, and a *client_oid* column replaces it. With these changes, the temporalization of this table is complete.

*The Policy Amendment Table.* According to the Table Type metadata table, the Policy Amendment table is an asserted version table. Prior to temporalization, the primary key of this table was *policy_amend_nbr*. From this column we derive the name *policy_amend_oid* for the first column in the bi-temporal primary key. We then add effective begin date and assertion begin date as the other two primary key columns. Policy amendment number itself is designated as the business key of this table, and appears in it as a non-key column. Policy amendment text is left unchanged. Episode begin date, effective end date, assertion end date and row create date are added as non-key columns. As before, unique constraints and indexes are augmented and are modified, as required.

*Policy_nbr* appears in the logical data model as a foreign key to the Policy table, and so the AVF must convert it into a temporal foreign key. So the foreign key declaration is dropped from the DDL, the policy number column is also dropped, and a *policy_oid* column replaces it. With these changes, the temporalization of this table is complete.

*The Wellness Program Category Table.* According to the Table Type metadata table, the Wellness Program Category table is an asserted version table. Prior to temporalization, the primary key of this table was *wellpgmcat_cd*. From this column we derive the name *wellpgmcat_oid* for the first column in the bi-temporal primary key. We then add effective begin date and assertion begin date as the other two primary key columns. Wellness program category code itself is designated as the business key of this table, and appears in it as a non-key column. Wellness program category name is left unchanged. Episode begin date, effective end date, assertion end date and row create date are added as non-key columns. As before, unique constraints and indexes are augmented and are modified, as required. With these changes, the temporalization of this table is complete.

*The Wellness Program Table.* According to the Table Type metadata table, the Wellness Program table is an asserted version table. Prior to temporalization, the primary key of this table was *wellpgm_nbr*. From this column we derive the name *wellpgm_oid* for the first column in the bi-temporal primary key. We then add effective begin date and assertion begin date as the other two primary key columns. Wellness program number itself is designated as the business key of this table, and appears in it as a non-key column. Wellness program name is left unchanged. Episode begin date, effective end date, assertion end date and row create date are added as non-key columns. As before, unique constraints and indexes are augmented and are modified, as required.

*Wellpgmcat_cd* code appears in the logical data model as a foreign key to the Wellness Program table, and so the AVF must convert it into a temporal foreign key. The foreign key declaration is dropped from the DDL, the wellness program category code column is also dropped, and a *wellpgmcat_oid* column replaces it. With these changes, the temporalization of this table is complete.

*The Wellness Program Enrollment Table.* Unlike the other tables in this sample database, Wellness Program Enrollment is an associative table, commonly called an "xref table". But its conversion to a temporal table follows the pattern we have already seen. The only difference is that this table has two foreign keys to convert to temporal foreign keys, not just one, and two columns in its original primary key.

According to the Table Type metadata table, the Wellness Program Enrollment table is an asserted version table. Prior to temporalization, the primary key of this table consisted of the two foreign keys *client_nbr* and *wellpgm_nbr*. But asserted version tables must have single-column object identifiers, and so instead of creating an object identifier for both client and wellness program, we create a single object identifier and name it *client_wellpgm_oid*. We then add effective begin date and assertion begin date as the other two primary key columns.

As we see in Figure 8.8, the business key of this table is the pair of temporal foreign keys. The other four non-key columns are left unchanged. Episode begin date, effective end date, assertion end date and row create date are added as non-key columns. As before, unique constraints and indexes are augmented and are modified, as required.

*Client_nbr* and *wellpgm_nbr* appear in the logical data model as foreign keys to the Client and Wellness Program tables, respectively. The foreign key declarations are dropped from the DDL, the client number and wellness program number columns are also dropped, and the *client_oid* and *wellpgm_oid* columns, respectively, replace them. With these changes, the temporalization of this table is complete.

In fact, the temporalization of the entire physical data model is now complete. The result is the Asserted Versioning physical data model shown in Figure 8.8. But an asserted version database is not simply one that contains one or more temporal tables. It is also a database that includes the code which enforces the semantic constraints without which those tables would just be a collection of columns with nothing particularly temporal about them at all.

## Generating Temporal Entity and Temporal Referential Integrity Constraints

If this temporalized physical data model were submitted to the DBMS, and an empty database were created from it, we could begin to populate the tables in the database right away. We could populate them using conventional SQL insert, update and delete statements. But we would have to be very careful. We already have some idea of what temporal entity integrity and temporal referential integrity are, but we have yet to see these integrity constraints at work. Some of the work they do is quite complex.

The AVF enforces temporal integrity as data is being updated, not as it is being read. Today's DBMSs do not support temporal integrity constraints on versions and episodes, so it is the AVF— or a developer-written framework—that must do it. Applying those constraints, the AVF would reject some temporal transactions because they would violate one or both of those constraints.

But if we write our transactions in native SQL, then whenever we do maintenance to the database, we will have to manually check the contents of the database, compare each transaction to those contents, and determine for ourselves whether or not the transactions both did what they were intended to do, and resulted in a temporally valid database state. Past experience has shown us that doing our own application-developed bi-temporal data maintenance, using standard SQL, is resource-intensive and error-prone. It is a job for a company's most experienced DBAs, and even they will have a difficult time with it. Having an enterprise standard framework like the AVF to carry out these operations significantly reduces the work involved in maintaining temporal data, and will eliminate the errors that would otherwise inevitably happen as temporal data is maintained.

Using a framework like the AVF, temporal transactions will be no more difficult to write than conventional transactions. The reason is that the AVF supports a temporal insert, temporal update and temporal delete transaction in which all temporal qualifiers on the transaction are expressed declaratively. These transactions also preserve a fundamentally important feature of standard insert, update and delete transactions. They allow one bi-temporal semantic unit of work to be expressed in one transaction.

Typically, a single standard SQL transaction will insert, update or delete a single row in a conventional table. And typically, the corresponding temporal transaction will require two or three physical transactions to complete. In addition, many temporal update transactions, as we will see, and many temporal delete cascade transactions too, can require a dozen or more physical transactions to complete. If we attempt to maintain a bi-temporal database ourselves, using standard SQL, then for each semantic intention we want to express in the database, we will have to figure out and write these multiple physical transactions ourselves. As Chapter 7 indicated, and as Chapters 9 through 12 will make abundantly clear, that is a daunting task.

# Redundancies in the Asserted Versioning Bi-Temporal Schema

An Asserted Versioning database is a physical implementation of a logical data model, a logical model which does not contain any mention of temporal data in the model itself. In fact, the logical data models of Asserted Versioning databases are indistinguishable from the logical data models of conventional databases.

## Apparent Redundancies in the Asserted Versioning Schema

However, some data modelers have objected to an apparent third normal form (3NF) violation in the bi-temporal schema common to all asserted version tables. They point to the effective end date, the assertion end date and the row creation date to support their claims. Their objections, in summary, are one or more of the following:

(i) The effective end date is redundant because it can be inferred from the effective begin date of the following version.

(ii) The assertion end date is redundant because it can be inferred from the assertion begin date of the next assertion of a version.

(iii) The row create date is redundant because it is the same as the assertion end date.

Now in fact, none of these objections are correct. As for the first objection, an effective end date *would* be redundant if every version of an object followed immediately after the previous version. If we could depend on that being true, which means if we could depend on there never being a requirement to support multiple episodes of the same object, then the effective end date would be redundant.

One could make the argument that all versions within one episode have versions that [meet] and so, within each episode, the end date could be inferred. Although that is true, we would still need an episode end date to mark the end of the episode. Furthermore, the end dates on each version significantly improve performance because both dates are searched on the same row, reducing the need, otherwise, for expensive subselects on every read.

Also, we are not interested in implementing just the minimal temporal requirements a specific business use may require, especially when it would be difficult and expensive to add additional functionality, such as support for multiple episodes (i.e. for temporal gaps between some adjacent versions of the same object), to a database already built and populated, and to a set of maintenance transactions and queries already written and in use. All asserted version tables are ready to support gaps between versions. On the other hand, as long as temporal trans-actions issued to the AVF do not specify an effective begin date, that capability of Asserted Versioning will remain unused and the mechanics of its use will remain invisible.

As for the second objection, an assertion end date would be redundant with the following asserted version's assertion begin date only if every assertion of a version followed the previous one without a gap of even a single clock tick in assertion time. But once again, we are not interested in implementing just the minimal temporal requirements a specific business use may require. All asserted version tables are ready to support deferred assertions, and deferred assertions may involve a gap in asser-tion time. On the other hand, as long as temporal transactions issued to the AVF do not specify an assertion begin date, that capability of Asserted Versioning will remain unused and the mechanics of its use will remain invisible.

In addition, as we will see in following chapters, single vers-ions can be replaced by multiple versions as new assertions are made, and vice versa. In that case, the logic for inferring asser-tion begin dates from the assertion end dates of other versions could become quite complex. This complexity could affect the performance, not only of maintenance transactions, but also of queries. The reason is that, if we followed this suggestion, it would be impossible to determine, from just the data on any one row, whether or not that row has an Allen relationship with the assertion time specified on a query. To determine that, we would need to know the assertion time period of the row, not just when that time period ended.

As for the third objection, a row create date would be redundant with an assertion end date if Asserted Versioning did not support deferred assertions. In fact, neither the standard temporal model, nor any more recent computer science research that we are aware of, includes deferred assertions. But Asserted Versioning does. Because it does, the AVF may insert rows into asserted version tables whose assertion begin dates are later than their row creation dates.

## A Real Redundancy in the Asserted Versioning Schema

But there is one redundancy that we did introduce into the Asserted Versioning schema. It was to add the episode begin date to every row. The episode begin date, as we all know by now, is the effective begin date of the effective-time earliest version of an episode. So it is not functionally dependent on the primary key of any row which is not the initial version of an episode.[2]

The primary use of this column is to indicate, for any version, when the episode that version is a part of began. It efficiently associates every version with the one episode it belongs to. Lacking this column, we would only be able to find all versions of an episode by looking for versions with the same *oid* that [meet], and we would only be able to distinguish one episode from the next one by looking for a [before] or [before$^{-1}$] relationship between adjacent versions with the same *oid*.

Together with that version's own effective end date, this tells us that the object that version designates has been continuously represented, in current assertion time, from the effective-time beginning of that version's episode to the effective-time end of that version. Since the parent managed object in a temporal referential integrity relationship is an episode, this means that when we are validating temporal referential integrity on a child version, all we need to do is find one parent version whose effective end date is not earlier than the effective end date of the new

---

[2]Interestingly enough, although clearly redundant, this replication of the effective begin date of each episode's initial version onto all other versions of the episode is not a violation of any relational normal form. Its presence involves no partial, transitive or multi-valued dependencies. For other examples of redundancies that are not caught by fully normalizing a database, see Johnston's articles in the archives at Information_Management.com (formerly DM Review), with links listed in the bibliography.

child version, and whose episode begin date is not later than the effective begin date of the new version. In other words, it enables us to do TRI checking from one parent-side row, rather than having to go back and find the row that begins that parent episode. This significantly improves performance for temporal referential integrity checking.

The result of TRI enforcement is to guarantee that the effective-time extent of any version representing a TRI child object completely [fills] the effective-time extent of one set of contiguous versions representing a TRI parent object.

In addition, note that the presence of this redundant column has little maintenance cost associated with it. As new versions are added to an episode, the episode begin date of the previous version is just copied onto that of the new version. Only in the rare cases in which an episode's begin date is changed will this redundancy require us to update all the versions in the episode.

## Glossary References

Glossary entries whose definitions form strong interdependencies are grouped together in the following list. The same glossary entries may be grouped together in different ways at the end of different chapters, each grouping reflecting the semantic perspective of each chapter. There will usually be several other, and often many other, glossary entries that are not included in the list, and we recommend that the Glossary be consulted whenever an unfamiliar term is encountered.

Allen relationships
contiguous
filled by
include

asserted version table
Asserted Versioning
Asserted Versioning database
Asserted Versioning Framework (AVF)

assertion begin date
assertion end date
assertion time
assertion time period

business key
reliable business key
unreliable business key

child object

clock tick
closed-open
granularity

conventional database
conventional table
conventional transaction
deferred assertion

design encapsulation
maintenance encapsulation
query encapsulation

effective begin date
effective end date
effective time
effective time period

episode
episode begin date

existence dependency

managed object

mechanics

object
object identifier
oid

parent episode
parent object

PERIOD datatype

represented

row creation date

temporal database

temporal entity integrity (TEI)
temporal foreign key (TFK)
temporal referential integrity (TRI)

temporal transaction
temporal update transaction

temporalize

version

# AN INTRODUCTION TO TEMPORAL TRANSACTIONS

**CONTENTS**

Temporal transactions are inserts, updates or deletes whose targets are asserted version tables. But temporal transactions are not submitted directly to the DBMS. The work that has to be done to manage conventional tables is straightforward enough that we can let users directly manipulate those tables. But bi-temporal tables, including asserted version tables, are too complex to expose to the transaction author. The difference between what the user wants done, and what has to take place to accomplish it, is too great. And so temporal transactions are the way that the query author tells us what she wants done to the database, without having to tell us how to do it. The mechanics of how her intentions are carried out are encapsulated within our Asserted Versioning Framework. All that the application accepting the transaction has to do is to pass it on to the AVF.

A DBMS can enforce such constraints as entity integrity and referential integrity, but it cannot enforce the significantly more complex constraints of their temporal analogs. It is the AVF which enforces temporal entity integrity and temporal referential integrity. It is the AVF which rejects any temporal

Managing Time in Relational Databases. Doi: 10.1016/B978-0-12-375041-9.00009-1

**191**

transactions that violate the semantic constraints that give bi-temporal data its meaning. It is the AVF that gives the user a declarative means of expressing her intentions with respect to the transactions she submits.

In the Asserted Versioning temporal model, the two bi-temporal dimensions are effective time and assertion time. If assertion time were completely equivalent to the standard temporal model's transaction time, then every row added to an asserted version table would use the date the transaction was physically applied as its assertion begin date. Important additional functionality is possible, however, if we permit rows to be added with assertion begin dates in the future. This is functionality not supported by the standard temporal model. But it comes at the price of additional complexity, both in its semantics and in its implementation.

Fortunately, it is possible to segregate this additional functionality, which is based on what we call *deferred transactions* and *deferred assertions*, and to discuss Asserted Versioning as though both its temporal dimensions are strictly analogous to the temporal dimensions of the standard temporal model. This makes the discussion easier to follow, and so this is the approach we will adopt. Deferred assertions, then, will not be discussed until Chapter 12.

## Effective Time *Within* Assertion Time

A row in a conventional table makes a statement. Such a row, in a conventional Policy table, is shown in Figure 9.1.

This row makes the following statement: "I represent a policy which has an object identifier of P861, a client of C882, a type of HMO and a copay of $15." The statement makes no explicit reference to time. But we all understand that it means "I represent a policy which exists at the current moment, and which at the current moment has an object identifier of . . . . . .".

This same row, with an effective time period attached, is shown in Figure 9.2.

It makes the following statement: "I represent a policy which has an object identifier of P861 and which, from January 2010 to

| oid | *client* | type | copay |
|------|------|------|------|
| P861 | C882 | HMO | $15 |

**Figure 9.1** A Non-Temporal Row.

| oid | eff-beg | eff-end | client | type | copay |
|-----|---------|---------|--------|------|-------|
| P861 | Jan10 | Jul10 | C882 | HMO | $15 |

**Figure 9.2** A Uni-Temporal Version.

July 2010, has a client of C882, a type of HMO and a copay of $15." In other words, the row shown in Figure 9.2 has been placed in a temporal *container*, and is treated as representing the object as it exists within that container, but as saying nothing about the object as it may exist outside that container.

If we were managing uni-temporal versioned data, that would be the end of the story. But if we are managing bi-temporal data, there is one more temporal tag to add. This same row, with an assertion time period attached, is shown in Figure 9.3.

It makes the following statement: "I represent the assertion, made on January 2010 but withdrawn on October 2010, that this row represents a policy which has an object identifier of P861 and which, from January 2010 to July 2010, has a client of C882, a type of HMO and a copay of $15." In other words, the row shown in Figure 9.2, as included in its first temporal container, has been placed in a second temporal container, and is treated as representing what we claim, within that second container, is true of the object as it exists within that first container, but as saying nothing about what we might claim about the object within its first container outside that second container.

From January to July, this statement makes a current claim about what P861 is like during that period of time. From July to October, this statement makes an historical claim, a claim about what P861 *was* like at that time. But from October on, this statement makes no claim at all, not even an historical one. It is simply a record of what we once claimed was true, but no longer claim is true.

All this is another way of saying (i) that a non-temporal row represents an object; (ii) that when that row is tagged with an effective time period, it represents that object as it exists during that period of time (January to July in our example); and (iii) that when that tagged row receives an additional time period tag, it represents our assertion, during the indicated period of time

| oid | eff-beg | eff-end | asr-beg | asr-end | client | type | copay |
|-----|---------|---------|---------|---------|--------|------|-------|
| P861 | Jan10 | Jul10 | Jan10 | Oct10 | C882 | HMO | $15 |

**Figure 9.3** A Bi-Temporal Row.

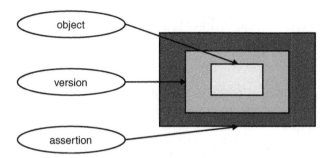

**Figure 9.4** Assertions Are About Versions Are About Objects.

(January to October in our example) that the effective-time tagged row represents that object as it is/was during the other indicated period of time (January to July).

So an effective time tag qualifies the representation of an object, while an assertion time tag qualifies the effective-time qualified representation of an object. Effective time containment turns a row representing an object into a version. Assertion time containment turns a row representing a version into an assertion of a version, i.e. into a temporally delimited truth claim.[1] This is illustrated in Figure 9.4.

Temporal integrity constraints govern the effective time relationships among bi-temporal rows. But, as we pointed out earlier, these effective time relationships apply only within *shared assertion time*. For example, when one version is asserted from January 2012 to April 2014, and another version of the same object is asserted from March 2012 to 12/31/9999, then the effective time periods of those two versions must not [intersect] from March 2012 to April 2014 in assertion time. But from January 2012 to March 2012, they neither [intersect] nor do not [intersect]. During those two periods of assertion time, the comparison doesn't apply. During those times, those two versions are what philosophers call "incommensurable".

In the following discussion of temporal integrity constraints, we will assume that all the rows involved exist in shared assertion time.

Note that it is effective time that exists with assertion time, and not vice versa. If the semantic containment were reversed,

---

[1]And if there were no versioning, and non-temporal statements were contained directly in assertion time, i.e. non-temporal rows were given an assertion time tag but not an effective time tag, then assertion time containment would turn non-temporal statements directly into temporally delimited truth claims.

it would be possible to have some rows which are in effect and which we assert to be true, and also have other rows which are in effect but which we do not assert are true. But when we say that a row is in effect from January to June, we are saying that it makes a true statement about what its object is like during that period of time. In other words, we are asserting that it is true.

Consider a row with an assertion time of [Mar 2012 – Aug 2012] and an effective time of [Jan 2012 – Dec 2012]. Clearly this means that, from March to August, we assert that this row makes a true statement about what its object was like from January to December. Barring deferred assertions, we can tell that on March 2012, we retroactively inserted this version, effective as of January 2012, and that on August 2012, we withdrew the assertion.

# Explicitly Temporal Transactions: The Mental Model

In every clock tick within a continuous period of effective time, an object is either represented by a row or not represented. If it is represented, there is business data which describes what that object is like during that clock tick. So our three temporal transactions affect the representation of an object in a period of time as follows:

(i) A temporal insert places business data representing an object into one or more clock ticks of effective time.

(ii) A temporal update replaces business data representing an object in one or more clock ticks of effective time.

(iii) A temporal delete removes business data representing an object from one or more clock ticks of effective time.

In all three cases, those clock ticks are contiguous with one another, as they must be since they constitute a continuous period of effective time. Let's call that continuous span of clock ticks the *target span* for a temporal transaction. A designated target span can be anywhere along the calendar timeline. It can also be open or closed, i.e. it can use either a normal date or 12/31/9999 to mark the end of the span.

When the user writes a temporal insert transaction, she is doing two things. First, she is designating a target span of clock ticks. Second, she is specifying business data that she wants inserted into the table, and that will occupy precisely that effective time target span within current assertion time. That current assertion time starts Now(), i.e. when the transaction is processed, and continues on until further notice. We can say that this transaction, like every transaction that accepts the default values for effective time, creates a version that describes what its object looks like *from now on*, and also that this transaction, like every transaction other than the deferred ones, creates an assertion that, *from now on*, claims that the version makes a true statement.

When the user writes a temporal update, she is also doing two things. First, she is designating a target span of clock ticks. Second, she is specifying a change in one or more columns of business data, a change that she wants applied to every version or part of a version of the designated object that falls, wholly or partially, within that effective time target span, a change that will be visible in current assertion time but not in past assertion time. She is not, however, necessarily specifying a change that will be applied to every clock tick in that target span, because a temporal update transaction does not require that the object it designates be represented in every clock tick within its target span—only that it be represented in at least one of those clock ticks.

A temporal delete is like a temporal update except that it specifies that every version or part of a version of the designated object that falls, wholly or partially, within that target span will be, in current assertion time, removed from that target effective timespan. Like a temporal update, a temporal delete does not require that its designated object occupy (be represented in) all of the clock ticks of the target span, only that it occupy at least one of them.

It follows that it is possible for more than one episode to be affected by an update or a delete. All episodes that fall within the target span of an update or delete transaction are affected. This includes parts of episodes as well as entire episodes. Given a target timespan, it is possible for one episode to begin outside that span and either extend into it or extend past the end of it, and also for one episode to begin within that span and either end within that span or extend past the end of it. By the same token, within either or both of those partially included target episodes, the start or end of the target span may or may not line up with the start or end of a specific version. In other words, one version may start outside a target span but extend into or even through it, and another version may begin within a target span and either end within it or extend past the end of it.

The details of how these transactions work will be discussed in the rest of this chapter. But we can already see that the mental image of designating a target span of clock ticks and then issuing a transaction whose scope is limited to that target span, is intuitively clear. But it is one thing to provide a clear mental image—

that of transactions as designating (i) an object, (ii) a span of time, (iii) business data and (iv) an action to take—but another thing to provide the details. To that task we now turn.

## A Taxonomy of Temporal Extent State Transformations

Because of the complexities of managing temporal data, we need a way to be sure that we understand how to carry out every possible *temporal extent state transformation* that could be specified against one or more asserted version tables. A temporal extent state transformation is one which, within a given period of assertion time, adds to or subtracts from the total number of effective-time clock ticks in which a given object is represented. We need a taxonomy of temporal extent state transformations.

As we explained in Chapter 2, a taxonomy is not just any hierarchical arrangement we happen to come up with. It is one whose components are distinguished on the basis of what they mean—and not, for example, on the basis of what they contain, as parts explosion hierarchies are. It is also a hierarchical arrangement whose components are, based on their meanings, mutually exclusive and jointly exhaustive. Because good taxonomies are like this, constructing them is a way to be sure that we haven't overlooked anything (because of the jointly exhaustive property) and haven't confused anything with anything else (because of the mutually exclusive property).

We begin with objects and episodes. The target of every temporal transaction is an episode of an object. Semantically, it is episodes which are created or destroyed, or which are transformed from one state into another state. *Physically,* of course, it is individual rows of data which are created and modified (but never deleted) in an asserted version table. But what we are concerned with here is semantics, not bits and bytes, not strings of letters and numerals. From a semantic point of view, *episodes* are the fundamental managed objects of Asserted Versioning.

Figure 9.5 shows our taxonomy. Under each leaf node, we have a graphic representing that transformation. A shaded rectangle represents an episode, and a non-shaded rectangle represents the absence of an episode. A short vertical bar separates the before-state, on the left-hand side, from the after-state, on the right-hand side, produced by a transformation.

Each of the nodes in our Allen relationship taxonomy are referred to, in the text, by surrounding the name of the node with

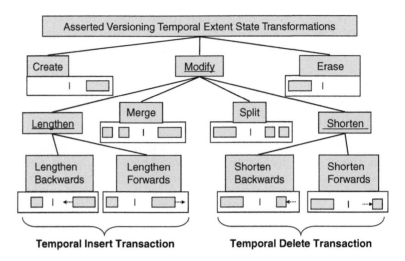

**Figure 9.5** A Taxonomy of Temporal Extent State Transformations.

brackets, for example as with [meets], [during$^{-1}$], [intersects], etc. We also underline the names of nodes which are not leaf nodes. We will use a similar convention for this taxonomy of temporal extent transformations, referring to each of its nodes by surrounding the name of the node with curly braces, for example as with {remove}, {shorten forwards}, {shorten}, etc.

With any type of thing we are concerned with, there are three basic things we can do with its instances. We can create an instance of it, modify an existing instance, or remove an instance. This is reflected in the three nodes of the first level underneath the root node.

Of course, in the case of episodes, the {erase} transformation is neither a physical nor a logical deletion. Instead, it is the action in which the entire episode is *withdrawn* from current assertion time into past assertion time.

{Create}, {modify} and {erase} are clearly jointly exhaustive of the set of all temporal extent transformations, and also mutually exclusive of one another. Thus, at its first two levels, this taxonomy is, as all taxonomies must be, a partitioning.

At the level of abstraction we are dealing with, there is no further breakdown of either the {create} or {erase} transformations. Of course, there are variations on those themes, as we will see in the next chapter. For example, we can create an episode retroactively, or in current time, or proactively, and similarly for modifying or erasing an episode.

As for the {modify} transformation, we achieve a partitioning by distinguishing transformations which change one episode into two episodes or vice versa, from transformations that transform episodes one for one, and then in the latter category, transformations that lengthen an episode's representation in effective time from transformations that shorten it. Thus, we extend the property of being a mathematical partitioning down to the third level of this taxonomy. And again, as with the {create} and {erase} transformations, there are similar variations.

Next, for both the {lengthen} and {shorten} transformations, it is possible to do so at the beginning or at the end of the episode. And so we complete this taxonomy with the assurance that no instance of any parent node can fail to be an instance of a child node of that parent, and also that every instance of any parent node exists as no more than one instance across the set of its child nodes.

Another way to reassure ourselves of the completeness of this taxonomy is to note its bilateral symmetry. If the diagram were folded along a vertical line running between the {merge} and {split} nodes, and also between the {lengthen forwards} and {shorten backwards} nodes, each transformation would overlay the transformation that is its inverse.

A third way to assure ourselves of completeness is to analyze the taxonomy in terms of its topology. On a line representing a timeline, we can place a line segment representing an episode. We can also remove a line segment from that line. Given a line segment, we can either lengthen it forwards or backwards, shorten it forwards or backwards, or split it. Given two line segments with no other segments between them, we can merge them (by lengthening one forwards towards the other and/or lengthening the other backwards towards the first, until they [meet]). There is nothing that can be done with the placement of segments on a line that cannot be done by means of combinations and iterations of these basic operations.

Finally, we need to be aware of the different scenarios possible under each of these nodes. As we have already pointed out, any of these transformations can result in changes to past, present or future effective time. Additional variations come into play when we distinguish between transformations that are applied to closed or to open episodes, and between transactions which leave an episode in a closed or open state.

With eight possible topological transformations, nine possible combinations of past, present and future effective time (three for the target and three for the transaction), and four possible open/closed combinations (two for the target and two for the transaction), we have a grand total of 288 scenarios. And this doesn't even take into consideration deferred assertions, which would at a minimum double the number of scenarios. Of course it might be possible to eliminate some of these scenarios as semantically impossible, i.e. as corresponding to no meaningful state and/or no meaningful transformation; but each one would still have to be analyzed.

We cannot analyze every one of these scenarios. Instead, our approach will be to analyze one variation of each temporal extent transformation, and then briefly discuss other variations which appear to be interestingly different.

## The Asserted Versioning Temporal Transactions

Figure 9.6 shows three episodes—A, B and C—located along a four-year timeline. Eight versions make up these three episodes, which are all episodes of the same object, policy P861. We will be referring to this diagram throughout our discussion of temporal transactions.

In the syntax used for the transactions shown below, values are associated with business data columns by means of their position in a bracket-delimited, comma-separated series of values. Except for the object identifier, which occupies the first position, the other six columns which implement Asserted Versioning are not included in this list, those other columns being effective begin date, effective end date, assertion begin date, assertion end date, episode begin date and row create date. And of those six temporal parameters, only the first three may be specified on a temporal transaction.

The syntax used in this book for temporal transactions is not the syntax in which those transactions will be submitted to the AVF. That is, it is not the syntax with which the AVF will be invoked. We use it because it is unambiguous and compact. The actual transactions supported by release 1 of the AVF can be seen at our website, AssertedVersioning.com.

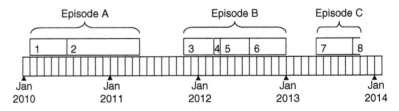

**Figure 9.6** Eight Versions and Three Episodes of Policy P861.

Every temporal transaction may supply an *oid*, a business key or both. In addition, every asserted version table has either reliable business keys, or unreliable ones. This gives us eight possible combinations of *oid*s with reliable or unreliable business keys, for each of our three temporal transactions.

For every temporal transaction, the first thing the AVF does is to perform edits and validity checks. As we will see below, these eight combinations are the checklist the AVF uses for its validity checks.

The edit checks work like this. Following the object identifier are comma-delimited places for the business data associated with the object. In this case, that business data is, in order, client, policy type and copay. Following this set of values is a set of three asserted version dates. The effective begin date defaults to the current date, but may be overridden with any date, past, present or future, that is not 12/31/9999. The effective end date defaults to 12/31/9999, but may be overridden with any other date that is at least one clock tick later than the effective begin date. Assertion dates on transactions will be discussed in Chapter 12. Until then, we assume that the assertion begin date on all transactions takes on its default value of the date current when the transaction takes place. The assertion end date can never be specified on temporal transactions, and is always set to 12/31/9999.

After doing edit checks to insure that each element of the transaction, including its data values, is well formed, the AVF does validity checks on the transaction as a whole. Only if a transaction passes both edit and validity checks will the AVF map it into one or more physical SQL transactions, submit those transactions to the DBMS, and monitor the results to insure that either all of them or none of them update the database, i.e. that they make up a semantically complete atomic unit of work.

## The Temporal Insert Transaction

The format of a temporal insert transaction is as follows:

```
INSERT INTO {tablename} [,,, ] eff_beg_dt, eff_end_dt,
asr_beg_dt
```

The validity checks work like this:
**(i) No *oid*, no business key, business key is reliable**. In this case, the AVF rejects the insert. The reason is that if the business key is reliable, an insert must provide it, even if it also provides an *oid*. Otherwise, it would be like an insert to a conventional table with a missing or incomplete primary key.

(ii) **No *oid*, no business key, business key is not reliable**. In this case, the AVF accepts the insert and assigns it a new *oid*. The reason is that if a business key is not reliable, it is not required on an insert transaction. Since no business key match logic will ever be carried out on tables with unreliable business keys, it doesn't matter if rows lacking those business keys make their way onto those tables.

(iii) **No *oid*, business key present, business key is reliable**. In this case, the AVF looks for a match on the business key. If it finds one, it assigns the *oid* of the effective-time latest matching row to the transaction. Otherwise, it assigns a new *oid* to the transaction. The reason is that *multiple appearances* of the same object, separated by gaps in time, should be recognized as multiple appearances of the *same object* whenever possible, and not as appearances of different objects.

(iv) **No *oid*, business key present, business key is not reliable**. In this case, the AVF accepts the insert and assigns it a new *oid*. The reason is that if the business key is not reliable, it doesn't matter, and so the AVF proceeds as though the business key were not there. Note that in this case, multiple temporal inserts which lack an *oid* but which contain the same business key value will result in multiple object identifiers all using that same value. Semantically, the business key will be a *homonym*, a single value designating multiple different objects. This, of course, is precisely what the "unreliable" means in "unreliable business key".

(v) ***Oid* present, no business key, business key is reliable**. In this case, the AVF rejects the insert. The reason is the same as it was for case (i); if the business key is reliable, an insert must provide it. Otherwise, it would be like an insert to a conventional table with a missing or incomplete primary key.

(vi) ***Oid* present, no business key, business key is not reliable**. In this case, the AVF accepts the insert and uses the *oid* supplied with it. The reason is that if the business key is not reliable, it doesn't matter, and so the AVF proceeds as though the business key were not there. And if the *oid* is already in use, that doesn't matter. If it is in use, and there is a collision in time periods, temporal entity integrity checks will catch it.

(vii) ***Oid* present, business key present, business key is reliable**. In this case, the AVF looks for a match on the business key. If it finds a match, and the *oid* of the matching row matches the *oid* on the transaction, the AVF accepts the transaction. If it finds a match, but the *oid* of the matching row does not match the *oid* on the transaction, the AVF rejects the transaction. If it does not find a match, and the *oid* on the transaction does not match any *oid* already in use, the AVF accepts the transaction. And if it does not find a match, but the *oid* on the transaction does match an *oid* already in use, the AVF rejects the transaction. The reason behind all this logic is that when both an *oid* and a reliable business key are present, any conflict makes the transaction invalid.

(viii) ***Oid* present, business key present, business key is not reliable**. In this case, the AVF accepts the insert and uses the *oid* supplied with it. The reason is that if the business key is not reliable, it doesn't matter, and so the AVF proceeds as though the business key were not there. And if the *oid* is already in use, that doesn't matter. If it is in use, and there is a collision in time periods, temporal entity integrity checks will catch it. Note that if the *oid* is in use, and there is no collision in time periods, then if the business key is a new one, the result of applying the transaction is to assign a new business key to an object, in clock ticks not previously occupied by that object.

### The Temporal Insert Transaction: Semantics

In a conventional table, if an object is not represented and the user wishes to represent it, she issues an insert transaction which creates a row that does just that. The insert transaction expresses not only her intentions, but also her beliefs. It expresses her intention to create a representation of an object, as it currently exists, in the target table. But it also expresses her belief that such a representation does not already exist. If she is mistaken in her belief, her transaction is rejected, which is precisely what she would expect and want to happen.

In an asserted version table, the question is not whether or not the object is already represented, but rather whether or not the object is already represented during all or part of the target timespan indicated on the transaction. If the user submits a temporal insert transaction, she also expresses both intention and belief. Her intention is to create a representation of an object in an effective time target span. Her belief is that such a representation does not already exist anywhere in that target span. If she is mistaken in her belief, her transaction is rejected, which is precisely what she would expect and want to happen.

Another aspect of the semantics of a temporal insert is the interpretation of its target span. If the transaction does not supply an effective end date, that date defaults to 12/31/9999. The result is that an open episode will be created. However, in the scenario shown in Figure 9.6, an open episode *cannot* be created, and the AVF will reject the attempt to create one. For if we tried to create an open episode with an effective begin date prior to version 7, that new episode would collide with one of the three episodes shown, and thus violate the *temporal entity integrity* (TEI) constraint. And if we tried to create an open episode, or in fact any episode, with an effective begin date on or after May 2013, it would collide with Episode C, whose effective end date is 12/31/9999.

It follows that there can be at most one open episode for an object, within any period of assertion time. No episode, open or closed, can be created later than an open episode because if it were created, it would occupy effective time already occupied by that open episode. And an open episode cannot be created earlier than any other episode, open or closed, for the same reason.

What of a temporal insert that specifies a non-12/31/9999 effective end date? Here the situation is more straightforward. Such transactions satisfy TEI just in case none of the clock ticks specified in the transaction's target span are already occupied by that object. And we should remember that because of our closed-open convention, TEI will still be satisfied if an episode already exists whose begin date has the same value as the end date of the transaction's target span, or one whose end date has the same value as the begin date of the transaction's target span, or if both such episodes are present.

### The Temporal Insert Transaction: Mechanics

The scope of a *conventional* insert is a single row in the target table. If the transaction is successful, the result is a new row added to the table. The scope of a *temporal* insert is a designated period of effective time, within current assertion time. So, in Figure 9.6, that scope cannot include any of the clock ticks already occupied by any of the three episodes shown there, but can include any other clock ticks. We should note that this means that the scope of the insert cannot be any clock tick from May 2013 forward. Since Episode C is open, it extends to 12/31/9999; consequently any other episode for the same object anywhere in the effective period starting with May 2013 would [intersect] that episode.

So a temporal insert of P861, given the state of the target table shown in Figure 9.6, can have an effective begin date which is any clock tick not occupied by any of the three episodes. What, then, of the effective end date? With a basic scenario temporal insert, both the effective begin and end dates are left to take on their default values which are, respectively, the date current when the transaction is applied, and 12/31/9999. But just as the effective begin date can be overridden on a transaction, so too can the effective end date.

What this means is that when a new episode is created, it does not need to be created as an open episode. If the user happens to know the effective end date for an episode of an object she is creating, she can specify this date on the temporal insert, as long as it is at least one clock tick later than the effective begin date, and does not [intersect] a time period already occupied by another episode of the same object.

In the scenario shown in Figure 9.6, in fact, a temporal insert would have to specify an effective end date. The reason is that no matter what the effective begin date is, an effective end date of 12/31/9999 would [intersect] one of the episodes already in the table.

For example, a temporal insert could place a new episode between the second two episodes, but given that our clock ticks only once a month, it would be a tight fit. In fact, there are only three possibilities. They are:

  **(i)** P861[Feb 2013 – Mar 2013]
 **(ii)** P861[Feb 2013 – Apr 2013]
**(iii)** P861[Mar 2013 – Apr 2013]

There are four ways in which Episode B could be {lengthened forwards}, the last listed of which would {merge} it with Episode C. They are:

  **(i)** P861[Jan 2013 – Feb 2013]
 **(ii)** P861[Jan 2013 – Mar 2013]
**(iii)** P861[Jan 2013 – Apr 2013]
 **(iv)** P861[Jan 2013 – May 2013]

And there are also four ways in which Episode C could be {lengthened backwards}, the first listed of which would {merge} it with Episode B. They are:

  **(i)** P861[Jan 2013 – May 2013]
 **(ii)** P861[Feb 2013 – May 2013]
**(iii)** P861[Mar 2013 – May 2013]
 **(iv)** P861[Apr 2013 – May 2013]

As we said earlier, no temporal insert would be valid that specified an effective time period of May 2013 or later. However, any temporal insert would be valid that specified an effective time period that ended on February 2010 or earlier because that insert would not result in a time period that [intersected] any time period for P861 already in the target table.

Sometimes we have no open episode of an object, but we may want to *wake up* the latest closed episode and change it to an open episode. It is only the latest episode of an object that can be transformed into an open episode, of course, because if it were not the latest, it would then collide with the next later episode and thus violate the TEI constraint.

So if a temporal insert specifies a 12/31/9999 end date, and no effective begin date is provided, the target span is [Now() − 12/31/9999]. An insert with this target timespan will wake up an existing episode of an object only if (i) there is a closed episode of the object already in the target table, and its effective end date is Now() (a situation which is very unlikely to occur when timestamps rather than dates are used to specify temporal parameters); and (ii) there are no representations of the object which begin in future effective time. So we cannot wake up a closed episode unless we supply an effective begin date on an insert transaction which matches the effective end date of an existing episode, and there are no other episodes of that object in later effective time.

Waking up a closed episode is a special case of the {lengthen episode forwards} transformation. But in every case, what the user must do to lengthen an episode forwards is to specify a target span whose effective begin date matches the effective end date of the last version of a closed episode, and whose effective end date does not [intersect] that of the next later episode of that object, if there is one. In this latter case, the episode is {lengthened forwards} because an unknown end date (represented by 12/31/9999) is replaced by a known end date.

## The Temporal Update Transaction

The format of a temporal update transaction is as follows:

```
UPDATE {tablename} [,,, ] eff_beg_dt, eff_end_dt, asr_beg_dt
```

The validity checks work like this:

**(i) No *oid*, no business key, business key is reliable**. In this case, the AVF rejects the update. The reason is that an update must attempt to find a match, and must be rejected if it cannot make that attempt. Lacking both an *oid* and a reliable business key, the transaction cannot be matched to what is already in the target table.

(ii) **No *oid*, no business key, business key is not reliable**. In this case, the AVF rejects the update, for the same reason as for case (i).

(iii) **No *oid*, business key present, business key is reliable**. In this case, the AVF looks for a match on the business key. If it finds one, it assigns the *oid* of the matching row to the transaction. Otherwise, it rejects the transaction. The reason is that reliable business keys are unique identifiers of objects, and that, because all temporal insert transactions to tables with reliable business keys must have a business key on the transaction, all existing rows for the same object will contain that reliable business key. This means that a temporal update with a non-matching reliable business key is just like a conventional update which cannot match a primary key. It is a mistaken update.

(iv) **No *oid*, business key present, business key is not reliable**. In this case, the AVF rejects the update. The reason is that if the business key isn't reliable, it doesn't matter if it's there or not, and so the AVF proceeds as though the business key were not there. Note that if we did attempt a match on the business key, and were successful, we might or might not have the right *oid* to assign to the transaction. We can't be sure because the AVF can't guarantee that an unreliable business key value is not being used by two or more *oid*s. If we use a match on a business key that may be associated with several different objects, then unless we have an *oid* supplied by the transaction itself, we have no way of knowing which *oid* is the correct target of the transaction.

(v) ***Oid* present, no business key, business key is reliable**. In this case, the AVF looks for a match on the *oid*. If it finds one, it accepts the transaction. Otherwise, it rejects it. The reason is obvious. Note that, unlike inserts, updates to tables with reliable business keys are not required to have the business key on the transaction.

(vi) ***Oid* present, no business key, business key is not reliable**. In this case, the AVF looks for a match on the *oid*. If it finds one, it accepts the transaction. Otherwise, it rejects it.

(vii) ***Oid* present, business key present, business key is reliable**. In this case, the AVF looks for a match on the business key. If it finds a match, and the *oid* of the matching row matches the *oid* on the transaction, the AVF accepts the transaction. If it finds a match, but the *oid* of the matching row does not match the *oid* on the transaction, the AVF rejects the transaction. If it does not find a match, and the *oid* on the transaction does not match any *oid* already in use, the AVF rejects the transaction. And if it does not find a match, but the *oid* on the transaction does match an *oid* already in use, the AVF rejects the transaction. The reason behind all this logic is that when both an *oid* and a reliable business key are present, any conflict makes the transaction invalid; and when a temporal update has an *oid* and business key that do agree, but that do not match anything on the target table, the temporal update fails the match, and is rejected.

(viii) **Oid present, business key present, business key is not reliable**. In this case, the AVF attempts to match on the *oid*. If it does, it accepts the transaction, and otherwise rejects it. Note that if the business key is a new one, then when the transaction is applied, it assigns a new business key to an object, in clock ticks already occupied by that object.

### The Temporal Update Transaction: Semantics

In a conventional table, if an object is represented and the user wishes to modify the row doing the representing, she issues an update transaction which overwrites the data to be changed with the data that changes it. The update transaction expresses not only her intentions, but also her beliefs and assumptions. It expresses her intention to update a representation of an object, but it also expresses her belief that such a representation already exists. If she is mistaken in her belief, her transaction is rejected, which is precisely what she would expect and want to happen.

In an asserted version table, the question is not whether or not the object is already represented, but rather whether or not the object is already represented, in current assertion time, within the effective-time target span indicated on the transaction. If the user submits a temporal update transaction, she also expresses both intention and belief. Her intention is to modify a currently asserted representation of an object in every clock tick within the target effective timespan. Her belief is that such a representation already exists in at least one clock tick within that target span. If she is mistaken in her belief, her transaction is rejected, which is precisely what she would expect and want to happen.

### The Temporal Update Transaction: Mechanics

Here are some examples that will illustrate how this interpretation of the target timespans on temporal update transactions works. Consider a temporal update with a [Nov 2011 – 12/31/9999] target timespan. This update affects all versions in

Episodes B and C shown in Figure 9.6. A temporal update with an [Apr 2012 – Oct 2013] scope affects entire versions, but partial episodes. It will update versions 5–7, i.e. the last two versions of Episode B and the first version of Episode C.

For our final example, let's consider an update that affects partial versions. Suppose that the temporal update specifies a target span of [Jan 2012 – May 2012]. January 2012 is the third clock tick within version 3, and is not the last clock tick within that version. So the AVF must split version 3 into two versions, the first covering [Nov 2011 – Jan 2012] and the second covering [Jan 2012 – Mar 2012]. Call these two versions 3a and 3b, respectively. In just the same way, the AVF must split version 5 into versions 5a and 5b. Version 5a's effective target span is [Apr 2012 – May 2012], and 5b's is [May 2012 – Aug 2012].

Versions 3, 4 and 5 are then withdrawn into past assertion time. Versions 3a and 5b *replace* the unaffected parts of versions 3 and 5, in current assertion time. Finally, the update is applied to 3b, 4 and 5a, which now *supercede* the versions that previously occupied that effective target span in current assertion time.

Notice that the semantics we have given to temporal updates which span episodes is that they do not "fill in the gaps" between episodes. Filling in the gaps is left to temporal inserts, whose job is to place the representation of an object into one or more clock ticks that did not previously contain one. By the same token, temporal updates cannot be used for *any* {lengthen} transformation. Since any such expansion puts the representation of an object into one or more previously unoccupied clock ticks, temporal inserts are used for all of them.

## The Temporal Delete Transaction

The format of a temporal delete transaction is as follows:

```
DELETE FROM {tablename} [,,, ] eff_beg_dt, eff_end_dt,
asr_beg_dt
```

The validity checks work exactly as they do for temporal update transactions. The reason is that a temporal update is equivalent to a temporal delete followed by a temporal insert. So for purposes of validity checking, exactly the same logic applies to both.

Other than supplying the business key when the object identifier is not known, there is no business data to specify on a temporal delete. The target timespan picks out the effective-time range which is to be left empty of any representation of the object, in current assertion time, after the transaction has completed. The delete withdraws any such representations into past assertion time, leaving those corresponding effective time clock ticks unoccupied by the object in current assertion time.

### The Temporal Delete Transaction: Semantics

In a conventional table, if an object is represented and the user wishes to delete it, she issues a delete transaction which deletes the one row representing the object. And once again, this kind of transaction expresses not only her intentions, but also her beliefs. It expresses her intention to delete a row representing an object, but it also expresses her belief that such a row is currently there to delete. If she is mistaken in her belief, her transaction is rejected, which is precisely what she would expect and want to happen.

In an asserted version table, the question is not whether or not the object is already represented, but rather whether or not the object is represented, in current assertion time, within the target effective time span. If the user submits a temporal delete transaction, she also expresses both intention and belief. Her intention is to remove the representation of an object from the indicated timespan. Her belief is that such a representation already exists in one or more of the clock ticks within that target span. If she is mistaken in her belief, her transaction is rejected, which is precisely what she would expect and want to happen.

### The Temporal Delete Transaction: Mechanics

The scope of a *conventional* delete is a single row in the target table. If the transaction is successful, the result is that the designated row is deleted from the table. The scope of a *temporal* delete is any set of one or more contiguous effective time clock ticks at least one of which contains a representation of the object. So, in Figure 9.6, it must include at least one of the clock ticks occupied by Episodes A, B or C.

In Chapter 7, we looked at a basic temporal delete transaction, submitted in December 2010, that specified a target timespan of [Now() – 12/31/9999], and we saw what the AVF did in response to that transaction. It found that an episode did exist whose effective time period [intersected] that target span. It split that episode into two parts. The part from the episode's begin date to (the then-current value of) Now() lay outside the target timespan, while the part from Now() to the end of the episode was found to lie entirely within the target timespan. This split occurred within the latest version of that episode. So the AVF split that version, withdrew it, and replaced the effective time earlier, unaffected part. Since the target timespan extended to 12/31/9999, no later part of the episode lay outside that target span, so nothing else was replaced. The transaction terminated a current episode as of Now(). But in doing so, it went through exactly the same steps that all temporal deletes go through.

## Glossary References

Glossary entries whose definitions form strong interdependencies are grouped together in the following list. The same glossary entries may be grouped together in different ways at the end of different chapters, each grouping reflecting the semantic perspective of each chapter. There will usually be several other, and often many other, glossary entries that are not included in the list, and we recommend that the Glossary be consulted whenever an unfamiliar term is encountered.

We note, in particular, that none of the nodes in our taxonomy of temporal extent transformations are included in this list. In general, we leave taxonomy nodes out of these lists, but recommend that the reader look them up in the Glossary.

---

12/31/9999
Now()

asserted version table
Asserted Versioning Framework (AVF)

assertion
assertion begin date
assertion end date
assertion time
shared assertion time

statement

transaction time

version

bi-temporal
uni-temporal

business data
business key
reliable business key
unreliable business key

clock tick

closed-closed
closed-open
open-closed
open-open

closed episode
episode
episode begin date
open episode

conventional table
conventional transaction

deferred assertion
deferred transaction

effective begin date
effective end date
effective time

incommensurable

intersect
occupied
represented

managed object
object
object identifier
oid

replace
supercede
terminate
withdraw

row creation date

target episode
target span

temporal transaction

temporal dimension

temporal entity integrity (TEI)
temporal referential integrity (TRI)

temporal extent
temporal extent state transformation

the alternative temporal model
the standard temporal model

# TEMPORAL TRANSACTIONS ON SINGLE TABLES

In the previous chapter, we looked at the "specs" of the three types of temporal transactions. In this chapter, we'll take those transactions out for a spin and see exactly how the AVF responds to each one. Its response has two parts. After performing the edit and validity checks described in the previous chapter, the AVF looks to see if applying a transaction would violate temporal entity integrity (TEI) or temporal referential integrity (TRI). If it would violate either one, the transaction is rejected.

Otherwise, the temporal transaction is translated into one or more physical transactions which are then submitted to the DBMS. If the DBMS finds that applying any of those physical transactions would violate an entity integrity or a referential integrity constraint, it will reject that transaction. In response, the AVF will stop processing the temporal transaction, undo

Managing Time in Relational Databases. Doi: 10.1016/B978-0-12-375041-9.00010-8

any changes that might have been made up to that point, and pass an error message back to the calling program.

But if all goes well, the transaction will continue on, and will update the database. In doing so, it will begin by preserving the original state of the version or versions about to be changed, doing this by *withdrawing* them into past assertion time. There is no preservation work to do with temporal inserts, but there is with both temporal updates and temporal deletes. After the preservation step, the AVF will place the representation of an object into one or more clock ticks, update the representation of an object in one or more clock ticks, or remove the representation of an object from one or more clock ticks.

*Temporal referential integrity (TRI)* is the subject of the next chapter. In this chapter, we will focus on *temporal entity integrity (TEI)*. TEI checks insure that, at any given moment of assertion time or during any given period of assertion time, no object may be represented in an effective time clock tick more than once.

TEI applies to both episodes and to versions within episodes. For episodes, it is the constraint that no two episodes of the same object, in the same period of assertion time, either are contiguous with one another or share even a single clock tick. Using the terminology from our Allen relationship taxonomy, it is the constraint that no two episodes of the same object, in the same period of assertion time, either [meet] or [intersect]. They share no clock ticks, and they all have at least one unoccupied clock tick between them. One is always [before] the other.

For versions within an episode, temporal entity integrity is the constraint that each effective-time adjacent pair of versions [meet] but do not [intersect]. They share no clock ticks, and have no unoccupied clock ticks between them.

That's the theory. Now let's put it to work.

## The Temporal Insert Transaction

A temporal insert transaction specifies a representation of an object (Figure 10.1). In the syntax we are using, that representation is the part of the transaction enclosed in brackets. It includes the object identifier (*oid*), if it is known to the user. If an *oid* is not provided on the transaction, the AVF attempts to find or create one according to the rules described in the previous chapter. Finally, the transaction either accepts the default values for its temporal parameters, or overrides one or more of them with explicit values.

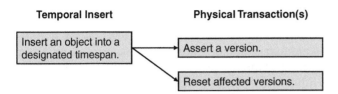

**Figure 10.1** The Temporal Insert Transaction: Temporal to Physical Mapping.

The end result, if successful, is that the transaction has an *oid*, an effective time period, and an assertion time period. The default effective time period for a temporal transaction is [Now() – 12/31/9999], but either effective date can be overridden. The default assertion time period is also [Now() – 12/31/9999]. In Chapter 12, we will see what happens if the assertion begin date default is overridden; but until then, we will assume that all transactions accept this default.

The temporal insert is the simplest of the three temporal transactions to implement. There are no existing versions to be withdrawn and then replaced and/or superceded. As long as not a single clock tick in the transaction's target timespan [intersects] the effective time period of some version of the same object that is already in the target table, the insert is valid. Otherwise, the transaction would violate TEI, and therefore is rejected by the AVF.

A valid insert is always carried out by creating one version. Sometimes the result is a new episode. Sometimes the result is to {lengthen an existing episode forwards}.[1] Sometimes, in being lengthened, an episode "bumps into" another episode and the two episodes are {merged}. When an insert creates a new episode, or {lengthens an episode forwards} (without bumping into the next episode), no other versions are affected. But otherwise, i.e. when {lengthening an episode backwards} or when {merging} two episodes, an insert does require some adjustment on the part of other versions.

---

[1]"{lengthen forwards}" is a two-word temporal extent state transformation name that, for the sake of readability, often needs a pronoun or a noun in the middle. For example, "{lengthen it forwards}" or "{lengthen an episode forwards}". In any of these alternative forms, however, it is still the {lengthen forwards} transformation that is being referred to. The same is true for the names "{lengthen backwards}", "{shorten forwards}" and "{shorten backwards}".

## Creating an Episode

Figure 10.2 depicts the history of policy P861 along a fragment of the calendar timeline, the fragment extending from January 2010 through January 2014. Let's recall that our examples all use, unless otherwise indicated, a clock that ticks once a month. And so, using our page-width-preserving notation, "Jan10" stands for January 1st, 2010, "May12" for May 1st, 2012, and so on. In the text, we will write, more concisely, "January 2010" and "May 2012", not bothering to indicate that the clock always starts the tick on the first moment of the first day of each month and lasts through the last moment of the last day of that month.

We emphasize here a point that we originally made in Chapter 3. A clock tick is a *logical* concept, not a *physical* one. It is the smallest unit of time that can intervene between two adjacent versions of the same object. Thus, if one version begins on the first of the month, then given the granularity for clock ticks used in the examples in this book, the next one *cannot* begin until the first of the next month.

A clock tick gap, in physical time, is whatever the duration of a clock tick happens to be. But the duration of a clock tick, in physical time, is not the issue. As far as recorded data is concerned, there is no duration. There are either clock ticks that happen between two rows of interest to us, or clock ticks that don't.

Unless otherwise indicated, these diagrams show the history of our policy as we currently believe it to be. In other words, it depicts the history of our policy in current assertion time.

Here is a temporal insert transaction, which takes place on August 2011.

```
INSERT INTO Policy [P861, C882, PPO, $30] Jan 2011, Mar 2011
```

This is a *retroactive* transaction because it is attempting to insert a representation of the policy into an effective time period that is already in the past. This transaction is directing us to insert its data into January 2011 and February 2011. Another way to express this target time period in English, using this example, would be "Starting on January 2011 and continuing up to but not including March 2011 . . . . ."

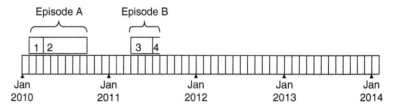

**Figure 10.2** Creating an Episode: Before the Transaction.

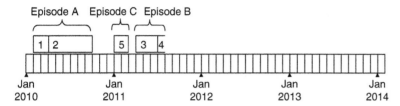

**Figure 10.3** Creating an Episode: After the Transaction.

Immediately prior to this transaction, the currently asserted life history of policy P861 is as shown in Figure 10.2. After the transaction is completed, that history will be the history of the policy as asserted up to (but not including) August 2011. The new currently asserted history of the policy will be as shown in Figure 10.3.

Episode C, as we have labeled it, is a single-version episode. Of course all episodes, when initially created, are single-version episodes. Using the in-line notation introduced in Chapter 6, this new episode looks like this:

```
P[P861[Jan11-Mar11][Aug11-9999][Jan11][C882, PPO, $30]
[Aug11]]
```

This example shows our business correcting a mistake. The mistake was forgetting to record that policy P861 was in effect for those two months until eight months after the fact. What probably happened is that in August, the policy holder filed a claim against the policy. The claim was rejected, the policy holder complained, people in the company did some research, the customer service representative apologized, the policy was retroactively created and, finally, the claim was processed.

New episodes can be created proactively, before they go into effect, just as easily as they can be created retroactively, after they go into effect. But in the scenario shown here, that is not possible. The reason is that Episode B is an open episode; it remains in effect until further notice. Its version 4 has an effective end date of 12/31/9999. Therefore, any attempt to proactively create a new episode, i.e. to create an episode that began sometime after August 2011, would violate temporal entity integrity.

## Lengthening an Episode Backwards

In the previous example, the mistake our company made was to fail to record that a policy was in effect until several months after the fact. Another kind of mistake is to get the effective begin date wrong. For example, Figure 10.3 shows the first episode of our policy becoming effective on February 2010. But let's suppose that the correct date was actually the month before that. How will we make this correction?

Because this correction will place data about an object into a clock tick where it previously was absent, it is carried out with a temporal insert transaction. Similarly, if we mistakenly place data about an object into a clock tick where it doesn't belong, we will need to use a temporal delete transaction to correct our mistake. So we should note that with temporal data, it is not just update transactions that can correct mistakes.

Immediately prior to this transaction, the currently asserted life history of policy P861 is as shown in Figure 10.3. It is still August 2011, and we now submit the following transaction to the AVF:

`INSERT INTO Policy [P861, C882, PPO, $30] Jan 2010, Feb 2010`

Immediately after this transaction is completed, that history will be the history of the policy as asserted from when the previous transaction was applied up to August 2011. The new currently asserted history of the policy will be as shown in Figure 10.4. The new version—version 6—looks like this:

`P[P861[Jan10-Feb10][Aug11-9999][Jan10][C882, PPO, $30]`
`[Aug11]]`

Unlike our first insert transaction, this one does not create a new episode; it extends an existing episode backwards in time. But in doing so, it changes that episode's begin date. As we can see from the schema common to all asserted version tables, the episode begin date is repeated on every version in an episode. And by extending this episode backwards, this transaction changes that episode's begin date. So as part of the atomic isolated unit of work started by this transaction, the AVF must also change the episode begin date on versions 1 and 2, the other two versions in the new Episode A. This is done by withdrawing those two versions and replacing them with versions identical to them except that they have the correct episode begin date. Those two replacement versions are versions 7 and 8, and the versions

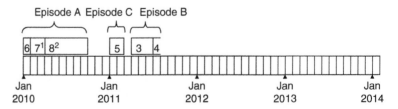

**Figure 10.4** Lengthening an Episode Backwards: After the Transaction.

they replace are shown as superscripts next to them. At the end of the transaction, versions 6, 7 and 8 make up the currently asserted Episode A, and all have an episode begin date of January 2010.

## Lengthening an Episode Forwards

Another thing we can use a temporal insert for is to {extend an episode forwards} in time. This is, naturally enough, much the same process as {extending an episode backwards}. In both cases, the timespan of the transaction must [meet] the timespan of an episode already in the table. The two timespans cannot [intersect], and they cannot have a gap between them.[2] However, {extending an episode forwards} is a little less work for the AVF than {extending an episode backwards} because extending forwards leaves the episode begin date unchanged on the other versions in the episode.

All of our temporal inserts, so far, have done retroactive work. So let's set up this next example as a proactive transaction. The main lesson to be learned is that the distinction between proactive and retroactive transactions is one *we* make, but not one that matters to the AVF. It is a matter of the relationship between when the transaction takes place, and what period of effective time it affects. As a relationship between a point in time and a period of time, the basic options are that the point in time can be earlier than the period of time, within the period of time, or later than the period of time. This gives us, against a current episode, proactive, current and retroactive temporal transactions.

To illustrate a proactive transaction, let's assume that it is now May 2010, and that at this point in time, our database looks as shown in Figure 10.5.

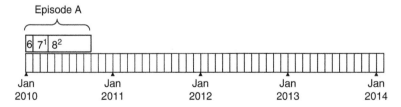

**Figure 10.5** Lengthening an Episode Forwards: Before the Transaction.

---

[2]In Allen relationship terms, one cannot be [before] the other. However, since one clearly is *before* the other, as we understand the word "before", Allen relationship terminology is, in this instance, somewhat unfortunate.

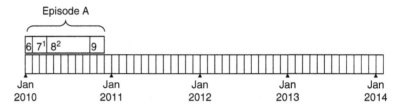

**Figure 10.6** Lengthening an Episode Forwards: After the Transaction.

It is May 2010, and the following transaction is submitted to the AVF:

```
INSERT INTO Policy [P861, C882, HMO, $25] Oct 2010, Dec 2010
```

Immediately after this transaction is completed, the history shown in Figure 10.5 will no longer be currently asserted. Instead, it will be the history of the policy as asserted from when the previous transaction was applied up to May 2010. The new currently asserted history of the policy will be as shown in Figure 10.6. Version 9 looks like this:

```
P[P861[Oct10-Dec10][May10-9999][Jan10][C882, HMO, $25]
[May10]]
```

Episode begin dates are not supplied on transactions. They are always determined by the AVF. In this case, the AVF sees that there is already a version of that same policy in the table whose effective end date [meets$^{-1}$] the effective begin date on the transaction. Because this match means that the episode is being extended forwards, the AVF assigns version 9 the episode begin date on the version it is contiguous with—in this case, version 8.

So now, on May 2010, we are claiming that we know several things about policy P861's future. We know that it will remain in effect until December 2010, i.e. through November 30th, 2010. We know that from May 2010 to October 2010, it will have the properties ascribed to it by version 8. We also know that in October and November of that year, it will be an HMO policy with a $25 copay.

We say we know this about the future. But, of course, as with any statement about the future, we may be wrong. However, since anyone viewing this data about the future will understand this, we are misrepresenting nothing.

## Merging Episodes

We have seen how temporal inserts can create new episodes and can extend existing episodes backwards and forwards. But when any but the latest episode of an object is extended forwards, there is an episode ahead of it to "bump into". Similarly, when any but the earliest episode of an object is extended backwards, there is an episode behind it to bump into.

In either case, however, a successful temporal insert will {merge} the two adjacent episodes together. The resulting episode will contain all the versions in both of the original episodes, and also the one version that caused them to {merge}.

To illustrate a temporal transaction merging two episodes, let's go all the way back to Figure 10.2 and assume that it is now January 2012. Immediately after this next transaction is completed, the history shown in Figure 10.2 will no longer be currently asserted. Instead, it will be the history of the policy as asserted from when the previous transaction was applied up to January 2012. The new currently asserted history of the policy will be as shown in Figure 10.7.

It is now January 2012, and the following transaction is submitted to the AVF:

```
INSERT INTO Policy [P861, C882, POS, $15] Oct 2010, Apr 2011
```

Version 7 looks like this:

```
P[P861[Oct10-Apr11][Jan12-9999][Feb10][C882, POS, $15]
[Jan12]]
```

The AVF sees that this transaction will {merge} two episodes. It can tell that because there are already two versions of that same policy in the table such that the effective end date of the earlier one [meets$^{-1}$] the effective begin date on the transaction, and the effective begin date of the later one [meets] the effective end date on the transaction. Because the result is a single episode, all versions in that episode must have the same episode begin date. Therefore, to complete the transaction, the AVF sets the episode begin date of version 7 to February 2010, and withdraws versions 3 and 4, replacing them with versions that are identical except that they remain in current assertion time and have an episode begin date of February 2010.

We have now discussed all the temporal extent transformations that are carried out in response to a temporal insert transaction. At the end of this chapter, we will review the

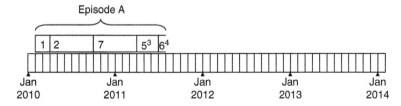

**Figure 10.7** Merging Adjacent Episodes: After the Transaction.

taxonomy of temporal extent transformations shown in Figure 9.5 (and repeated as Figure 10.21) to be sure that we have demonstrated that each of them can be produced by one of the three temporal transactions.

In the meantime, let's turn to temporal update transactions. But before we do, let's note that update transactions do not bring about temporal extent transformations. A temporal extent transformation necessarily involves adding the representation of an object to one or more clock ticks, or removing the representation of an object from one or more clock ticks. Temporal updates do neither. They simply change business data on versions that [intersect] a designated target range.

## The Temporal Update Transaction

A temporal update transaction specifies (i) an object, (ii) a value for one or more columns of business data, and (iii) a target effective timespan, which we sometimes also call a target *range* for the transaction. The transaction includes the object identifier (*oid*), if it is known to the user. If an *oid* is not provided on the transaction, the AVF attempts to find or create one according to the rules described in the previous chapter. Finally, the transaction either accepts the default values for its temporal parameters, or overrides one or more of them with explicit values.

Although a temporal update does not alter the temporal extent of an object, it is still the most complex of the three temporal transactions to implement. There are always existing versions that must be *withdrawn*. If parts of those versions do not [intersect] the transaction's target range, those parts must be *replaced*. Then the parts of versions or entire versions that do [intersect] the target range must be *superceded* with versions that contain the new data.

As long as even a single clock tick in the transaction's target range [intersects] the effective time period of some version of the specified object, the temporal update is valid because it means that there is data for the transaction to modify. A valid update is always carried out by creating one new version for every version found within the target range, as well as a new version for every part of a version found within the target range. These versions are the ones that supercede, in current assertion time, the versions that fall within the timespan of the transaction. A valid update will also create a new version for those parts of versions, if any, that do not [intersect] the target range. These new versions contain no new business data. They are simply replacements for those parts of withdrawn versions that were unaffected by the update.

A temporal update's target range may include part of an episode or version, an entire episode or version, multiple episodes or versions, or any combination thereof. But a temporal update never creates a new episode, and never adds to or subtracts from the total count of clock ticks occupied by its referenced object.

We will need only a single example to illustrate the most important variations of temporal updates. We begin with a sample database whose rows 1–6 represent the versions 3–8 shown in Figure 10.4. This is the sample database shown in Figure 10.9. Row 1 represents version 7, the currently asserted replacement for version 1. Row 2 represents version 8, the currently asserted replacement for version 2. Rows 3–6 represent versions 3–6.

We will show none of the past assertion history that led to this database state, but only the six versions that are currently asserted. But because this is a relatively complex transaction, we will illustrate its progress one physical transaction at a time.

The mapping shown in Figure 10.8 illustrates the steps the AVF will go through to complete the temporal update.

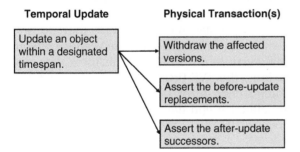

**Figure 10.8** The Temporal Update Transaction: Temporal to Physical Mapping.

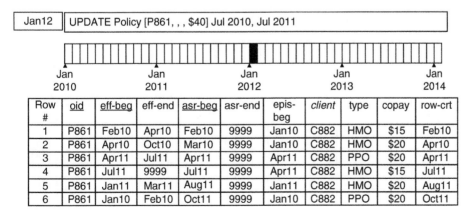

| Row # | oid | eff-beg | eff-end | asr-beg | asr-end | epis-beg | client | type | copay | row-crt |
|---|---|---|---|---|---|---|---|---|---|---|
| 1 | P861 | Feb10 | Apr10 | Feb10 | 9999 | Jan10 | C882 | HMO | $15 | Feb10 |
| 2 | P861 | Apr10 | Oct10 | Mar10 | 9999 | Jan10 | C882 | HMO | $20 | Apr10 |
| 3 | P861 | Apr11 | Jul11 | Apr11 | 9999 | Apr11 | C882 | PPO | $20 | Apr11 |
| 4 | P861 | Jul11 | 9999 | Jul11 | 9999 | Apr11 | C882 | HMO | $15 | Jul11 |
| 5 | P861 | Jan11 | Mar11 | Aug11 | 9999 | Jan11 | C882 | HMO | $20 | Aug11 |
| 6 | P861 | Jan10 | Feb10 | Oct11 | 9999 | Jan10 | C882 | PPO | $20 | Oct11 |

**Figure 10.9** Updating a Policy: Before the Transaction.

We begin by withdrawing the affected versions. The transaction specifies the timespan [Jul 2010 – Jul 2011]. Part of version 8, and all of versions 5 and 3, [fill$^{-1}$] this timespan. So the first step is to withdraw these three versions. Since no assertion begin date was explicitly specified on the transaction, that date defaults to Now(), January 2012. The result is shown in Figure 10.10. Using a convention described previously, we enclose in angle brackets the row numbers of all rows which are part of this atomic, isolated unit of work and, because these rows are now withdrawn, we show them shaded.

Only part of row 2 (version 8) [intersects] the range of the transaction. Since row 2 has been withdrawn into past assertion time, the next thing we must do is to replace, in current assertion time, that part of the version that the transaction is not concerned with. To do this, the AVF creates a version whose effective time period extends from version 8's effective begin date up to the effective begin date of the transaction, July 2010. The result is row 7, shown in Figure 10.11.

The rest of version 8 does [fill$^{-1}$] the range of the transaction, as do all of versions 5 and 3. The versions which take the place of these two versions are not replacements, because they do not contain identical business data. Instead, they are versions which *supercede* the original versions with the new business data. To supercede these versions, the AVF first creates a version whose effective time period extends from the transaction's effective begin date up to the effective end date of version 8. The result is row 8, shown in Figure 10.12.

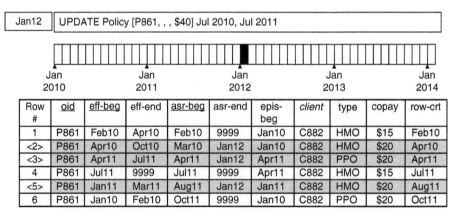

| Jan12 | UPDATE Policy [P861, , , $40] Jul 2010, Jul 2011 |
|-------|---------------------------------------------------|

| Row # | oid | eff-beg | eff-end | asr-beg | asr-end | epis-beg | client | type | copay | row-crt |
|-------|------|---------|---------|---------|---------|----------|--------|------|-------|---------|
| 1 | P861 | Feb10 | Apr10 | Feb10 | 9999 | Jan10 | C882 | HMO | $15 | Feb10 |
| <2> | P861 | Apr10 | Oct10 | Mar10 | Jan12 | Jan10 | C882 | HMO | $20 | Apr10 |
| <3> | P861 | Apr11 | Jul11 | Apr11 | Jan12 | Apr11 | C882 | PPO | $20 | Apr11 |
| 4 | P861 | Jul11 | 9999 | Jul11 | 9999 | Apr11 | C882 | HMO | $15 | Jul11 |
| <5> | P861 | Jan11 | Mar11 | Aug11 | Jan12 | Jan11 | C882 | HMO | $20 | Aug11 |
| 6 | P861 | Jan10 | Feb10 | Oct11 | 9999 | Jan10 | C882 | PPO | $20 | Oct11 |

**Figure 10.10** Updating a Policy: Withdrawing the Versions in the Target Range.

| Jan12 | UPDATE Policy [P861, , , $40] Jul 2010, Jul 2011 |
|---|---|

| Row # | oid | eff-beg | eff-end | asr-beg | asr-end | epis-beg | client | type | copay | row-crt |
|---|---|---|---|---|---|---|---|---|---|---|
| 1 | P861 | Feb10 | Apr10 | Feb10 | 9999 | Jan10 | C882 | HMO | $15 | Feb10 |
| <2> | P861 | Apr10 | Oct10 | Mar10 | Jan12 | Jan10 | C882 | HMO | $20 | Apr10 |
| <3> | P861 | Apr11 | Jul11 | Apr11 | Jan12 | Apr11 | C882 | PPO | $20 | Apr11 |
| 4 | P861 | Jul11 | 9999 | Jul11 | 9999 | Apr11 | C882 | HMO | $15 | Jul11 |
| <5> | P861 | Jan11 | Mar11 | Aug11 | Jan12 | Jan11 | C882 | HMO | $20 | Aug11 |
| 6 | P861 | Jan10 | Feb10 | Oct11 | 9999 | Jan10 | C882 | PPO | $20 | Oct11 |
| <7> | P861 | Apr10 | Jul10 | Jan12 | 9999 | Jan10 | C882 | HMO | $20 | Jan12 |

**Figure 10.11** Updating a Policy: Replacing the Unaffected Part of Version 2.

| Jan12 | Update Policy [P861, , , $40] Jul 2010, Jul 2011 |
|---|---|

| Row # | oid | eff-beg | eff-end | asr-beg | asr-end | epis-beg | client | type | copay | row-crt |
|---|---|---|---|---|---|---|---|---|---|---|
| 1 | P861 | Feb10 | Apr10 | Feb10 | 9999 | Jan10 | C882 | HMO | $15 | Feb10 |
| <2> | P861 | Apr10 | Oct10 | Mar10 | Jan12 | Jan10 | C882 | HMO | $20 | Apr10 |
| <3> | P861 | Apr11 | Jul11 | Apr11 | Jan12 | Apr11 | C882 | PPO | $20 | Apr11 |
| 4 | P861 | Jul11 | 9999 | Jul11 | 9999 | Apr11 | C882 | HMO | $15 | Jul11 |
| <5> | P861 | Jan11 | Mar11 | Aug11 | Jan12 | Jan11 | C882 | HMO | $20 | Aug11 |
| 6 | P861 | Jan10 | Feb10 | Oct11 | 9999 | Jan10 | C882 | PPO | $20 | Oct11 |
| <7> | P861 | Apr10 | Jul10 | Jan12 | 9999 | Jan10 | C882 | HMO | $20 | Jan12 |
| <8> | P861 | Jul10 | Oct10 | Jan12 | 9999 | Jan10 | C882 | HMO | $40 | Jan12 |
| <9> | P861 | Apr11 | Jul11 | Jan12 | 9999 | Apr11 | C882 | PPO | $40 | Jan12 |
| <10> | P861 | Jan11 | Mar11 | Jan12 | 9999 | Jan11 | C882 | HMO | $40 | Jan12 |

**Figure 10.12** Updating a Policy: Superceding the Affected Versions.

The last step for the AVF is to insert rows 9 and 10. Row 9 supercedes row 3 (version 3 in Figure 10.4), and row 10 supercedes row 5 (version 5). The temporal update transaction is now complete. The atomic unit of work is over, and the DBMS can release its locks on the rows involved in this transaction. These rows are no longer isolated, but are now part of the database.

### Restricted and Unrestricted Temporal Transactions

The temporal update transactions discussed in this book are *restricted* temporal updates. By that we mean that these transactions designate a specific object, a span of effective time, and a value for one or more columns of business data, and then change all representations of that object, in all clock ticks within that timespan, to those new values. But limited to only restricted update transactions, Asserted Versioning could not, for example, change the copay amounts on *all* policies within a target timespan *provided* that the original amounts are less than a certain value. Instead, the AVF could only change all copay amounts within that timespan, for a single object, to that new value.

Obviously, a series of carefully designed restricted temporal updates could produce any desired result, and do so across any set of objects. But just as obviously, it would be a tedious process. And because of the careful analysis required, it would also be an error-prone process.

As we go to press, these limitations on temporal update transactions have been removed. Release 1 of our Asserted Versioning Framework now supports *unrestricted* temporal update transactions, ones which will update multiple objects within a target timespan, and will do so based on WHERE clause qualifying criteria. The AVF also now supports unrestricted temporal deletes as well.

In addition, instead of requiring the user to write transactions in a proprietary format required by an Application Programming Interface (API) we were developing, the AVF now accepts temporal insert, update and delete transactions written as native SQL. This is done by means of Instead of Triggers, as described in the section Ongoing Research and Development, in Chapter 16.

Our new support for unrestricted temporal transactions, written as native SQL statements, can be found on our website AssertedVersioning.com.

## The Temporal Delete Transaction

A temporal delete transaction specifies an object and a target range for the transaction (Figure 10.13). It includes the object identifier, if it is known to the user. If an *oid* is not provided on the transaction, the AVF attempts to find one according to the rules described in the previous chapter. Finally, the transaction either accepts the default values for its temporal parameters, or overrides one or more of them with explicit values.

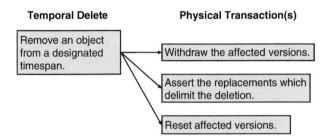

**Figure 10.13** The Temporal Delete Transaction: Temporal to Physical Mapping.

A temporal delete is the inverse of a temporal insert. A temporal insert always increases the total number of clock ticks occupied by an object. A temporal delete always decreases the total number of those clock ticks.

As long as even a single clock tick in the transaction's target timespan [intersects] the effective time period of some version of the same object, the delete is valid because it means that there is data in one or more clock ticks for the delete to move into past assertion time.

A temporal delete's target range may include part of an episode or version, an entire episode or version, multiple episodes or versions, or any combination thereof. But a temporal delete never creates a new episode or version in clock ticks that were previously unoccupied, just as a temporal insert never removes one from clock ticks that were previously occupied.

## Deleting One or More Episodes

We will begin with the set of three episodes shown in Figure 10.14. These are the current episodes A, B and C after being updated as shown in Figure 10.12. We have also reset the version numbers so they correspond to the row numbers in Figure 10.12.

To completely remove an episode from current assertion time, we do not need to provide the exact begin and end dates of the episode, but simply need to include its effective time

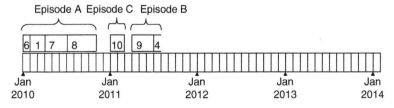

**Figure 10.14** Deleting an Episode: Before the Transaction.

period in the transaction's target timespan. If that target timespan includes that of the episode, the result is to remove the entire episode, i.e. to {erase} that episode from current assertion time.

It is now March 2012, and either of the following two transactions is submitted to the AVF:

```
DELETE FROM Policy [P861] Jan 2010, Nov 2010
```

or

```
DELETE FROM Policy [P861] Jan 2010, Dec 2010
```

These two temporal delete transactions have the same result. They both {erase} Episode A, the episode consisting of versions 6, 1, 7 and 8. The author of the transaction will not be confused by this fact provided she remembers that a delete transaction simply stops asserting the presence of an object anywhere in the effective timespan indicated on the transaction. Both timespans shown here contain exactly the same occupied clock ticks.

Withdrawing these versions is the first of the three physical transaction steps shown in Figure 10.15. As for the other two steps, neither of them is needed to complete this temporal transaction. The reason is that since an entire episode is being {erased}, and the object is represented nowhere else in the target timespan, no other episodes are affected. We can think of the empty clock tick or clock ticks that exist on both ends of an episode as insulating other episodes from whatever happens to just that one episode.

## Shortening an Episode Forwards

We still currently assert episodes C and B in Figure 10.14. It is now May 2012, and the following transaction is submitted to the AVF:

```
DELETE FROM Policy [P861] Jan 2011, May 2011
```

This transaction will {erase} Episode C, and {shorten Episode B forwards} by one month.

| Row # | oid | eff-beg | eff-end | asr-beg | asr-end | epis-beg | client | type | copay | row-crt |
|-------|------|---------|---------|---------|---------|----------|--------|------|-------|---------|
| <1> | P861 | Feb10 | Apr10 | Feb10 | Mar12 | Jan10 | C882 | HMO | $15 | Feb10 |
| 2 | P861 | Apr10 | Oct10 | Mar10 | Jan12 | Jan10 | C882 | HMO | $20 | Apr10 |
| 3 | P861 | Apr11 | Jul11 | Apr11 | Jan12 | Apr11 | C882 | PPO | $20 | Apr11 |
| 4 | P861 | Jul11 | 9999 | Jul11 | 9999 | Apr11 | C882 | HMO | $15 | Jul11 |
| 5 | P861 | Jan11 | Mar11 | Aug11 | Jan12 | Jan11 | C882 | HMO | $20 | Aug11 |
| <6> | P861 | Jan10 | Feb10 | Oct11 | Mar12 | Jan10 | C882 | PPO | $20 | Oct11 |
| <7> | P861 | Apr10 | Jul10 | Jan12 | Mar12 | Jan10 | C882 | HMO | $20 | Jan12 |
| <8> | P861 | Jul10 | Oct10 | Jan12 | Mar12 | Jan10 | C882 | HMO | $40 | Jan12 |
| 9 | P861 | Apr11 | Jul11 | Jan12 | 9999 | Apr11 | C882 | PPO | $40 | Jan12 |
| 10 | P861 | Jan11 | Mar11 | Jan12 | 9999 | Jan11 | C882 | HMO | $40 | Jan12 |

**Figure 10.15** Deleting an Episode.

| Row # | oid | eff-beg | eff-end | asr-beg | asr-end | epis-beg | client | type | copay | row-crt |
|-------|-----|---------|---------|---------|---------|----------|--------|------|-------|---------|
| 1 | P861 | Feb10 | Apr10 | Feb10 | Mar12 | Jan10 | C882 | HMO | $15 | Feb10 |
| 2 | P861 | Apr10 | Oct10 | Mar10 | Jan12 | Jan10 | C882 | HMO | $20 | Apr10 |
| 3 | P861 | Apr11 | Jul11 | Apr11 | Jan12 | Apr11 | C882 | PPO | $20 | Apr11 |
| 4 | P861 | Jul11 | 9999 | Jul11 | 9999 | Apr11 | C882 | HMO | $15 | Jul11 |
| 5 | P861 | Jan11 | Mar11 | Aug11 | Jan12 | Jan11 | C882 | HMO | $20 | Aug11 |
| 6 | P861 | Jan10 | Feb10 | Oct11 | Mar12 | Jan10 | C882 | PPO | $20 | Oct11 |
| 7 | P861 | Apr10 | Jul10 | Jan12 | Mar12 | Jan10 | C882 | HMO | $20 | Jan12 |
| 8 | P861 | Jul10 | Oct10 | Jan12 | Mar12 | Jan10 | C882 | HMO | $40 | Jan12 |
| <9> | P861 | Apr11 | Jul11 | Jan12 | May12 | Apr11 | C882 | PPO | $40 | Jan12 |
| <10> | P861 | Jan11 | Mar11 | Jan12 | May12 | Jan11 | C882 | HMO | $40 | Jan12 |

**Figure 10.16** Shortening an Episode Forwards: After Step 1.

Because the delete transaction {shortens Episode B forwards}, it alters the episode begin date. Specifically, it changes that begin date from April 2011 to May 2011. This transaction will require all three of the physical transaction steps shown in Figure 10.13.

The first physical transaction step withdraws versions 9 and 10. The result is shown in Figure 10.16. These versions have been withdrawn, as all versions are, by overwriting their assertion end dates. The overwrites which withdraw rows into past assertion time do not lose information, however, as overwrites of business data do. This is because we always know what the assertion end date was before the row was withdrawn. In all cases, it was 12/31/9999. This is guaranteed because (i) all versions are created with an assertion end date of 12/31/9999, and (ii) the AVF will never alter an assertion end date that is not 12/31/9999.

In comparing the transaction's time period to that of the episode, we see that it completely includes version 10 but only [overlaps] version 9. So, having withdrawn version 9, we must now replace it with a version identical to it except that its effective time period begins on May 2011. But because version 9 is the first version of Episode B, it changes the episode begin date of the episode from April 2011 to May 2011. This, in turn, affects version 4, which is the second version in that episode. Consequently, we must withdraw version 4, and replace it with a version that is identical to it except for having the new episode begin date. The result of all this work is shown in Figure 10.17.

Episode C has been {erased}, completely withdrawn into past assertion time. Episode B has been {shortened forwards} by one month.

The first delete transaction we considered covered an entire episode, {removing} that episode by withdrawing all its versions into past assertion time. This delete transaction, however, left part

| Row # | oid | eff-beg | eff-end | asr-beg | asr-end | epis-beg | client | type | copay | row-crt |
|---|---|---|---|---|---|---|---|---|---|---|
| 1 | P861 | Feb10 | Apr10 | Feb10 | Mar12 | Jan10 | C882 | HMO | $15 | Feb10 |
| 2 | P861 | Apr10 | Oct10 | Mar10 | Jan12 | Jan10 | C882 | HMO | $20 | Apr10 |
| 3 | P861 | Apr11 | Jul11 | Apr11 | Jan12 | Apr11 | C882 | PPO | $20 | Apr11 |
| 4 | P861 | Jul11 | 9999 | Jul11 | May12 | Apr11 | C882 | HMO | $15 | Jul11 |
| 5 | P861 | Jan11 | Mar11 | Aug11 | Jan12 | Jan11 | C882 | HMO | $20 | Aug11 |
| 6 | P861 | Jan10 | Feb10 | Oct11 | Mar12 | Jan10 | C882 | PPO | $20 | Oct11 |
| 7 | P861 | Apr10 | Jul10 | Jan12 | Mar12 | Jan10 | C882 | HMO | $20 | Jan12 |
| 8 | P861 | Jul10 | Oct10 | Jan12 | Mar12 | Jan10 | C882 | HMO | $40 | Jan12 |
| <9> | P861 | Apr11 | Jul11 | Jan12 | May12 | Apr11 | C882 | PPO | $40 | Jan12 |
| <10> | P861 | Jan11 | Mar11 | Jan12 | May12 | Jan11 | C882 | HMO | $40 | Jan12 |
| <11> | P861 | May11 | Jul11 | May12 | 9999 | May11 | C882 | PPO | $40 | May12 |
| <12> | P861 | Jul11 | 9999 | May12 | 9999 | May11 | C882 | HMO | $15 | May12 |

**Figure 10.17** Shortening an Episode Forwards: After Step 2.

of a target episode in current assertion time. It withdrew part but not all of that episode, bringing about the temporal extent transformation in which an episode is {shortened forwards}.

In this way, a temporal delete is different from a non-temporal delete. Non-temporal deletes remove the one and only row representing an object from the database. Temporal deletes remove some but not necessarily all of the possibly multiple rows representing an object, and may also remove part but not necessarily all of any one (or two) of those rows. And, of course, temporal deletes do not physically remove any data from the database. They just withdraw assertions and end the effective time of versions, so that at any point in time, what used to be the case can be recreated exactly as it was then.

## Shortening an Episode Backwards

A temporal delete can also {shorten an episode backwards} in time. This happens when the transaction's target range [overlaps] later clock ticks in the episode (and perhaps additional clock ticks as well) while one or more earlier clock ticks are not [overlapped].

{Shortening an episode backwards} is easier than {shortening it forwards} because it doesn't alter the episode's begin date. Since the episode's begin date remains the same, the only versions in the episode that are affected by the transaction are those which [overlap] the transaction's target range. If we're really fortunate, the target range will line up on version boundaries. An example would be a temporal delete whose target range is [Jul 2011 – 12/31/9999] against the episode still asserted in Figure 10.17. In this case, the timespan on this transaction [*equals*] the effective time of version 12.

When a temporal delete's timespan lines up on a version boundary within a target episode, then all that has to be done is to withdraw the affected versions. Doing so, in this case, leaves an episode whose effective time extends from May 2011 to July 2011. So the effective end date, July 2011, of this previous version, row 11, would designate the end of the episode.

## Splitting an Episode

{Splitting} an episode is a little more interesting than either {shortening an episode backwards} or {shortening an episode forwards}. The reason is that, from the point of view of the earlier of the two resulting episodes, {splitting} is {shortening an episode backwards}, while from the point of view of the later of the two resulting episodes, it is {shortening an episode forwards}. From the point of view of the "internals" of AVF processing, of course, it is simply another case of removing the representation of an object from a series of clock ticks, the case in which those clock ticks are contained within the clock ticks of a single episode.

Let's begin with the life history of policy P861 as represented in the table in Figure 10.15 and as graphically illustrated in Figure 10.14. In that table, versions (row numbers) 9 and 4 constitute a currently asserted episode, one which extends from April 2011 to 12/31/9999.

It is now February 2012. Note that this is one month before the {shorten forwards} transaction, described in the previous section, is processed. That's why we're going back to Figure 10.15, rather than to Figure 10.16. The following transaction is submitted to the AVF:

```
DELETE FROM Policy [P861] May 2011, Dec 2012
```

Policy P861 exists, in current assertion time, in every clock tick from May 2011 to December 2012. As we can see from version 9, it also exists for exactly one clock tick prior to that timespan. And as we can see from version 4, it exists past December 2012, into the indefinite future.

The first physical transaction step in this deletion is to withdraw versions 9 and 4 since each of them has at least one clock tick included in the timespan specified by the temporal delete. The result is shown in Figure 10.18.

Having {erased} the entire episode, the next step is to replace those parts of those versions which lie outside the scope of the transaction. For version 9, [Apr 2011 – May 2011] is the single clock tick that must be replaced. For version 4, [Dec 2012 – 12/31/9999] is the effective timespan that must be replaced. The result is shown in Figure 10.19.

| Row # | oid | eff-beg | eff-end | asr-beg | asr-end | epis-beg | client | type | copay | row-crt |
|---|---|---|---|---|---|---|---|---|---|---|
| 1 | P861 | Feb10 | Apr10 | Feb10 | Mar12 | Jan10 | C882 | HMO | $15 | Feb10 |
| 2 | P861 | Apr10 | Oct10 | Mar10 | 9999 | Jan10 | C882 | HMO | $20 | Apr10 |
| 3 | P861 | Apr11 | Jul11 | Apr11 | 9999 | Apr11 | C882 | PPO | $20 | Apr11 |
| <4> | P861 | Jul11 | 9999 | Jul11 | Feb12 | Apr11 | C882 | HMO | $15 | Jul11 |
| 5 | P861 | Jan11 | Mar11 | Aug11 | 9999 | Jan11 | C882 | HMO | $20 | Aug11 |
| 6 | P861 | Jan10 | Feb10 | Oct11 | Mar12 | Jan10 | C882 | PPO | $20 | Oct11 |
| 7 | P861 | Apr10 | Jul10 | Jan12 | Mar12 | Jan10 | C882 | HMO | $20 | Jan12 |
| 8 | P861 | Jul10 | Oct10 | Jan12 | 9999 | Jan10 | C882 | HMO | $40 | Jan12 |
| <9> | P861 | Apr11 | Jul11 | Jan12 | Feb12 | Apr11 | C882 | PPO | $40 | Jan12 |
| 10 | P861 | Jan11 | Mar11 | Jan12 | 9999 | Jan11 | C882 | HMO | $40 | Jan12 |
| 11 | P861 | Jun10 | Jul10 | Mar12 | 9999 | Jun10 | C882 | PPO | $20 | Mar12 |

**Figure 10.18** Splitting an Episode: After Step 1.

| Row # | oid | eff-beg | eff-end | asr-beg | asr-end | epis-beg | client | type | copay | row-crt |
|---|---|---|---|---|---|---|---|---|---|---|
| 1 | P861 | Feb10 | Apr10 | Feb10 | Mar12 | Jan10 | C882 | HMO | $15 | Feb10 |
| 2 | P861 | Apr10 | Oct10 | Mar10 | 9999 | Jan10 | C882 | HMO | $20 | Apr10 |
| 3 | P861 | Apr11 | Jul11 | Apr11 | 9999 | Apr11 | C882 | PPO | $20 | Apr11 |
| <4> | P861 | Jul11 | 9999 | Jul11 | Feb12 | Apr11 | C882 | HMO | $15 | Jul11 |
| 5 | P861 | Jan11 | Mar11 | Aug11 | 9999 | Jan11 | C882 | HMO | $20 | Aug11 |
| 6 | P861 | Jan10 | Feb10 | Oct11 | Mar12 | Jan10 | C882 | PPO | $20 | Oct11 |
| 7 | P861 | Apr10 | Jul10 | Jan12 | Mar12 | Jan10 | C882 | PPO | $20 | Jan12 |
| 8 | P861 | Jul10 | Oct10 | Jan12 | 9999 | Jan10 | C882 | PPO | $40 | Jan12 |
| <9> | P861 | Apr11 | Jul11 | Jan12 | Feb12 | Apr11 | C882 | PPO | $40 | Jan12 |
| 10 | P861 | Jan11 | Mar11 | Jan12 | 9999 | Jan11 | C882 | HMO | $40 | Jan12 |
| 11 | P861 | Jun10 | Jul10 | Mar12 | 9999 | Jun10 | C882 | PPO | $20 | Mar12 |
| <12> | P861 | Apr11 | May11 | Feb12 | 9999 | Apr11 | C882 | PPO | $40 | Feb12 |
| <13> | P861 | Dec12 | 9999 | Feb12 | 9999 | Dec12 | C882 | HMO | $15 | Feb12 |

**Figure 10.19** Splitting an Episode: After Steps 2 and 3.

The second physical transaction step in carrying out a temporal delete is to assert the replacement versions which delimit the time period of the deletion. This is done with versions 12 and 13. Version 12 replaces the one clock tick from version 9 that was not included in the range of the delete. Version 13 replaces the clock ticks from December 2012 to 12/31/9999 from version 4 that were not included in the range of the delete.

The third physical transaction step resets any versions that need their episode begin dates reset. That is version 13. Version 4, which it replaces, belongs to an episode which began on July 2011. That episode has been {shortened forwards} by the transaction so that it now begins on December 2012, the effective begin date of what is now its only version.

# Completeness Checks

We have now used all three temporal transactions, in a variety of situations. There are several ways to categorize the situations which temporal transactions might encounter, but we concluded, a couple of chapters ago, that we could not provide an example for all of them. Nonetheless, we would like some assurance that any semantically valid request to transform one or more asserted version tables from one state to another state can be made with temporal transactions and can be carried out with the physical transactions that the AVF maps them into.

We know of two ways to do this. One is with the Allen relationships. The other is with our taxonomy of temporal extent state transformations. The relationship of these two ways of demonstrating completeness is this. While we will use the Allen relationships to compare temporal transactions to their target episodes, we will use the temporal extent state transformations to compare before and after states of a target database.

## An Allen Relationship Completeness Check

First of all, it is well established that the Allen relationships are a mutually exclusive and jointly exhaustive set of all the possible relationships between two time periods along a common timeline that are based on the temporal precedence and succession of one to the other (Figure 10.20). We ourselves derived precisely those Allen relationships as the leaf nodes in a taxonomy of our own invention. Since taxonomies are tools for demonstrating mutual exclusion and joint coverage of an original root node, this is further proof, if any were needed, of the validity of the Allen relationships.

In the case of temporal transactions, one of those two Allen relationship time periods is the effective time period specified on the transaction. The other time period is the effective time period of each episode and version to which those transactions may apply.

We should also remind ourselves that when we compare any two time periods in effective time, we are assuming that they exist in shared assertion time. When one of those time periods is on a transaction, that assertion time cannot begin in the past, and usually begins Now(); and the assertion time specified on the transaction always extends to 12/31/9999.

[Before], [before$^{-1}$]. When a temporal transaction's effective time is non-contiguous with that of any episodes of the same object already in the target table, a temporal insert will {create} a new episode of the object. In Allen relationship terms, this

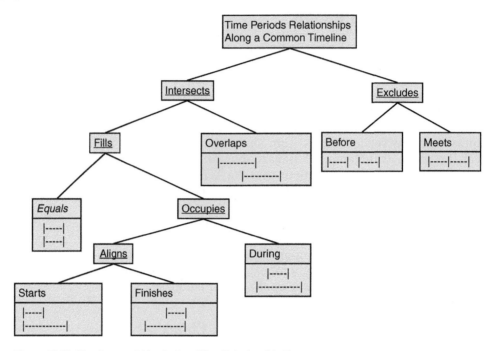

**Figure 10.20** The Asserted Versioning Allen Relationship Taxonomy.

means that, for any episode of the same object already in the target table, the effective time period specified on a temporal insert is either [before] or [before$^{-1}$] that episode. Another way of making the same point is to say that the time period on the transaction is *non-contiguous* with the time period of any episode of the same object.

If the effective time period on a temporal update or delete transaction is either [before] or [before$^{-1}$] the effective time period of every episode of the same object already in the target table, then the temporal transaction is invalid. It is equivalent to a conventional transaction trying to update or delete a row that isn't there.

[Meets], [meets$^{-1}$]. When a temporal transaction's effective time [meets] or [meets$^{-1}$] that of an episode of the same object already in the target table, a temporal insert will result in one or the other of the {lengthen} transformations, depending on whether the transaction's timespan is later than or earlier than that of the episode. Also, if a temporal insert transaction's effective time both [meets] one episode and [meets$^{-1}$] an adjacent episode, the result will be a {merge} transformation.

The [before], [before$^{-1}$], [meets] and [meets$^{-1}$] relationships are subtypes, in our taxonomy, of the [excludes] relationship. And we can now see why this is an important group of relationships to define. Temporal insert transactions are valid only if they have an [excludes] relationship with every other episode of the same object already in the target table. And by the same token, temporal update and temporal delete transactions are valid only if there is at least one episode of the same object already in the target table with which they do not have an [excludes] relationship. So now that we are through with the [excludes] branch of the Allen taxonomy, we have exhausted all the Allen relationship possibilities for temporal insert transactions.

We will discuss how temporal delete transactions work with the remaining Allen relationships. We will not explicitly discuss temporal updates because temporal updates are semantically equivalent to temporal deletes followed by the insertion of updated versions which supercede those versions wholly or partially withdrawn. And so there are no Allen relationships possible for temporal updates that are not also possible for temporal deletes.

[Starts]. If a temporal delete transaction's effective time begins on the same clock tick as that of an episode, but ends earlier than the episode ends, it will withdraw all versions wholly or partially included within its timespan. If one version is partially within the timespan, the temporal delete will replace the part of that withdrawn version not within its timespan. In either case, the result is a {shorten backwards} transformation on that episode.

[Starts$^{-1}$]. If a temporal delete transaction's effective time begins on the same clock tick as that of an episode, but ends after the episode ends, the transaction will {erase} the episode; and, in addition, it will withdraw all other versions, for the same object, that are wholly or partially included within its timespan.

Those other versions will exist within one or more later episodes. On any of those episodes wholly included within the transaction's timespan, there will be an {erase} transformation on them, as well. The last episode within the transaction's timespan may be wholly or partially included within that timespan. If it is wholly contained, there will be an {erase} transformation on it. Otherwise, there will be a {shorten forwards} transformation. If the end of the transaction's timespan does not fall on a version effective time boundary, then the temporal delete will replace the part of that withdrawn version that is not within its timespan.

[Finishes]. If a temporal delete transaction's effective time ends on the same clock tick as that of an episode, but begins after that episode begins, it will withdraw all versions wholly or partially included within its timespan. If one version is partially within the timespan, the temporal delete will replace the part of that withdrawn version not within its timespan. In either case, the result is a {shorten forwards} transformation on that episode.

[Finishes$^{-1}$]. If a temporal delete transaction's effective time ends on the same clock tick as that of an episode, but begins before that episode begins, it will {erase} the episode; and, in addition, it will withdraw all other versions, for the same object, that are wholly or partially included within its timespan.

Those other versions will exist within one or more earlier episodes. On any of those episodes wholly included within the transaction's timespan, there will be an {erase} transformation on them, as well. The earliest episode within the transaction's timespan may be wholly or partially included within that timespan. If it is wholly contained, there will be an {erase} transformation on it. Otherwise, there will be a {shorten backwards} transformation. If the start of the transaction's timespan does not fall on a version effective time boundary, then the temporal delete will replace the part of that withdrawn version that is not within its timespan.

[During]. If a temporal delete transaction's effective time begins after that of an episode, and ends before that episode ends, then the transaction will withdraw all versions wholly or partially included within its timespan. At most two versions can be partially included in that timespan, those being the ones at the begin and/or end of the timespan. This delete transaction carries out a {split} transformation on the episode in question.

[During$^{-1}$]. If a temporal delete transaction's effective time begins before that of an episode, and ends after that episode ends, then the transaction will {erase} the one or more episodes wholly included within its timespan. In addition, as well as any number of additional episodes wholly included within the transaction's timespan, there may be one or two episodes only partially included within the transaction's timespan. If there is an earlier but partially included episode, the delete transaction will do a {shorten backwards} transformation on it. If there is a later but partially included episode, the delete transaction will result in a {shorten forwards} transformation. In either case, the partially included episode may or may not have a partially included version; in other words, the transaction's timespan may or may not align on version boundaries. In either case, a partially included version is {split}, and the part outside the transaction's timespan is replaced.

[*Equals*]. If a temporal transaction's effective time [*equals*] that of one episode of the same object already in the target table, a temporal delete will {erase} that episode.

[Overlaps]. If a temporal delete transaction's effective time [overlaps] that of an episode, then either it begins after the episode begins and before it ends, and ends after the episode ends; or else it begins before the episode begins and ends after the episode begins but before it ends. In either case, the transaction will withdraw all versions wholly or partially included within the timespan of the transaction. At most one version can be partially included. If there is such a version, a temporal delete will replace the part of the partially included version that is outside the timespan of the transaction. The result is to either {shorten the episode backwards} or {shorten it forwards}, depending on whether the episode began before or after the transaction's timespan.

We have now demonstrated that every Allen relationship between a transaction and a target is valid for an insert, an update or a delete. So although we have not worked through a separate example for each Allen relationship, we can now be confident that there are no temporal precedence and succession relationships between a transaction's time period and that of a target episode that Asserted Versioning temporal transactions cannot handle.

## A Temporal Extent Transformation Completeness Check

A second completeness check uses the taxonomy of Asserted Versioning temporal extent transformations presented in Chapter 9. After presenting that taxonomy, we argued there that the taxonomy is mutually exclusive and demonstrably complete. Its completeness was demonstrated by showing that all possible single-transformation topological transformations of two line segments are represented in the taxonomy.

Our second completeness check will use this taxonomy to review all extent-altering state transformations, and be sure that all of them can be brought about by valid temporal transactions.

This completeness check has proven to be easier to complete than we had originally anticipated. As indicated in Figure 10.21, all the transformations on the left-hand side of the diagram can be brought about by means of a temporal insert transaction. Indeed, each of those transformations was explicitly mentioned in the previous section. All the transformations on the right-hand

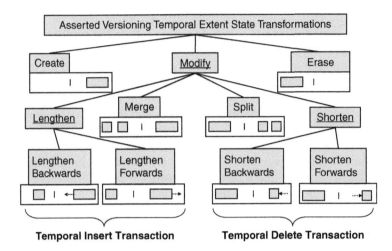

**Figure 10.21** A Taxonomy of Asserted Versioning Temporal Extent Transformations.

side of the diagram can be brought about by means of a temporal delete transaction. Again, each of those transformations was explicitly mentioned in the previous section.

## Glossary References

Glossary entries whose definitions form strong inter-dependencies are grouped together in the following list. The same glossary entries may be grouped together in different ways at the end of different chapters, each grouping reflecting the semantic perspective of each chapter. There will usually be several other, and often many other, glossary entries that are not included in the list, and we recommend that the Glossary be consulted whenever an unfamiliar term is encountered.

We note, in particular, that none of the nodes in the two taxonomies referenced in this chapter are included in this list. In general, we leave taxonomy nodes out of these lists since they are long enough without them.

12/31/9999
clock tick
Now()
until further notice
Allen relationships

adjacent
include
contiguous

asserted version table
Asserted Versioning Framework (AVF)
assertion begin date
assertion end date
assertion time

business data

effective begin date
effective end date
effective time

episode
episode begin date
open episode
lock

object
object identifier
oid

occupied
represented

past assertion

physical transaction
temporal transaction
temporal parameter
temporal insert transaction
temporal update transaction
temporal delete transaction
transaction timespan

proactive transaction
retroactive transaction

replace
supercede
withdraw

temporal entity integrity (TEI)
temporal referential integrity (TRI)

temporal extent state transformation

version

# TEMPORAL TRANSACTIONS ON MULTIPLE TABLES

In the previous two chapters, we discussed temporal transactions and the temporal entity integrity constraint to which they must conform. We saw that, just as conventional entity integrity applies to the non-temporal representations of objects by those managed objects we call rows, temporal entity integrity (TEI) applies to the temporal representations of objects by those managed objects we call episodes and versions. TEI is the constraint that, within shared assertion time, no two versions of the same object may occupy the same effective time clock tick, and that no two episodes of the same object may do so either. In short, it is the constraint that no two *representations* of the same object may occupy the same effective time clock ticks.

In this chapter, we discuss temporal transactions and the temporal referential integrity constraint to which they must conform. Conventional referential integrity (RI), at the level of types rather than instances, is a relationship between two relational tables (not necessarily distinct). At the level of instances, it is a relationship between two rows of relational tables (which are, however, necessarily distinct).

An RI relationship between a child row and a parent row is based on an *existence dependency* between the objects they represent. In our examples, policies are objects which are existence-dependent on clients, who are also objects. Reflecting that fact, and precisely because of it, rows in Policy tables are referentially dependent on rows in Client tables.

Existence dependency, of course, does not have to be a cause-and-effect dependency between two physical objects, although that is one kind of existence dependency. For example, as we just pointed out, there is an existence dependency of policies on clients; yet neither policies nor clients are physical objects. A policy is a contract, an agreement recognized in civil law. A client is a party to such a contract. The existence dependency of a policy on a client is thus a dependency of one legal object on another, a dependency defined in the world of law, not in the world of physics.

In this chapter, we will see how *temporal referential integrity (TRI)* is referential integrity applied to the temporalized representations of objects by two types of managed objects—episodes and versions. A TRI relationship between a child managed object and a parent managed object is based on an existence dependency between the objects which those managed objects represent.

In either an RI or a TRI relationship between a managed object representing a policy and one representing a client, a client may exist without a related policy, but a policy cannot exist without a related client.[1] These "mays" and "cannots", as far as RI is concerned, are enforced on the managed objects which are rows, by the DBMS, in accordance with rules declared to it in DDL statements as constraints. These "mays" and "cannots", as far as TRI is concerned, are enforced on the managed objects which are versions and episodes, by the AVF, in accordance with rules declared to it as entries in metadata tables.

---

[1] Throughout this book, we have been referring to the individuals who own policies as "clients". But in fact, the health insurance industry refers to these individuals as "members", i.e. members of insurance plans. We made the terminological change because the word "member", used in this way, is unfamiliar outside the health insurance industry.

# Temporal Managed Objects and Temporal Referential Integrity

Temporal referential integrity relates a child *version* to a parent *episode*. It is important to understand why this is so, to understand why TRI is not a relationship between episodes and other episodes, or between versions and other versions.

## Child Managed Objects

First of all, the child managed object in a TRI relationship cannot be an episode. The reason is that within the same episode, the owning parent object can change over time. For example, as policy episodes P861-A and P861-C in Figure 11.1 illustrate, different versions within the same episode can have different temporal foreign keys (TFKs), which means that they can designate different parent objects. Of course, since those

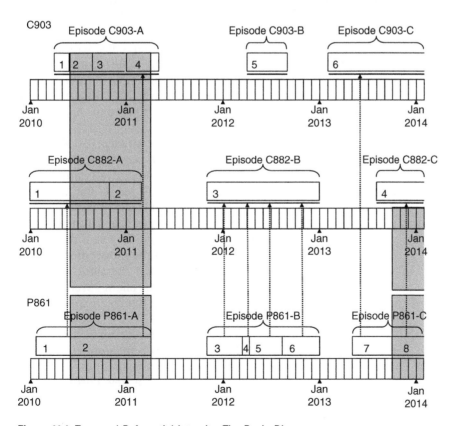

**Figure 11.1** Temporal Referential Integrity: The Basic Diagram.

versions are versions of the same child object, temporal entity integrity constraints insure that they represent those different parent objects at different points in effective time. If the child managed object in the TRI relationship were an entire policy episode, then every time a policy changed the client it is related to, we would need to create a new episode of the policy.

But by definition, there is always at least one clock tick between versions of the same object that belong to different episodes. So if a change in a TFK value always resulted in a new episode, then the first two versions of P861 would become two episodes, but episodes between which there is no temporal gap. And that is a contradiction.

## Parent Managed Objects

On the other side of the relationship, the parent managed object in a TRI relationship must be an episode and not a version. If it were a version, then when that version in the parent episode was updated, the TRI relationship to that version would no longer be valid. The reason is that an update always ends the assertion time period of the version it supercedes, withdrawing that original version into past assertion time. Consequently, since temporal integrity constraints apply only among objects that share assertion time, the referenced version would no longer exist in the child's still-current assertion timespan, and so the reference to it would become invalid.

Besides being *mechanically* incorrect, as we have just shown, it would also be *semantically* incorrect to use versions as the parent managed objects in temporal referential integrity relationships. To see why, let's consider non-temporal referential integrity, "regular RI". If our two tables were non-temporal tables rather than asserted version tables, then clearly changes that happen to the parent client would have no effect on that RI relationship. For example, a client could change her name without affecting the fact that she owns policy P861. Therefore, if the same semantic change—the same name change for the same client—were applied to a temporal representation of that client, the result should have no effect on that TRI relationship.

So the semantics are the same whether the objects involved are represented in conventional tables or in asserted version tables. But in asserted version tables, those changes will withdraw the current assertion, replace it with a new current assertion that has the same business data but an effective end date of Now(), and then supercede it with another new current assertion that has the updated business data and an effective begin date of Now().[2] So if it were those versions that were the parents in a TRI relationship, this process would continually invalidate temporal foreign keys (TFKs) by ending the assertion time of the versions they refer to.

## Temporal Referential Integrity: The Basic Diagram

Figure 11.1 is the basic diagram we will use in our discussion of temporal referential integrity. It consists of timelines for three objects. Besides policy P861, there is a timeline for client C882 and for client C903. The dotted-line vertical arrows represent temporal foreign key (TFK) relationships from a child version to a parent episode. Parent episodes are underlined to emphasize that those vertical arrows are not pointing to specific versions, but rather to entire episodes.

The shaded rectangle on the left covers the effective time period of version 2 of episode P861-A, which extends from July 2010 to May 2011. It graphically illustrates that the effective time period of this version is wholly included in the effective time period of an episode of its parent object, client C903, that episode being C903-A. It also graphically shows why a TRI relationship is between a child version and a parent episode. No single version of C903-A could be a TRI parent to P861-A(2), because no single version of C903-A covers [Jul 2010 – May 2011], the effective time period for P861-A(2).[3]

The shaded rectangle on the right covers [Oct 2013 – 12/31/9999]. This is the effective time period of P861-C(8). In this case, a single parent version effective time includes (i.e. [fills⁻¹]) that child version, but that is merely happenstance. For example, suppose that we wanted to change client C882's name from "Smith" to "Jones", effective May 2014. This would make the effective time period of C882-C(4) [Sep 2013 – May 2014]. But if that happens, there would be no version of C882-C that could

---

[2]This, of course, is a description of a *basic* temporal update transaction. But a similar description of the mechanics of non-basic temporal updates leads to the same conclusion, that TFKs do not point to specific versions in a parent asserted version table.

[3]We use the notation X-{A, B, . . . . . Z} to denote an episode of an object. Thus, C882-B denotes episode B of client C882. We use the notation E(n) to denote a version of an episode. Thus, P861-A(2) denotes version 2 of policy P861, included within episode A. Note, however, that it only *happens* to denote the second version of that episode. For example, P861-C(8) denotes version 8 of that policy, but that version is the second version of that episode, not the eighth one.

be a TRI parent to P861-C(8). The new C882-C(5) goes into effect on May 2014, so its effective time period does not cover the earlier clock ticks in P861-C(8). And C882-C(4) ends its effectivity on May 2014, so its effective time period does not cover the ongoing effectivity of P861-C(8), whose effective time period is, once again, [Oct 2013 – 12/31/9999].

As in the previous chapter, we assume for now that all relationships exist within current assertion time, and that all temporal transactions specify an assertion time of [Now() – 12/31/9999]. We also assume that delete transactions against clients cascade down to the policies that they own, in accordance with the metadata declaration made in the Temporal Foreign Key metadata table, shown in Figure 8.4.

We can read the somewhat schizophrenic history of policy P861 from this diagram.[4] Think of a vertical line running from the top to the bottom of the diagram, and initially positioned at January 2010. As time passes, this line moves to the right. The history of P861 is recorded in the begin and end dates of its versions. So as that line reaches each such date, there is a change in the state of P861.

As Figure 11.1 shows, the policy was originally owned by client C882. The only episode of C882 whose effective time period included that of P861, at the time P861-A(1) was created, was C882-A. And so that became the episode of client C882 that the policy pointed to.

The next thing that happened was that, on July 2010, P861 changed hands. At that time, ownership was transferred to client C903. The only episode of C903 that existed at that time was C903-A, and so that became the parent episode to P861, beginning on that date. This change of ownership is recorded in version 2 of P861-A. Note that C903-A became effective on April 2010, two months after P861-A did. If episodes were the child managed objects in TRI relationships, then this relationship would be invalid. But they are not. C882-A is the parent to P861-A(1). C903-A is the parent to P861-A(2).

The third event in the life of P861 was a delete cascade issued against client C903. As of May 2011, C903 was no longer a client. Because C903 owned policy P861 at that point in time, the policy's existence was terminated on that same date, May 2011.

---

[4]Schizophrenic in that the policy can't make up its mind which client it belongs to. As unlikely as such a policy history might be, in the real world, it will have to serve as an example of how TRI relationships are managed.

The next event in the life of this policy occurred in November 2011. It took place as part of the same event in which client C882 was reinstated. On that date, a second episode of client C882 began, and a second episode of policy P861 began also, and was designated as a policy owned by C882. After that, three changes occurred to the policy between November 2011 and January 2013, but none of them changed the ownership of the policy.

The fifth event in the life of the policy was that client C882 asked to terminate her relationship with our company as of January 2013. Since she owned P861 at that time, and would still own it on that termination date, the policy was terminated along with the client.

Four months later, on May 2013, policy P861 was reinstated and assigned to client C902. So a third episode of the policy was created, P861-C. It was an open-ended episode, one with an effective end date of 12/31/9999, and so the only owner that could be assigned to it would be one with an open-ended episode that began on or before May 2013. Fortunately, client C903 had such an episode, having been reinstated, after a 5-month absence, with episode C903-C.

With this information as part of our production data, we know, at any point in the history of policy P861, who its owner was and when and for how long she had been the owner. For any claims submitted for medical services provided to either C903 or C882, no matter how delayed the filing of those claims may have been, we know exactly when each client was covered by that policy and exactly when she was not covered by it—an essential piece of information needed to pay claims correctly.

And we don't have to go digging in archival storage, or historical data warehouses, for that information—which, in a high transaction volume claims processing system, is a very good thing. That historical data exists in the same table as data about current policies and their current owners. The service date on the claim selects the correct version of the policy, and that version points to its owner. If its owner is not the person for whom the claim is submitted, the claim is rejected.

# Foreign Keys and Temporal Foreign Keys

Before proceeding, let's remind ourselves of the difference between (i) foreign keys (FKs), the relationships they implement and the constraints they impose, and (ii) temporal foreign keys (TFKs), the relationships they implement and the constraints they impose.

A foreign key is a column in a relational table whose job is to relate rows to other rows.[5] If the foreign key column is declared to the DBMS to be nullable, then any row in that table may or may not contain a value in its instance of that column. But if it does contain a value, that value must match the value of the primary key of a row in the table declared as the target table for that foreign key. For non-nullable foreign keys, of course, *every* row in the source table must contain a valid value in its foreign key column.

In addition, once the FK relationship is declared to the DBMS, the DBMS is able to guarantee that the two managed objects—the child row and the parent row—accurately reflect the existence dependency between the objects they represent. It does so by enforcing the constraint expressed in the declaration, the constraint that if the child row's FK points to a parent row, that parent row must have existed in its table at the time the child row was added to its table, and must continue to exist in the parent table for as long as the child row exists in its table and continues to point to that same parent.

This is a somewhat elaborate way of describing something that most of us already understand quite well, and that few of us may think is worth describing quite so carefully—that foreign keys relate child rows to parent rows and that, in doing so, they reflect a relationship that exists in the real world. We have gone to this length in order to be very clear about both the semantics and the mechanics of foreign keys—semantics described in our talk about objects, and mechanics in our talk about managed objects—and to place the descriptions at a level of generality where the semantics and mechanics of TFKs can be seen as analogous to those of the more familiar FKs. So if we use an "X/Y" notation in which the "X" term is part of the referential integrity description and the "Y" term is part of the temporal referential integrity description, we have a description which makes it clear that temporal referential integrity really is temporalized referential integrity, that TRI is RI as it applies to temporal data. That description is given in the following paragraph.

Once the FK/TFK relationship is declared to the DBMS/AVF, the DBMS/AVF is able to guarantee that the two managed objects—the child row/version and the parent row/episode— accurately reflect the existence dependency between the objects they represent. Each does so by enforcing the constraint expressed in the declaration, the constraint that if the FK/TFK in the child row/version points to a parent row/episode, that parent

---

[5]We will assume that all primary and foreign keys consist of single columns, since the complications that arise with multi-column keys are irrelevant to this discussion.

row/episode must have existed in its table/be currently asserted and currently effective at the time the child row/version was added to its table, and must continue to exist/be currently asserted and currently effective in the parent table for as long as the child row/version exists/is currently asserted and currently effective in its table and continues to point to that same parent.

## TFKs: A Data Part and a Function Part

As a data element, a TFK is a column in an asserted version table whose job is to relate child managed objects to parent managed objects. Of course, the same may be said of FKs. The difference is that the parent managed object of a FK is a non-temporal row, while the parent managed object of a TFK is a group of possibly many rows. A TRI child table is an asserted version table that contains a TFK. A TRI parent table is an asserted version table referenced by a TFK. The FK reference is a data value, and is unambiguous; but the TFK reference, as a data value, is not unambiguous.

So as a data element, all a TFK can do is designate the object on which the object represented by its own row is existence dependent. There may be any number of versions representing that object in the parent table, and those versions may be grouped into any number of episodes scattered along the assertion and effective time timelines. So *as a data value*, a TFK reference is incomplete.

For example, a TFK data value in a Policy table references all the episodes in a Client table which represent the client on which that policy is existence dependent, that being the client whose *oid* matches the data value in the TFK. To complete the reference, we need to identify, from among those episodes, the one episode which was in effect when the policy version went into effect, and will remain in effect as long as that policy version remains in effect.

What is needed to complete the reference is a function. We will name this function $f$TRI. It has the following syntax:

```
fTRI(PTN, TFK, [eff-beg-dt – eff-end-dt])
```

*PTN* is the name of the parent table which this TFK points to. Given the TFK and effective time period of a version in a TRI child table, the AVF searches the parent table for an episode whose versions have that *oid* as part of their primary key, and whose effective time period fully includes the effective time period designated by the function. If there is such an episode, it is the TRI parent episode of that version, and the $f$TRI function evaluates to *True*. If there is no such episode, then the function evaluates to *False*, and that version will never be added to the database because if it were, it would violate TRI.

If the AVF finds such an episode, in carrying out this function, it does not have to check further to insure that there is only one such episode. If there were more than one, then those episodes would be in TEI conflict across all their clock ticks which [intersect]. The AVF does not allow TEI violations to occur, so if there is a TRI parent episode for the TFK reference, there is only one of them.

For example, the *oid* value in the TFK of P861-A(2) picks out client C903. Before the AVF added that version to the database, it used the *f*TRI function to determine whether or not it was referentially valid.[6] That TRI validation check would look something like this:

```
IF ISTRUE(fTRI(Client, C903, [Jul10 - 9999])) THEN
        {add the version}

ELSE
        {notify the calling program of a TRI error}

ENDIF
```

Together, the explicit and implicit parts of the TFK, its data element part and its function part, complete an unambiguous reference from a TFK to the one episode which satisfies the TRI constraint on the relationship from that version to that episode.

Note that this description of a TFK is a semantic description, not an implementation-level description. The *f*TRI function is one component of a TFK. Its representation here is obviously not source code that could be compiled or interpreted. But however it is expressed, whether in the AVF or in some other framework based on these concepts, it is a function; and without it, the columns of data we call TFKs are not TFKs. Those columns of data are simply those components of TFKs which can be expressed as data.

## Temporal Transactions and Associative Tables

In a non-temporal database, an associative table, often informally referred to as an *xref* table, implements a many-to-many relationship between two other tables. Each of those other tables

---

[6]This is a logical description of what the AVF does. It does not imply that the AVF code makes a single function call to carry out its TRI checks, let alone that it calls a function named *f*TRI.

is a parent to the xref table, which is thus RI dependent on both of them.

Each row in the xref table has two FKs, one to a parent row in one table and one to a parent row in another table (or, possibly, in the same table). As we already know, this dual RI dependency means that a row cannot be inserted into the xref table unless both its parent rows already exist in the database, and neither parent row can be deleted as long as that xref row remains in the database.

## TRI with Multiple TFKs

If a child version has two or more TFKs, the effective timespan of an episode of each of the objects which those TFKs reference must fully include the effective timespan of the version. If either of them did not, that would be a TRI violation.

So consider an associative asserted version table, whose versions each contain two TFKs. What of the Allen relationships between the two parent episodes related by any version in this table? Are there any constraints on those parent episodes?

In fact, there are. Those two effective timespans must [intersect]. If they did not [intersect], then there would be no clock tick when both were in effect, and so no clock tick in which an xref row, TRI dependent on both parents, could exist.

Consider an example in which we have a customer episode C773-B with an effective timespan from March 2013 until further notice, which we will write as C773-B[Mar 2013 – 12/31/9999], and also a salesperson episode S217-D[Sep 2013 – Dec 2013]. What can we say of the effective timespan of a version in an asserted version associative table relating that customer episode to that salesperson episode?[7]

First, that associative table version cannot have an effective begin date prior to September 2013 because that would make the start of its effective time period earlier than the start of S217-D. By the same token, that version cannot have an effective end date after December 2013 because that would make the end of its effective time period later than the end of S217-D.

So knowing what we do of the two parent episodes, what is the maximum effective timespan that would be valid for the

---

[7]As a complete aside, we note that the in-line notations developed in Chapter 6 and elsewhere in this book, for example the S217-D[Sep 2013 – Dec 2013] notation developed in this chapter, might be the basis for a degree of automated semantic interoperability between structured and semi-structured representations of temporal data.

child version? It is the later of the two parents' begin dates, and the earlier of their end dates. This gives a maximum effective timespan of the xref table child version of [Sep 2013 – Dec 2013], which happens to be the effective timespan of its parent salesperson episode. This is because the salesperson episode occurs [during] the customer episode.

Next, let's consider an example that does not involve 12/31/9999. Suppose that the effective timespans of our parent episodes are like this: C773-B[Mar 2013 – Jun 2013] and S217-D [Sep 2013 – Dec 2013]. Using our earlier/later rule, the maximum effective timespan of the xref version happens to be the same as it was in the previous case: [Sep 2013 – Dec 2013].

But this isn't the end of the story. In our first example, the two parent episodes [intersected], and the timespan during which they intersected was that widest timespan possible for the child version. But in this second example, the parent episodes do not [intersect]. C773-B ceases being in effect three months before S217-D begins to be in effect.

An associative table version cannot have two non-intersecting TRI parents because there would then be no effective time clock ticks shared by the parents, and therefore no clock ticks in which both TRI relationships are satisfied.

In summary: the effective timespan of an xref row must be fully included in the effective timespans of both of its parent episodes. It follows that if there are no effective time clock ticks which those parent episodes have in common, no version which is TRI dependent on both of them can exist in the database. It also follows that if there are one or more clock ticks which those two parent episodes do have in common, the widest extent of the effective time period of the TRI dependent version is precisely that set of [intersecting] clock ticks.

## Temporal Delete Options

The three options for standard delete transactions are (i) RESTRICT, (ii) SET NULL, and (iii) CASCADE. As applied to temporal delete transactions, the RESTRICT option is straightforward. For example, suppose there is a RESTRICT option on deletes applied to the Client table, and suppose that the database is populated as shown in Figure 11.1. Episode C903-B could be deleted in its entirety because no policies are dependent on it. Episode C882-A could be deleted from the single clock tick January 2010, or from July 2010 through April 2011 because the resulting episode, removed from any of those months, will still satisfy the TRI relationship from P861-A(1). But an attempt to remove client C903 from January 2011, for example, would be restricted because a dependent child—P861-A(2)—is TRI dependent on it during that month.

As for the SET NULL option, its temporal form is not as straightforward. It means that if a temporal delete would violate a TRI constraint, and the SET NULL option is in effect for that table, then the TFK in the child row that would otherwise be orphaned will be set to NULL. In the last example just mentioned, if the delete option was SET NULL, episode C903-A would be split into two episodes by removing it from January 2011. P-861A(2) would be split into three versions, with effective time periods of [Jul 2010 – Jan 2011], [Jan 2011 – Feb 2011] and [Feb 2011 – May 2011]. The TFK in the middle of the three versions would then be set to NULL.

But the temporal form of the CASCADE option is both mechanically and semantically even more complex than this. As for its semantics, a temporal delete cascade will attempt to remove both the parent object, and all its dependent children, from the clock ticks specified in the transaction. For example, if we specified a temporal delete cascade on client C882 for the effective time period [Jul 2012 – Jan 2013], we would find that episode P861-B would be subject to a {shorten backwards} transformation for those six clock ticks. This would remove P861-B(6) from current assertion time, and would also shorten P861-B(5) by one clock tick. But this should cause no concern. We already understand the mechanics of temporal extent state transformations.

# Temporal Referential Integrity Applied to Temporal Transactions

## A Temporal Insert Transaction

Let's assume that the Client and Policy tables are as shown in Figure 11.1, and let's begin by considering a temporal insert of P861 which has a TFK of C903. In order to satisfy TRI constraints, every clock tick in the effective time period specified on the transaction must already be occupied by C903. So there are only a limited number of effective time spans that can validly be specified by a temporal insert transaction, in this situation. They are:

(i) The three months of [Feb 2013 – May 2013], or the two months of [Mar 2013 – May 2013] or the month of [Apr 2013 – May 2013], each of which will {lengthen P861-C backwards}.

**(ii)** The two months of [Feb 2013 – Apr 2013], which will create a new episode between P861-B and P861-C.

Let's be sure we understand why these are the only possibilities. To begin with, the existing episodes of C903, the parent object, cover the effective time clock ticks [Apr 2010 – May 2011], [Apr 2012 – Sep 2012] and [Feb 2013 – 12/31/9999]. So if all the clock ticks in a new version of P861 fall anywhere within any one of those three ranges, that version will satisfy TRI; and otherwise, it won't.

However, this is a temporal insert transaction, and therefore none of the clock ticks in the new version being created can already be occupied by another version of P861. This is the TEI constraint applied to temporal insert transactions. This rules out [Feb 2010 – May 2011], [Nov 2011 – Jan 2013] and [May 2013 – 12/31/9999]. So, eliminating these clock ticks that are already occupied by P861 from the clock ticks occupied by C903, we are left with only the three clock ticks of February, March and April 2013.

## A Temporal Update Transaction

By definition, temporal updates neither add a representation of an object to a clock tick nor remove a representation of an object from a clock tick. But they can still cause temporal referential constraints to be violated. They can do so by changing the TFK value in one or more clock ticks.

For example, suppose a temporal update is submitted which specifies that in November and December of 2012, P861's owning client should be C903. The transaction looks like this:

```
UPDATE Policy [P861, C903,, ] Nov 2012, Jan 2013
```

The problem is that there is no representation of C903 in either of those two clock ticks. The function $f$TRI(Client, C903, [Nov12 – Jan13]) will evaluate to *False*. Therefore, the AVF will restrict this transaction because of TRI constraints. This is the equivalent of working with a non-temporal table, and trying to change a FK value to point to a parent row that does not, at that time, exist.

## A Temporal Delete Transaction

A temporal delete withdraws its target object from one or more effective time clock ticks. In the process, it may {erase} an entire episode from current assertion time, or {split} an episode in two, or {shorten} an episode either forwards or backwards, or do several of these things to one or more episodes with one and the same transaction.

With a conventional referential integrity relationship, a parent row cannot be deleted as long as any child row exists with a foreign key pointing to it. So with a temporal referential integrity relationship, a parent managed object cannot be withdrawn from any clock ticks as long as any of those clock ticks are occupied by a child managed object. Either the delete will be restricted, the referencing TFKs will be set to NULL, or the delete will cascade to the dependent children and also remove them from those same clock ticks.

So let's assume that the RESTRICT option is being used, and let's consider the first episode of client C903, episode C903-A. A temporal delete against C903 will withdraw the representation of C903 from one or more effective time clock ticks. But C903 cannot be withdrawn from the effective time period [Jul 2010 – May 2011], because P861-A(2), with its TFK of C903, is TRI dependent on it. On the other hand, C903-A may be {shortened forwards} by means of a delete transaction which withdraws it from any or all of the three clock ticks April, May or June 2010, because during those three clock ticks, it has no dependent policies.

To generalize: any temporal delete transactions, using the RESTRICT option, can be processed against C903 without violating temporal referential integrity as long as they do not withdraw it from any clock ticks which are occupied by any version that has a TFK of C903.

To take just one more example, and continuing to assume that the RESTRICT option is in effect, let's consider C882-C. It may be removed from either or both of the clock ticks August 2013 and September 2013, by either {splitting} it or {shortening it forwards}. But P861-C(8) occupies the effective time period [Oct 2013 – 12/31/9999], and is TRI dependent on client C882, specifically on the single-version episode C882-C. Therefore, the object C882 cannot be removed from those clock ticks, and therefore the only clock ticks that C882-C episode can be withdrawn from are August 2013 and September 2013.

### A Temporal Delete Cascade

We will conclude this chapter with a row-level analysis of a temporal delete cascade to client C903, removing the representation of that client from the effective time period [Oct 2010 – Mar 2011]. This temporal delete against C903 will withdraw the representation of P861 from those five months. The result, as we will see, will be to {split} episode C903-A into two episodes, and also to {split} episode P861-A into two episodes.

We begin with the delete cascade transaction itself. Let's assume that it is taking place on November 2013. The transaction looks like this:

```
DELETE FROM Client [C903,, ] Oct2010, Mar2011
```

The temporal foreign key metadata table (Figure 8.4) directs the AVF to apply the delete cascade option to this temporal transaction. After the transaction successfully completes, the database will no longer assert that client C903 is in effect in the time period [Oct 2010 – Mar 2011]. Also, the database will no longer assert that there are any policies owned by this client that are in effect during those same five months.

Figure 11.2 shows the current state of the Client and Policy tables, as represented in Figure 11.1. However, we have removed the history of how the tables reached those states. In other words, in Figure 11.2 we do not show the withdrawn assertions that were part of the history leading up to that state of the database. Instead, we show only the currently asserted versions of our two clients and one policy.

The first step is to apply the delete transaction to its target, client C903. Within the target timespan of [Oct 2010 – Mar 2011],

**Client Table**

| Row # | oid | eff-beg | eff-end | asr-beg | asr-end | epis-beg | client-nbr | client-nm | row-crt |
|---|---|---|---|---|---|---|---|---|---|
| 1 | C903 | Apr10 | Jun10 | Apr10 | 9999 | Apr10 | X457 | Jones | Apr10 |
| 2 | C903 | Jun10 | Sep10 | Jun10 | 9999 | Apr10 | X457 | Roberts | Jun10 |
| 3 | C903 | Sep10 | Jan11 | Sep10 | 9999 | Apr10 | X457 | Colbert | Sep10 |
| 4 | C903 | Jan11 | May11 | Jan11 | 9999 | Apr10 | D834 | Powers | Jan11 |
| 5 | C903 | Apr12 | Sep12 | Apr12 | 9999 | Apr12 | D834 | Smith | Apr12 |
| 6 | C903 | Feb13 | 9999 | Feb13 | 9999 | Feb13 | D834 | Williams | Feb13 |
| 7 | C882 | Jan10 | Nov10 | Jan10 | 9999 | Jan10 | Z119 | Cooper | Jan10 |
| 8 | C882 | Nov10 | Mar11 | Nov10 | 9999 | Jan10 | Z119 | Matthews | Nov10 |
| 9 | C882 | Nov12 | Jan13 | Nov12 | 9999 | Nov12 | Z119 | Smith | Nov12 |
| 10 | C882 | Aug13 | 9999 | Aug13 | 9999 | Aug13 | Z119 | Nelson | Aug12 |

**Policy Table**

| Row # | oid | eff-beg | eff-end | asr-beg | asr-end | epis-beg | client | type | copay | row-crt |
|---|---|---|---|---|---|---|---|---|---|---|
| 1 | P861 | Feb10 | Jul10 | Feb10 | 9999 | Feb10 | C882 | PPO | $20 | Feb10 |
| 2 | P861 | Jul10 | May11 | Jul10 | 9999 | Feb10 | C903 | PPO | $20 | Jul10 |
| 3 | P861 | Nov11 | Mar12 | Nov11 | 9999 | Nov11 | C882 | HMO | $30 | Nov11 |
| 4 | P861 | Mar12 | Apr12 | Nov11 | 9999 | Nov11 | C882 | POS | $40 | Mar12 |
| 5 | P861 | Apr12 | Aug12 | Apr12 | 9999 | Nov11 | C882 | POS | $50 | Apr12 |
| 6 | P861 | Aug12 | Jan13 | Aug12 | 9999 | Nov11 | C882 | PPO | $40 | Aug12 |
| 7 | P861 | May13 | Oct13 | Mag13 | 9999 | May13 | C903 | PPO | $40 | May13 |
| 8 | P861 | Oct13 | 9999 | Oct13 | 9999 | May13 | C882 | PPO | $40 | Oct13 |

**Figure 11.2** A Temporal Delete Cascade: Before the Transaction.

there are two currently asserted versions of C903. They are C903 (r3 & r4).[8] To remove the representation of C903(r3) from this timespan, we need to {shorten it backwards}, changing its effective end date from January 2011 to October 2010. To remove the representation of C903(r4) from this timespan, we need to {shorten it forwards}, changing its effective begin date from January 2011 to March 2011. In the process, this will {split} episode C903-A into two episodes.

The result of applying this temporal delete to the Client table is shown in the upper table in Figure 11.3. C903(r3 & r4) have been withdrawn into past assertion time. They are now part of the assertion history of this table, a record of what we used to assert is true, but no longer do. In their place are C903(r11 & r12). Everything, in current assertion time, is as it was except that a "hole" has been created in C903's effective time. C903 is no longer asserted to be a client of ours from October 2010 to March 2011.

**Client Table**

| Row # | oid | eff-beg | eff-end | asr-beg | asr-end | epis-beg | client-nbr | client-nm | row-crt |
|---|---|---|---|---|---|---|---|---|---|
| 1 | C903 | Apr10 | Jun10 | Apr10 | 9999 | Apr10 | X457 | Jones | Apr10 |
| 2 | C903 | Jun10 | Sep10 | Jun10 | 9999 | Apr10 | X457 | Roberts | Jun10 |
| <3> | C903 | Sep10 | Jan11 | Sep10 | Nov13 | Apr10 | X457 | Colbert | Sep10 |
| <4> | C903 | Jan11 | May11 | Jan11 | Nov13 | Apr10 | D834 | Powers | Jan11 |
| 5 | C903 | Apr12 | Sep12 | Apr12 | 9999 | Apr12 | D834 | Smith | Apr12 |
| 6 | C903 | Feb13 | 9999 | Feb13 | 9999 | Feb13 | D834 | Williams | Feb13 |
| 7 | C882 | Jan10 | Nov10 | Jan10 | 9999 | Jan10 | Z119 | Cooper | Jan10 |
| 8 | C882 | Nov10 | Mar11 | Nov10 | 9999 | Jan10 | Z119 | Matthews | Nov10 |
| 9 | C882 | Nov12 | Jan13 | Nov12 | 9999 | Nov12 | Z119 | Smith | Nov12 |
| 10 | C882 | Aug13 | 9999 | Aug13 | 9999 | Aug13 | Z119 | Nelson | Aug13 |
| <11> | C903 | Sep10 | Oct10 | Nov13 | 9999 | Apr10 | X457 | Colbert | Nov13 |
| <12> | C903 | Mar11 | May11 | Nov13 | 9999 | Mar11 | D834 | Powers | Nov13 |

**Policy Table**

| Row # | oid | eff-beg | eff-end | asr-beg | asr-end | epis-beg | *client* | type | copay | row-crt |
|---|---|---|---|---|---|---|---|---|---|---|
| 1 | P861 | Feb10 | Jul10 | Feb10 | 9999 | Feb10 | C882 | PPO | $20 | Feb10 |
| <2> | P861 | Jul10 | May11 | Jul10 | Nov13 | Feb10 | C903 | PPO | $20 | Jul10 |
| 3 | P861 | Nov11 | Mar12 | Nov11 | 9999 | Nov11 | C882 | HMO | $30 | Nov11 |
| 4 | P861 | Mar12 | Apr12 | Nov11 | 9999 | Nov11 | C882 | POS | $40 | Mar12 |
| 5 | P861 | Apr12 | Aug12 | Apr12 | 9999 | Nov11 | C882 | POS | $50 | Apr12 |
| 6 | P861 | Aug12 | Jan13 | Aug12 | 9999 | Nov11 | C882 | PPO | $40 | Aug12 |
| 7 | P861 | May13 | Oct13 | May13 | 9999 | May13 | C903 | PPO | $40 | May13 |
| 8 | P861 | Oct13 | 9999 | Oct13 | 9999 | May13 | C882 | PPO | $40 | Oct13 |
| <9> | P861 | Jul10 | Oct10 | Nov13 | 9999 | Feb10 | C882 | PPO | $40 | Nov13 |
| <10> | P861 | Mar11 | May11 | Nov13 | 9999 | Mar11 | C882 | PPO | $40 | Nov13 |

**Figure 11.3** A Temporal Delete Cascade: After the Transaction.

[8]Client C903, rows 3 and 4 in the illustration.

As in the previous chapter, withdrawn rows are shaded, and rows which are part of the atomic and isolated unit of work that carries out the temporal transaction are marked with angle brackets. The isolation property of this transaction means that the rows marked with angle brackets are not visible from the moment the first physical transaction reads its target row to the moment the last physical transaction writes its data to the table.

The second table affected by this transaction is the Policy table. Here there is a single version of a policy owned by C903 that exists in the transaction's timespan. P861(r2)'s effective time begins prior to the transaction's timespan, and extends past the end of the transaction's timespan. The transaction thus splits the version which, in turn, {splits} the episode.

The first step is to withdraw P861(r2) into past assertion time. The second step is to replace it with two rows which are identical to it except that they leave a 5-month "hole" in P861's currently asserted effective time.

The first of these two newly asserted versions is shown as P861(r9) in Figure 11.3. Its effective begin date (and everything else except its effective end date) is the same as it is in P861 (r2). But its effective end date is October 2010, the start of the delete transaction's timespan.

The second of these two newly asserted versions is shown as P861(r10) in Figure 11.3. Its effective end date is the same as P861(r2)'s effective end date. But its effective begin date is March 2011, the end of the delete transaction's timespan. Everything else on P861(r10) is the same as it is on P861(r2), with one exception. P861(r10) begins a new episode of P861 because there is a currently asserted effective time gap between it and the next earliest clock tick that contains a representation of P861. So the episode begin date is changed to the effective begin date of that row itself.

Figure 11.1 is the graphic illustration of these two tables prior to applying the delete cascade transaction. It corresponds to the state of the tables shown in Figure 11.2. Figure 11.4 is the graphic illustration of these same two tables after applying the delete cascade transaction. The "hole" in currently asserted effective time, for both client C903 and policy P861, is shown as the cross-hatched areas in the illustration. It corresponds to the state of the tables shown in Figure 11.3.

The temporal delete directed the AVF to remove the representation of client C903 from October 2010 to March 2011; and that is what the AVF has done. Metadata directed the AVF to cascade this temporal delete to all dependent managed objects. The only such object was policy P861; and the AVF has removed the representation of that object from those five months.

Everything, in current assertion time, is now as it was except that a "hole" has been created in the effective time shared by C903 and

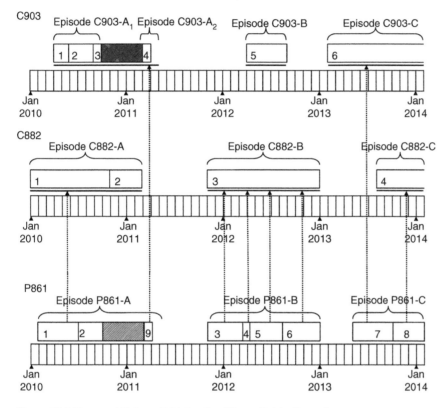

**Figure 11.4** Temporal Referential Integrity: After a Delete Cascade.

P861. C903 is no longer asserted to be a client of ours from October 2010 to March 2011. And the policy owned by C903 is no longer asserted to be in effect during that same period of time. Our delete cascade is complete, and the new state of the database is now visible to its users. (We should therefore remove the angle brackets from the row numbers in Figure 11.3. We have left them there to make it easier to see the rows involved in the transaction.)

# Glossary References

Glossary entries whose definitions form strong interdependencies are grouped together in the following list. The same glossary entries may be grouped together in different ways at the end of different chapters, each grouping reflecting the semantic perspective of each chapter. There will usually be several other, and often many other, glossary entries that are not included in the list, and we recommend that the Glossary be consulted whenever an unfamiliar term is encountered.

We note, in particular, that none of the nodes in the two taxonomies referenced in this chapter are included in this list.

In general, we leave taxonomy nodes out of these lists since they are long enough without them.

---

12/31/9999
clock tick
Now()
Allen relationships

include

asserted version table
assertion time
shared assertion time

Asserted Versioning Framework (AVF)

child managed object
parent managed object

episode
open episode

object
oid
managed object

existence dependency
temporal foreign key (TFK)
temporal referential integrity (TRI)

instance
type

mechanics
semantics

occupied
represented

terminate
replace
supercede
withdraw

temporal entity integrity (TEI)

temporal extent state transformation

temporalize

version
effective begin date
effective end date
effective time
effective time period

---

# 12

# DEFERRED ASSERTIONS AND OTHER PIPELINE DATASETS

We normally think of inserting a row into a table as the same thing as claiming, or asserting, that the statement which that row makes is true. From that point of view, a distinction between the physical act of creating a row in a table, and the semantic act of claiming that what the row says is true, is a distinction without a difference.

This is why, we surmise, the computer science community calls the second of their two bi-temporal dimensions "transaction time", an expression with obvious physical connotations. Yet while a transaction is a physical act, an assertion is not. It is a semantic act. And while the semantic act can't happen before the physical one, we see no reason why it can't happen after it, and a number of advantages that result if it can.

With the standard temporal model, the rows inserted into bi-temporal tables begin to be asserted on the date they are physically inserted into the database. With Asserted Versioning, this is the default for those rows; but Asserted Versioning permits

Managing Time in Relational Databases. Doi: 10.1016/B978-0-12-375041-9.00012-1

this default to be overridden. Temporal transactions may be submitted, and physical rows created in response to them, prior to the date on which those rows will begin to be asserted.

To put it the other way around, an Asserted Versioning temporal transaction may be submitted with an assertion begin date in the future, so that the row the transaction creates will have a row creation date earlier than its assertion begin date. The row will be physically part of the table, but it won't be asserted. It won't be anything we show to the world, anything we are yet willing to claim makes a true statement. It will be a row which is physically in the same table as the rows which make up the currently asserted production data in that table. But semantically, it will be distinct from those rows.

We will say that transactions like these are *deferred transactions*, and that what they place in the database are *deferred assertions*. Unlike rows in conventional tables, deferred assertions do not represent true statements. They do not have a truth value at all, because we do not yet attribute a truth value to them. By the same token, as described in earlier chapters, Asserted Versioning rows which are withdrawn into past assertion time also do not represent true statements. They do not have a truth value at all, because we no longer attribute a truth value to them. They are a record of what we once claimed was true, just as deferred assertions are a record of what we may eventually claim is true.

For the most part, we need not concern ourselves with these logical subtleties. But neither should we ignore them completely, because they will help us understand this important functionality of Asserted Versioning which distinguishes it from the standard temporal model and from all other computer science work on bi-temporal data that we are aware of. So before we get on with the task of understanding what deferred assertions are and how to manage them, we should look a little more closely at the logical and semantic foundation on which the distinction between assertions and statements is based.

## The Semantics of Deferred Assertion Time

Data describes objects. Conventional tables represent types of objects. Rows in those tables represent instances of those types, and describe those instances.

We create and maintain the data in these tables. Those who access this data assume that we believe that the data is correct and that each row makes a true statement about the object it represents. They understand, of course, that we may sometimes be wrong; but they assume that our intention is to be truthful, and that we take reasonable care to be accurate. Without those assumptions, the creation and maintenance of data would be a pointless activity.

So underlying the activity of creating, maintaining and consuming data lies the matter of what we claim or assert to be true. For purposes of this discussion, we will take the following ways of describing our relationship to the data we create, maintain and retrieve as equivalent. A row in a conventional table, we may say, indicates:

(i) What we *accept* as a true statement of what the object it represents is like.

(ii) What we *agree* is a true statement of what that object is like.

(iii) What we *assent* to as a true statement of what that object is like.

(iv) What we *assert* is a true statement of what that object is like.

(v) What we *believe* is a true statement of what that object is like.

(vi) What we *claim* is a true statement of what that object is like.

(vii) What we *know* is a true statement of what that object is like.

(viii) What we *say* is a true statement of what that object is like. And

(ix) What we *think* is a true statement of what that object is like.

Whatever semantic differences there may be between accepting, agreeing, assenting, asserting, believing, claiming, knowing, saying and thinking—and such differences are of great importance in such fields as epistemology, linguistics and the foundations of logic—these differences make no difference as far as bi-temporal data management is concerned. The fundamental difference for our purposes is between *ontology* and *epistemology*, between talk about what the world is like, and talk about what we think it is like.

A more thorough discussion of the semantics of statements and assertions is outside the scope of this book, but the reader should be aware that there is more here than meets the eye. For one thing, assertions are not statements. They are what philosophers call *speech acts*, ones made by means of statements. A statement is true or false. That is a relationship between the statement and the object it represents and describes.[1] An assertion is either made or not made. But that is not a relationship between a statement and an object. It is a relationship between a statement and the person who does or does not assert it.

We sometimes say, in rough equivalence, that we believe or do not believe that a statement is true. But just as assertions are not statements, beliefs are neither statements nor assertions. Beliefs are what philosophers call *propositional attitudes.* In fact, assent, assert, claim and say are all speech acts; they are things we *do* with words. But believe, know and think are propositional attitudes; they are cognitive stances we take with respect to those words. (Accept and agree could be one or the other, depending on whether they refer to behavior or to a behavioral disposition.)

## Assertions, Statements and Time

Conventional tables are the bread and butter of IT. The data in those tables represent both what things are currently like and also what we currently believe those things are like. They represent both what things are like now and what we now believe they are like.

There is a timeline along which persistent objects are located, and a timeline along which we hold various beliefs. Data in conventional tables is "pinned", along both timelines, to the moving point in time we call "the present" and which, in this book, we designate as *Now()*. The maintenance of conventional data is an ongoing effort to keep up with the changes that follow in the trail of that moving point.

But as well as the present, there are the past and the future. So if we "unpin" data along both these timelines, we end up with nine possible ways that data and time may be related.

In this section, we will use the terminology of beliefs even though, as we said previously, the nine different terms we listed there are equivalent, as far as our discussions in this book are concerned. This chapter is about assertions, and so we initially tried to write this section using that terminology. But it seems to us that the argument is easier to follow using the language of beliefs. Nonetheless, we are speaking about assertions, albeit in the more colloquial language of beliefs. Not all assertions, of course; and not all beliefs. Rather, as we said earlier, assertions that statements made by rows in database tables

---

[1]Assuming, that is, a pre-critical correspondence theory of truth which, for purposes of clarifying the semantics of bi-temporal data, seems to us perfectly adequate.

|  | what we used to believe | what we currently believe | what we will believe |
|---|---|---|---|
| **what things used to be like** | (i) what we used to believe things used to be like | (iv) what we currently believe things used to be like | (vii) what we will believe things used to be like |
| **what things are like** | (ii) what we used to believe things are like now | (v) what we currently believe things are like now | (viii) what we will believe things are like now |
| **what things will be like** | (iii) what we used to believe things will be like | (vi) what we currently believe things will be like | (ix) what we will believe things will be like |

**Figure 12.1** Facts, Beliefs and Time.

are true statements, and beliefs that those statements are true statements.

Using the terminology of beliefs, we may say that the rows in tables in relational databases may relate data to time in any of nine ways. So where "thing" means, more precisely, "persistent object", we can organize these nine relationships of rows to time as shown in Figure 12.1.

In Asserted Versioning, beliefs are what we assert by means of rows in our tables, and facts are what those rows describe about the objects they represent. Columns, in Figure 12.1, from left to right, represent past, present and future beliefs. Rows, in that same illustration, from top to bottom, represent past, present and future facts. Temporalized beliefs are represented by rows with assertion time periods. Temporalized facts are represented by rows with effective time periods, i.e. by versions.[2]

But temporal transactions cannot insert, update or delete all nine types of rows. Specifically, temporal transactions cannot insert, update or delete rows making statements about what we used to believe, statements of type (i), (ii) or (iii).

It's important to understand why this is so. Temporal transactions create new rows in temporal tables. But these rows represent beliefs, and we can't *now* make a statement about what we *used to* believe. On the other hand we can, of course, now make a statement about what used to be true. To understand what the two temporal dimensions of bi-temporal data really mean, we need to understand why distinctions like these ones are valid—why, in this case, we *can* make statements about how things used to be, but *cannot* make statements about what we used to think about them.

---

[2]Of course, since we cannot know the future, we cannot state with certainty either what the facts will be, or what we will believe. Instead, "what things will be like" should be taken as shorthand for "what things may turn out to be like", and "what we will believe" should be taken as shorthand for "what we may come to believe".

So why can't we? Surely we make statements about what we used to believe all the time. For example, we can now state that we used to believe that Bernie Madoff was an honest man. If we can make such statements in ordinary conversation, why can't we make them as transactions that will update a database?

The reason is that in a database, as we said, a belief is expressed by the presence of a row in a table. No row, no belief. So if we write a transaction today that creates a row stating that we believed something yesterday, we are creating a row that states that we believed something at a time when there was no row to represent that belief. Given that the beliefs we are talking about are beliefs that certain statements about persistent objects are true, and given that those statements are the statements made by rows in tables, it would be a logical contradiction to state that we had such a belief at a point or period in time during which there was no row to represent that belief.[3]

This leaves us six combinations of beliefs and what they are about that we can, without logical contradiction, modify by means of a temporal transaction. Asserted Versioning recognizes all six combinations. But the standard temporal model does not permit data to be located in future belief time, and so it does not recognize combinations (vii), (viii) or (ix) as meaningful. It does not attempt to develop a data management framework within which we can make statements about what we may in the future believe.

Future beliefs, and their representation in temporal tables as not yet asserted rows, are precisely what make the difference between the assertion time dimension of Asserted Versioning and the transaction time dimension of the standard temporal model. Without it, the two temporal dimensions of Asserted Versioning are semantically equivalent to the two temporal dimensions of the standard temporal model. Without it, assertion time is equivalent to transaction time.

But is it valid to locate data in future belief time? After all, as we noted in a footnote a short while ago, we can be certain about what we once believed and about what we currently believe, but we cannot be certain about what we will believe. On the other hand, a lack of certainty is not the same thing as a logical contradiction. There is nothing logically invalid about making statements about what we think was, is or may come to be true. By the same token, there is nothing logically invalid about making

---

[3]In fact, we offer this as a statement of what we will call the *temporalized extension* of the Closed World Assumption (CWA). All too briefly: the CWA is about the relationship of a collection of statements to the world. Its temporalized extension is about the relationship of beliefs (assertions, claims, etc.) to each of those statements.

statements about what we currently believe or may come to believe was, is or may turn out to be true. The only logical contradition is the one already noted, that because of the temporalized extension of the CWA, it is a logical contradiction to create a row representing a statement about what, prior to the time the row was created, we then believed/asserted to be true.

We should now have a clear idea of what deferred transactions and deferred assertions are. They are the data in categories (vii), (viii) and (ix) of Figure 12.1. We understand that neither the standard temporal model nor, for that matter, any more recent computer science work on bi-temporality that we are aware of, recognizes data which represents what we are not yet willing to assert is true about what things were like, are like or may turn out to be like.

Before discussing deferred transactions and deferred assertions, we want to explain how they are one subtype of a more generalized concept, of something we call *pipeline datasets*. Once we have done that, the remainder of this chapter will focus on deferred transactions and deferred assertions, and the business value of *internalizing* them. Then, in the next chapter, we will look at several other kinds of pipeline datasets, and the business value of internalizing them as well.

# The Internalization of Pipeline Datasets

We begin by introducing some new terminology. *Dataset* is an older technical term, and up to this point in the book, we have used it to refer to any physical collection of data. Going forward, we would like to narrow that definition a bit. From now on, when we talk about *datasets*, we will mean physical files, tables, views or other managed objects in which the managed object itself represents a type and contains multiple managed objects each of which represent an instance of that type. Thus, comma-delimited files are datasets, as are flat files, indexed files and relational tables themselves. A graphic image is not a dataset, in this narrower sense of the term, nor is a CLOB (a character large object).

*Production datasets* are datasets that contain production data. *Production data* is data that describes the objects and events of interest to the business. It is a semantic concept. *Production databases* are the collections of production datasets which the business recognizes as the official repositories of that data. Production databases consist of *production tables*, which are production datasets whose data is designated as always reliable and always available for use.

When production data is being worked on, it may reside in any number of production datasets, for example in those datasets we call *batch transaction files*, or *transaction tables*, or *data staging areas*. Once we've got the data just right, we use it to transform the production tables that are its targets. The transformation may be carried out by applying insert, update and delete transactions to the production tables. At other times, the transformation may be a merge of data we've been working on into those tables, or a replacement of some of the data in those tables with the data we've been working on.

When data is extracted from production tables, it has an intended destination. That destination may be another database or a business user, either of which may be internal to the business or external to it. Sometimes that data is delivered directly to its destination. At other times, it must go through one or more intermediate stages in which various additional transformations are applied to it. When first extracted from production tables, this data is usually said to be contained in *query result sets*. As that data moves farther away from its point of origin, and through additional transformations, the resulting production datasets tend to be called things like *extracts*. At its ultimate destinations, it is manifested as the content displayed on *screens* or in *reports*, or as data that has just been acquired by downstream organizations, perhaps to supply their own databases as datasets which tend to be call *feeds*.

Let's make the metaphor underlying this description a little more explicit by using the concept of *pipelines*. *Pipeline production datasets* (*pipeline datasets*, for short) are points at which data comes to rest along the *inflow pipelines* whose termination points are production tables, or along the *outflow pipelines* whose points of origin are those same tables. The points of origin of inflow pipelines may be external to the organization or internal to it; and the data that flows along these pipelines are the acquired or generated transactions that are going to update production tables. The termination points of outflow pipelines may also be either internal to the organization, or external to it; and we may think of the data that flows along these pipelines as the result sets of queries applied to those production tables.

There may be many points at which incoming production data comes to rest, for some period of time, prior to resuming its journey towards its target tables. Similarly, there may be many points at which outgoing data comes to rest, for some period of time, prior to continuing on to its ultimate destinations. These points at which production data comes to rest are these pipeline datasets.

But these points of rest, and the movement of data from one to another, exist in an environment in which that data is also at risk. The robust mechanisms with which DBMSs maintain the security and integrity of their production tables are not available to those pipeline datasets which exist outside the production database itself.

All in all, pipeline data flowing towards production tables would cost much less to manage, and would be managed to a higher standard of security and integrity, if that data could be moved immediately from its points of origin directly into the production tables which are its points of destination. Let's see now if this is as far-fetched a notion as it may appear to be to many IT professionals. We will look at deferred transactions and deferred assertions in this chapter, and consider other pipeline datasets in the next chapter.

# Deferred Assertions

We will discuss deferred transactions and deferred assertions, and how they work, by means of a series of scenarios in which deferred transactions are applied to sample data.

## A Deferred Update to a Current Episode

We begin with an open episode of policy P861. As shown in Figure 12.2, the current version in this episode—P861(r4)—has an [Aug 2012 – 12/31/9999] effective time period.[4] It also has an [Aug 2012 – 12/31/9999] assertion time period. From this, we know that there is no representation of this object anywhere else in the production table, in either temporal dimension, from August 2012 until further notice.

By now we should know how to read an asserted version table like this. The episode extends from an effective begin date of

**Policy Table**

| Row # | oid | eff-beg | eff-end | asr-beg | asr-end | epis-beg | client | type | copay | row-crt |
|---|---|---|---|---|---|---|---|---|---|---|
| 1 | P861 | Nov11 | Mar12 | Nov11 | 9999 | Nov11 | C882 | HMO | $20 | Nov11 |
| 2 | P861 | Mar12 | Apr12 | Mar12 | 9999 | Nov11 | C882 | PPO | $50 | Mar12 |
| 3 | P861 | Apr12 | Aug12 | Apr12 | 9999 | Nov11 | C882 | HMO | $30 | Apr12 |
| 4 | P861 | Aug12 | 9999 | Aug12 | 9999 | Nov11 | C882 | POS | $40 | Aug12 |

**Figure 12.2** A Current Episode: Before the Deferred Assertion.

[4]The notation "P861(r4)" indicates row #4 in the referenced figure, in this case Figure 12.2. The policy identifier is not strictly necessary, and is included just to remind us which object we are talking about.

November 2011 to an effective end date of 12/31/9999. Every version in this episode is currently asserted.

We will now submit a deferred temporal update. Again, we assume that it is now January 2013. That transaction looks like this:

```
UPDATE Policy [P861,,, $55] May 2012, Jul 2012, Jan 2090
```

The three temporal parameters following the bracketed data are the effective begin date, effective end date and assertion begin date. All temporal updates discussed so far have accepted the default value for the assertion begin date, that value being Now(). Here, with our first deferred transaction, we override that default with a future date.

There are several things to note about this transaction. First of all, the object specified in this transaction is policy P861, and the transaction's effective timespan is May 2012 to July 2012, i.e. the two months of May and June 2012. The assertion begin date is January 2090, a date which is several decades in the future.

The first thing the AVF does is to split one or more rows in the Policy table into multiple rows such that one or a contiguous set of those rows has the *oid* and the effective timespan specified on the transaction. When a set of one or more contiguous asserted version rows, and a temporal transaction, have the same *oid* and also the same effective time period, we will say that they *match*.

Since the transaction specifies an effective timespan of [May 2012 – July 2012], the AVF modifies the current assertions for P861 so that one version matches the transaction. That is P861 (r6), as shown in Figure 12.3.

This results in a set of rows that are semantically equivalent to the original row, those rows being P861(r5, r6 & r7). They cover the same effective time period as the original row; and they contain the same business data as the original row. Note

**Policy Table**

| Row # | oid | eff-beg | eff-end | asr-beg | asr-end | epis-beg | clinet | type | copay | row-crt |
|---|---|---|---|---|---|---|---|---|---|---|
| 1 | P861 | Nov11 | Mar12 | Nov11 | 9999 | Nov11 | C882 | HMO | $20 | Nov11 |
| 2 | P861 | Mar12 | Apr12 | Mar12 | 9999 | Nov11 | C882 | PPO | $50 | Mar12 |
| <3> | P861 | Apr12 | Aug12 | Apr12 | Jan13 | Nov11 | C882 | HMO | $30 | Apr12 |
| 4 | P861 | Aug12 | 9999 | Aug12 | 9999 | Nov11 | C882 | POS | $40 | Aug12 |
| <5> | P861 | Apr12 | May12 | Jan13 | 9999 | Nov11 | C882 | HMO | $30 | Jan13 |
| <6> | P861 | May12 | Jul12 | Jan13 | 9999 | Nov11 | C882 | HMO | $30 | Jan13 |
| <7> | P861 | Jul12 | Aug12 | Jan13 | 9999 | Nov11 | C882 | HMO | $30 | Jan13 |

**Figure 12.3** A Current Episode: Effective Time Alignment.

that, in Figure 12.3, we have not yet created the deferred assertion. We have just realigned version boundaries, within current assertion time, as a preliminary step to carrying out the update. Prior to this realignment, the effective timespan of the transaction was located [during] the effective time period of P861 (r3). Now the effective timespan of the transaction [*equals*] the effective time period of P861(r6), and so the transaction *matches* that asserted version.

The result of this alignment is shown in Figure 12.3. P861(r3) has been withdrawn into past assertion time, into an assertion time period that ends on January 2013. P861(r5, r6 & r7) have replaced it in current assertion time, in assertion time periods that begin on January 2013 (and not, let it be noted, on January 2090). Again, we use angle brackets on row numbers to indicate rows that are part of an atomic and isolated unit of work, a series of physical modifications to the database that must together all succeed or all fail, and a set of rows that are not visible in the database until the unit of work completes.

Note that P861(r5, r6 & r7) have the same episode begin date and the same business data as row 3. In addition, their three effective time periods cover exactly the same clock ticks as the withdrawn P861(r3). These three rows, together, are semantically equivalent to P861(r3). They represent the same object in exactly the same effective time clock ticks; and in every such clock tick, they attribute the same business data to that object.

Nor has the assertion time in the table been altered, either. Prior to this transaction, the statement made by P861(r3) was asserted from April 2012 to 12/31/9999. Midway into the transaction, at the point shown in Figure 12.3, the table still asserts that from April 2012 to 12/31/9999, P861 was owned by client C882, was an HMO policy, and had a copay of $30. It asserts this because the statement made by the logical conjunction of P861 (r6, r7 & r8) is truth-functionally equivalent to the statement made by P861(r6), and the assertion times of [Apr 2012 – Jan 2013] and [January 2013 – 12/31/9999] both [meet] and, together, [*equal*] the original assertion time of P861(r3), before it was withdrawn. At this point in the transaction, we have performed *syntactic surgery* on the target table, but have in no way altered its semantic content.

There is now one and only one row in the target table that matches the transaction. It is P861(r6). The AVF next *withdraws* P861(r6), moving it into *closed assertion time*, i.e. giving it an assertion time period with a non-12/31/9999 assertion end date. It does so by giving P861(r6) an assertion end date that matches the assertion begin date on the transaction, thus

**Policy Table**

| Row # | oid | eff-beg | eff-end | asr-beg | asr-end | epis-beg | clinet | type | copay | row-crt |
|---|---|---|---|---|---|---|---|---|---|---|
| 1 | P861 | Nov11 | Mar12 | Nov11 | 9999 | Nov11 | C882 | HMO | $20 | Nov11 |
| 2 | P861 | Mar12 | Apr12 | Mar12 | 9999 | Nov11 | C882 | PPO | $50 | Mar12 |
| <3> | P861 | Apr12 | Aug12 | Apr12 | Jan13 | Nov11 | C882 | HMO | $30 | Apr12 |
| 4 | P861 | Aug12 | 9999 | Aug12 | 9999 | Nov11 | C882 | POS | $40 | Aug12 |
| <5> | P861 | Apr12 | May12 | Jan13 | 9999 | Nov11 | C882 | HMO | $30 | Jan13 |
| <6> | P861 | May12 | Jul12 | Jan13 | Jan90 | Nov11 | C882 | HMO | $30 | Jan13 |
| <7> | P861 | Jul12 | Aug12 | Jan13 | 9999 | Nov11 | C882 | HMO | $30 | Jan13 |
| <8> | P861 | May12 | Jul12 | Jan90 | 9999 | Nov11 | C882 | HMO | $55 | Jan13 |

**Figure 12.4** Withdrawing a Current Assertion into Closed Assertion Time, and Superceding It.

preserving the assertion time continuity of this effective time history of P861.

The next thing the AVF does is to make a copy of P861(r6), apply the copay update to that copy, and give it an assertion time period of [Jan 2090 – 12/31/9999]. This becomes P861(r8), the row that *supercedes* row 6. This row is the deferred assertion.

The result is shown in Figure 12.4.

Note that this closed assertion is still current. It is currently January 2013, and so Now() still falls between the assertion begin and end dates of P861(r6), and will continue to do so until January 2090. So a closed assertion time period is one with a non-12/31/9999 end date. Some closed assertion time periods are past; they are no longer asserted. But others are current, like this one. And yet others may be assertion time periods that lie entirely in the future.

Note that this process is *almost* identical to the familiar process of withdrawing a version into past assertion time and superceding it with a row in current assertion time. The only difference is that the withdrawn assertion is moved into closed but still *current* assertion time, and the superceding assertion is placed into *future* assertion time.

At this point, both P861(r3 & r6) are *locked*. The AVF will never modify P861(r3) because it is already located in past assertion time. But P861(r6) is also locked, even though it is still currently asserted. The AVF treats any row with a non-12/31/9999 assertion end date as locked. The reason all such rows are locked, including those whose assertion time periods are not yet past, is that the database contains a later assertion which otherwise matches the locked assertion.

In this case, P861(r6) is locked because the Policy table now contains a later assertion that was created from it. That later assertion was supposedly written and submitted based on then-current knowledge of the contents of the database, specifically of what the database then asserted about what P861 was like in May and June of 2012. If that description is allowed to change before the later assertion became current, then all bets are off.

Another way to think about the locking associated with deferred transactions and deferred assertions is that it *serializes* those transactions. If a process about to update a row in a database does not first lock that row from other updates, then another update process could read the row before the first process is complete. Then, whichever process physically updates that row on the database first, its changes will be lost, overwritten by the changes made by the process which updates the database last. This could happen with deferred assertions if they were not serialized.

The mechanics of deferred assertion locking are simple. Every temporal transaction has an assertion begin date, either the default date of Now() or an explicitly supplied future date. Temporal updates and temporal deletes begin their work by withdrawing the one or more versions which represent an object in any clock ticks included in the transaction's effective timespan. The versions they withdraw are those versions located in the most recent period of assertion time. That may be current assertion time, and usually is. But when a deferred transaction has been applied to versions in current assertion time, it closes their assertion periods with the same date that begins the assertion period of the deferred assertion it creates, just as the deferred update we are discussing closed P861(r6) and superceded it with P861(r8). And it creates a version that exists in future assertion time. Deferred transactions may then be applied to that deferred assertion, and we will explain how to do that in the next section.

Note what is *not* locked. The episode itself is not locked. Out of the entire currently asserted effective time period from November 2011 to 12/31/9999, for P861, only two months have been locked. Inserts, updates and deletes can continue to take place against any of the other clock ticks in the episode occupied by P861—or, for that matter, against any clock ticks not occupied by P861.

We have now completed the deferred transaction. As directed by the transaction, the AVF has created a version of P861, for the effective time months of May and June 2012, that will not be asserted until January 2090. If nothing happens between now and January 2090, then at that time, the database will stop asserting that P861 had a copay amount of \$30 in May and June of 2012, and begin asserting, instead, that it had a copay amount of \$55 during those two long-ago months.

## A Deferred Update to a Deferred Assertion

Now we have a deferred assertion. Next, let's consider an update which will apply to that deferred assertion. This transaction takes place on February 2013.

```
UPDATE Policy [P861,,, $50] May 2012, Jun 2012, Jan 2090
```

Apparently, sometime in the month after the first deferred update, we decided that the copay update should have been increased to \$50, not to \$55, for the month of May 2012. To process this second deferred update, the AVF begins its work by looking for versions already in the target table, with the same *oid*, whose effective time periods [intersect] the effective timespan specified on the transaction. It ignores past assertions, because database modifications neither affect past assertions nor are affected by them.

The effective timespan for P861 that the AVF is looking for is [May 2012 – Jun 2012]. The AVF finds two rows—P861(r6 & r8) (as shown in Figure 12.4)—whose effective time includes that of the timespan on the transaction. Both rows have the same *oid* as the transaction, and both include the effective-time clock tick of May 2012.

P861(r6), however, is locked because there is a later assertion about the same object that includes all its effective time clock ticks. It is P861(r8) that is the latest assertion which has an effective time period that [intersects] that of the transaction.[5] That row's time period, to be more precise, [starts$^{-1}$] the effective time period on the transaction.

So the target of the deferred update must be P861(r8). It is the latest, i.e. future-most, assertion about the month of May 2012, in the life of P861.

Next, because P861(r8) includes June as well as May, the first thing the AVF does is to split that row to create a semantically

---

[5]As we said in Chapter 3, we will refer to Allen relationships by using the relationship name enclosed in brackets. And as we said in Chapter 9, we will refer to temporal extent state transformations by using the transformation name enclosed in braces. In both cases, when we refer to non-leaf nodes in either taxonomy, we will underline the name. Thus we can say that one time period [meets] another, or that one time period [intersects] another. We italicize the Allen relationship name *equals*, as we explained in Chapter 3, to mark the fact that, unlike all other Allen relationships, it has no distinct inverse.

**Policy Table**

| Row # | oid | eff-beg | eff-end | asr-beg | asr-end | epis-beg | clinet | type | copay | row-crt |
|---|---|---|---|---|---|---|---|---|---|---|
| 1 | P861 | Nov11 | Mar12 | Nov11 | 9999 | Nov11 | C882 | HMO | $20 | Nov11 |
| 2 | P861 | Mar12 | Apr12 | Mar12 | 9999 | Nov11 | C882 | PPO | $50 | Mar12 |
| 3 | P861 | Apr12 | Aug12 | Apr12 | Jan13 | Nov11 | C882 | HMO | $30 | Apr12 |
| 4 | P861 | Aug12 | 9999 | Aug12 | 9999 | Nov11 | C882 | POS | $40 | Aug12 |
| 5 | P861 | Apr12 | May12 | Jan13 | 9999 | Nov11 | C882 | HMO | $30 | Jan13 |
| 6 | P861 | May12 | Jul12 | Jan13 | Jan90 | Nov11 | C882 | HMO | $30 | Jan13 |
| 7 | P861 | Jul12 | Aug12 | Jan13 | 9999 | Nov11 | C882 | HMO | $30 | Jan13 |
| <8> | P861 | May12 | Jul12 | Jan90 | Jan90 | Nov11 | C882 | HMO | $55 | Jan13 |
| <9> | P861 | May12 | Jun12 | Jan90 | 9999 | Nov11 | C882 | HMO | $55 | Feb13 |
| <10> | P861 | Jun12 | Jul12 | Jan90 | 9999 | Nov11 | C882 | HMO | $55 | Feb13 |

**Figure 12.5** A Deferred Assertion: Effective Time Alignment.

equivalent pair of rows, one of which matches the transaction. This is shown in Figure 12.5. P861(r8) has been withdrawn. In its place, the AVF has created the two rows P861(r9 & r10).

P861(r8) has been withdrawn into closed assertion time, but that assertion time is neither past nor present assertion time. It is *empty assertion time*, because the time period [Jan 2090 – Jan 2090] includes no clock ticks, not a single one.

## Reflections on Empty Assertion Time

In all our dealings with temporal transactions, the assertion date specified on the transaction (or accepted as a default) is used both as the assertion end date of the withdrawn row and also as the assertion begin date of the row or rows that replace and/or supercede it. In this way, our transactions build an unbroken succession of assertions about what the object in question is like during the unbroken extent of the episode's effective time.

P861(r8) cannot be withdrawn into past assertion time because it hasn't been asserted yet. But it also can't be allowed to remain in future assertion time because if P861(r9 and/or r10) are ever updated, they and P861(r8) would make different statements about what P861 was like at the same point in time, i.e. in either May or June 2012. In other words, P861(r8) can't be allowed to remain in future assertion time because it would then be a TEI conflict waiting to happen.

This is why the AVF moved it into *empty* assertion time. This is the semantically correct thing to do. With P861(r9 & r10) now in the database, which together *match* P861(r8), and with both being in yet-to-come assertion time, one of them had to go.

Creating P861(r9 & r10) is a preparatory move made by the AVF, to isolate a single deferred assertion that will match the update transaction. So P861(r8) was the correct one to go. Having nowhere in past assertion time to go, and obviously not belonging in current assertion time, it went to the only place it could go—into non-asserted time, i.e. into empty assertion time.

A row in empty assertion time, however, is a row that never was asserted and never will be asserted. So there is an argument for simply physically deleting the row rather than moving it into empty assertion time. For one thing, Asserted Versioning cannot keep track of *when* it was moved into empty assertion time. The only physical date on an asserted version table is the row creation date, and the movement of a row into empty assertion time is a physical update, for which there is no corresponding date.

For another thing, since a row in empty assertion time never was asserted, and never will be asserted, what information does it contain that would justify retaining it in the database? Well, in fact, a row in empty assertion time *is* informative. The information it contains is information about an intention. At one point in time, we apparently intended that the business data on that row would one day be asserted. Perhaps we intended to deceive someone with that business data. In that case, that row is a record of an intent to deceive. By retaining the row, we retain a record of that intent.

Non-deferred transactions are always against currently asserted versions which have a 12/31/9999 assertion end date. They withdraw those target versions by ending their assertions on the same clock tick that their replacement and/or superceding versions begin to be asserted. The result is to withdraw those target versions into past assertion time, but leave no assertion time gap between them and the results of the transaction.

Deferred transactions against those same currently asserted versions do the same thing. They withdraw them by ending their assertions on the same clock tick that their replacement and/or superceding versions will begin to be asserted. But being deferred, those replacement and/or superceding versions begin on some future date. Using that future date as the assertion end date of the target versions, those target versions are withdrawn, but into current assertion time. This current assertion time, however, has a definite, non-12/31/9999, end date, and so we say that their assertion periods are current but *closed*. If nothing happens in the meantime, then when that date comes to pass, the current closed assertions will fall into past assertion time, and the deferred assertions which replaced and/or superceded them will fall into current assertion time. The mechanics of withdrawal supports these different semantics correctly, just as it supported the semantics of non-deferrals correctly.

Deferred update and delete transactions may also have deferred assertions as their target. However, for any *oid* and any effective-time clock tick, the target of a deferred update or delete transaction must be the *latest* assertion of that effective-time clock tick for that object because, if it were not, it would violate the serialization property of deferred assertions (as described earlier, in the section *A Deferred Update to a Current Episode*). And the AVF guarantees that this will be so because any but the latest assertion will be locked; it will be on a row with a non-12/31/9999 assertion end date.

The mechanics of the AVF does its job, as in the first two cases, by ending the withdrawn assertions on the same clock tick that their replacement and/or superceding versions begin to be asserted.

For example, P861(r8) has an assertion begin date of January 2090. If a deferred update transaction targeting P861(r8) specified any assertion date later than that, then it would leave P861 (r8) to become currently asserted on January 2090, and to remain currently asserted until whatever assertion end date the transaction assigned to it. That's an ordinary enough case, and perhaps we should not be surprised that the machinery of deferral works correctly for it. But in fact, the deferred update we are discussing here specifies an assertion date of January 2090, the same date as the begin date on the target deferred assertion. And this is not so ordinary a case.

But in this case, too, what the mechanics achieves is precisely what the semantics demands. In this case, P861(r8)'s assertion end date is set to January 2090, with the result that its assertion time period is [Jan 2090 – Jan 2090]. With a closed-open convention for representing periods of time, this is an empty time period, one including not a single clock tick. It makes it as though P861(r8) had never been. It makes that row one which never was asserted and never will be asserted. For such rows, we will say, the transaction *overrides* them. So, to override a row is to withdraw it into empty assertion time prior to its ever being asserted in the first place.

What the semantics demands is a replacement row and a superceding row to cover the months of May and June 2012 in the life of P861, and for both those rows to begin to be asserted on January 2090. With P861(r9 & r10), that's exactly what it gets. There is now a target row which exactly matches the update transaction, and the transaction can now proceed on to completion.

## Completing the Deferred Update to a Deferred Assertion

The remaining analysis is straightforward. P861(r9) matches the deferred update transaction. P861(r10) is of no interest to the transaction because its effective time period does not share even a single clock tick with the effective timespan of the transaction.

Having created a target row which matches the transaction, the AVF now updates that row with the new copay amount. Note that it does not withdraw P861(r9) and supercede it with a new row. It could do that, but there is no need to do so because we are still in the midst of an atomic and isolated unit of work. At this point, the change to the copay amount is recorded. At this point, the update is complete. The result is shown in Figure 12.6.

As directed by the transaction, the AVF has created a version of P861, for the effective time period of May 2012, that will not be asserted until January 2090. The first deferred update changed the copay amount for P861, for the month of May 2012, from $30 to $55. This second deferred update corrected the copay amount which the first one set to $55. It changed it to $50.

Once again, we retain the angle brackets in the illustration to make it easy to identify the rows involved in the transaction. But the transaction, at this point, is complete. All DBMS locks are released, and all the rows in Figure 12.6 are now visible in the database. P861(r9 & r10) are not locked. P861(r8) has been overridden by those next two rows, and moved into empty assertion time. But note that P861(r6) is still both currently asserted and locked.

**Policy Table**

| Row # | oid | eff-beg | eff-end | asr-beg | asr-end | epis-beg | clinet | type | copay | row-crt |
|-------|------|---------|---------|---------|---------|----------|--------|------|-------|---------|
| 1 | P861 | Nov11 | Mar12 | Nov11 | 9999 | Nov11 | C882 | HMO | $20 | Nov11 |
| 2 | P861 | Mar12 | Apr12 | Mar12 | 9999 | Nov11 | C882 | PPO | $50 | Mar12 |
| 3 | P861 | Apr12 | Aug12 | Apr12 | Jan13 | Nov11 | C882 | HMO | $30 | Apr12 |
| 4 | P861 | Aug12 | 9999 | Aug12 | 9999 | Nov11 | C882 | POS | $40 | Aug12 |
| 5 | P861 | Apr12 | May12 | Jan13 | 9999 | Nov11 | C882 | HMO | $30 | Jan13 |
| 6 | P861 | May12 | Jul12 | Jan13 | Jan90 | Nov11 | C882 | HMO | $30 | Jan13 |
| 7 | P861 | Jul12 | Aug12 | Jan13 | 9999 | Nov11 | C882 | HMO | $30 | Jan13 |
| <8> | P861 | May12 | Jul12 | Jan90 | Jan90 | Nov11 | C882 | HMO | $55 | Jan13 |
| <9> | P861 | May12 | Jun12 | Jan90 | 9999 | Nov11 | C882 | HMO | $55 | Feb13 |
| <10> | P861 | Jun12 | Jul12 | Jan90 | 9999 | Nov11 | C882 | HMO | $55 | Feb13 |

**Figure 12.6** Completing the Deferred Update.

Does the business really intend to leave the database in this state? Does it really intend to continue saying until 2090 that in May and June 2012, P861 has a copay of $30, even though it apparently knows that the correct amount is $50 in May and $55 in June? Well, it certainly doesn't seem very likely.

## The Near Future and the Far Future

Deferred assertions may be located in the *near future* or the *far future*. Deferred assertions located in the near future will become current assertions as soon as enough time has passed. In a real-time update situation, a near future deferred assertion might be one with an assertion begin date just a few seconds from now. In a batch update situation, a near future deferred assertion might be one that does not become currently asserted until midnight, or perhaps even for another several days. What near future deferred assertions have in common is that, in all cases, the business is willing to wait for these assertions to *fall into currency*, i.e. to become current not because of some explicit action, but rather when the passage of time reaches their begin dates.

Deferred assertions may be created in *near future assertion time*, or moved to it from *far future assertion time* when the business approves of those assertions becoming production data. Deferred assertions may also be placed in or moved to far future assertion time. Such are our two deferred assertions shown above, which will not become current until nearly eight decades from now. It is unlikely, of course, that the business intends to wait that long. So once the business reviews those assertions and approves them, it will want them to become current assertions as soon as possible. It will do that by moving them into near future assertion time.

Assertions located in the far future are, for one reason or another, not ready to be applied to the production database. For example, they may be transactions that are created by assembling data from multiple sources. One of those sources arrives before the others, and so can create only incomplete transactions. Rather than managing those incomplete transactions as an inflow pipeline dataset, the user can submit them to the AVF using a far future assertion begin date, such as one several decades from now, or perhaps several hundred or several thousand years from now. As the other data sources begin to provide their contributions to those transactions, deferred update transactions override the deferred assertions placed there by earlier data sources. Eventually, the transactions are completed. Once approved, they can be moved into near future assertion time, ready to *fall into currency* in the near future, on the same clock tick that the assertions they replace and/or supercede *fall out of currency* and into assertion time history.

And there are any number of other reasons for assembling updates in far future assertion time. One is that a group of updates may be so important that the business wants a careful review and approve process before they are applied to production tables. Another is to create a group of assertions that the business can use for simulations or forecasts.

Once far future deferred assertions are ready to become production data, they must be moved into near future assertion time. Located close to Now(), those deferred assertions will then quickly fall into currency. They will quickly become currently asserted production data.

What we need now is a transaction that will move assertions from the far future to the near future. We will call it the *approval transaction*.

## Approving a Deferred Assertion

When a deferred transaction is applied to the database, it *locks* all prior but not yet past assertions for that object and that effective time period by setting the assertion end date to a non-12/31/9999 date. It withdraws matching current assertions, and either withdraws matching deferred assertions, or overrides them, or withdraws an earlier portion of them and overrides the remaining portion. The deferred transaction then creates a deferred assertion for the specified object in the specified effective time period, whose assertion begin date is set to the assertion begin date specified on the transaction.

For example, the first of the deferred transactions we looked at locked the effective time months of May and June 2012 for policy P861, and then created a deferred assertion for that policy in those two months. The second deferred transaction focused in on the month of May 2012, isolating it by splitting the deferred assertion P861(r8) into the two semantically equivalent deferred assertions P861(r9 & r10), and overriding P861(r8) with those two deferred assertions. Next, with P861(r9) representing the policy during May 2012, the deferred transaction applied the new copay amount to that row, completing the transaction and the atomic unit of work, ending the isolation of those rows and making them visible in the database, accessible to queries that specify assertions deferred until 2090.

As shown in Figure 12.6, the Policy table now contains only three deferred assertions that have not been overridden. One is P861(r6), whose withdrawal has been deferred until January 2090. The other two are P861(r9 & r10). They constitute a single *deferred assertion group*, that group being defined by the future assertion date that they share.

A deferred assertion group is another managed object introduced by Asserted Versioning but not supported by relational theory, relational technology, other temporal models, or ongoing research in the field. It is a designated collection of one or more rows which consist of assertions in the same future assertion period of time, and, transitively, any earlier non-past assertions that are locked because of them. These deferred assertion groups can contain assertions for different episodes of the same object, and for different objects in the same or in different tables.

Besides its own currently asserted production data, a production table may contain any number of deferred assertion groups. These deferred assertion groups are the *internalization* of inflow pipeline datasets. They are the internalization of collections of transactions which are not currently production data.

Usually, these collections are called batch transaction datasets. Typically, there may be any number of batch transaction datasets in which *pending* transactions are accumulated as they are acquired or created. One by one, on a scheduled or as-needed basis, these batch datasets are processed against their target databases, and production tables are updated. But with asserted version tables as the target production tables, these batch datasets aren't necessary. Transactions scheduled to be processed on a later date can be submitted immediately, with that later date as the assertion begin date.

Let us assume that the business has now reviewed the deferred assertion group and approved the assertions in it to become current as soon as possible. It is now March 2013, and so the next opportunity to update the database is April 2013.

The AVF moves deferred assertions backwards in time with a special temporal update transaction. This transaction takes deferred assertions in the far future and moves them into the near future.

But before we move P861(r9 & r10) backwards in assertion time, consider P861(r6). P861(r9 & r10) were created as *assertion-time contiguous* with P861(r8), which itself was created as assertion-time contiguous with P861(r6). The idea was that, on January 2090, when P861(r6) ceased being asserted, it would *hand-off* to P861(r8) on precisely that clock tick. But then a second deferred update was applied, which overrode P861(r8) with P861(r9 & r10), and then updated P861(r9).

When we originally created P861(r9 & r10), that future clock tick was January 2090. We are now about to change the assertion begin date on those two assertions to April 2013.

But if we do so, and do nothing about P861(r6), we will create a TEI violation. If we do nothing about P861(r6), then from January 2013 to January 2090, P861(r6) will assert that P861's copay amount in May 2012 was $30, but P861(r9) will assert that it was $50. So even though P861(r6) exists in a closed period of assertion time, it can, and indeed in this case must, be overridden. So rather than thinking of the approval transaction as changing the assertion begin date on one or more deferred assertions, we should think of it as changing the *hand-over* clock tick between locked assertions and the deferred assertions that are being moved backwards in assertion time.

The approval transaction looks like this:[6]

```
UPDATE Policy [ ]., Jan 2090, Apr 2013
```

This transaction is unlike the standard temporal update transaction in that its temporal parameters are both assertion dates. As indicated by the commas, there are no effective time dates on this transaction. And although a standard transaction can have one assertion date, this transaction has two assertion dates.

The first assertion date on the approval transaction is the *assertion group date*. The second is the *assertion approval date*.

The transaction proceeds as an atomic (all-or-nothing, and isolated) unit of work. For all assertions whose assertion begin date matches the assertion group date, it changes their assertion begin dates to the approval date. This is shown in Figure 12.7. P861(r9 & r10) have been moved from far future (2090) into near future (2013) assertion time. As soon as April 2013 occurs, those two rows will fall into currency.

The approval transaction is almost complete, but it has one thing left to do. As shown in Figure 12.6, P861(r6) has a January 2090 assertion end date prior to the approval transaction. If nothing is done, then in less than a month after the approval transaction is applied, P861(r9 &r10) will be in TEI conflict with P861(r6), and will remain so for several decades.

---

[6]As we have noted before, these examples do not use the syntax that will be used in release 1 of the AVF. The temporal data in these transactions is shown in a refinement of a comma-delimited positional notation.

**Policy Table**

| Row # | oid | eff-beg | eff-end | asr-beg | asr-end | epis-beg | clinet | type | copay | row-crt |
|-------|------|---------|---------|---------|---------|----------|--------|------|-------|---------|
| 1 | P861 | Nov11 | Mar12 | Nov11 | 9999 | Nov11 | C882 | HMO | $20 | Nov11 |
| 2 | P861 | Mar12 | Apr12 | Mar12 | 9999 | Nov11 | C882 | PPO | $50 | Mar12 |
| 3 | P861 | Apr12 | Aug12 | Apr12 | Jan13 | Nov11 | C882 | HMO | $30 | Apr12 |
| 4 | P861 | Aug12 | 9999 | Aug12 | 9999 | Nov11 | C882 | POS | $40 | Aug12 |
| 5 | P861 | Apr12 | May12 | Jan13 | 9999 | Nov11 | C882 | HMO | $30 | Jan13 |
| 6 | P861 | May12 | Jul12 | Jan13 | Apr13 | Nov11 | C882 | HMO | $30 | Jan13 |
| 7 | P861 | Jul12 | Aug12 | Jan13 | 9999 | Nov11 | C882 | HMO | $30 | Jan13 |
| 8 | P861 | May12 | Jul12 | Jan90 | Jan90 | Nov11 | C882 | HMO | $55 | Jan13 |
| <9> | P861 | May12 | Jun12 | Apr13 | 9999 | Nov11 | C882 | HMO | $55 | Apr13 |
| <10> | P861 | Jun12 | Jul12 | Apr13 | 9999 | Nov11 | C882 | HMO | $55 | Apr13 |

**Figure 12.7** Approving a Deferred Assertion Group.

This is because the override work of the approval transaction is incomplete. P861(r9 & r10) match P861(r6), which exists in current but closed assertion time. But in order to make room in near future assertion time, the AVF must withdraw any earlier assertions that would conflict with the assertions being moved backwards in time by the approval transaction. So, using the same withdraw/override mechanics it has always used, the AVF sets the assertion end date on P861(r6) to the assertion begin date of the two rows it has moved into near future assertion time, that date being April 2013.

The approval transaction is now complete. The deferred assertions have been moved into near future time, and are waiting to fall into currency. The database is in the state shown in Figure 12.7.

And, once again, we find that our mechanics, applied to a situation never anticipated for it, produces results that accurately express the correct semantics. For with its approval transaction, the business told us that we could update the copay amount for P861 in May of 2012 as soon as possible. As soon as possible is April 2013. So our database now shows the incorrect claim about P861 in May of 2012 continuing until that as soon as possible correction, and that correction, as the two rows P861(r9 & r10), taking over on that same clock tick.

In this way, multiple deferred assertions can be managed as a single group. For example, if we are adding 1000 clients to our database, then if all 1000 clients are assigned the same future assertion date, a single approval transaction can be used to assert all of them at once.

## Deferred Assertions and Temporal Referential Integrity

Deferred update and delete transactions, like their non-deferred cousins, lock matching assertions that were already in the database at the time those transactions were carried out. It locks them by giving them a non-12/31/9999 assertion end date. In the case of a non-deferred update or delete, these locked assertions exist in past assertion time. But in the case of a deferred transaction, the locked assertions remain in current assertion time, and their assertion time periods [meet] the assertion time periods of the deferred assertions that replace or supercede them.

When an approval transaction is applied to a group of deferred assertions, those assertions are moved backwards in assertion time, usually to just a few clock ticks later than the current moment in time. Then, with the passage of those few clock ticks, those deferred assertions become current assertions.

In moving backwards in assertion time, those approved assertions override any locked matching assertions. In overriding them, it "sets them to naught" almost literally, by setting their assertion end dates to match their assertion begin dates, thus moving them into empty assertion time.

But there is one last issue to deal with. We have emphasized that semantic constraints do not exist across assertion time periods. But if a TRI child managed object is moved backwards into an earlier period of assertion time, one which begins before the assertion time period containing its parent managed object, then the TRI relationship between them will be broken. The assertion time movement will make the child managed object a referential "orphan" until the passage of time reaches the beginning of the assertion time period of the parent managed object.

So the AVF must block any such movement, or else insure that as part of the same atomic and isolated unit of work, parent and child managed objects are moved together so as to preserve the referential relationships.

It turns out that this isn't always easy to do, especially when the related managed objects exist in different deferred assertion groups. The problem is that, as long as an approval transaction is not applied, the assertion time of any TRI deferred parent is guaranteed to include the assertion time of all of its deferred children. But by applying an approval transaction, we may break the inclusion relationship by moving the start of the assertion time of the approved children to a date prior to the beginning assertion time of the not-yet-approved parent. We are working on the problem as this book goes to press. We know that the problem is not insoluble. But we also know that it *is* difficult.

## Glossary References

Glossary entries whose definitions form strong interdependencies are grouped together in the following list. The same glossary entries may be grouped together in different ways at the end of different chapters, each grouping reflecting the semantic perspective of each chapter. There will usually be several other, and often many other, glossary entries that are not included in the list, and we recommend that the Glossary be consulted whenever an unfamiliar term is encountered.

We note, in particular, that the nine terms used to refer to the act of giving a truth value to a statement, listed in the section *The Semantics of Deferred Assertion Time*, are not included in this list. Nor are nodes in our Allen Relationship taxonomy or our State Transformation taxonomy included in this list.

---

12/31/9999
clock tick
closed-open
Now()

Allen relationships

approval transaction
assertion group date
deferred assertion group
deferred assertion
deferred transaction
empty assertion time
fall into currency
fall out of currency
far future assertion time
near future assertion time
override
lock
retrograde movement

Asserted Versioning Framework (AVF)

assertion begin date
assertion end date
assertion time period

assertion time
assertion
closed assertion

conventional table

dataset

episode
open episode

statement

hand-over clock tick

instance
type

managed object
object
oid
persistent object
thing

occupied
represented
match
replace
supercede
withdraw

pipeline dataset
inflow pipeline dataset
inflow pipeline
outflow pipeline dataset
outflow pipeline
production data
production database
production dataset
production table

row creation date

temporal dimension

temporal entity integrity (TEI)
temporal foreign key (TFK)
temporal referential integrity (TRI)

the standard temporal model

transaction table

transaction time

version
effective begin date
effective end date
effective time period

# RE-PRESENTING INTERNALIZED PIPELINE DATASETS

**CONTENTS**

In Chapter 12, we introduced the concept of *pipeline datasets*. These are files, tables or other physical datasets in which the managed object itself represents a type and contains multiple managed objects each of which represents an instance of that type, and which in turn themselves contain instances of other types. Using the language of tables, rows and columns, these managed objects are tables, the instances they contain are rows, and those last-mentioned types are the columns of those tables, whose instances describe the properties and relationships of the objects represented by those rows.

Because our focus is temporal data management at the level of tables and rows, and not at the level of databases, we have discussed pipeline datasets as though there were a distinct set of them for each production table. Figure 13.1 shows one conventional table, and a set of eight pipeline datasets related to it.

Managing Time in Relational Databases. Doi: 10.1016/B978-0-12-375041-9.00013-3

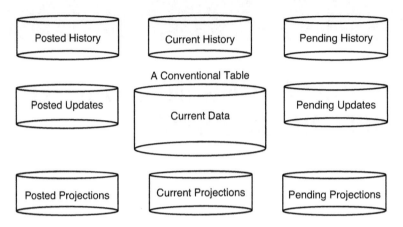

**Figure 13.1** Physically Distinct Pipeline Datasets.

What Figure 13.1 illustrates is a simplification of the always complex and usually messy physical database environment which IT departments everywhere must manage. Pipeline datasets may often contain data targeted at, or derived from, several tables within that database. They do not necessarily target, or derive from, single tables within a database. In addition, the IT industry has only the broadest of categories of pipeline datasets, categories such as batch transaction tables, logfiles of processed transactions, history tables, or staging areas where unusually complicated data transformations are carried out before the data is moved back into the production tables from whence it originated.

Figure 13.1 shows eight different types of pipeline datasets surrounding a conventional table of current data. These nine datasets align with the set of nine categories of temporal data which we introduced in Chapter 12.

Given a bi-temporal framework of two temporal dimensions, in each of which data can exist in the past, the present or the future, this set of nine categories is what results from the intersection of those two temporal dimensions. In addition, since the past, present and future are clear and distinct within each temporal dimension, and since each dimension is clear and distinct from the other, the result of this intersection is a set of nine categories which are themselves clear and distinct, which are, precisely, jointly exhaustive and mutually exclusive. Like our taxonomies, they cover all the ground there is to cover, and they don't overlap. Like our taxonomies, they are what mathematicians call a partitioning of their domain. Like our taxonomies, they assure us that in our discussions, we won't overlook anything and we won't confuse anything with anything else.

In the previous chapter, we showed how to physically *internalize* one particular kind of pipeline dataset within the production tables which are their destinations or points of origin. We showed how to turn them from distinct physical collections of data into logical collections of data that share residence in a single physical table.

The internalization of pipeline datasets is illustrated in Figure 13.2. These internalizations of pipeline datasets are not themselves managed objects to either the operating system or the DBMS. They are managed objects only to the AVF. The operating system recognizes and manages database instances, but is neither aware of nor can manage tables, rows, columns or the other managed objects that exist within database instances. As for the DBMS, once these pipeline datasets are internalized, all it sees is the production table itself, and the columns and rows of that table.

In this chapter, we show how to *re-present* these internalized datasets as queryable objects. We use the hyphenated form "re-present" advisedly. We do mean that we will show how to *represent* those internalized datasets as queryable objects, in the ordinary sense of the word "represent". But we also wish to emphasize that we are re-presenting, i.e. presenting again, things whose presence we had removed.[1] Those things are the physical

An Asserted Version Table

| Posted History | Current History | Pending History |
| --- | --- | --- |
| Posted Updates | Current Data | Pending Updates |
| Posted Projections | Current Projections | Pending Projections |

**Figure 13.2** Internalized Pipeline Datasets.

---

[1]We also wish to avoid confusion with our technical term *represent*, in which an object, we say, is represented in an effective time clock tick within an assertion time clock tick just in case business data describing that object exists on an asserted version row whose assertion and effective time periods contain those clock tick pairs.

pipeline datasets which, in the previous chapter, we showed how to *internalize* within the production tables which are their destinations or points of origin.

For example, we show how to provide, as queryable objects, all the pending transactions against a production table, or a logfile of posted transactions that have already been applied to that table, or a set of data from that table which we currently claim to be true, or that same set of data but as it was originally entered and prior to any corrections that may have been made to it.

We do not claim that any of these eight types of pipeline dataset correspond to data that supports a specific business need. For the most part, that will *not* be the case. For example, auditors will frequently want to look at Posted History pipeline datasets, i.e. at the rows that belong to that logical category of temporal data. But they will usually want to see current assertions about the historical past of the objects they are interested in, along with those past assertions. The current assertions about historical data are logically part of, as we will see, the Posted Updates pipeline dataset. So to provide queryable objects corresponding to their specific business requirements, auditors will usually write queries directly against asserted version tables, queries that combine and filter data from any number of these pipeline datasets.

To take another example, the Pending Projections pipeline dataset does not distinguish data in the near assertion time future from data in the far assertion time future. Yet deferred assertions with an assertion begin date that will become current an hour from now serve an entirely different business purpose than deferred assertions whose assertion begin date is January 1st, 5000. So to provide queryable objects corresponding to real business requirements, we will often have to write queries that filter out rows from within a single pipeline dataset, and combine rows from multiple pipeline datasets.

## Internalized Pipeline Datasets

We can say what things used to be like, what they are like, and also what they will be like. These statements we can make are statements about, respectively, the past, the present and the future. In a table in a database, each row makes one such statement. In conventional tables, however, the only rows are ones that make statements about the present.

These things we say represent what we claim is true. Of course, as we saw in Chapter 12, we can equally well say that they represent what we accept as true, agree is true, assent to or assert as true, or believe, know or think is true. For now, we'll just call them our truth claims, or simply our claims, about the statements made by rows in our tables.

Besides what we currently claim is true, there are also claims that we once made but are no longer willing to make. These are statements that, based on our current understanding of things, are not true, or should no longer be considered as reliable sources of information. It is also the case that we may have statements—whether about the past, the present or the future—that we are not yet willing to claim are true, but which nonetheless are "works in progress" that we intend to complete and that, at that time, we will be willing to claim are true. Or perhaps they are complete, and we are pretty certain that they are correct, but we are waiting on a business decision-maker to review them and approve them for release as current assertions. The former is a set of transactions about to be applied to the database. The latter is a set of data in a staging area, either waiting for additional work to be performed on it, or waiting for review and approval.

So if statements may be about what things were, are or will be like, and claims about statements may have once been made and later repudiated, or be current claims, or be claims that we are not yet willing to make but might at some time in the future be willing to make, then the intersection of facts and claims creates a matrix of nine temporal combinations. That matrix is shown in Figure 13.3.[2]

| | what we used to claim | what we currently claim | what we will claim |
|---|---|---|---|
| **what things used to be like** | what we used to claim things used to be like | what we currently claim things used to be like | what we will claim things used to be like |
| **what things are like** | what we used to claim things are like now | what we currently claim things are like now | what we will claim things are like now |
| **what things will be like** | what we used to claim things will be like | what we currently claim things will be like | what we will claim things will be like |

**Figure 13.3** Facts, Claims and Time.

[2]With the substitution of the word "claims" for "beliefs", this is the same matrix shown in Figure 12.1. Chapter 12 also contains a discussion of the interchangeability of "claims", "beliefs" and several other terms. We note, however, that "claims" is a stronger word than "beliefs" in this sense, that some of the things we *believe* are true are things we are nonetheless not yet willing to *claim* are true. We take "claims", and "asserts" or "assertions", to be synonymous, and the other equivalent terms discussed in Chapter 12 to be terminological variations that appear more or less suitable in different contexts.

The reason we are interested in the intersection of facts and claims is that rows in database tables are both. All rows in database tables represent *factual claims*. One aspect of the row is that it represents a statement of fact. The other aspect is that it represents a claim that that statement of fact is, in fact, true. This is just as true of conventional tables as it is of asserted version tables.

When dealing with periods of time, as we are, the past includes all and only those periods of time which end before Now(). The future includes all and only those periods of time which begin after Now(). The present includes all and only those periods of time which include Now().

Every row in a bi-temporal table is tagged with two periods of time, which we call assertion time and effective time. Consequently, every row falls into one of these nine categories. Conventional tables contain rows which exist in only one of these nine temporal combinations. They are rows which represent current claims about what things are currently like. But since conventional tables do not contain any of the other eight categories of rows, their rows don't need explicit time periods to distinguish them from rows in those other categories. And in conventional tables, of course, they don't have them.

Both the assertion and the effective time periods of conventional rows are co-extensive with their physical presence in their tables. They begin to be asserted, and also go into effect, when they are created; and they remain asserted, and also remain in effect, until they are deleted. They don't keep track of history because they aren't interested in it. They don't distinguish updates which correct mistakes in data from updates which keep data current with a changing reality, ultimately because the business doesn't notice the difference, or is willing to tolerate the ambiguity in the data.

So conventional tables, all in all, are a poor kind of thing. They do less than they could, and less than the business needs them to do. They overwrite history. They don't distinguish between correcting mistakes and making changes to keep up with a changing world. And these conventional tables, as we all know, make up the vast majority of all persistent object tables managed by IT departments.

We put up with tables like these because the IT profession isn't yet aware that there is an alternative and because, by dint of hard work, we can make up for the shortcomings of these tables. Data which falls into one of the other eight categories can usually be found somewhere, or reconstructed from data that can be found somewhere. If all else fails, DBMS archives and backups, and their associated transaction logs, will usually enable us to recreate any state that the database has been in. They will allow us to re-present six of the nine temporal categories we have identified.[3]

The three categories that cannot be re-presented from backups and logfiles are the three categories of future claims— things we are going to make our databases say (unless we change our minds) about what things once were like, or are like now, or may be like in the future. Future claims often start out as scribbled notes on someone's desk. But once inside the machine, they exist in transaction datasets, in collections of data that are intended, at some time or other, to be applied to the database and become currently asserted data.

In the previous chapter, we called the eight categories of data which are not current claims about the present, *pipeline datasets*, collections of data that exist at various points along the pipelines leading into production tables or leading out from them. As physically separate from those production tables, these collections of data are generally not immediately available for business use. Usually, IT technical personnel must do some work on these physical files or tables before a business user can query them for information.

This takes time, and until the work is complete, the information is not available. By the time the work is complete, the business value of the information may be much reduced. This work also has its costs in terms of how much time those technicians must spend to prepare that data to be queried. In addition, even without special requests for information in them, these physical datasets, taken together, constitute a significant management cost for IT.

With multiple points of rest in the pipelines leading into and out of production database tables, there are multiple points at which data can be lost. For example, data can be accidentally deleted before any copies are made. For datasets in the *inflow* pipelines, and which have not yet made it into the database itself, the only recourse for lost data is to reacquire or recreate the data. If prior datasets in the pipeline have already been

---

[3]That's the idea, anyway. In reality, this "data of last resort" isn't always there when we go looking for it. Backups and logfiles are rarely kept forever, so the data we need may have been purged or written over. There will inevitably be occasional intervals during which the system hiccupped, and simply failed to capture the data in the first place. If the data is still available, it might not be in a readily accessible format because of schema changes made after it was captured.

legitimately deleted (legitimately because the data had success-fully made it to the next downstream point), then we may have to go all the way back to the original point at which the data was first acquired or created. This can impose significant delays in getting the data to its consumers, and significant costs in reacquiring or recreating it and in moving it, for a second time, down the pipeline. And this risk is quite real because, prior to making it into the database, the backups and logfiles which pro-tect data once it has reached the DBMS are not yet available.

By internalizing these datasets within the production tables whose data they contain, we eliminate the costs of managing them, including the costs of recovering from mistakes made in managing them. We now turn to the task of re-presenting what were physically distinct managed objects, external to production tables. We re-present them as queryable objects, showing how queries can produce result sets containing exactly the data that would have been in those physical datasets, had we not internalized them.

## Pipeline Datasets as Queryable Objects

We emphasize once more that most business queries for temporal data will *not* focus on data from a single one of these eight internalized pipeline datasets. Together with currently asserted current data, these eight other categories of temporal data constitute a partitioning of all bi-temporal data. Like the Allen relationship queries we will discuss in the next chapter, we focus on these queries *in spite of* the fact that they are not real-world business queries. We focus on them because, as a set, they are guaranteed to be complete. If these eight categories of pipeline datasets can be internalized, then we can be *certain* that any real-world business dataset—one des-tined to update a production table, or one derived from a pro-duction table—can also be internalized. In the next chapter, once we have seen that any Allen relationship against asserted version data can be expressed in a query, we will be similarly *certain* that any query whatsoever can be expressed against asserted version tables.

In each case, we will illustrate these queries in the context of CREATE VIEW statements. From the point of view of the semantics involved, there is no difference between direct queries and SQL VIEW statements. But actual VIEW statements lend a little more substance to the notion of re-presenting internalized pipeline datasets as queryable objects.

## Posted History: Past Claims About the Past

The Posted History dataset consists of all those rows in an asserted version table which lie in both the assertion time past and also in the effective time past. Its subject matter is things as they used to be. Its rows are claims about what is now part of history which we are no longer willing to make. Posted History is a record of all the times we got it wrong about what is now the past, up to but not including our current claims about that past. Those current claims, of course, are the ones in which we finally, we hope, got it right.

Here is the view which re-presents Posted History. With the suffix "Post_Hist" standing for "posted history", it looks like this:

```
CREATE VIEW V_Policy_Post_Hist
AS SELECT oid, asr_beg_dt, asr_end_dt, eff_beg_dt, eff_end_dt,
          client, type, copay

FROM Policy_AV
       WHERE asr_end_dt <= Now()
       AND eff_end_dt <= Now()
```

Note that Posted History is a bi-temporal collection of data. Neither temporal dimension is restricted to a point in time, and so both time periods must be included on all rows in the view. The unique identifier for this or for any other bi-temporal view of an asserted version table, is the combination of *oid*, assertion time period and effective time period.

Because Asserted Versioning manages the two pairs of dates as PERIOD datatypes, either or both can be used to represent the time period. So, in an asserted version table and, therefore, in any bi-temporal view based on it, any of the following are unique identifiers: {*oid* + *asr-beg* + *eff-beg*}, {*oid* + *asr-end* + *eff-beg*}, {*oid* + *asr-beg* + *eff-end*}, or {*oid* + *asr-end* + *eff-end*}. In addition, the identifiers will remain unique even if we add either one or two more dates from the date pairs to them. For example, {*oid* + *asr-beg* + *eff-beg* + *eff-end*} is also unique.

|  | what we used to claim | what we currently claim | what we will claim |
|---|---|---|---|
| **what things used to be like** | what we used to claim things used to be like |  |  |
| **what things are like** |  |  |  |
| **what things will be like** |  |  |  |

**Figure 13.4** Posted History.

This is important to know when creating indexes for performance, as described in Chapter 15.

Any report about the effective-time past can be either an *as-was* or an *as-is* report. If it is an *as-is* report, it can be produced from Current History. But if it is an *as-was* report, it can be produced only from Posted History.

## Posted Updates: Past Claims About the Present

The Posted Updates dataset consists of all those rows in an asserted version table which lie in the assertion time past but in the effective time present. Its subject matter is things as they currently are. Its rows are claims about these things which we are no longer willing to make. Posted Updates are a record of all the times we got it wrong about what is now the present, up to but not including our current claims about that present. Those current claims, of course, are the ones in which we finally, we hope, got it right.

Here is the view which re-presents Posted Updates. With the suffix "Post_Upd" standing for "posted updates", it looks like this:

```
CREATE VIEW V_Policy_Post_Upd
AS SELECT oid, asr_beg_dt, asr_end_dt, eff_beg_dt, eff_end_dt,
          client, type, copay

FROM Policy_AV
     WHERE asr_end_dt <= Now()
     AND eff_beg_dt <= Now() AND eff_end_dt > Now()
```

The Posted Updates dataset is also a bi-temporal collection of data, and so both time periods must be included on all rows in the view. The unique identifier for this or for any other bi-temporal view of an asserted version table, is the combination of *oid*, any one or both of the assertion dates, and any one or both of the effective dates.

| | what we used to claim | what we currently claim | what we will claim |
|---|---|---|---|
| what things used to be like | | | |
| what things are like | what we used to claim things are like now | | |
| what things will be like | | | |

**Figure 13.5** Posted Updates.

## Posted Projections: Past Claims About the Future

The Posted Projections dataset consists of all those rows in an asserted version table which lie in the assertion time past but in the effective time future. Its subject matter is things as they might have turned out to be. Its rows are claims about these things which we are no longer willing to make. Posted Projections are a record of all the times we got it wrong about what currently lies in the future, up to but not including our current claims about that future. Those current claims, of course, are the ones in which we finally, we hope, got it right.

Here is the view which re-presents Posted Projections. With the suffix "Post_Proj" standing for "posted projections", it looks like this:

```
CREATE VIEW V_Policy_Post_Proj
AS SELECT oid, asr_beg_dt, asr_end_dt, eff_beg_dt, eff_end_dt,
          client, type, copay

FROM Policy_AV
        WHERE asr_end_dt <= Now()
        AND eff_beg_dt > Now()
```

The Posted Projections dataset is also a bi-temporal collection of data, and so both time periods must be included on all rows in the view. The unique identifier for this or for any other bi-temporal view of an asserted version table, is the combination of *oid*, any one or both of the assertion dates, and any one or both of the effective dates.

The rows in this view are mistakes which never became effective. In a more sinister light, they are forecasts which never came true, and which those making them perhaps knew or suspected would never come true. Note, however, that we can certainly be held responsible for statements about what never came to be. We can be held responsible for a statement made by any row that has ever existed in current assertion time. In this case, these rows were once asserted. Once upon a time, they were claims made about what the future will be like. Bernie Madoff is in jail for making such claims.

| | what we used to claim | what we currently claim | what we will claim |
|---|---|---|---|
| what things used to be like | | | |
| what things are like | | | |
| what things will be like | what we used to claim things will be like | | |

**Figure 13.6** Posted Projections.

Of course, we can always be mistaken about what the future will be like. But that's not the point about responsibility. The point is that we made those claims. Due allowance will be made for the fact that they were claims about the future.

If they turn out to be false, that doesn't necessarily mean that we intended to mislead others. In making those claims, we may have taken all due diligence, and simply have made a responsible but mistaken projection. On the other hand, we may have been irresponsible, we may *not* have taken due diligence. On the basis of nothing more than a hunch, we may have presented to the world, as actionable projections responsibly made, statements about what we merely guessed the future might be like.

So assertions are not just claims that statements are true, although that is an often convenient shorthand for saying what assertions are. More precisely, assertions are claims that statements are not only true, but are also actionable, that they are good enough for their intended uses. And since statements about the future are neither true nor false, at the time they are made, the best that we can assert about them is that they are responsibly made, and are therefore actionable.

## Current History: Current Claims About the Past

The Current History dataset consists of all those rows in asserted version tables which lie in the assertion time present but in the effective time past. Its subject matter is things as they used to be. Its rows are current claims about what is now the past. Current History is a record of what we currently believe things used to be like.

Here is the view which re-presents Current History. With the suffix "Curr_Hist" standing for "current history", it looks like this:

```
CREATE VIEW V_Policy_Curr_Hist
AS SELECT oid, eff_beg_dt, eff_end_dt, client, type, copay
FROM Policy_AV
        WHERE asr_beg_dt <= Now() AND asr_end_dt > Now()
        AND eff_end_dt <= Now()
```

| | what we used to claim | what we currently claim | what we will claim |
|---|---|---|---|
| **what things used to be like** | | what we currently claim things used to be like | |
| **what things are like** | | | |
| **what things will be like** | | | |

**Figure 13.7** Current History.

The Current History dataset is a uni-temporal collection of data. It re-presents, as a queryable object, what is usually called a *history table*, a table of all versions of objects, up to but not including the current version.

Because there cannot be two current assertions about the same object during the same or overlapping periods of effective time, assertion time is not needed in this view. All the rows in this dataset are currently asserted rows. And so only one time period is part of this view. The unique identifier of the data in the view is {*oid* + *eff-beg* + *eff-end*}. In fact, with just either one of those two dates, it is still a unique identifier.

In history tables as they are currently used in IT, assertion time differences are not recorded. Some history tables will be *as-was* tables, i.e. tables in which each row remains exactly as it was when it became history. Others will be *as-is* tables, i.e. tables in which errors in the history table data are corrected as they are discovered, but corrected by means of overwriting the original data. In yet other cases, there is no explicit policy defining the history table as an *as-is* or an *as-was* table; and so if we use the history table, for example, to recreate a report as it was originally run, we will probably produce a report with a mixture of data as originally entered, together with other data that has been corrected, with no way to tell which is which.

Asserted Versioning supports both kinds of history. The Posted History dataset is equivalent to an *as-was* history table. The Current History dataset is equivalent to an *as-is* history table, a table which tells us what we currently believe the past to have been like. As such, it is a currently asserted version table. So if it is used to rerun reports as of some point in past effective time, those reports will reflect all corrections made to that data since that time.

Queries supporting specific business requests for information can, of course, be written against these internalizations of pipeline datasets. For example, if we are interested only in 2009's historical data, as we currently claim that data to be, we can issue a query against this view which selects just that data. That query looks like this:

```
SELECT oid, eff_beg_dt, eff_end_dt, client, type, copay
FROM Policy_V_Curr_Hist
    WHERE eff-beg >= 01/01/2009 AND eff_end_dt < 01/01/2010
```

## Current Data: Current Claims About the Present

The Current Data dataset consists of all those rows in an asserted version table which lie in the assertion time present and also in the effective time present. Its subject matter is things as they are now. Its rows are claims about these things which we currently make. Current Data is what most of our database tables contain. It is a record of what we currently believe things are currently like.

If our asserted version table previously existed as a conventional table, there are likely to be any number of production queries that reference it. To make the conversion of this table to an asserted version table transparent to these queries, we must rename the table and use its original name as the name of this view. This is why we have renamed such tables by appending "_AV" to them. Doing this for the Policy table we are using in these examples, we renamed it as Policy_AV.

Here is a view preliminary to the one which does re-present Current Data. This view contains all currently asserted current versions.

```
CREATE VIEW Policy_CACV
AS SELECT oid, client, type, copay
FROM Policy_AV
        WHERE asr_beg_dt <= Now() AND asr_end_dt > Now()
        AND eff_beg_dt <= Now() AND eff_end_dt > Now()
```

In the original non-temporal table, there was one row per object. Since each oid uniquely identifies an object, and since there can only be one row for each object that is currently asserted as being currently in effect, this view also contains one row per object. In addition, since, at every point in time, the original table contains rows that represent what we currently believe the objects described by those rows are currently like, an asserted version table of currently asserted current versions will contain, moment for moment, exactly the same business data.

Like the conventional Policy row, this view uses exactly one row to re-present one policy. But unlike the conventional Policy table, these rows include *oids*, not the column or columns that were the primary key in the original conventional table. And they

| | what we used to claim | what we currently claim | what we will claim |
|---|---|---|---|
| **what things used to be like** | | | |
| **what things are like** | | what we currently claim things are like now | |
| **what things will be like** | | | |

**Figure 13.8** Current Data.

include temporal foreign keys, not the column or columns that were the foreign keys in the original table.

So we do not yet have a view which re-presents the original conventional table. The Current Data dataset is row-to-row equivalent to the original table in terms of its contents, but not in terms of its schema. We do not yet have a view to which all queries against the original table can be redirected. That view must replace the oid in Policy_CACV with the original primary key, and replace the TFK with the original foreign key. And it must have the same name as the original table. Here is that view:

```
CREATE VIEW Policy
AS SELECT policy_nbr AS P.policy_nbr, policy_type AS P.
policy_type,
      copay_amt AS P.copay_amt, client_nbr AS C.client_nbr
FROM Policy_CACV P
      JOIN Client C
      ON C.client_oid = P.client_oid
```

The most frequently used view of any asserted version table is likely to be this current data view. These are precisely those rows that make up the complete contents of a conventional non-temporal table.

## Current Projections: Current Claims About the Future

The Current Projections dataset consists of all those rows in an asserted version table which lie in the assertion time present but in the effective time future. Its subject matter is things as they may turn out to be. Its rows are claims about these things which we currently make. Current Projections are a record of what we currently believe things are going to be like; and, of course, we shouldn't make such claims unless we are pretty sure that's how they will turn out to be. If we aren't pretty sure about them, then we should make them, if we make them at all, as *pending* projections.

|  | what we used to claim | what we currently claim | what we will claim |
|---|---|---|---|
| what things used to be like |  |  |  |
| what things are like |  |  |  |
| what things will be like |  | what we currently claim things will be like |  |

**Figure 13.9** Current Projections.

Here is the view which re-presents Current Projections. With the suffix "Curr_Proj" standing for "current projections", it looks like this:

```
CREATE VIEW V_Policy_Curr_Proj
AS SELECT oid, eff_beg_dt, eff_end_dt, client, type, copay
FROM Policy_AV
        WHERE asr_beg_dt <= Now() AND asr_end_dt > Now()
        AND eff_beg_dt > Now()
```

As we can see, effective time is explicitly represented in this view, and so the view is a collection of uni-temporal versioned data. As such, it has the unique identifier that all version tables have—{*oid* + *eff-beg*+ *eff-end*}, in which the two dates are not merely two dates, but each the semantically complete representative of a PERIOD datatype.

The Current Projections dataset is the collection of all future versions in an asserted version table that we currently assert as making actionable statements. A simple example of a current projection is a version that shows a change in a policy's copay amount that will go into effect next month. The version exists in current assertion time but in future effective time.

## Pending History: Future Claims About the Past

The Pending History dataset consists of all those rows in an asserted version table which lie in the assertion time future but in the effective time past. Its subject matter is things as they used to be. Its rows are claims which we are not yet willing to make about what is now part of history. Pending History is a record of what we may eventually be willing to say the past was like, once we've got all our facts straight.

Here is the view which re-presents Pending History. With the suffix "Pend_Hist" standing for "pending history", it looks like this:

| | what we used to claim | what we currently claim | what we will claim |
|---|---|---|---|
| **what things used to be like** | | | what we will claim things used to be like |
| **what things are like** | | | |
| **what things will be like** | | | |

**Figure 13.10** Pending History.

```
CREATE VIEW V_Policy_Pend_Hist
AS SELECT oid, asr_beg_dt, asr_end_dt, eff_beg_dt, eff_end_dt,
      client, type, copay

FROM Policy_AV
      WHERE asr_beg_dt > Now()
      AND eff_end_dt <= Now()
```

Pending History is history as it will look once we get around to correcting it. One reason we might have pending history is that we have some information about what is needed to correct the past, but not all the information we need. Once that deferred assertion about the past is complete, we can then apply it. Another reason we might have pending history is that we have one or more corrections to the past, but those corrections can't be released until they are approved. Once approval is given, we can apply them, and those deferred assertions about the past will become current assertions about the past.

## Pending Updates: Future Claims About the Present

The Pending Updates dataset consists of all those rows in an asserted version table which lie in the assertion time future but in the effective time present. Its subject matter is things as they currently are. Its rows are claims about these things which we are not yet willing to make. The Pending Updates dataset is a record of what we may eventually (or soon) be willing to say things are like right now.

Here is the view which re-presents Pending Updates. With the suffix "Pend_Upd" standing for "pending updates", it looks like this:

```
CREATE VIEW Policy_Pend_Upd
AS SELECT oid, asr_beg_dt, asr_end_dt, eff_beg_dt, eff_end_dt,
client, type, copay
FROM Policy_AV
      WHERE asr_beg_dt > Now()
      AND eff_beg_dt <= Now() AND eff_end_dt > Now()
```

|  | what we used to claim | what we currently claim | what we will claim |
|---|---|---|---|
| what things used to be like |  |  |  |
| what things are like |  |  | what we will claim things are like now |
| what things will be like |  |  |  |

**Figure 13.11** Pending Updates.

Pending Updates exist in what we called, in the previous chapter, either the assertion-time *near future* or the assertion-time *far future*. Those in the near future have an assertion begin date close enough to Now() that the business is willing to let the passage of time make them current. Near future deferred assertions would typically have a begin date that will become current in the next few seconds, hours, days or weeks. In a conventional database, pending updates are transactions accumulated in an external batch transaction file, or perhaps in a batch transaction table within the database.

Far future deferred assertions are the internalization of data located in what are often called staging areas. They are collections of data that are usually more complicated than usual to update. By placing them in far future assertion time, we guarantee that they will not inadvertently become current assertions simply because of the passage of time. They can become current assertions only when, presumably after a review-and-approve process, the business releases them into near-future assertion time.

## Pending Projections: Future Claims About the Future

The Pending Projections dataset consists of all those rows in an asserted version table which lie in both the assertion time future and in the effective time future. Its subject matter is things as they may turn out to be. Its rows are claims about what currently lies in the future, but claims which we are not yet willing to make. Pending Projections are a record of what we may eventually be willing to say things are going to be like.

Here is the view which re-presents Pending Projections. With the suffix "Pend_Proj" standing for "pending projections", it looks like this:

```
CREATE VIEW Policy_Pend_Proj
AS SELECT oid, asr_beg_dt, asr_end_dt, eff_beg_dt, eff_end_dt,
client, type, copay
```

| | what we used to claim | what we currently claim | what we will claim |
|---|---|---|---|
| what things used to be like | | | |
| what things are like | | | |
| what things will be like | | | what we will claim things will be like |

**Figure 13.12** Pending Projections.

```
FROM Policy_AV
        WHERE asr_beg_dt > Now()
        AND eff_beg_dt > Now()
```

As we have seen with our other re-presented pipeline datasets, Pending Projections include both the assertion and effective time period as part of the unique identifier because both temporal dimensions are specified as ranges, and neither as points in time.

## Mirror Images of the Nine-Fold Way

As we said in Chapter 9, effective time exists within assertion time. First, logically speaking, we make a statement about how things are. Next, logically speaking, we make a truth claim about that statement.

Most of our queries against bi-temporal tables will specify a point in assertion time—most commonly Now()—and then ask for rows asserted at that point in time that were in effect at some point or period of effective time. For example, we might ask for all policies that were in effect on August 23, 2008, as we currently believe them to have been. Or we might ask for all policies which we currently claim were in effect any time in the first half of 2008.

Pinning down a point in assertion time, and then asking for versions of objects claimed at that point in time to be correct, is the general form that queries will take when posed by business users. But we can look at bi-temporal data from the opposite point of view as well. We can pin down a point or period in effective time, and ask for everything we ever asserted about things at that point in time.

It would not be too misleading to call this the *auditor's* point of view. From this point of view, we are interested in the history of our claims about what is true, not in the history of what actually happened out there in the world. Of course, we could also ask for all future assertions about a given point in effective time. But auditors, by the nature of their work, have little interest in future assertions. By the same token, they are very interested in past assertions, along with current ones. So an auditor's mirror-image of the nine categories reduces to a set of six categories, those shown in Figure 13.13.

These views that auditors are interested in are physically the same ones we have already described. The "mirror-image" is in perspective, not in content.

|  | what we used to claim | what we currently claim |
|---|---|---|
| **what things used to be like** | what we used to claim things used to be like | what we currently claim things used to be like |
| **what things are like** | what we used to claim things are like now | what we currently claim things are like now |
| **what things will be like** | what we used to claim things will be like | what we currently claim things will be like |

**Figure 13.13** The Auditor's Mirror Image of the Nine-Fold Way.

# The Value of Internalizing Pipeline Datasets

The cost of managing physical pipeline datasets is high. This cost is seldom discussed because it is universally thought to be just an inevitable cost of doing business. Bringing down this cost is a matter of doing all those various things that IT management has done for decades, and continues to do. Quality control procedures are put in place so errors don't creep into our databases and later have to be backed out. The platform costs of storing, transforming, and moving data into and out of pipeline datasets are controlled by minimizing redundancy, and by moving datasets up and down the storage hierarchy. Software that sets up and runs production schedules minimizes the human costs of scheduling work involving these pipeline datasets.

But the work of managing pipeline datasets is tedious. And whenever the management of these datasets is a one-off kind of thing, i.e. whenever the development group has to manage these datasets rather than the IT Operations group that handles scheduled maintenance, errors in managing them are not uncommon.

Asserted Versioning does not offer a way to more efficiently *manage* pipeline datasets. It offers a way to *eliminate* them and, consequently, eliminate the totality of their management costs! There will always be some circumstances in which data must be manipulated in external pipeline datasets. But these can become the exception rather than the rule.

In place of these pipeline datasets, Asserted Versioning stores the information contained in those pipeline datasets *internally*, within the production tables that are their sources and destinations. Pending transactions can be stored within the production tables themselves. Posted transactions can be, too. Data staging areas can also exist as semantically distinct sets of rows, physically contained within production tables. Pipeline datasets, then, cease to exist as distinct physical objects. They become virtualized, as semantically distinct collections of rows all physically existing within the same tables, re-presented in different views.

We may think that the principal cost elimination benefit of internalizing pipeline datasets is that it reduces the number of distinct datasets that programs, SQL and production scheduling software have to identify and manage. This is a reduction in the cost of the mechanics of pipeline datasets. Instead of assembling data from multiple tables, it already exists all in one place.

But the more significant cost reduction has to do with the semantics of pipeline datasets. With all data about the same things in the same place, we will, all of us, find all of it when we go looking for it. The most junior member of the business community will find the same set of data for his queries that the most senior member does. There won't be differences in completeness of the source data, or quality of that data, as there so often are in today's business world and today's collections of business data.

When we need any of this data, we won't have to go looking for it. All of the data about what we once thought was true, or what we currently think is true, or what we are not yet willing to assert is true, will be available by simply changing the assertion point-in-time selection criterion on views and queries. By changing that predicate in a WHERE clause to a past point in assertion time, we will be able to access the internalized re-presentation of posted transactions. By changing the predicate to a future point in time, we will be able to access the internalized re-presentation of pending transactions.

By the same token, we will be able to access historical data about what things used to be like from the same table that contains data about what they are like right now, and that may also contain data about what those things are going to be like sometime in the future. Again, it will be as easy as changing a predicate in a WHERE clause.

# Glossary References

Glossary entries whose definitions form strong interdependencies are grouped together in the following list. The same glossary entries may be grouped together in different ways at the end of different chapters, each grouping reflecting the semantic perspective of each chapter. There will usually be several other, and often many other, glossary entries that are not included in the list, and we recommend that the Glossary be consulted whenever an unfamiliar term is encountered.

We note, in particular, that none of the nine types of pipeline dataset are included in this list. In general, we leave category sets out of these lists, but recommend that the reader look them up in the Glossary.

as-is
as-was

Asserted Versioning Framework (AVF)

assertion time

statement

conventional table
non-temporal table

deferred assertion
far future assertion time
near future assertion time

instance
type

managed object
object
oid
queryable object

pipeline dataset
inflow pipeline
outflow pipeline
internalization of pipeline datasets
re-presentation of pipeline datasets

production database
production table

temporal dimension

temporal transaction

version

# ALLEN RELATIONSHIP AND OTHER QUERIES

In this chapter, we examine each of the thirteen Allen relationships, as well as each non-leaf node in the taxonomy of Allen relationships which we introduced in Chapter 3. We describe the Allen relationships as they hold between two time periods, between a time period and a point in time, and also between two points in time. We show how these relationships are expressed in terms of time periods represented with the closed-open convention, and we provide a sample query for each one.

After a section in which we illustrate how much simpler these queries would be to express if we had a PERIOD datatype, we conclude this chapter by discussing queries which involve temporal joins.

Figure 14.1 shows our taxonomy of the Allen relationships. Those relationships are the leaf nodes in this taxonomy. Every leaf node has an inverse relationship, except the [*equals*] relationship. We italicize that relationship name to emphasize that it has no inverse. So counting the [*equals*] relationship, and the six leaf nodes and their inverses, we have the full set of thirteen Allen relationships. We also underline the non-leaf node relationships in the taxonomy, to emphasize that they are relationships *we* have defined, and are not one of the Allen relationships.

Managing Time in Relational Databases. Doi: 10.1016/B978-0-12-375041-9.00014-5

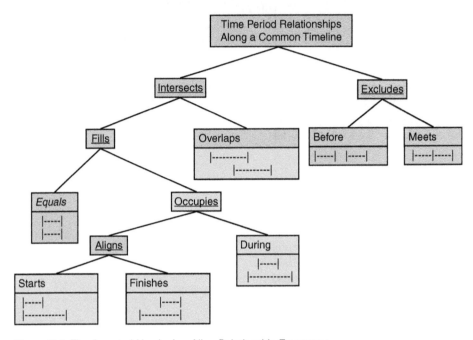

**Figure 14.1** The Asserted Versioning Allen Relationship Taxonomy.

Many of the Allen relationships are used by the AVF to enforce TEI and TRI. For example, as we pointed out in Chapter 3, the [intersects] relationship is important because it defines TEI. If two asserted versions of the same object share even a single effective time clock tick, within shared assertion time, then they [intersect], and violate TEI. Otherwise, they don't. The [fills] relationship is important because it defines TRI. If a TRI relationship fails, it is because there is no episode of the referenced parent object which temporally includes, i.e. [fills$^{-1}$], that of the child version. The [before] relationship is important because it distinguishes episodes from one another. Every episode of an object is non-contiguous with every other episode of the same object, and so one of them must be [before] the other.

As for queries issued by business users, we have found that many ad hoc queries, and perhaps the majority of them, are queries about *episodes*, not about versions. That is, they are queries that want (i) the begin and end date of the episode and, for business data, (ii) the last version of past episodes, the current version of current episodes, or the latest version of future episodes. Because of the importance of episodes to queries, the SQL examples in this chapter will select episodes. The last, current or latest version contains the business data. The episode begin date that is on every version, and the version's own effective end date, provide the effective time period of the episode itself.

We also note that the SQL in many of the following examples does not represent typical queries that a business would write. Each of these queries focuses on one specific Allen relationship, and show how to express it in SQL. In particular, these sample queries do not include typical join criteria. Instead, the only join criteria used in these examples are two time periods and the Allen relationship between them.

Another reason these sample queries don't look very real world is that they select from two of the tables in our sample database that don't have much to do with one another. In particular, there is no TRI relationship between them. They are the Policy and Wellness Program tables. If we had used, for example, the Client and Policy tables instead, many of the queries would have been more realistic.

But TRI-related tables cannot illustrate all of the Allen relationships. In fact, every instance of a TRI relationship involves a parent and a child time period that is an instance of one of seven of the Allen relationships. This leaves six other Allen relationships that TRI-related tables cannot illustrate.

Nevertheless, as overly simple and unrealistic as most of these sample queries may be, they are the foundation for all queries that express temporal relationships. No query will ever need to express a temporal relationship that is not one of these relationships. So if we know how to write the temporal predicates in these queries, we will know how to write any temporal predicate for any query.

## Allen Relationship Queries

The value of reviewing all the Allen relationships in terms of queries against asserted version tables is that, as we already know, the Allen relationships are exhaustive. There are no positional relationships along a common timeline, among time periods and/or points in time, other than those ones. Thus, by showing how to write a query for each one of them, as well as for the groups of them identified in our taxonomy, we will have provided the basic material out of which any query against any assertion version table may be expressed.

In addition to the thirteen Allen relationships themselves, our taxonomy provides five additional relationships, each of which is a logical combination of two or more Allen relationships. And these combinations are not formed simply by stringing together Allen relationships with OR predicates. Although they are, necessarily, logically equivalent to the OR'd set of those relationships, they are often much simpler expressions, easier to understand and faster when executed.

In these sample queries, we will not include predicates for assertion time, and will pretend that our sample tables are uni-temporal versioned tables. This eliminates unnecessary detail from these examples. We will do this by using two version table views, shown below: *V_Wellness_Program_Curr_Asr* and *V_Policy_Curr_Asr*. The former is a view of all currently asserted Wellness Program versions. The latter is a view of all currently asserted Policy versions.

```
CREATE VIEW V_Wellness_Program_Curr_Asr AS
SELECT * FROM Wellness_Program_AV
      WHERE asr_beg_dt <= Now()
      AND asr_end_dt > Now()

CREATE VIEW V_ Policy _Curr_Asr AS
SELECT * FROM Policy_AV
      WHERE asr_beg_dt <= Now()
      AND asr_end_dt > Now()
```

In these example queries, as we said before, we will be selecting episodes, not versions. For the two tables used in this chapter, these are the views which provide episodes as queryable managed objects:

```
CREATE VIEW V_Wellness_Program_Epis AS
SELECT wp.wellpgm_oid, wp.epis_beg_dt, wp.eff_end_dt
AS epis_end_dt, wp.welllpgm_nm, wp.wellpgm_nbr,
wp.wellpgm_cat_cd
FROM V_Wellness_Program_Curr_Asr AS wp
      WHERE wp.eff_end_dt =
          (SELECT MAX(wpx.eff_end_dt)
          FROM V_Wellness_Program_Curr_Asr AS wpx
             WHERE wpx.wellpgm_oid = wp.wellpgm_oid
             AND wpx.epis_beg_dt = wp.epis_beg_dt)

CREATE VIEW V_Policy_Epis AS
SELECT pol.policy_oid, pol.epis_beg_dt, pol.eff_end_dt AS
epis_end_dt, pol.policy_type, pol.copay_amt,
pol.client_oid, pol.policy_nbr
FROM V_Policy_Curr_Asr AS pol
      WHERE pol.eff_end_dt =
          (SELECT MAX(px.eff_end_dt)
          FROM V_Policy_Curr_Asr px
          WHERE px.policy_oid = pol.policy_oid
          AND px.epis_beg_dt = pol.epis_beg_dt)
```

These episode views are the query-side work of defining an episode datatype. The AVF presents episodes as maintainable managed objects. These views present episodes as queryable managed objects.

This is a very important point. Both computer science research and IT practice have shown the importance of the concept of a string of one or more contiguous clock ticks with a known location in time. SQL does not directly support this concept; and so instead, we, and others, have to write code to exclude gaps and overlaps occurring in the timespan between a pair of dates or timestamps. A PERIOD datatype is the direct support needed for this concept. This datatype implements this concept at the correct *level of abstraction*.

By the same token, our own research and practice has shown the importance of the concept of an episode, a string of one or more contiguous and non-overlapping versions of the same object. Without that concept, and the concepts of objects and versions on which it depends, there is also no concept of temporal entity integrity and temporal referential integrity. Without that concept, collections of rows are defined, as needed, within each SQL statement. As we can see with both the standard and alternative temporal models, their SQL insert, update and delete statements do result in bi-temporal data that satisfies what we call TEI and TRI. Their SQL queries do find episodes, when they need them, past assertions when they need them, and so on. But the *level of abstraction is wrong*, for the same reason that getting the same results with a pair of dates that one would get with a PERIOD datatype is wrong.

So we now have two views which externalize, as queryable managed objects, the best data we currently have (i.e. our currently asserted data) about policy episodes and wellness program episodes. Now, using these two views, we will define another view that we will use to illustrate each of the Allen relationships. This is the view *V_Allen_Example*. This view will keep the examples as small and easy to understand as possible, eliminating all extraneous and repetitive detail while focusing on the Allen relationships themselves. Here is the *V_Allen_Example* view:

```
CREATE VIEW V_Allen_Example AS
SELECT wp.wellpgm_oid, pol.policy_oid,
       wp.epis_beg_dt AS wp_epis_beg_dt,
       wp.epis_end_dt AS wp_epis_end_dt,
       pol.epis_beg_dt AS pol_epis_beg_dt,
       pol.epis_end_dt AS pol_epis_end_dt
```

```
FROM V_Wellness_Program_Epis AS wp,
     V_Policy_Epis AS pol
     WHERE wp.wellpgm_nm = 'Diabetes'
     AND wp.epis_beg_dt >= '1/1/2009'
     AND wp.epis_beg_dt <= '12/31/2009'
```

As we said previously, these queries are not intended to represent realistic scenarios. Their sole purpose is to demonstrate that all Allen relationships can be expressed as queries against asserted version tables. Note in particular that the two tables in this view are not correlated by a key, whereas they normally would be correlated with a join predicate. This is so we can see how the Allen relationships correlate the two tables using dates.

## Time Period to Time Period Queries

Allen relationships may relate two time periods, or a time period to a point in time, or two points in time. We will represent time periods, using our closed-open notation, as follows:

Period 1: [eff_beg_dt$_1$ - eff_end_dt$_1$]. Referred to as P$_1$.
Period 2: [eff_beg_dt$_2$ - eff_end_dt$_2$]. Referred to as P$_2$.

*Eff_beg_dt$_1$* is earlier than *eff_end_dt$_1$*, and *eff_beg_dt$_2$* is earlier than *eff_end_dt$_2$*. This is true even for the limiting case of a time period that includes only a single clock tick.

### P$_1$ [starts] P$_2$

This is a pair of relationships, one the inverse of the other.[1] In the non-superscripted relationship, the first time period is the shorter one. Figure 14.2 shows this relationship, and its place in our taxonomy. The two dashed lines in the illustration graphically represent P$_1$ and P$_2$, with P$_1$ being the upper dashed line.

The predicate for this relationship, as it holds between two time periods expressed as pairs of dates using the closed-open convention, is:

```
(eff_beg_dt₁ = eff_beg_dt₂)
AND (eff_end_dt₁ < eff_end_dt₂)
```

It says that P$_1$ and P$_2$ begin at the same time, but that P$_1$ is the first to end, and is therefore the shorter of the two time periods.

The inverse of this relationship is: P$_1$ [starts$^{-1}$] P$_2$. In the superscripted relationship, the first time period is the longer one. The predicate for this relationship, as it holds between

---

[1]The names of the Allen relationships are standard. They were provided by Allen in his original article, and continue to be used throughout the computer science literature.

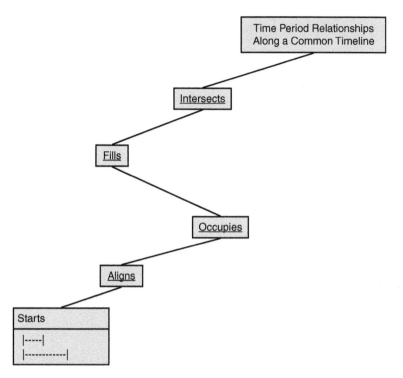

**Figure 14.2** $P_1$ [starts] $P_2$.

two time periods expressed as pairs of dates using the closed-open convention, is:

```
(eff_beg_dt₁ = eff_beg_dt₂)
AND (eff_end_dt₁ > eff_end_dt₂)
```

It says that $P_1$ and $P_2$ begin at the same time, but that $P_1$ is the last to end, and is therefore the longer of the two time periods.

Consider the following request for information: which policies began when the Diabetes Management Wellness Program for 2009 began, but ended while that program was still going on?

The SQL written to fulfill this request is:

```
SELECT * FROM V_Allen_Example
    WHERE pol_eff_beg_dt = wp_eff_beg_dt
    AND pol_epis_end_dt < wp_epis_end_dt
```

## $P_1$ [finishes] $P_2$

This is a pair of relationships, one the inverse of the other. In the non-superscripted relationship, the first time period is the shorter one. Figure 14.3 shows this relationship, and its place

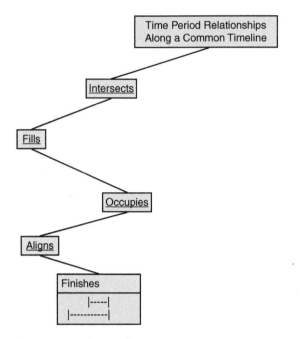

**Figure 14.3** $P_1$ [finishes] $P_2$.

in our taxonomy. The two dashed lines in the illustration graphically represent $P_1$ and $P_2$, with $P_1$ being the upper dashed line.

The predicate for this relationship, as it holds between two time periods expressed as pairs of dates using the closed-open convention, is:

```
(eff_beg_dt₁ > eff_beg_dt₂)
AND (eff_end_dt₁ = eff_end_dt₂)
```

It says that $P_1$ and $P_2$ end at the same time, but that $P_1$ is the last to begin, and is therefore the shorter of the two time periods.

The inverse of this relationship is: $P_1$ [finishes$^{-1}$] $P_2$. In the superscripted relationship, the first time period is the longer one. The predicate for this relationship, as it holds between two time periods expressed as pairs of dates using the closed-open convention, is:

```
(eff_beg_dt₁ < eff_beg_dt₂)
AND (eff_end_dt₁ = eff_end_dt₂)
```

It says that $P_1$ and $P_2$ end at the same time, but that $P_1$ is the first to begin, and is therefore the longer of the two time periods.

Consider the following request for information: which policies began prior to the Diabetes Management Wellness Program for 2009, and ended when that program ended?

The SQL written to fulfill this request is:

```
SELECT * FROM V_Allen_Example
      WHERE pol_eff_beg_dt > wp_eff_beg_dt
      AND pol_epis_end_dt = wp_epis_end_dt
```

## $P_1$ *[aligns]* $P_2$

This not an Allen relationship. It is the node in our taxonomy of Allen relationships which includes the [starts], [starts$^{-1}$], [finishes] and [finishes$^{-1}$] relationships.

The predicate for this relationship, as it holds between two time periods expressed as pairs of dates using the closed-open convention, is:

```
((eff_beg_dt₁ = eff_beg_dt₂) AND (eff_end_dt₁ < eff_end_dt₂))
OR ((eff_beg_dt₁ > eff_beg_dt₂) AND (eff_end_dt₁ =
eff_end_dt₂))
AND NOT((eff_beg_dt₁ = eff_beg_dt₂) AND (eff_end_dt₁ =
eff_end_dt₂))
```

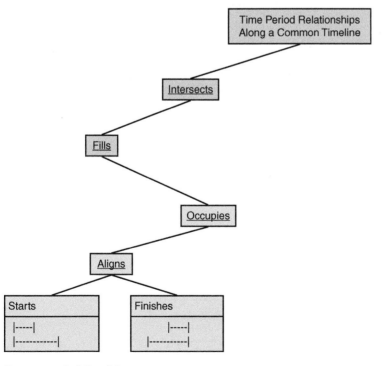

**Figure 14.4** $P_1$ [aligns] $P_2$.

It says that $P_1$ and $P_2$ either start or end at the same time, but do not both start and end at the same time.

This relationship has no inverse.

Consider the following request for information: which policies either began when the Diabetes Management Wellness Program for 2009 began, or ended when that program ended, but not both?

The SQL written to fulfill this request is:

```
SELECT * FROM V_Allen_Example
      WHERE ((pol_eff_beg_dt = wp_eff_beg_dt
         AND pol_epis_end_dt < wp_epis_end_dt)

      OR (pol_eff_beg_dt > wp_eff_beg_dt
         AND pol_epis_end_dt = wp_epis_end_dt))

      AND NOT(pol_eff_beg_dt = wp_eff_beg_dt
         AND pol_epis_end_dt = wp_epis_end_dt)
```

### $P_1$ [during] $P_2$

This is a pair of relationships, one the inverse of the other. In the non-superscripted relationship, the first time period is the shorter one.

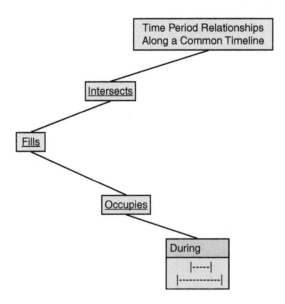

**Figure 14.5** $P_1$ [during] $P_2$.

The predicate for this relationship, as it holds between two time periods expressed as pairs of dates using the closed-open convention, is:

```
(eff_beg_dt₁ > eff_beg_dt₂)
AND (eff_end_dt₁ < eff_end_dt₂)
```

It says that $P_1$ starts after $P_2$ and ends before $P_2$.

The inverse of this relationship is: $P_1$ [during$^{-1}$] $P_2$. In the superscripted relationship, the first time period is the longer one. The predicate for this relationship, as it holds between two time periods expressed as pairs of dates using the closed-open convention, is:

```
(eff_beg_dt₁ < eff_beg_dt₂)
AND (eff_end_dt₁ > eff_end_dt₂)
```

It says that $P_1$ starts before $P_2$ and ends after $P_2$.

Consider the following request for information: which policies began after the Diabetes Management Wellness Program for 2009 began, and ended before that program ended?

The SQL written to fulfill this request is:

```
SELECT * FROM V_Allen_Example
        WHERE pol_eff_beg_dt > wp_eff_beg_dt
        AND pol_epis_end_dt < wp_epis_end_dt
```

## $P_1$ [occupies] $P_2$

This not an Allen relationship. It is the node in our taxonomy of Allen relationships which includes the [starts], [starts$^{-1}$], [finishes], [finishes$^{-1}$], [during] and [during$^{-1}$] relationships. In other words, it combines the [during] relationships with the [aligns] relationships. These are all the relationships in which one time period includes all the clock ticks that are in the other time period, but also includes at least one additional clock tick.

In the non-superscripted relationship, the first time period is the shorter one. The predicate for this relationship, as it holds between two time periods expressed as pairs of dates using the closed-open convention, is:

```
((eff_beg_dt₁ >= eff_beg_dt₂) AND (eff_end_dt₁
<= eff_end_dt₂))
AND NOT((eff_beg_dt₁ = eff_beg_dt₂) AND (eff_end_dt₁ =
eff_end_dt₂))
```

It says that $P_1$ doesn't start before $P_2$, doesn't end after $P_2$, but doesn't match $P_2$. The idea behind it is that every clock tick that is in $P_1$ is also in $P_2$, but that there is at least one clock tick in $P_2$ that is not also in $P_1$.

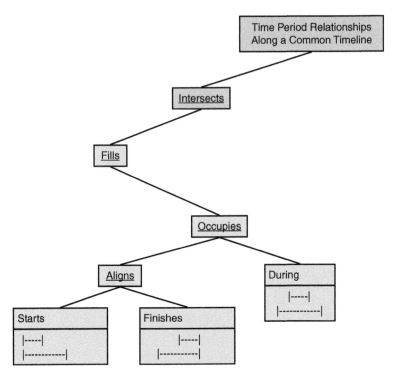

**Figure 14.6** $P_1$ [occupies] $P_2$.

The inverse of this relationship is: $P_1$ [occupies$^{-1}$] $P_2$. In the superscripted relationship, the second time period is the shorter one. The predicate for this relationship, as it holds between two time periods expressed as pairs of dates using the closed-open convention, is:

```
((eff_beg_dt1 <= eff_beg_dt2) AND (eff_end_dt1
>= eff_end_dt2))
AND NOT((eff_beg_dt1 = eff_beg_dt2) AND (eff_end_dt1 =
eff_end_dt2))
```

It says that $P_1$ doesn't start after $P_2$, doesn't end before $P_2$, and doesn't match $P_2$. The idea behind it is that there is no clock tick in $P_2$ which is not also in $P_1$, but that there is at least one clock tick in $P_1$ which is not also in $P_2$.

Throughout the book, whenever $P_1$ [occupies$^{-1}$] $P_2$, we will say that $P_1$ *is occupied by* $P_2$.

Consider the following request for information: which policies began on or after the Diabetes Management Wellness Program for 2009 began, and ended on or before that program ended, but did not both start and end at the same times as that program started and ended?

The SQL written to fulfill this request is:

```
SELECT * FROM V_Allen_Example
      WHERE pol_eff_beg_dt >= wp_eff_beg_dt
      AND pol_epis_end_dt <= wp_epis_end_dt
      AND NOT (pol_eff_beg_dt = wp_eff_beg_dt
         AND pol_epis_end_dt = wp_epis_end_dt)
```

## $P_1$ [equals] $P_2$

This is a single relationship, and has no inverse.

The predicate for this relationship, as it holds between two time periods expressed as pairs of dates using the closed-open convention, is:

```
(eff_beg_dt₁ = eff_beg_dt₂)
AND (eff_end_dt₁ = eff_end_dt₂)
```

It says that $P_1$ and $P_2$ both start and end at the same time.

Consider the following request for information: which policies began when the Diabetes Management Wellness Program for 2009 began, and ended when that program ended?

The SQL written to fulfill this request is:

```
SELECT * FROM V_Allen_Example
      WHERE pol_eff_beg_dt = wp_eff_beg_dt
      AND pol_epis_end_dt = wp_epis_end_dt
```

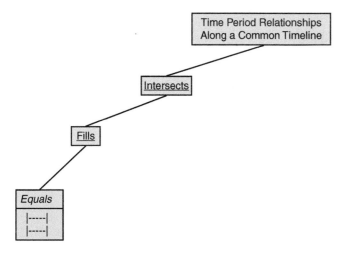

**Figure 14.7** $P_1$ [equals] $P_2$.

### $P_1$ [fills] $P_2$

This not an Allen relationship. It is the node in our taxonomy of Allen relationships which includes the [starts], [starts$^{-1}$], [finishes], [finishes$^{-1}$], [during], [during$^{-1}$] and [equals] relationships. In other words, it combines the [equals] relationship with the [occupies] relationships.

In the non-superscripted relationship, the first time period is either the same duration or the shorter one. The predicate for this relationship, as it holds between two time periods expressed as pairs of dates using the closed-open convention, is:

```
(eff_beg_dt1 >= eff_beg_dt2)
AND (eff_end_dt1 <= eff_end_dt2)
```

It says that $P_1$ doesn't start before $P_2$ and doesn't end after $P_2$. The idea behind it is that it includes every relationship in which $P_2$ has every clock tick that $P_1$ has.

The inverse of this relationship is: $P_1$ [fills$^{-1}$] $P_2$. In the superscripted relationship, the first time period is either the same duration or the longer one. The predicate for this relationship, as it holds between two time periods expressed as pairs of dates using the closed-open convention, is:

```
(eff_beg_dt1 <= eff_beg_dt2)
AND (eff_end_dt1 >= eff_end_dt2)
```

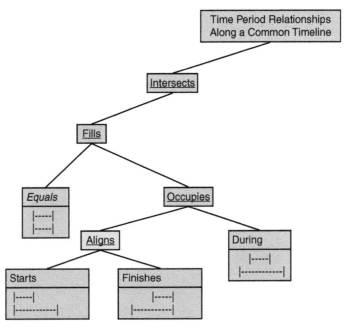

**Figure 14.8** $P_1$ [fills] $P_2$.

It says that $P_1$ doesn't start after $P_2$ and doesn't end before $P_2$. The idea behind it is that it includes every relationship in which every clock tick in $P_2$ is also in $P_1$. Throughout the book, whenever $P_1$ [fills$^{-1}$] $P_2$, we will say that $P_1$ *is filled by* $P_2$.

Note that in the case where both begin dates are identical, and both end dates are identical, $P_1$ both fills and is filled by $P_2$.

This is a particularly useful group of Allen relationships because a parent and child in a temporal relationship satisfy temporal referential integrity just in case the child's time period [fills] the parent's time period.

Consider the following request for information: which policies began on or after the Diabetes Management Wellness Program for 2009 began, and also ended on or before that program ended?

The SQL written to fulfill this request is:

```
SELECT * FROM V_Allen_Example
    WHERE pol_eff_beg_dt <= wp_eff_beg_dt
    AND pol_epis_end_dt >= wp_epis_end_dt
```

### $P_1$ [overlaps] $P_2$

This is a pair of relationships, one the inverse of the other. In the non-superscripted relationship, the first time period is the earlier one. The predicate for this relationship, as it holds between two time periods expressed as pairs of dates using the closed-open convention, is:

```
(eff_beg_dt₁ < eff_beg_dt₂)
AND (eff_end_dt₁ > eff_beg_dt₂)
AND (eff_end_dt₁ < eff_end_dt₂)
```

It says that $P_1$ starts before $P_2$ starts and ends after $P_2$ starts but before $P_2$ ends.

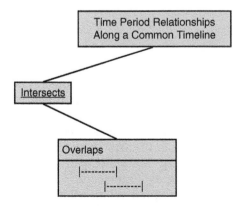

**Figure 14.9** $P_1$ [overlaps] $P_2$.

The inverse of this relationship is: $P_2$ [overlaps$^{-1}$] $P_1$. In the superscripted relationship, the first time period is the later one. The predicate for this relationship, as it holds between two time periods expressed as pairs of dates using the closed-open convention, is:

```
(eff_beg_dt₁ > eff_beg_dt₂)
AND (eff_beg_dt₁ < eff_end_dt₂)
AND (eff_end_dt₁ > eff_end_dt₂)
```

It says that $P_1$ starts after $P_2$ starts and before $P_2$ ends, and ends after $P_2$ ends.

Consider the following request for information: which policies began before the Diabetes Management Wellness Program for 2009, and ended while that program was still going on? The SQL written to fulfill this request is:

```
SELECT * FROM V_Allen_Example
      WHERE pol_eff_beg_dt < wp_eff_beg_dt
      AND pol_epis_end_dt > wp_eff_beg_dt
      AND pol_epis_end_dt < wp_epis_end_dt
```

### $P_1$ [intersects] $P_2$

This not an Allen relationship. It is the node in our taxonomy of Allen relationships which includes the [starts], [starts$^{-1}$], [finishes], [finishes$^{-1}$], [during], [during$^{-1}$], [equals], [overlaps] and [overlaps$^{-1}$] relationships. In other words, it combines the [overlaps] relationships with the [fills] relationships.

In the non-superscripted relationship, the first time period is the earlier one. The predicate for this relationship, as it holds between two time periods expressed as pairs of dates using the closed-open convention, is:

```
(eff_beg_dt₁ <= eff_beg_dt₂)
AND (eff_end_dt₁ > eff_beg_dt₂)
```

It says that $P_1$ starts no later than $P_2$ starts, and ends after $P_2$ starts. The idea behind it is that it includes every relationship in which $P_1$ and $P_2$ have at least one clock tick in common and in which $P_1$ is the earlier time period.

The limiting case is that in which $P_1$ ends at the same time $P_2$ starts. So let $P_1$ be [4/15/2010 – 5/13/2010] and let $P_2$ be [5/12/2010 – 9/18/2010]. The clock tick they share is 5/12/2010.

The inverse of this relationship is: $P_1$ [intersects$^{-1}$] $P_2$. The first time period in this non-superscripted relationship is the later one. The predicate for this relationship, as it holds between

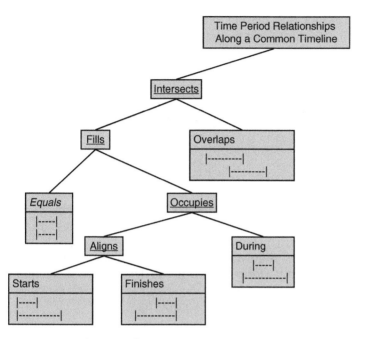

**Figure 14.10** $P_1$ [intersects] $P_2$.

two time periods expressed as pairs of dates using the closed-open convention, is:

```
(eff_beg_dt₁ >= eff_beg_dt₂)
AND (eff_beg_dt₁ < eff_end_dt₂)
```

It says that $P_2$ starts no later than $P_1$ starts, and ends after $P_1$ starts. The idea behind it is that it includes every relationship in which $P_1$ and $P_2$ have at least one clock tick in common and in which $P_1$ is the earlier time period.

All pairs of time periods that share at least one clock tick satisfy one or the other of these two predicates. So the predicate that expresses the truth condition for all time periods that share at least one clock tick is:

```
((eff_beg_dt₁ < eff_end_dt₂)
AND (eff_end_dt₁ > eff_beg_dt₂))
```

It says that either one of the clock ticks in $P_1$ is also in $P_2$ or that one of the clock ticks in $P_2$ is also in $P_1$. The idea behind it is that it covers all the cases where two time periods have at least one clock tick in common, regardless of which is the later time period.

It is interesting to look at this relationship in terms of what falls outside its scope. For any two relationships that share at least one clock tick, neither ends before the other begins. Otherwise, they could not share a clock tick. Looking at [includes] in terms of what falls outside its scope, we can express it as follows:

```
NOT(eff_end_dt₁ <= eff_beg_dt₂) AND NOT(eff_beg_dt₁
>= eff_end_dt₂)
```

And for those who like as few NOTs as possible, a logical rule (one of the transformation rules known as the De Morgan's equivalences) gives us the following predicate:

```
NOT((eff_end_dt₁ <= eff_beg_dt₂) OR (eff_beg_dt₁
>= eff_end_dt₂))
```

In other words, if two things are both not true, then it isn't true that either of them is true! On such profundities are the rules of logic constructed.

Consider the following request for information: which policies share any clock tick with the Diabetes Management Wellness Program for 2009?

The SQL written to fulfill this request is:

```
SELECT * FROM V_Allen_Example
       WHERE pol_eff_beg_dt < wp_epis_end_dt
       AND pol_epis_end_dt > wp_eff_beg_dt
```

Notice how this SQL is much simpler than the OR'd collection of all of the conditions that make up the leaf nodes of its Allen relationships.

### $P_1$ [before] $P_2$

This is a pair of relationships, one the inverse of the other. In the non-superscripted relationship, the first time period is the earlier one.

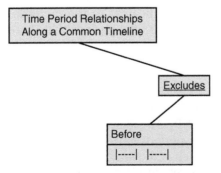

**Figure 14.11** $P_1$ [before] $P_2$.

The predicate for this relationship, as it holds between two time periods expressed as pairs of dates using the closed-open convention, is:

```
(eff_end_dt₁ < eff_beg_dt₂)
```

It says that after $P_1$ ends, there is at least one clock tick before $P_2$ begins. For example, consider the case where *eff_end_dt₁* is 5/13/2014 and *eff_beg_dt₂* is 5/14/2014. Because of the closed-open convention, the last clock tick in $P_1$ is 5/12/2014, and so there is one clock tick gap between the two time periods, that clock tick being 5/13/2014.

The inverse of this relationship is: $P_1$ [before$^{-1}$] $P_2$. In the superscripted relationship, the first time period is the later one. The predicate for this relationship, as it holds between two time periods expressed as pairs of dates using the closed-open convention, is:

```
(eff_beg_dt₁ > eff_end_dt₂)
```

It says that before $P_1$ begins, there is at least one clock tick after $P_2$ ends. For example, consider the case where *eff_beg_dt₁* is 5/14/2014 and *eff_end_dt₂* is 5/13/2014. Because of the closed-open convention, the last clock tick in $P_2$ is 5/12/2014, and so there is one clock tick gap between the two time periods, that clock tick being 5/13/2014.

Throughout this book, if it isn't important which time period comes first, we will simply say that the two time periods are non-contiguous.

This is a particularly useful pair of relationships because they distinguish episodes of the same object from one another. Two adjacent versions—versions of an object with no other version of the same object between them—belong to different episodes just in case the earlier one is [before] the later one. Of two adjacent episodes of the same object, one is [before] the other, and the other is [before$^{-1}$] the former.

Consider the following request for information: which policies ended at least one date before the Diabetes Management Wellness Program for 2009 began?

The SQL written to fulfill this request is:

```
SELECT * FROM V_Allen_Example
       WHERE pol_epis_end_dt < wp_eff_beg_dt
```

## $P_1$ [meets] $P_2$

This is a pair of relationships, one the inverse of the other. In the non-superscripted relationship, the first time period is the earlier one.

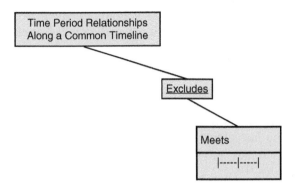

**Figure 14.12** $P_1$ [meets] $P_2$.

The predicate for this relationship, as it holds between two time periods expressed as pairs of dates using the closed-open convention, is:

$(eff\_end\_dt_1 = eff\_beg\_dt_2)$

It says that after $P_1$ ends, $P_2$ begins on the very next clock tick. There is no clock tick gap between them. Say that both dates are 5/13/2004. This means that the last clock tick in $P_1$ is 5/12/2004 and the first clock tick in $P_2$ is 5/13/2004, and so there are no clock ticks between the two time periods.

The inverse of this relationship is: $P_2$ [meets$^{-1}$] $P_1$. In the superscripted relationship, the first time period is the later one. The predicate for this relationship, as it holds between two time periods expressed as pairs of dates using the closed-open convention, is:

$(eff\_beg\_dt_1 = eff\_end\_dt_2)$

It says that before $P_1$ begins, $P_2$ ends on the previous clock tick. There is no clock tick gap between them.

This is a particularly useful relationship because it defines a collection of versions of the same object that belong to the same episode. Every adjacent pair of versions of the same object that do not share any clock ticks, i.e. in which neither includes the other, and which also do not have a single clock tick between them, belong to the same episode. The earlier version of the pair meets the later one; the later version is met by the earlier one.

Throughout this book, if it isn't important which of two time periods that meet come first, we will simply say that the two time periods are contiguous.

Consider the following request for information: which policies ended immediately before the Diabetes Management Wellness Program for 2009 began?

The SQL written to fulfill this request is:

```
SELECT * FROM V_Allen_Example
        WHERE pol_epis_end_dt = wp_eff_beg_dt
```

### $P_1$ [excludes] $P_2$

This not an Allen relationship. It is the node in our taxonomy of Allen relationships which includes the [before], [before$^{-1}$], [meets] and [meets$^{-1}$] relationships.

In the non-superscripted relationship, the first time period is the earlier one. The predicate for this relationship, as it holds between two time periods expressed as pairs of dates using the closed-open convention, is:

```
(eff_end_dt₁ <= eff_beg_dt₂)
```

It says that $P_2$ starts either immediately after the end of $P_1$, or later than that. The idea behind it is that it includes every relationship in which $P_1$ and $P_2$ have no clock ticks in common and in which $P_1$ is the earlier time period.

The inverse of this relationship is: $P_1$ [excludes$^{-1}$] $P_2$. The first time period in this non-superscripted relationship is the later one. The predicate for this relationship, as it holds between two time periods expressed as pairs of dates using the closed-open convention, is:

```
(eff_beg_dt₁ >= eff_end_dt₂)
```

It says that $P_2$ ends either immediately before the start of $P_1$, or earlier than that. The idea behind it is that it includes every relationship in which $P_1$ and $P_2$ have no clock ticks in common and in which $P_1$ is the later time period.

All pairs of time periods that share no clock ticks satisfy one or the other of these two predicates. So the predicate that

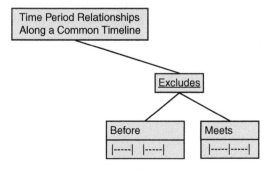

**Figure 14.13** $P_1$ [excludes] $P_2$.

designates all and only those time periods that share no clock ticks is:

```
(eff-end-dt₁ <= eff-beg-dt₂) OR (eff-beg-dt₁ >= eff-end-dt₂)
```

It says that either $P_2$ starts after $P_1$ ends or ends before $P_2$ starts. The idea behind it is that regardless of which time period comes first, they share no clock ticks.

It should be the case that two time periods [exclude] one another if and only if they do not [intersect] one another. If so, then if we put a NOT in front of the predicate for the [intersects] relationship, we should get a predicate which expresses the [excludes] relationship.[2] Putting a NOT in front of the [intersects] relationship, we get:

```
NOT((eff_beg_dt₁ < eff_end_dt₂)
AND (eff_end_dt₁ > eff_beg_dt₂))
```

This is a statement of the form NOT(X AND Y). The first thing we will do is transform it, according to the De Morgan's rules, into (NOT-X OR NOT-Y). This gives us:

```
NOT(eff_beg_dt₁ < eff_end_dt₂)
OR NOT(eff_end_dt₁ > eff_beg_dt₂)
```

Next, we can replace *NOT(eff_beg_dt₁ < eff_end_dt₂)* with *(eff_beg_dt₁ >= eff_end_dt₂)*, and *NOT(eff_end_dt₁ > eff_beg_dt₂)* with *(eff_end_dt₁ <= eff_beg_dt₂)*. This gives us:

```
(eff_beg_dt₁ >=eff_end_dt₂) OR (eff_end_dt₁ <= eff_beg_dt₂)
```

Finally, by transposing the two predicates, we get:

```
(eff_end_dt₁ <= eff_beg_dt₂) OR (eff_beg_dt₁ >= eff_end_dt₂)
```

And this is indeed the predicate for the [excludes] relationship, demonstrating that [excludes] is indeed logically equivalent to NOT[intersects].

Consider the following request for information: which policies either ended before the Diabetes Management Wellness Program for 2009 began, or began after that program ended? The SQL written to fulfill this request is:

```
SELECT * FROM V_Allen_Example
      WHERE (pol_epis_end_dt <= wp_eff_beg_dt
      OR pol_eff_beg_dt >= wp_epis_end_dt)
```

---

[2]Since, at the time we are writing this paragraph, we haven't done this, it is an excellent way of finding out if we have made any logical mistakes so far.

## Point in Time to Period of Time Queries

A point in time is a period of time that includes only one clock tick. Thus, using the closed-open convention, a point in time, $T_1$, is identical to the period of time $[T_1 - T_2]$ where $T_2$ is the next clock tick after $T_1$. The only difference is in the notation. In the following discussions, we will use the simpler notation, $T_1$, for the point in time.

In this section, we consider periods of time that are longer than a single clock tick. Periods of time that are one clock tick in length are points in time, and we consider Allen relationships between two points in time later.

Given that $P_1$ is longer than a single clock tick, it may or may not share a clock tick with $T_1$. If it does, then $T_1$ [occupies] $P_1$. Otherwise, either one is [before] the other, or else they [meet].

In Asserted Versioning databases, all temporal periods are delimited with the same point in time granularities. When comparing time periods to time periods, the logic in the AVF does not depend on the granularity of the clock ticks used in temporal parameters, as long as all of them are the same. The clock ticks could be months (as they are in the examples throughout this book), days, seconds or microseconds of any size. As we noted in Chapter 3, the AVF can carry out its temporal logic without caring about granularity specifically because of the closed-open convention.

However, when comparing a point in time to a period of time, we must be aware of the granularity of the clock tick, and must often either add a clock tick to a point or period in time, or subtract a clock tick from a point or period in time. Consequently, we need to specify the clock tick duration used in the specific implementation to correctly perform this arithmetic. We will use "*f*CTD", standing for "clock tick duration", as the name of a function that converts an integer into that integer number of clock ticks of the correct granularity. So, for example, in:

```
eff_end_dt - fCTD(1)
```

*f*CTD takes on the value of one clock tick. If the granularity is a month, as it is in most of the examples in this book, the result will be to subtract one month from the effective end date. If the granularity is a millisecond-level timestamp, it will subtract one millisecond from that date. The *f*CTD function determines the granularity for a specific Asserted Versioning database from the miscellaneous metadata table, shown as Figure 8.7 in Chapter 8.

Different DBMSs use different date formats for date literals. It is also dependent on the default language and the date format currently set. These formats are shown in Figure 14.14.

| Name | Layout | Example |
|------|--------|---------|
| ISO | yyyy-mm-dd | 2010-09-25 |
| USA | mm/dd/yyyy | 09/25/2010 |
| EUR | dd.mm.yyyy | 25.09.2010 |
| JIS | yyyy-mm-dd | 2010-09-25 |

**Figure 14.14** Date Formats for Date Literals.

We used the USA format in parts of the book, so we will assume that the default date format in our sample DBMS is the same.

Different DBMSs use different syntax for date arithmetic. SQL Server would use something like this:

```
AND DATEADD(DAY, -1, pol.eff_end_dt) > '07/15/2010'
```

where DAY is the granularity (which can also be abbreviated as DD or D), while DB2 might use:

```
AND (pol.eff_end_dt - 1 DAY) > '07/15/2010'
```

with the reserved word DAY indicating the granularity. We will use the T-SQL format for our examples, and will assume our clock tick granularity is one month, to keep it in synch with the examples used in the book. However, in real-world databases, the granularity would more likely be a day, a second or a microsecond. This $f$CTD translation could be built into a reusable database function as part of the framework based on metadata.

### $T_1$ [starts] $P_1$

This is a pair of relationships, one the inverse of the other. In the non-superscripted relationship, the first time period is the point in time, i.e. the single clock-tick time period. Figure 14.15 shows this relationship, and its place in our taxonomy. The two dashed lines in the illustration graphically represent $T_1$ and $P_1$, with $T_1$ being the upper dashed line.

The predicate for this relationship, as it holds between a period of time expressed as a pair of dates using the closed-open convention, and a point in time, is:

```
(T₁ = eff_beg_dt)
```

It says that $T_1$ starts at $P_1$.

Consider the following request for information: which policies begin on the same date as the 2009 Diabetes Management Wellness Program?

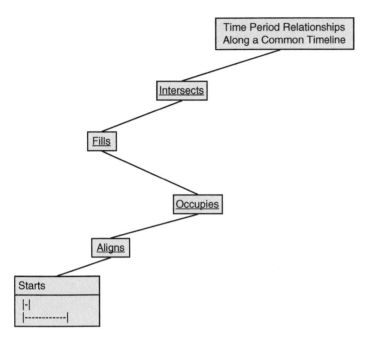

**Figure 14.15** $T_1$ [starts] $P_1$.

The SQL written to fulfill this request is:

```
SELECT * FROM V_Allen_Example
       WHERE pol_eff_beg_dt = wp_eff_beg_dt
```

### $T_1$ [finishes] $P_1$

This is a pair of relationships, one the inverse of the other. In the non-superscripted relationship, the first time period is the point in time, i.e. the single clock-tick time period. Figure 14.16 shows this relationship, and its place in our taxonomy. The two dashed lines in the illustration graphically represent $T_1$ and $P_1$, with $T_1$ being the upper dashed line.

The predicate for this relationship, as it holds between a period of time expressed as a pair of dates using the closed-open convention, and a point in time, is:

```
(T₁ = eff_end_dt - fCTD(1))
```

Since the effective end date of a time period is the next clock tick after the last clock tick in that time period, this predicate says that $P_1$ ends on the clock tick that is $T_1$.

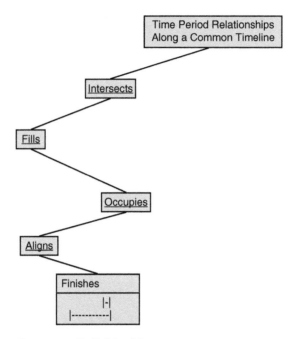

**Figure 14.16** $T_1$ [finishes] $P_1$.

Consider the following request for information: which policies began on the same date as the 2009 Diabetes Wellness Management Program ended?

The SQL written to fulfill this request is:

```
SELECT * FROM V_Allen_Example
        WHERE pol_eff_beg_dt = DATEADD(MONTH, -1,
        wp_epis_end_dt)
```

### $T_1$ [during] $P_1$

This is the relationship in which a single clock tick occurs after the start of a period of time, and before that period of time ends. Figure 14.17 shows this relationship, and its place in our taxonomy. The two dashed lines in the illustration graphically represent $T_1$ and $P_1$, with $T_1$ being the upper dashed line.

The predicate for this relationship, as it holds between a period of time expressed as a pair of dates using the closed-open convention, and a point in time, is:

```
(eff_beg_dt < T₁) AND (eff_end_dt − fCTD(1) > T₁)
```

It says that $T_1$ occurs during $P_1$ just in case $P_1$ starts before $T_1$ and ends after $T_1$.

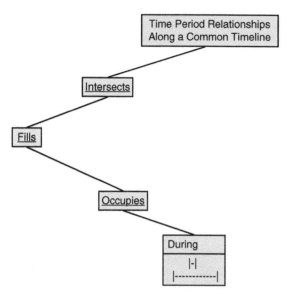

**Figure 14.17** $T_1$ [during] $P_1$.

Consider the following request for information: which policies began before the 2009 Diabetes Wellness Management Program started, and ended after it started?

The SQL written to fulfill this request is:

```
SELECT * FROM V_Allen_Example
      WHERE pol_eff_beg_dt < wp_eff_beg_dt
      AND DATEADD(MONTH, −1, pol_epis_end_dt) > wp_eff_beg_dt
```

## $T_1$ [occupies] $P_1$

This not an Allen relationship. It is the node in our taxonomy of Allen relationships which, when one of the time periods is a point in time, includes the [starts], [finishes], and [during] relationships. In other words, it combines the [during] relationships with the [aligns] relationships. These are all the relationships in which a time period (of more than one clock tick) includes a point in time.

The predicate for this relationship, as it holds between a period of time expressed as a pair of dates using the closed-open convention, and a point in time, is:

```
(eff_beg_dt <= T₁) AND (eff_end_dt > T₁)
```

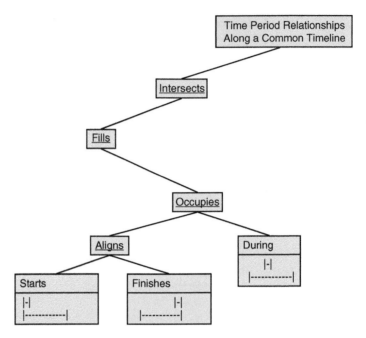

**Figure 14.18** $T_1$ [occupies] $P_1$.

It says that $P_1$ occupies $T_1$ just in case $P_1$ starts on or before $T_1$ and ends on or after $T_1$.

Consider the following request for information: which policies began on or before the 2009 Diabetes Management Wellness Program started, and ended on or after it started?

The SQL written to fulfill this request is:

```
SELECT * FROM V_Allen_Example
      WHERE pol_eff_beg_dt <= wp_eff_beg_dt
      AND pol_epis_end_dt > wp_eff_beg_dt)
```

### $T_1$ [before] $P_1$

The predicate for this relationship, as it holds between a period of time expressed as a pair of dates using the closed-open convention, and a point in time, is:

```
(T₁ + fCTD(1) < eff_beg_dt)
```

It says that $P_1$ starts at least one clock tick after $T_1$; similarly T occurs at least one clock tick before $P_1$ starts.

The inverse of this relationship is: $P_1$ [before$^{-1}$] $T_1$. In this superscripted relationship, the time period is later than the point

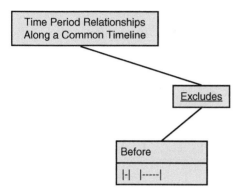

**Figure 14.19** $T_1$ [before] $P_1$.

in time. The predicate for this relationship, as it holds between two time periods expressed as pairs of dates using the closed-open convention, is:

```
(eff_end_dt < T₁)
```

It says that $P_1$ ends at least one clock tick before $T_1$.

It follows that to pick out those versions or episodes which are non-contiguous with a given point in time, the predicate is:

```
(T₁ + fCTD(1) < eff_beg_dt) OR (eff_end_dt < T₁)
```

Consider the following request for information: which policies have a temporal gap between when they began and when the 2009 Diabetes Management Wellness Program ended? The SQL written to fulfill this request is:

```
SELECT * FROM V_Allen_Example
      WHERE wp_epis_end_dt
      < pol_eff_beg_dt
```

## $T_1$ [meets] $P_1$

The predicate for this relationship, as it holds between a period of time expressed as a pair of dates using the closed-open convention, and a point in time, is:

```
(T₁ + fCTD(1) = eff_beg_dt)
```

It says that $P_1$ starts immediately after $T_1$.

The inverse of this relationship is: $P_1$ [meets$^{-1}$] $T_1$. In this superscripted relationship, the time period is earlier than the point in time. The predicate for this relationship, as it holds

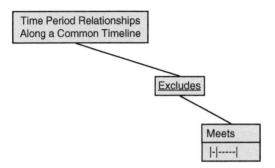

**Figure 14.20** $T_1$ [meets] $P_1$.

between two time periods expressed as pairs of dates using the closed-open convention, is:

```
(eff_end_dt = T₁)
```

It says that $P_1$ ends immediately before $T_1$.

It follows that to pick out those versions, or episodes which are contiguous with a given point in time, the predicate is:

```
(T₁ + fCTD(1) = eff_beg_dt) OR (eff_end_dt = T₁)
```

Consider the following request for information: which policies began at the same time the 2009 Diabetes Management Wellness Program ended?

The SQL written to fulfill this request is:

```
SELECT * FROM V_Allen_Example
      WHERE wp_epis_end_dt =
      pol_eff_beg_dt
```

## $P_1$ [excludes] $T_1$

This not an Allen relationship. It is the node in our taxonomy of Allen relationships which includes the [before], [before$^{-1}$], [meets] and [meets$^{-1}$] relationships.

The predicate for this relationship is:

```
(T₁ + fCTD(1)) <= eff_beg_dt) OR (eff_end_dt <= T₁)
```

It says that $P_1$ starts after $T_1$ or ends before $T_1$. Note that if a time period's effective end date is $T_1$, that time period ended the day before $T_1$.

Consider the following request for information: which policies ended anytime before the 2009 Diabetes Management Wellness Program began or started anytime after the 2009 Diabetes Management Wellness Program began? Note that this is not

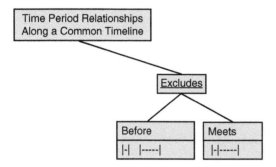

**Figure 14.21** P$_1$ [excludes] T$_1$.

the same as a request for policies which ended [before] the 2009 Diabetes Management Wellness Program began.

The SQL written to fulfill this request is:

```
SELECT * FROM V_Allen_Example
      WHERE (pol_epis_end_dt <= wp_eff_beg_dt
      OR DATEADD(MONTH, +1, wp_eff_beg_dt) <=
      pol_eff_beg_dt)
```

## Point in Time to Point in Time Queries

Another special set of Allen relationships consists of the relationships between two points in time, T$_1$ and T$_2$. There are only three such relationships. One point in time may precede another and be non-contiguous with it, or precede the other and be contiguous with it, or be the same as the other.

### T$_1$ [before] T$_2$

The predicate for this relationship, as it holds between two points in time, expressed as points in time, is:

$$((T_1 + fCTD(1)) < T_2)$$

It says that T$_1$ comes before T$_2$, and that there is at least one clock tick between it and T$_2$. Note that because of the requirement for this one clock tick gap, the Allen relationship [before] does not mean the same thing as "before" in ordinary language.

The inverse of this relationship is: T$_1$ [before$^{-1}$] T$_2$. The predicate for this relationship, as it holds between two points in time, expressed as points in time, is:

$$((T_1 - fCTD(1)) > T_2)$$

It says that T$_1$ comes after T$_2$, and that there is at least one clock tick between it and T$_2$.

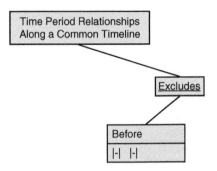

**Figure 14.22** $T_1$ [before] $T_2$.

## $T_1$ [meets] $T_2$

The predicate for this relationship, as it holds between two points in time, expressed as points in time, is:

$$((T_1 + fCTD(1)) = T_2)$$

It says that $T_1$ comes immediately before $T_2$.

The inverse of this relationship is: $T_1$ [meets$^{-1}$] $T_2$. The predicate for this relationship, as it holds between two points in time, expressed as points in time, is:

$$((T_1 - fCTD(1)) = T_2)$$

It says that $T_1$ comes immediately after $T_2$.

## $T_1$ [equals] $T_2$

The predicate for this relationship, as it holds between two points in time, expressed as points in time, is:

$$(T_1 = T_2)$$

It says that $T_1$ and $T_2$ are equal if and only if they occur on the same clock tick.

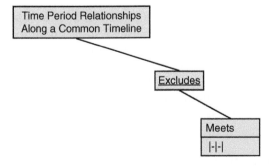

**Figure 14.23** $T_1$ [meets] $T_2$.

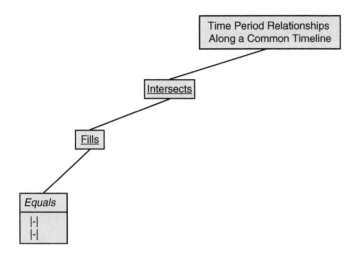

**Figure 14.24** $T_1$ [*equals*] $T_2$.

# A Claims Processing Example

With the Asserted Versioning queries developed and discussed in this book, we have generally chosen to sacrifice realism in the examples in order to guarantee completeness of coverage. For example, in Chapter 13 we developed and discussed SQL views of nine categories of bi-temporal data, eight of those categories being what we called pipeline datasets. And yet few real-world collections of bi-temporal data, we acknowledged, would correspond to precisely one of those nine categories of data (with the one exception of currently asserted current versions of data, the category which corresponds to the data in a conventional table). Completeness of coverage was guaranteed, however, because those nine categories are a mathematical partitioning of all possible combinations of past, present and future assertion and effective time data.

Thus far in Chapter 14, we have developed and discussed SQL predicates, and SQL statements illustrating their use, each corresponding to one of the Allen relationships or one of the nodes in our taxonomy of Allen relationships. We have reviewed all possible Allen relationships, and taxonomic groupings of them, between pairs of time periods, between a time period and a point in time, and between two points in time. Once again, completeness of coverage has been guaranteed because of the use of a mathematical partitioning of all possible types of queries. But once again, the examples have not been very realistic.

In this section, we move on from completeness to verisimilitude. Having used a simplified set of health insurance data throughout this book, we continue by developing a query about claims issued against policies held by clients.

Claims data has not been used, so far, and so we begin with the SQL definition of a simplified Adjudicated Claims table.

```
CREATE TABLE dbo.Adjud_Claim (
      claim_rowid    int        identity,
      policy_oid     int        null,
      claim_amt      money      null,
      service_dt     datetime   default getdate()    null,
      adjud_dt       datetime   null,
      row_crt_dt     datetime   default getdate()    not null)
```

This Adjudicated Claims table is *not* an asserted version table. It is an event table, not a persistent object table, and each of its rows represent an event on which an insurance claim was adjudicated. As an event, each claims adjudication has no persistence. It happens, and then it's over.

In the Adjudicated Claims table, *policy_oid* is not a foreign key, because there is no table for which it is the primary key. The Policy table is an asserted version table, and its primary key is the combination of *policy_oid* with assertion begin date and effective begin date. Nor is *policy_oid* a temporal foreign key, because Asserted Versioning does not recognize and manage referential relationships between non-temporal tables and asserted version tables. For example, the AVF may temporally delete a policy after several claims have been adjudicated that reference that policy, and it may temporally delete those policies effective at some point in time prior to the adjudication of those claims. It is the responsibility of the application which manages the Adjudicated Claims table to make sure it is not adjudicating claims against terminated policies.

Returning to our query, for each adjudicated claim, it will show the client number and name, the policy number, type and copay amount, and the claim service date, amount, and adjudication date.

For the policy associated with the claim, this query picks out the version of the policy that was in effect on the service date. Clearly, we are not interested in any other version of the policy. In particular, we are not interested in the version of the policy that is in effect when the query is run, or in the version of the policy that was in effect on the adjudication date. Those versions may in fact be correct, but we can't count on it. We want to see the version that was in effect at the time the medical service was rendered.

But there is more to picking out the correct policy data than this. We need, not simply the correct version, but the appropriate assertion of that version. For it is possible that, between the service date and the adjudication date or after the adjudication date, we found an error in the data about the policy as it was on the service date.

Say that the service date is 9/24/2009 and the adjudication date is 12/07/2009, and that between those two dates, we discovered and corrected an error in the version of the policy that was in effect on 9/24/2009, and then again after the adjudication another correction was made to the policy for the effective period of the service. This means that we have three rows representing the same version of the same policy, both purporting to describe the policy as it was on 9/24/2009. Which one do we want?

We want the one that was used to adjudicate the claim, of course, that being the assertion that was current on the adjudication date, 12/07/2009. So we want policy data that was effective on the service date, and asserted as of the adjudication date whether it was right or wrong because we want to see the source of the Explanation of Benefits (EOB) as the customer sees it.

This query also returns the client number and name of the client that owns the policy. Like most persistent object data, of course, that name may have changed over time. In this sample query, we choose to use the client data that was currently asserted at the time that the row in the Adjudicated Claims table was physically created.

Finally, we include one selection criterion on the query. We select those adjudicated claims where the claim amount is greater than the client's copay amount. These, of course, are the claims for which a payment will be made by the insurance company to the service provider.

Here is the query we have described.

```
SELECT c.client_nbr, c.client_nm,
        p.policy_nbr, p.policy_type, p.copay_amt,
        cl.service_dt, cl.claim_amt, cl.adjud_dt
    FROM Claim cl
    INNER JOIN Policy_AV p
        ON p.policy_oid = cl.policy_oid
        AND p.eff_beg_dt <= cl.service_dt
        AND p.eff_end_dt > cl.service_dt
        AND p.asr_beg_dt <= cl.adjud_dt
        AND p.asr_end_dt > cl.adjud_dt
    INNER JOIN Client_AV c
        ON c.client_oid = p.client_oid
```

```
            AND c.eff_beg_dt <= cl.row_crt_dt
            AND c.eff_end_dt > cl.row_crt_dt
            AND c.asr_beg_dt <= cl.row_crt_dt
            AND c.asr_end_dt > cl.row_crt_dt
        WHERE cl.claim_amt > p.copay_amt
        ORDER BY cl.adjud_dt, c.client_nbr, p.policy_nbr,
        p.eff_beg_dt;
```

To conclude this section, we show what this query might look like if the SQL language supported PERIOD datatypes, and also our taxonomy of Allen relationships. We suppose that the taxonomy node [fills$^{-1}$] is represented by the reserved word INCLUDES. With a SQL language like this, the Asserted Versioning schema no longer has pairs of dates to represent its two time periods. Instead, it has the single columns *asr_per* and *eff_per*.

```
SELECT c.client_nbr, c.client_nm,
        p.policy_nbr, p.policy_type, p.copay_amt,
        cl.service_dt, cl.claim_amt, cl.adjud_dt
    FROM Claim cl
    INNER JOIN Policy_AV p
        ON p.policy_oid = cl.policy_oid
        AND p.eff_per INCLUDES cl.service_dt
        AND p.asr_per INCLUDES cl.adjud_dt
    INNER JOIN Client_AV c
        ON c.client_oid = p.client_oid
        AND c.eff_per INCLUDES cl.row_crt_dt
        AND c.asr_per INCLUDES cl.row_crt_dt
    WHERE cl.claim_amt > p.copay_amt
    ORDER BY cl.adjud_dt, c.client_nbr, p.policy_nbr,
    p.eff_beg_dt;
```

In either form, what is striking about the query is its simplicity relative to the complexity of the bi-temporal semantics that underlies it. Unlike queries in the standard temporal model and, for that matter, uni-temporal queries in the alternative temporal model as well, this query does not assemble a collection of rows and then proceed to check for temporal gaps and temporal overlaps within sub-selected collections of those rows. Asserted Versioning enforces bi-temporal semantics once, as the data is being created and modified, rather than each time the data is queried.

## In Other Words

With appropriate temporal extensions to the SQL language, the expression of all thirteen Allen relationships, and of this and other relationships which are combinations of those thirteen relationships, would be greatly simplified. The first thing that is needed to support predicates for these relationships is to provide a PERIOD datatype, as we discussed in Chapter 3. With that datatype available, SQL could express each of the relationships we have discussed with one binary predicate relating two time periods (not two pairs of dates).

For example, instead of having to request data associated with two time periods such that the first starts before the second and ends after the second starts but before the second ends, we could simply request data associated with two time periods such that the first [overlaps] the second.

Or, instead of having to request data associated with two time periods such that the first doesn't start after the second and doesn't end before the second, we could simply request data associated with two time periods such that the first [fills] the second.

It is clearly easier to think about what information one wants from the database at the higher level of abstraction provided by this new datatype and these new relationships, rather than at the level of abstraction in which begin and end dates have to be used, as they are in the original formulation of the example. And it is just as clearly easier to write the corresponding SQL.

But even with today's SQL which lacks these temporal extensions, Asserted Versioning manages assertion and effective time date pairs as user-defined PERIOD datatypes, and supports all the Allen relationships as well as the other relationships in our Allen relationship taxonomy. Asserted Versioning thus provides a migration path to the day when these extensions are supported in the SQL standard and in commercial DBMSs.

# Glossary References

Glossary entries whose definitions form strong interdependencies are grouped together in the following list. The same glossary entries may be grouped together in different ways at the end of different chapters, each grouping reflecting the semantic perspective of each chapter. There will usually be several other, and often many other, glossary entries that are not included in the list, and we recommend that the Glossary be consulted whenever an unfamiliar term is encountered.

We note, in particular, that none of the nodes in the Asserted Versioning taxonomy of Allen relationships are included in this list. In general, we leave taxonomy nodes out of these lists since they are long enough without them.

Allen relationships

Asserted Versioning Framework (AVF)

episode

clock tick
closed-open
contiguous
granularity

effective begin date
effective end date

object

PERIOD datatype
point in time
time period

temporal entity integrity (TEI)
temporal referential integrity (TRI)

the alternative temporal model
the standard temporal model

version

# OPTIMIZING ASSERTED VERSIONING DATABASES

One concern about Asserted Versioning is with how well it will perform. We believe that with recent improvements in technology, and with the use of the physical design techniques described in this chapter, Asserted Versioning databases can achieve performance very close to that of conventional databases. This is especially true for queries, which are usually the most frequent kind of access to any relational database. The AVF, our own implementation of Asserted Versioning, is designed to operate well with large data volume databases supporting a high volume of mixed-type data retrieval requests.

Managing Time in Relational Databases. Doi: 10.1016/B978-0-12-375041-9.00015-7

# Bi-Temporal, Conventional, and Non-Temporal Databases

In this section, we compare data volumes and response times in bi-temporal and in conventional databases. We find that differences in both data volumes and response times are generally quite small, and are usually not good reasons for hesitating to implement bi-temporal data in even the largest databases of the world's largest corporations.

## Data Volumes in Bi-Temporal and in Conventional Databases

It might seem that a bi-temporal database will have a lot more data in it than a conventional database, and will consequently take a lot longer to process. It is true that the size of a bi-temporal database will be larger than that of an otherwise identical database which contains only current data about persistent objects. But in our consulting engagements, which span several decades and dozens of clients, we have found that in most mission-critical systems, temporal data is jury-rigged into ostensibly non-temporal databases.

There are any number of ways that this may happen. For example, in some systems a version date is added to the primary key of selected tables. In other systems, more advanced forms of best practice versioning (as described in Chapter 4) are employed. Sometimes, history will be captured by triggering an insert into a history table every time a particular non-temporal table is modified. Another approach is to generate a series of periodic snapshot tables that capture the state of a non-temporal table at regular intervals.

Of course, a database with no temporal data at all will certainly be smaller than the same database with temporal data. But adding up the overhead associated with embedded best practice versioning, or with triggered history, periodic snapshots or some combination of these and other techniques, the amount of data in a so-called non-temporal database may be as much or even more than the amount of data in a bi-temporal database.

Throughout this book, we have been using the terms "non-temporal database" and "conventional database" as equivalent expressions. But now we have a reason to distinguish them. From now on, we will call a database "non-temporal" only if it contains no temporal data about persistent objects at all.[1] And from now on, we will use the term "conventional database" to refer to databases that may or may not contain temporal data about persistent objects (and that usually do), but that do not contain explicitly bi-temporal tables and instead incorporate temporal data by using variations on one or more of the ad hoc methods we have described.

## Response Times in Bi-Temporal and in Conventional Databases

At the level of individual tables, a table lacking temporal data will clearly have less data than an otherwise identical table that also contains temporal data. But even if a table has more data than another table, it may perform nearly as well as that other table because response times are usually not linear to the amount of data in the target table.

Response times will be approximately linear to the amount of data in the table in the case of full table scans, but will almost never be linear for direct access reads. A direct (random) read to a table with five million rows will perform almost as well as a direct read to a table with only one million rows, provided that the table is indexed properly and that the number of non-leaf index *levels* is the same. And, in most cases, they will be the same, or very close to it.

In addition, when adding in the overhead of triggers of an exponentially growing number of dependents, and of the often inefficient SQL used to access and maintain data in conventional databases, it is likely that using the AVF to manage temporal data in an Asserted Versioning database will prove to be a more efficient method of managing temporal data than directly invoking DBMS methods to manage temporal data in a conventional database.

# The Optimization Drill: Modify, Monitor, Repeat

Performance optimization, also known as "performance tuning", is usually an iterative approach to making and then monitoring modifications to an application and its database. It

---

[1]The point of adding "about persistent objects", of course, is to distinguish between objects and events, as we did in our taxonomy in Chapter 2. So a "non-temporal database", in this new sense, may contain event tables, i.e. tables of transactions. And it may also contain fact-dimension data marts. What it may not contain is data about any historical (or future) states of persistent objects.

could involve adjusting the configuration of the database and server, or making changes to the applications and the SQL that maintain and query the database. As authors of this book, we can't participate in the specific modify and monitor iterative processes being carried on by any of our readers and their IT organizations. But we can describe factors that are likely to apply to any Asserted Versioning implementation.

These factors include the number of users, the complexity of the application and the SQL, the volatility of the data, and the DBMS and server platform. The major DBMSs may optimize varying configurations differently, and may have extensions that can be used to simplify and improve a "plain vanilla" implementation of Asserted Versioning.

In this chapter, we will take a broad brush approach and, in general, discuss optimization techniques that apply to the temporalization of any relational database, regardless of what industry its owning organization is part of, and regardless of what types of applications it supports. Each reader will need to review these recommendations and determine if and how they apply to specific databases and applications that she may be responsible for.

To repeat once more as we read the following sections, although we use the term "date" in this book to describe the delimiters of assertion and effective time periods, those delimiters can actually be of any time duration, such as a day, minute, second or microsecond. We use a month as the clock tick granularity in many of our examples. But in most cases, a finer level of granularity will be chosen, such as a timestamp representing the smallest clock tick supported by the DBMS.

# Performance Tuning Bi-Temporal Tables Using Indexes

Many indexes are designed using something similar to a B-tree (balanced tree) structure, in which each node points to its next-level child nodes, and the leaf nodes contain pointers to the desired data. These indexes are used by working down from the top of the hierarchy until the leaf node containing the desired pointer is reached. Each pointer is a specific index value paired with the physical address, page or row id of the row that matches that value. From that point, the DBMS can do a direct read and retrieve the I/O page that contains the desired data.

B-tree indexes for bi-temporal tables work no differently than B-tree indexes for non-temporal tables. Knowing how these indexes work, our design objective is to construct indexes that will optimize the speed of access to the most frequently accessed data. In bi-temporal tables, we believe, that will almost always be the currently asserted current versions of the objects represented in those tables. As index designers, our task is two-fold. First, we need to determine the best columns to index on. Then we need to arrange those columns in the best sequence.

## General Considerations

The physical sequence of columns within an index has a significant impact on the performance of queries that use that index. Our objective is to get to the desired row in a table with the minimum amount of I/O activity against the index, followed by a single direct read to the table itself. So in determining the sequence of columns in an index, a good idea is to put the most frequently used lookup columns in the leftmost (initial) nodes of the index. These columns are often the columns that make up the business key, or perhaps some other identifier such as the primary key, or a foreign key.

Against asserted version tables, most queries will be similar to queries against non-temporal tables except that a few temporal predicates will be added to the queries. These temporal predicates eliminate rows whose assertion time periods and/or effective time periods are not what the query is looking for.

An object that is represented by exactly one row in a non-temporal table may be represented by any number of rows in a temporal table. But for normal business use, the one current row in the temporal table, i.e. the row which corresponds to that one row in the non-temporal table, is likely to be accessed much more frequently than any of the other rows. Unless we properly combine temporal columns with non-temporal columns in the index, access to that current row may require us to scan through many past or future rows to get to it.

Of course, we are talking about both a scan of index leaf pages, as well as the more expensive scan of the table itself. When specific rows are being searched for, and when they may or may not be clustered close to one another in physical storage, we want to minimize any type of scan.

Another important consideration in determining the optimal sequence of columns in an index is that optimizers may decide not to use a column in an index unless values have been provided for all the columns to its left, those being the columns that help to more directly trace a path through the higher levels of the index tree, using the columns that *match* supplied predicates. So if we design an index with its temporal columns too far to the right, and with unqualified columns prior to them, a scan might still be triggered whenever the optimizer looks for the one current row for the object being queried. On the other hand, as we will see, the solution is not to simply make the temporal columns left-most in the index.

There will usually be many more non-current rows for an object, in an asserted version table, than the one current row for that object. The table may contain any number of rows representing the history of the object, and any number of rows representing anticipated future states of the object. The table may contain any number of no longer asserted rows for that object, as well as rows that we are not yet prepared to assert. So what we want the optimizer to do is to jump as directly as possible to the one currently asserted current version for an object, without having to scan though a potentially large number of non-current rows.

## Indexes to Optimize Queries

Let's look at an example. We will assume that it is currently September 2011. So the next time the clock ticks, according to the clock tick granularity used in this book, it will be October 2011.

In the table shown in Figure 15.1, there are nine rows representing the object whose object identifier is 55. Three of those rows are historical versions. Their effectivity periods are past. They represent past states of the object they refer to. We designate them with "pe" (past effective) in the state column of the table.[2]

Another three of those rows are no longer asserted. Their assertion periods are past. They represent claims that we once made, claims that the statements which those rows made about the objects which they represented were true statements. But now we no longer make those claims. They exist in the assertion time past. We designate these rows with "pa" (past asserted) in the state column of the table.

---

[2]The state and row # columns are not columns of the table itself. They are metadata about the rows of the table, just like the row # column in the tables shown in other chapters in this book.

| state | row # | oid | eff-beg | eff-end | asr-beg | asr-end | data |
|-------|-------|-----|---------|---------|---------|---------|------|
| pa | 1 | 55 | Jan09 | 9999 | Jan09 | Feb09 | Apples |
| pe | 2 | 55 | Jan09 | Mar09 | Feb09 | 9999 | Apples |
| pa | 3 | 55 | Mar09 | 9999 | Feb09 | Jun09 | Berries |
| pe | 4 | 55 | Mar09 | Jun09 | Jun09 | 9999 | Berries |
| pa | 5 | 55 | Jun09 | 9999 | Jun09 | Aug09 | Cherries |
| pe | 6 | 55 | Jun09 | Aug09 | Aug09 | 9999 | Cherries |
| cc | 7 | 55 | Aug09 | 9999 | Aug09 | Oct12 | Kiwi |
| fa | 8 | 55 | Aug09 | Dec13 | Oct12 | 9999 | Kiwi |
| fa | 9 | 55 | Dec13 | 9999 | Oct12 | 9999 | Grapes |

**Figure 15.1** A Bi-Temporal Table.

Two of those rows are not yet asserted. They are deferred assertions. We are not yet willing to claim that the statements made by those rows are true statements. We designate these rows with "fa" (future asserted) in the state column of the table.

There is one current row representing the object whose identifier is 55. This row is currently asserted and, within current assertion time, became effective in August 2009 and will remain in effect until further notice. Note, however, that it will remain asserted only until October 2012. At that time, if nothing in the data changes, the database will cease to say that the data for object 55 is Kiwi from August 2009 until further notice. Instead, it will say that data for object 55 is Kiwi from August 2009 to December 2013, and that from December 2013 until further notice, it will be Grapes. We designate this earlier, but current, row with "cc" (currently asserted current version) in the state metadata column of the table.

The SQL to retrieve the one current row for object 55 is:

```
SELECT data
FROM mytable
      WHERE oid = 55
      AND eff_beg_dt <= Now() AND eff_end_dt > Now()
      AND asr_beg_dt <= Now() AND asr_end_dt > Now()
```

Most optimizers will use the index tree to locate the *row id* (*rid*) of the qualifying row or rows using, first of all, the columns that have *direct matching predicates*, such as EQUALS or IN, columns which are sometimes called *match columns*. These optimizers will also use the index tree for a column with a range predicate, such as BETWEEN or LESS THAN OR EQUAL TO (<=), *provided that* it is the first column in the index or the first column following the direct match columns.

Together, the direct match predicates and the first range predicate determine a starting position for a search of the index, that position being the first value found within the range specified on the first range predicate. And because of the match columns to the left of that first range column in the index, that first range predicate will direct us to the branch of the index tree where all the leaf node pointers point to rows in the target table which satisfy those match predicates as well that first range predicate. The most important thing to note here is that we get to this starting point in the search of the index *without doing a scan*. Our strategy is to get to the desired result using an index with little or no scanning.

Once we reach that starting point, all of the entries matching both the direct match predicates and also that first range predicate will be scanned. For all rows qualified by that scan, each of them will be scanned by the remaining predicates in the index. The index entries get narrowed down to a small set of pointers to all the rows in the table which match those search criteria whose columns appear on that index.

After the index scan is exhausted, it may still be necessary to scan the table itself. Although our goal is to have no scans at all, it isn't always possible to completely avoid them. Frequency of reads and updates, and other conditions, also need to be considered.

This is why the sequence of columns in an index is so important. Most important of all is to choose the correct range predicate column to place immediately after the common match predicate columns. To put the same point in other words: most important of all is to get positioned into the index for the desired row without resorting to scanning.

Suppose that the sequence of columns in the index is {*oid, eff_beg_dt, asr_beg_dt*}. In this case, using Figure 15.1, the optimizer will match on the 55, and then apply the LESS THAN OR EQUAL TO predicate to the second indexed column, *eff_beg_dt*. If the current date is September 2011, there are eight rows where *eff_beg_dt* is less than or equal to the current date. So those eight rows will be scanned, and after that the other criteria will be applied while being scanned. Is this the best sequence of columns for this index, given that most queries will be looking for the one current row for an object, lost in a forest of non-current assertions and/or non-current versions for that same object?

In this proposed sequence of columns, the effective begin date immediately follows the match columns, and the next column is the assertion begin date. So after matching, and then filtering on effective begin date, the index will be scanned for the remaining criteria including assertion begin date. And the same eight rows will be qualified by that scan. Finally, the DBMS will use the *row ids* (*rids*) of the qualifying rows, and read the table itself. If the table is physically clustered on exactly this sequence of columns, we might get all eight rows in one I/O. On the other hand, in the worst case, it would require eight I/Os just to find the one current row. Since physical I/Os are one of the main causes of performance problems, reducing them is one of our main opportunities for optimization. And this particular sequence of index columns doesn't seem to do a good job in reducing I/O, either in the index or in the table itself.

Since there are probably more rows for object 55's past than for its future, we might consider reversing the sort order on the effective begin date index column, and make it descending instead of ascending. But even with a descending sort order, there are still the same eight rows that qualify and need further filtering. In fact, most rows in a temporal database usually have an effective begin date less than Now(). So effective begin date does not appear to be a good column to place immediately after the last match column in the index.

Another approach is to put all four temporal columns in the index. This might improve things, but it also has serious flaws. One problem is that some optimizers might ignore columns if the earlier columns do not match with EQUALS predicates (e.g. *List Prefetch* in earlier versions of DB2). And even if these four columns are used by the optimizer, an index scan may still be needed. *Index performance for asserted version tables is most strongly affected by the one temporal column in the index that follows immediately after the match columns.*

As we have now seen, effective begin date is not a good choice for that column position. Neither is assertion begin date, and for much the same reasons, as almost all rows have an assertion begin date earlier than the assertion begin date on the most frequently retrieved row, the current row for the object.

There are two remaining candidates for the column position that immediately follows the match columns: effective end date and assertion end date. In the table in Figure 15.1, there are the same number of rows with an assertion end date greater than Now() as there are rows with an effective end date greater than Now(). The ratio is determined by the number of updates to open-ended versions (ones with 12/31/9999 effective end dates) compared to the number of versions created with known effective end dates.

For example, a policy might have a known effective end date when it is created, whereas a client would normally not have one. So for a policy table, there would be fewer rows with an effective end date greater than Now(), because there would be fewer rows with a 12/31/9999 effective end date to withdraw into past assertion time. For a client table, it would be a toss-up. Since one withdrawn row is created for every temporal update, the number of rows for that object with an assertion end date greater than Now(), and the number of rows with an effective end date greater than Now() would tend to be roughly equal.

There is also an update performance issue with including the assertion end date anywhere in the index. Every time an episode is updated, a currently asserted row is withdrawn; and so its assertion end date is changed. This would require an update to the index, if the assertion end date is in that index; and it would happen every time a temporal update or a temporal delete is processed. By leaving the assertion end date out of the index, these frequent updates will not affect the index.

By a process of elimination, we have come to {*oid, eff_end_dt*} as the sequence of columns that will best optimize the performance of queries looking for the currently asserted current versions of objects. In this case, the optimizer will match on the 55, and then apply the GREATER THAN predicate to the second indexed column, *eff_end_dt* such as *"eff_end_dt > Now()"*. But for tables whose updates usually result in a version with a 12/31/9999 effective end date, the effective end date will not separate the currently asserted current version from the withdrawn versions for the same object. The best way to do that is to add the assertion end date as the last column in the index, giving us {*oid, eff_end_dt, asr_end_dt*}. Even though it will require an index scan to filter the assertions, doing so will often reduce the number of I/Os to the main table.

As we noted earlier, however, the assertion end date is updated every time a temporal update is carried out. It is updated as the then-current row is withdrawn into past assertion time, making room for the row or rows that replace it, or else replace and supercede it. So these physical updates will require a physical update to the corresponding index entry as well.

The decision of whether or not to include the assertion end date in an index designed to optimize access to the currently asserted current versions of objects, therefore, requires careful analysis of the specific situation. For policies and similar kinds of entities, where the effective end dates are usually known in advance, most withdrawn assertions will have an effective end date less than that of the currently asserted current version for the policy. This means that there is less need for the assertion end date in the index. But for clients and similar kinds of entities, where the effective end dates are usually not known in advance, many withdrawn assertions will contain an effective end date equal to that of the currently asserted current version, specifically the 12/31/9999 effective end date. This means that there is greater need for the assertion end date in the index, to push all those past assertions aside and allow us to get to the currently asserted current version more directly.

Generalizing from this specific case, our conclusion is that the sequence of columns for an asserted version table should begin with the match predicates for that table, starting with the most frequently used ones. After that, the effective end date should be the next column in the index. For tables in which most rows are created with a known (non-12/31/9999) effective end date, nothing else is needed in the index. But for tables in which most rows are created with a 12/31/9999, "until further notice", effective end date, we recommend that the assertion end date be added to the index, right after the effective end date.

## Currency Flags

Given the sensitivity of index use to range predicates, and the fact that currently asserted current versions will be the most frequently accessed (and frequently updated) rows in an asserted version table, it is tempting to consider the use of flags rather than dates to indicate currency. Flags can be used as match predicates, performing much better than dates used as range predicates.

Some implementations of historical data do use a flag to mark current rows. But this doesn't work for versions. For one thing, a current version can cease to be current with the passage of time. For another thing, if future versions are supported, they can become current with the passage of time. And it is impossible to guarantee that whenever a current version ceases to be current, the flag marking it as current will be changed on the exact clock tick when it stopped being current. Similarly, it is impossible to guarantee that whenever a future version becomes current, the flag marking it as non-current will be changed on the exact clock tick when it first becomes current.

For these reasons, currency flags are unreliable for versioned data. We cannot count on them to always tell us exactly which rows are current right now, and which rows are not. This may be acceptable for some business data requirements, but our implementation of Asserted Versioning is an enterprise solution, and must also work for databases where a request for current data will return current data no matter how recently it became current.

A currency flag doesn't work for assertions, either. Since asserted version tables support deferred transactions and deferred assertions, the same passage of time can move a currently asserted row into the past, and can also move a deferred assertion into current assertion time. And again, it is nearly impossible to maintain these flags on the exact clock tick when the change occurs. So there will be times when Now() does fall between begin and end dates, while currency flags indicate that it does not.

But as we will now explain, match predicate flags *can* be used in place of or in addition to range predicate dates in an index. A key insight is this: a currency flag must never classify a current row as non-current. But if that flag happens to classify a small number of non-current rows as current, that's not a problem. The objective for the index is to get us close for the most common access. The rest of the predicates in the query, or in the maintenance transaction, will get us all the way there, all the way to exactly the rows we want.

### Using a Currency Flag to Optimize Queries

While many queries will look for versions that are no longer effective, or perhaps not yet effective, the vast majority of queries will look for versions that are currently asserted, versions that represent our best current knowledge of how things used to be, are, or may be at some point in the future. So it seems that there is greater potential improvement in query performance if we focus on assertion time.

We will call our current assertion time flag the *circa flag* (*circa-asr-flag*). It distinguishes between rows which are definitely known to be in the assertion time past from all other rows. All asserted version rows are created with an assertion begin date of Now() or an assertion begin date in the future. They are all created as either current assertions or deferred assertions. When they are created, their circa flag is set to 'Y', indicating that we cannot rule out the possibility that they are current assertions.

One way that a row can find itself in the assertion time past is for the AVF to *withdraw* that row in the process of completing a temporal update or a temporal delete transaction. When it does this, the AVF will also set that row's circa flag to 'N'. At that point, both the flag and the row's assertion end date say the same thing. Both say that the row is definitely not a currently asserted row. (Both also say that the row is definitely not a deferred assertion, either; but the purpose of the flag is to narrow down the search for current assertions.)

The second way that a row can become part of past assertion time is by the simple passage of time. Whenever a temporal update transaction takes place, the assertion time specified on the transaction is used for both the assertion end date of the row being updated, and also for the assertion begin date of the row which updates it. Usually that assertion time is Now(), and so usually the result of the transaction is to immediately withdraw the row being updated into past assertion time and to immediately assert the row which supercedes it.

But when that temporal update is a deferred transaction, something different happens. Suppose that it is April 2013 right now, and a temporal update transaction is processed which has a future assertion date of July 2013. Just as with a non-deferred update, both the assertion end date of the version being updated, and also the assertion begin date of the version updating it, are given the assertion date specified on the transaction.

After this transaction, the original row has an assertion end date three months in the future. For those three months, it remains currently asserted. But after those three months have passed, i.e. once we are into the month of July 2013, that row will exist in the assertion time past. But it was not withdrawn; that is, it did not become assertion time past because of an explicit action on the part of the AVF. Instead, it has "fallen" into the past. We will say that it *fell out of currency.*

Because the row was not withdrawn by the AVF, its circa flag remains 'Y' even though its assertion end date has become earlier than Now(). And as long as its circa flag remains 'Y', this flag, by itself, will not exclude the row during an index search. However, as we will see, additional components come into play, components which will exclude that row.

Since the AVF itself cannot update circa flags on rows as they fall into the past, we will need to periodically run a separate process to find and update those flags. This can be done with the following SQL statement:

```
UPDATE mytable
      SET circa_asr_flag = 'N'
      WHERE circa_asr_flag = 'Y'
      AND asr_end_dt < Now()
```

This update does not need to be run every second or every minute or every hour. It can be run as needed, during off hours such as nights or weekends, when system resources are more available.

How would we use this flag in an index? This flag could be used as the first column after the other direct matching columns

| state | row # | oid | circa | eff-end | asr-beg | asr-end | eff-beg | data |
|-------|-------|-----|-------|---------|---------|---------|---------|---------|
| pa | 1 | 55 | N | 9999 | Jan09 | Feb09 | Jan09 | Apples |
| pa | 3 | 55 | N | 9999 | Feb09 | Jun09 | Mar09 | Berries |
| pa | 5 | 55 | N | 9999 | Jun09 | Aug09 | Jun09 | Cherries |
| pe | 2 | 55 | Y | Mar09 | Feb09 | 9999 | Jan09 | Apples |
| pe | 4 | 55 | Y | Jun09 | Jun09 | 9999 | Mar09 | Berries |
| pe | 6 | 55 | Y | Aug09 | Aug09 | 9999 | Jun09 | Cherries |
| fa | 8 | 55 | Y | Dec13 | Oct12 | 9999 | Aug09 | Kiwi |
| cc | 7 | 55 | Y | 9999 | Aug09 | Oct12 | Aug09 | Kiwi |
| fa | 9 | 55 | Y | 9999 | Oct12 | 9999 | Dec13 | Grapes |

**Figure 15.2** A Bi-Temporal Table with a Circa Flag.

in the index, for example: {*oid, circa_asr_flag, eff_end_dt*}. If the assertion end date were used instead of the circa flag, then the effective end date would require an index scan, prior to reaching the desired index entries. But by replacing the assertion end date with a match predicate, the effective end date becomes the first range predicate following the match predicates, and consequently can be processed without doing a scan.

Let's assume that it is now September 2011, and that the table we are querying is as shown in Figure 15.2. The circa flag has been added to the table shown in Figure 15.1, columns have been rearranged, and the rows from the original table have been resequenced on the index columns. Those columns are shown with their column headings shaded.

Note that row 7 has a non-12/31/9999 assertion end date. Its assertion end date is still in the future because the AVF processed a deferred temporal update against that row. That deferred temporal update created the deferred assertion which is row 8. In a year and a month, on October 2012, two rows will change their assertion time status, and will do so "quietly", simply because of the passage of time. Row 7 will fall into the assertion time past and, at the same moment, row 8 will fall into the assertion time present.

Row 7 will cease to be currently asserted on that date. However, its circa flag will remain unchanged. As far as the flag can tell us, it remains a *possibly current* row. Also, row 8 will become currently asserted on that date. It was a possibly current row all along, and now it has become an actually current one. But its circa flag remains unchanged. That flag does not attempt to distinguish possibly current rows from actually current ones.

At some point, the SQL statement shown earlier will run. It will change the circa flag on row 7 to 'N', indicating that row 7 is definitely not a currently asserted row, and can never become one.

The following query will correctly filter and select the currently asserted current version of object 55 regardless of when the query is executed, and regardless of when the flag reset process is run. This is a query against the table shown in Figure 15.2, and let's assume that it is now September 2011.

```
SELECT data
FROM mytable
      WHERE oid = 55
      AND circa_asr_flag = 'Y'
      AND eff_beg_dt <= Now() AND eff_end_dt > Now()
      AND asr_beg_dt <= Now() AND asr_end_dt > Now()
```

Processing this query, and using the index, the optimizer will:
  **(i)** Match exactly on the predicate {*oid* = *55*}
 **(ii)** Match exactly on the predicate {*circa_asr_flag*= *'Y'*}; and
**(iii)** Then, using its first range predicate, {*eff_end_dt* > Now()}, it will position and start the index scan on the row with the first effective end date later than now, that row being row 8.

We have reached the first range predicate value, and have done so using only the index tree. At this point, an index scan begins; but we have already eliminated a large number of rows from the query's result set without doing any scanning at all.

When there are no more future effective versions found in the index scan, we will have assembled a list of index pointers to all rows which the index scan did not disqualify. But in this example, there *is* one more row with a future effective begin date, that being row 7. So, from its scan starting point, the index will scan rows 8, 7 and 9 and apply the other criteria. If some of the other columns are in the index, it will probably apply those filters via the index. If no other columns are in the index, it will go to the target table itself and apply the criteria that are not included in the index. Doing so, it will return a result set containing only row 7. Row 7's assertion end date has not yet been reached, so it is still currently asserted. And the assertion begin dates for rows 8 and 9 have not yet been reached, so they are not yet currently asserted.

In many cases, there will be no deferred assertions or future versions, and so the first row matched on the three indexed columns will be the only qualifying row. Whenever that is the case, we won't need the other temporal columns in the index. So restricting the index to just these three columns will keep the index smaller, enabling us to keep more of it in memory. This will improve performance for queries that retrieve the current row of objects that have no deferred assertions or future versions, but will be slightly slower when retrieving the current rows of objects that have either or both.

To understand how this index produces correct results whether it is run before or after the circa flag update process changes any flag values, let's assume that it is now November 2012, and the flag update process has not yet adjusted any flag values. In September, row 7 was the current row, and our use of the index correctly led us to that row. Now it is October, and the current row is row 9. Without any changes having been made to flag values, how does the index correctly lead us to this different result?

Prior to this tick of the clock, the table contained a current assertion with an October 2012 end date, and a deferred assertion with an October 2012 begin date. Because flag values haven't changed, our first three predicates will qualify the same three rows, rows 7, 8 and 9. But now row 7 will be filtered out because right now, November 2012 is past the assertion end date of October 2012. Row 9 will be filtered out because the effective begin date of December 2013 has not yet been reached. But row 8 meets all of the criteria and is therefore returned in the result set.

If the update of the circa flag is run on January 2013, let's say, it will change row 7's flag from 'Y' to 'N' because the assertion end date on that row is, when the process is run, in the past. Now, if our same query is run again, there will only be two rows to scan, two currently asserted rows. The SQL will correctly filter those two rows by their effective time periods, returning only the one row which is, at that time, also currently in effect.

Recall that the purpose of the circa flag is to optimize access to the most frequently requested data, that being current assertions about what things are currently like, i.e. currently asserted and currently effective rows. We note again that rows which make current assertions about what things are currently like are precisely the rows we find in non-temporal tables. Rather than being some exotic kind of bi-temporal construct, they are actually the "plain vanilla" data that is the only data found in most of the tables in a conventional database. For queries to such data, asserted version tables containing a circa flag, and having the index just described, will nearly match the performance of non-temporal tables.

### Other Uses of the Circa Flag

While we have said that the purpose of this flag is to improve the performance of queries for currently asserted and currently effective data, it will also help the performance of queries for currently asserted but *not* currently effective versions by filtering out most withdrawn assertions and also versions no longer in effect as of the desired period of time. Another way to use the circa flag is to make it the *first* column in this index or in another index, and use it to create a separate *partition* for those past assertions whose circa flag also designates them as past. As we have said, this may not be all past assertions; but it will be most of them.

This will keep the index entries for current and deferred assertions together, and also separate from the index entries for assertions definitely known to be past assertions, resulting in a better buffer hit ratio. In fact, the index could be used as both a clustering and a partitioning index, in which case it would also keep more of the current rows in the target table in memory. To the circa flag eliminating definitely past assertions, and the *oid* column specifying the objects of interest, we also recommend adding the effective end date which will filter out past versions. The recommended clustering and partitioning index, then, is: {*circa_asr_flag, oid, eff_end_dt*}.

The circa flag can also be added to other search and foreign key indexes to help improve performance for current data. For example, a specialized index could be created to optimize searches for current Social Security Number data (currently asserted current versions of that data). The index would be: {*SSN, circa_asr_flag, eff_end_dt*}.

In this example, we have placed the circa flag after the SSN column so that index entries for all asserted version rows for the same SSN are grouped together. This means that the index will provide a slightly lower level of performance for queries looking for current SSN data than a {*circa_asr_flag, oid, eff_end_dt*} index, assuming we know the *oid* in addition to the SSN. But unlike that circa-first index, this index is also helpful for queries looking for *as-was* asserted data, that data being the mistakes we have made in our SSN data.

If we are looking for *past* assertions, it may also improve performance to code the circa flag using an IN clause. Some optimizers will manage short IN clause lists in an index look-aside buffer, effectively utilizing the predicate as though it were a match predicate rather than a range predicate.

In the following example, we follow standard conventions in showing program variables (e.g. those in a COBOL program's WORKING STORAGE section) as variable names preceded by the colon character. Also following COBOL conventions, we use hyphens in those variables. This convention was used, rather than generic Java or other dynamically prepared SQL with "?" parameter markers, to give an idea of the variables' contents.

```
SELECT data
FROM mytable
      WHERE SSN = :my-ssn
      AND eff_beg_dt <= :my-as-of-dt
      AND eff_end_dt > :my-as-of-dt
      AND asr_beg_dt <= :my-as-of-dt
      AND assertion end date > :my-as-of-dt
      AND circa_asr_flag IN ('Y', 'N')
```

In processing this query, a DB2 optimizer will first match on SSN. After that, still using the index tree rather than a scan, it will look aside for the effective end date under the 'Y' value for the circa flag, and then repeat the process for the 'N' value. This uses a *matchcols* of three; whereas without the IN clause, an index scan would begin right after the SSN match. However, we only recommend this for SQL where *:my_as_of_dt* is not guaranteed to be Now(). When that as-of date is Now(), using the EQUALS predicate ({*circa_asr_flag* = 'Y'}) will perform much better since the 'N's do not need to be analyzed.

Query-enhancing indexes like these are not always needed. For the most part, as we said earlier, these indexes are specifically designed to improve the performance of queries that are looking for the currently asserted current versions of the objects they are interested in, and in systems that require extremely high *read* performance.

## Indexes to Optimize Temporal Referential Integrity

Temporal referential integrity (TRI) is enforced in two directions. On the insert or temporal expansion of a child managed object, or on a change in the parent object designated by its temporal foreign key, we must insure that the parent object is present in every clock tick in which the child object is about to be present. On the deletion or temporal contraction of a parent managed object, we must RESTRICT, CASCADE or SET NULL that transformation so that it does not leave any "temporal orphans" after the transaction is complete.

In this section, we will discuss the performance considerations involved in creating indexes that support TRI checks on both parent and child managed objects.

### Asserted Versioning's Non-Unique Primary Keys

First, and most obviously, each parent table needs an index whose initial column will be that table's object identifier (*oid*). The object identifier is also the initial column of the primary key (PK) of all asserted version tables. It is followed by two other primary key components, the effective begin date and the assertion begin date.

We need to remember that these physical PKs do not explicitly define the logical primary keys used by the AVF because the AVF uses date *ranges* and not specific dates or pairs of dates. Because of this, a unique index on the primary key of an asserted version table does not guarantee temporal entity integrity. These primary keys guarantee *physical* uniqueness; they guarantee that no two rows will have identical primary key values. But they do not guarantee *semantic* uniqueness, because they do not prevent multiple rows with the same object identifier from specifying [overlapping] or otherwise [intersecting] time periods.

The PK of an asserted version table can be any column or combination of columns that physically distinguish each row from all the other rows in the table. For example, the PK could be the object identifier plus a sequence number. It could be a single surrogate identity key column. It could be a business key plus the row create date. We have this freedom of choice because asserted version tables more clearly distinguish between semantically unique identifiers and physically unique identifiers than do conventional tables.

But this very freedom of choice poses a serious risk to any business deciding to implement its own Asserted Versioning framework. It is the risk of implementing Asserted Versioning's concepts one project at a time, one database at a time, one set of queries and maintenance transactions at a time. It is the risk of proliferating point solutions, each of which may work correctly, but which together pose serious difficulties for queries which range across two or more of those databases. It is the risk of failing to create an *enterprise implementation* of bi-temporal data management.

The semantically unique identifier for any asserted version table is the combination of the table's object identifier and its two time periods. And to emphasize this very important point once again: two pairs of dates are indeed used to represent two time periods, but they are not equivalent to two time periods. What turns those pairs of dates into time periods is the Asserted Versioning code which guarantees that they are treated as the begin and end delimiters for time periods.

Given that there should be one enterprise-wide approach for Asserted Versioning primary keys, what should it be? First of all, an enterprise approach requires that the PK of an asserted version table must not contain any business data. The reason is that if business data were used, we could not guarantee that the same number of columns would be used as the PK from one asserted version table to the next, or that column datatypes would even be the same. These differences would completely eliminate the interoperability benefits which are one of the objectives of an enterprise implementation. But beyond that restriction, the choice of an enterprise standard for Asserted Versioning primary keys, in a proprietary implementation of Asserted Versioning concepts, is up to the organization implementing it.

We have now shown how the choice of columns beyond the object identifier—the choice of the effective end date and the assertion end date, and optionally a circa flag—is used to minimize scan costs in both indexes and the tables they index. We next consider, more specifically, indexes whose main purpose is to support the checks which enforce temporal referential integrity.

### Indexes on TRI Parents

As we have explained, a temporal foreign key (TFK) never contains a full PK value. So it never points to a specific parent row. This is the principal way in which it is different from a conventional foreign key (FK), and the reason that current DBMSs cannot enforce temporal referential integrity.

A complete Asserted Versioning temporal foreign key is a combination of a column of data and a function. That column of data contains the object identifier of the object on which the child object is existence-dependent. That function interprets pairs of dates on the child row being created (by either an insert or an update transaction) as time periods, and pairs of dates on the parent episode as time periods. With that information, the AVF enforces TRI, insuring that any transformation of the database will leave it in a state in which the full extent of a child version's time periods are included within its parent episode's time periods. It also enforces temporal entity integrity (TEI), insuring that no two rows representing the same object ever share a pair of assertion time and effective time clock ticks.

The AVF needs an index on the parent table to boost the performance of its TRI enforcement code. We do not want to perform scans while trying to determine if a parent object identifier exists, and if the effective period of the dependent is included within a single episode of the parent. The most important part of this index on the parent table is that it starts with the object identifier.

The AVF uses the object identifier and three temporal dates. First, it uses the parent table's episode begin date, rather than its effective begin date, because all TRI time period comparisons are between a child version and a parent episode. So we will consider the index sequence as described earlier to reduce scans, but then add the episode begin date.

Instead of creating a separate index for TRI parent-side tables, we could try to minimize the number of indexes by re-using the primary key index to:

(i) Support uniqueness for a row, because some DBMS applications require a unique PK index for single-row identification.

(ii) Help the AVF perform well when an object is queried by its object identifier; and

(iii) Improve performance for the AVF during TRI enforcement.

So we recommend an index whose first column is the object identifier of the parent table. Our proposed index is now {*oid*, . . . .}. Next, we need to determine if we expect current data reads to the table to outnumber non-current reads or updates.

If we expect current data reads to dominate, then the next column we might choose to use is the circa flag. If this flag is used as a higher-level node in the index, then TRI maintenance in the AVF can use the {*circa_asr_flag* = 'Y'} predicate to ignore most of the rows in past assertion time. This could significantly help the performance of TRI maintenance. Using the circa flag, our proposed index is now {*oid*, *circa_asr_flag*. . . . .}. The assumption here is that the DBMS allows updates to a PK value with no physical foreign key dependents because the circa flag will be updated.

Just as in any physical data modeling effort, the DBA or Data Architect will need to analyze the tradeoffs of indexing for reads vs. indexing for updates. The decision might be to replace a single multi-use index with several indexes each supporting a different pattern of access. But in constructing an index to help the performance of TRI enforcement, the next column should be the effective end date, for the reasons described earlier in this chapter. Our proposed index is now {*oid*, *circa_asr_flag*, *eff_end_dt*, . . . .}.

After that, the sequence of the columns doesn't matter much because the effective end date is used with a range predicate, so direct index matching stops there. However, other columns are needed for uniqueness, and the optimizer will still likely use any additional columns that are in the index and qualified as criteria, filtering on everything it got during the index scan rather than during the more expensive table scan.

If the circa flag is not included in the index, and the DBMS allows the update of a primary key (with no physical dependents), then the next column should be the assertion end date. Otherwise, the next column should be the assertion begin date. In either case, we now have a unique index, which can be used as the PK index, for queries and also for TRI enforcement. Finally, to help with TRI enforcement, we recommend adding the episode begin date. This is because the parent managed object in any TRI relationship is always an episode.

Depending on whether or not the circa flag is included, this unique index is either

```
{oid, circa_asr_flag, eff_end_dt, asr_beg_dt, epis_beg_dt}
```

or

```
{oid, eff_end_dt, asr_end_dt, epis_beg_dt}
```

Let's be sure we understand why both indexes are unique. The unique identifier of any object is the combination of its *oid*, assertion time period and effective time period. In the primary key of asserted version tables, those two time periods are represented by their respective begin dates. But because the AVF enforces temporal entity integrity, no two rows for the same object can share both an assertion clock tick and an effective clock tick. So in the case of these two indexes, while the assertion begin date represents the assertion time period, the effective *end* date represents the effective time period. Both indexes contain an object identifier and one delimiter date representing each of the two time periods, and so both indexes are unique.

### Indexes on TRI Children

Some DBMSs automatically create indexes for foreign keys declared to the DBMS, but others do not. Regardless, since Asserted Versioning does not declare its temporal foreign keys using SQL's Data Definition Language (DDL), we must create our own indexes to improve the performance of TRI enforcement on TFKs.

Each table that contains a TFK should have an index on the TFK columns primarily to assist with delete rule enforcement, such as ON DELETE RESTRICT, CASCADE or SET NULL. These indexes can be multi-purpose as well, also being used to assist with general queries that use the *oid* value of the TFK. We should try to design these indexes to support both cases in order to minimize the system overhead otherwise required to maintain multiple indexes.

When a temporal delete rule is fired from the parent, it will look at every dependent table that uses the parent's *oid*. It will also use the four temporal dates to find rows that fall within the assertion and effective periods of the related parent.

The predicate to find dependents in any contained clock tick would look something like this:

```
WHERE parent_oid = :parent-oid
      AND eff_beg_dt < :parent-eff-end-dt
      AND eff_end_dt > :parent-eff-beg-dt
      AND circa_asr_flag = 'Y' (if used)
      AND asr_end_dt >= Now()
      (might have deferred assertion criteria, too)
```

In this SQL, the columns designated as parent dates are the effective begin and end dates specified on the delete transaction.

In an index designed to enhance the performance of the search for TRI parent–child relationships, the first column should be the TFK. This is the *oid* value that relates a child to a parent.

Temporal referential integrity checks are never concerned with withdrawn assertions, so this is another index in which the circa flag will help performance. If we use this flag, it should be the next column in the index. However, if this is the column that will be used for clustering or partitioning, the circa flag should be listed first, before the *oid*.

For TRI enforcement, the AVF does not use a simple BETWEEN predicate because it needs to find dependents with *any* overlapping clock ticks. Instead, it uses an [intersects] predicate.

Two rules used during TRI delete enforcement are that the effective begin date on the episode must be less than the effective end date specified on the delete transaction, and that the effective end date on the episode must be greater than the effective begin date on the transaction.

Earlier, we pointed out that for current data queries, there are usually many more historical rows than current and future rows, and for that reason we made the next column the effective end date rather than the effective begin date. These same considerations hold true for indexes assisting with temporal delete transactions.

Therefore, our recommended index structure for TFK indexes, which can be used for both TRI enforcement by the AVF, and also for any queries looking for parent object and child object relationships, where the *oid* mentioned is the TFK value, is either {*parent_oid, circa_asr_flag, eff_end_dt. . . . .*} or {*parent_oid, eff_end_dt, asr_end_dt. . . . .*}.

Other temporal columns could be added, depending on application-specific uses for the index.

# Other Techniques for Performance Tuning Bi-Temporal Tables

In an Asserted Versioning database, most of the activity is row insertion. No rows are physically deleted; and except for the update of the assertion end date when an assertion is withdrawn, or the update of the assertion begin date when far future deferred assertions are moved into the near future, there are no physical updates either. On the other hand, there are plenty of reads, usually to current data. We need to consider these types of access, and their relative frequencies, when we decide which optimization techniques to use.

## Avoiding MAX(dt) Predicates

Even if Asserted Versioning did not support logical gap versioning, we would keep both effective end dates and assertion end dates in the Asserted Versioning bi-temporal schema. The reason is that, without them, most accesses to these tables would require finding the MAX(dt) of the designated object in assertion time, or in effective time within a specified period of assertion time. The performance problem with a MAX(dt) is that it needs to be evaluated for each row that is looked at, causing performance degradation exponential to the number of rows reviewed.

Experience with the AVF and our Asserted Versioning databases has shown us that eliminating MAX(dt) subqueries and having effective and assertion end dates on asserted version tables, dramatically improves performance.

## NULL vs. 12/31/9999

Some readers might wonder why we do not use nulls to stand in for unknown future dates, whether effective end dates or assertion end dates. From a logical point of view, NULL, which is a marker representing the absence of information, is what we should use in these date columns whenever we do not know what those future dates will be.

But experience with the AVF and with Asserted Versioning databases has shown that using real dates rather than nulls helps the optimizer to consistently choose better, more efficient access paths, and matches on index keys more directly.

Without using NULL, the predicate to find versions that are still in effect is:

```
eff_end_dt > Now()
```

Using NULL, the semantically identical predicate is:

```
(eff_end_dt > Now() OR eff_end_dt IS NULL)
```

The OR in the second example causes the optimizer to try one path and then another. It might use index look-aside, or it might scan. Either of these is less efficient than a single GREATER THAN comparison.

Another considered approach is to coalesce NULL and the latest date recognizable by the DBMS, giving us the following predicate:

```
COALESCE(eff_end_dt, '12/31/9999') > Now()
```

But functions normally cannot be resolved in standard indexes, and so the COALESCE function will normally cause a scan. Worse yet, some DBMSs will not resolve functions until all data is read and joined. So frequently, a lot of extra data will be assembled into a preliminary result set before this COALESCE function is ever applied.

The last of our three options is a simple range predicate (such as GREATER THAN) without an OR, and without a function. If the end date is unknown, and the value we use to represent that unknown condition is the highest date (or timestamp) which the DBMS can recognize, then this simple range predicate will return the same results as the other two predicates. And given that the highest date a DBMS can recognize is likely to be far into the future, it is unlikely that business applications will ever need to use that date to represent that far-off time. In SQL Server, for example, that highest date is 12/31/9999. So as long as our business applications do not need to designate that specific New Year's Eve nearly 8000 years from now, we are free to use it to represent the fact that a value is unknown. Using it, we can use the simple range predicate shown earlier in this section, and reap the benefits of the excellent performance of that kind of predicate.

## Partitioning

Another technique that can help with performance and database maintenance, such as backups, recoveries and reorganizations, is partitioning. There are several basic approaches to partitioning.

One is to partition by a date, or something similar, so that the more current and active data is grouped together, and is more likely to be found in cache. This is a common partitioning strategy for on-line transaction processing systems.

Another is to partition by some known field that could keep commonly accessed smaller groups of data together, such as a low cardinality foreign key. The benefit of this approach is that it directs a search to a small well-focused collection of data located on the same or on adjacent I/O pages. This strategy improves performance by taking advantage of sequential prefetch algorithms.

A third approach is to partition by some random field to take advantage of the parallelism in data access that some DBMSs support. For these DBMSs, the partitions define parallel access paths. This is a good strategy for applications such as reporting and business intelligence (BI) where typically large scans could benefit from the parallel processing made possible by the partitioning.

Some DBMSs require that the partitioning index also be the clustering index. This limits options because it forces a trade-off between optimizing for sequential prefetch and optimizing for parallel access. Fortunately, DBMS vendors are starting to separate the implementation of these two requirements.

Another limitation of some DBMSs, but one that is gradually being addressed by their vendors, is that whenever a row is moved between partitions, those entire partitions are both locked. This forces application developers to design their processes so that they never update a partitioning key value on a row during prime time, because doing so locks the source and destination partitions until the move is complete. As we noted, more recent releases of DBMSs reduce the locking required to move a row from one partition to another.

A good partitioning strategy for an Asserted Versioning database is to partition by one of the temporal columns, such as the assertion end date, in order to keep the most frequently accessed data in cache. As we have pointed out, that will normally be currently asserted current versions of the objects of interest to the query.

For an optimizer to know which partition(s) to access, it needs to know the high order of the key. For direct access to the other search criteria, it needs direct access to the higher nodes in the key, higher than the search key. Therefore, while one of the temporal dates is good for partitioning, it reduces the effectiveness of other search criteria. To avoid this problem, we might want to define two indexes, one for partitioning, and another for searching.

The better solution for defining partitions that optimize access to currently asserted versions is to use the circa flag as the first column in the partitioning index. The best predicate would be {*circa_asr_flag* = 'Y'} for current assertions. For DBMSs which support index-look-aside processing for IN predicates, the best predicate might be {*circa_asr_flag IN ('Y', 'N')*} when it is uncertain if the version is currently asserted. With this predicate, the index can support searches for past assertions as well as searches for current ones. Otherwise, it will require a separate index to support searches for past assertions.

## Clustering

Clustering and partitioning often go together, depending on the reason for partitioning and the way in which specific DBMSs support it. Whether or not partitioning is used, choosing the best clustering sequence can dramatically reduce I/O and improve performance.

The general concept behind clustering is that as the database is modified, the DBMS will attempt to keep the data on physical pages in the same order as that specified in the clustering index. But each DBMS does this a little differently. One DBMS will cluster each time an insert or update is processed. Another will make a valiant attempt to do that. A third will only cluster when the table is reorganized. But regardless of the approach, the result is to reduce physical I/O by locating data that is frequently accessed together as physically close together as possible.

Early DBMSs only allowed one clustering index, but newer releases often support multiple clustering sequences, sometimes called *indexed views* or *multi-dimensional clustering*.

It is important to determine the most frequently used access paths to the data. Often the most frequently used access paths are ones based on one or more foreign keys. For asserted version tables, currently asserted current versions are usually the most frequently queried data.

Sometimes, the right combination of foreign keys can provide good clustering for more than one access path. For example, suppose that a policy table has two low cardinality TFKs, product type and market segment, and that each TFK value has thousands of related policies.[3] We might then create this clustering index:

```
{circa_asr_flag, product_type_oid, market_segment_oid,
eff_end_dt, policy_oid}
```

The circa flag would cluster most of the currently asserted rows together, keeping them physically co-located under the lower cardinality columns. Clustering would continue based on

---

[3]*Low cardinality* means that there are fewer distinct values for the field in the table which results in more rows having a single value.

effective date, and then by the higher cardinality object identifier of the table. This will provide access via the product type *oid*, and will tend to cluster the data for current access for three other potential search indexes:

  **(i)** {*product_type_oid, circa_asr_flag, eff_end_dt*};

 **(ii)** {*market_segment_oid, circa_asr_flag, eff_end_dt*}; or

**(iii)** {*policy_oid, circa_asr_flag, eff_end_dt*}.

## Materialized Query Tables

Materialized Query Tables (MQTs), sometimes called Indexed Views, are extremely helpful in optimizing the performance of Asserted Versioning databases. They are especially helpful when querying currently asserted current versions.

Some optimizers will automatically determine if an MQT can be used, even if we do not explicitly specify one in the SQL FROM clause. Some DBMSs will let us specifically reference an MQT. Certain implementations of MQTs do not allow volatile variables and system registers, such as Now() or CURRENT TIMESTAMP in the definition, because the MQTs would be in a constant rebuild state. For example, we could not code the following in the definition of the MQT:

```
asr_end_dt > Now()
```

However, we could code a literal such as:

```
asr_end_dt > '01/01/2010'
```

This would work, but obviously the MQT would have to be recreated each time the date changed. Another option is to create a single row table with today's date in it, and join to that table. For example, consider a Today table with a column called today's date. An MQT table would be joined to this table using a predicate like {*asr_end_dt > Today.todays_dt*}. Then, we could periodically increment the value of *todays_dt* to rebuild the MQT.

However, this is another place where we recommend the circa flag. If we have it, we can just use the {*circa_asr_flag = 'Y'*} predicate in the MQT definition. This will keep the overhead low, will keep maintenance to a minimum, and will segregate past assertion time data, thereby getting better cache/buffer utilization.

We can also create something similar to the circa flag for the effective end date. This would be used to include currently *effective* versions in an MQT. However, for the same reasons we cannot use Now() in an assertion time predicate, we cannot use {*eff_end_dt > Now()*} in MQT definitions because of the volatile system variable Now(). So instead, we can use an effective time flag, and code a {*circa_eff_flag* = 'Y'} predicate in the MQT definition.

MQTs could also be helpful when joining multiple asserted version tables together.

With most MQT tables, we have a choice of refreshing them either periodically or immediately. Our choice depends on what the DBMS permits, and the requirements of specific applications and specific MQTs.

## Standard Tuning Techniques

In addition to tuning techniques specific to Asserted Versioning databases, there are general tuning techniques that are just as applicable to temporal tables as to conventional or non-temporal ones.

*Use Cache Profligately.* Per-unit memory costs, like per-unit costs for other hardware components, are falling. Multi-gigabyte memory is now commonplace on personal computers, and tera-byte memories are now found on mainframe computers. Try to get as many and as much of your indexes in cached buffers as you can. Reducing physical I/O is essential to good performance.

*Use Parameter Markers.* If we cannot use static SQL for a frequently executed large data volume query, then the next best thing is to prepare the SQL with parameter markers. Many optimizers will perform a hashed compare of the SQL to the database dynamic prepared SQL cache, then a direct compare of the SQL being prepared, looking for a match. If it finds a match, it will avoid the expensive access path determination optimization process, and will instead use the previously determined access path rather than trying to re-optimize it.

The reason for the use of parameter markers rather than literals for local predicates is that with cache matching, the optimizer is much more likely to find a match. For example, a prepared statement of

```
SELECT * FROM mytable WHERE oid = 55
```

does not match

```
SELECT * FROM mytable WHERE oid = 44
```

causing the statement to be re-optimized. But a prepared SQL statement of

```
SELECT * FROM mytable WHERE oid = ?
```

will find a match whether the value of the parameter marker is 44, 55, or any other number, and in most cases will not need to be re-optimized.

*Use More Indexes.* Index other common search columns such as business keys. Also, use composite key indexes when certain combinations of criteria are often used together.

*Eliminate Sorts.* Try to reduce DBMS sorting by having index keys match the ORDER BY or GROUP BY sequence after EQUALS predicates.

*Explain/Show Plan.* Know the estimated execution time of the SQL. Incorporate SQL tuning into the system development life cycle.

*Monitor and Tune.* Some monitoring tools will identify the SQL statements that use the most overall resources. But as well as the single execution overhead identified in the Explain (Show Plan), it is important to also consider the frequency of execution of the SQL statements. For example, a SQL statement that runs for 6 seconds but is called only 10 times per hour uses a lot fewer resources than another that runs only 60 milliseconds, but is called 10,000 times per hour—in this case, 1 minute vs. 10 minutes total time. The query it is most important to optimize is the 60 millisecond query.

*Use Optimization Hints Cautiously.* Most optimizers work well most of the time. However, once in a while, they just don't get it right. It's getting harder to force the optimizer into choosing a better access path, for example by using different logical expressions with the same truth conditions, or by fudging catalog statistics. However, most optimizers support some type of *optimization hints*. Use them sparingly, but when all else fails, and the optimizer is being stubborn, use them.

*Use Isolation Levels.* Specify the appropriate Isolation Level to minimize locks and lock waits. Isolation levels of Cursor Stability (CS) or Uncommitted Read (UR) can significantly improve the throughput compared to more restrictive levels such as Repeatable Read (RR). However, keep in mind that a temporal update usually expands into several physical inserts and updates to the objects. So make sure that less restrictive isolation levels are acceptable to the application.

## Glossary References

Glossary entries whose definitions form strong interdependencies are grouped together in the following list. The same glossary entries may be grouped together in different ways at the end of different chapters, each grouping reflecting the semantic perspective of each chapter. There will usually be several other, and often many other, glossary entries that are not included in the list, and we recommend that the Glossary be consulted whenever an unfamiliar term is encountered.

12/31/9999

Asserted Versioning Framework (AVF)

assertion
assertion begin date
assertion end date
assertion time period

bi-temporal database
conventional database
non-temporal database

circa flag

clock tick
time period

deferred assertion

effective begin date
effective end date
effective time period

episode begin date

object
object identifier
oid

fall out of currency
withdraw

temporal column

temporal entity integrity (TEI)
temporal foreign key (TFK)
temporal referential integrity (TRI)

version

# CONCLUSION

In the Preface, we listed four objectives for this book. Those objectives were to explain how to support:

 **(i)** Seamless access to temporal data;
 **(ii)** The encapsulation of temporal data structures and processes;
**(iii)** The internalization of pipeline datasets; and
 **(iv)** The enterprise contextualization of this functionality.

Let's see whether we have achieved these objectives.

## Seamless Access to Temporal Data

We've known all along that, with enough hard work, we can almost always pull together any data that the business asks for—past or present versions of objects of interest, current data about those versions or past data about them. And we now know how to extend the range of what we can pull together to include future data as well, in either or both of our two temporal dimensions—although we emphasize, again, that it is only the

Managing Time in Relational Databases. Doi: 10.1016/B978-0-12-375041-9.00016-9

Asserted Versioning temporal model that recognizes future assertion time.

But the hard work has to be paid for. And sometimes the results are flawed. Sometimes we don't pull together all the data relevant to a business request, because we overlook some sources we should have known about. Sometimes we don't pull together the best or most current copy of relevant data because we don't know how to tell the best from the rest. And often, by the time the hard work is over and the data is assembled, that data has lost some business value, or perhaps has become completely irrelevant, simply because too much time has gone by.

When data requests are for our best data about what things are currently like, we are usually able to respond rapidly. Usually, the data is already available, ready to be queried from within application programs, or by means of tools available to business analysts or researchers. This is the data we have been calling conventional data. In the terminology we have developed, conventional data consists of currently asserted current versions of the persistent objects we are interested in.

But past, present or future assertions about past, present or future versions give us nine temporal categories of data, and conventional data is only one of those nine. As requests for data in one or more of those other eight categories become more frequent, it becomes more important to reduce the work involved in satisfying those requests. As it becomes increasingly important to provide that data as quickly as possible, scavenger hunts for scattered data are less and less acceptable as a standard procedure.

This increasing importance of past and future data points to an obvious end-state. First, all nine bi-temporal categories of data should be as quickly and easily available as conventional data already is. Secondly, seamless access across data from multiple categories should be just as easy, and just as quick.

Asserted version tables are that end-state. Asserted version tables can contain any number of rows representing the same object, and those tables can include rows from any or all of those nine bi-temporal categories. This means that when data about one or more objects, in any of those categories, is requested, all of that data is immediately available and ready to be queried. There is no assembly and/or transformation work to be done to get that data ready for querying. There is no delay between the business request for data, and its availability in queryable form.

The majority of queries against bi-temporal data are point-in-time queries. A point in assertion time, and a point in effective time, are specified. As for assertion time, when Now() is specified, the result is an as-is query, a query returning our best and current data about what an object used to be like, is like, or may eventually be like. When a past point in time is specified, the result is an as-was query, a query returning data about the past, present or future which was asserted at some past point in time. As for queries specifying future assertion time, they are queries about internalized batch transaction datasets, about what our data is going to look like if and when we apply those transactions.

Queries which specify an assertion point in time, but either no effective time or else an effective range of time, are queries which return versioned data. So clearly, queries can return result sets all of whose rows reside in one of the nine bi-temporal categories or result sets whose rows are drawn from several of those bi-temporal categories. In this way, *seamless access* across those categories is provided. By containing all this data in production tables, there is no delay between a request for that data and when a query can be written against it.

We conclude that Asserted Versioning *does* provide real-time seamless access to the full range of bi-temporal data.

# Encapsulation of Temporal Data Structures and Processes

Asserted version tables are complex. There are two time periods, and each is expressed as a pair of dates. Surrogate keys are required. Temporal foreign keys are no kind of foreign key that a DBMS can recognize. If these bi-temporal components of data schemas must be designed and expressed in logical data models, the work required of those data modelers will be more complex than work on equivalent non-temporal models. Asserted Versioning shields data modelers from this temporal design work by means of its support for *design encapsulation*.

The semantic constraints that make bi-temporal data meaningful are complex. They involve extensive checks for temporal gaps, temporal contiguity and temporal overlaps. Temporal relationships between referential parent and child data are especially complex. The code that is required to make temporal foreign keys carry out a temporalized version of the same work that conventional foreign keys do is not simple code. Asserted Versioning shields developers and DBAs from this programming work by means of its support for *maintenance encapsulation*. This also shields those who write maintenance transactions from the complexities involved in writing what is often a lengthy series of SQL insert and update statements, all to carry out what, to the business, is a single action for example, "Extend the start date on policy P861 back to the beginning of the year".

Query encapsulation is provided for both ad hoc queries and production queries. Ad hoc queries, usually written by business analysts and researchers who are not IT technical specialists, may benefit from a rich set of views which hides much of the temporal selection and join criteria that might otherwise be difficult for those authors to write. Production queries, written by developers and DBAs, will generally not make use of views. But because Asserted Versioning insures that all data being queried already satisfies temporal entity integrity and temporal referential integrity constraints, it eliminates the need to filter out violations of those constraints from query result sets. In this way, Asserted Versioning eliminates much of the complexity that would otherwise have to be written into queries that directly access asserted version tables. In this way, Asserted Versioning provides as simple a target as possible for both ad hoc queries and production queries and, in doing so, provides the *query encapsulation* that assists both kinds of query authors.

## Design Encapsulation

Data modeling is usually on a project's critical path. That's because it is difficult to write code when you don't know what the database is going to look like! Database schemas come first; code comes after that.

The first thing the data modeler must do, with respect to temporal data, is to get the temporal requirements right. This can often be difficult because while IT and technically conversant business people usually have developed a business/IT *pidgin* that enables them to communicate clearly, there is no such pidgin for temporal requirements. But with Asserted Versioning, and its extensive Glossary, the material for such a pidgin does exist.

For example, technically conversant business people often understand IT people when they say things like "No, you don't really want a referential integrity relationship between salespersons and clients, because you want to be able to add a client before you assign a salesperson to him and, for that matter, be able to add a salesperson before you assign her a client". The modeler may be right or wrong; but both she and the business lead on the project understand what she's saying.

Now think of trying to explain temporal referential integrity with the language only of overlaps and gaps, and begin and end dates, all involving a set of rows in a pair of tables. Both the business analyst and the DBA will have to use the language of physical data and relationships among physical data to express semantic constraints, to express what are often called *business rules*. Those would be difficult conversations, and misunderstandings would inevitably result because of the mismatch between semantic requirements and the ability to talk about them in only physical terms.

But Asserted Versioning provides the concept of temporal referential integrity, and such related concepts as temporal foreign keys and episode to version temporal extent relationships. And TRI really is RI extended across two temporal dimensions, not a new concept which has no connection to concepts the business and technical members of the project team are already familiar with. And so, using the Asserted Versioning concepts of objects, episodes, versions, assertions, TEI and TRI, the modeler and the business lead can communicate at a level of abstraction appropriate to the content of the conversation. The terminology introduced by Asserted Versioning, and defined in its Glossary, is the basis for an extension of the business/IT pidgin to cover temporal data.

Once temporal requirements are clarified, Asserted Versioning provides a set of metadata tables (or ERwin UDPs) to capture those requirements. Expressing those requirements as metadata is straightforward, as we saw in Chapter 8. But expressing them in the logical data model, i.e. the one the modeler writes, is often complex, as the chapter on the subject in Dr. Snodgrass's book shows us.[1]

We believe that if it were necessary to express temporal requirements in data models, that requirement might add 25% or more to the total modeling effort on a typical project, and might extend the timeline for completing the model by at least that much. But by expressing temporal requirements separately from the logical data model, we both reduce the total amount of work to do in this phase of the project and also shorten the timeline along the critical path because clarifying temporal requirements, and building or extending the non-temporal logical data model, is work that can be done in parallel. This also means that existing logical data models can continue to function, without modification, as the data models for databases some or all of whose conventional tables have been and may continue to be converted to asserted version tables.

---

[1]See Chapter 11 in that book, the chapter entitled *Temporal Database Design*. In that chapter, Dr. Snodgrass takes 56 pages to describe how to express temporal data requirements in a logical data model.

We conclude that Asserted Versioning *does* provide design encapsulation for bi-temporal data, and also temporal upward compatibility for logical data models and conventional databases.

## Maintenance Encapsulation

Maintenance encapsulation protects both the user of the database, and the developers who have to write the code that maintains it.

This book contains several scenarios which show a temporal transaction—one written by a person—being applied to an Asserted Versioning database. The early scenarios, such as those in Chapter 7, are relatively simple. One temporal insert transaction is usually translated into one physical SQL transaction. But a temporal delete transaction, even one which does not cascade, may require three or more physical transactions to carry it out. Temporal update transactions will require a combination of physical update and physical insert transactions. Temporal retroactive transactions may require several dozen physical transactions to complete.

Asserted Versioning's maintenance encapsulation relieves the user of the burden of writing these SQL maintenance transactions. Because of this encapsulation, the user can instead, using the Instead Of functionality of the AVF, write a single insert, update or delete statement. The AVF will carry out the intentions expressed in those transactions, no matter how many physical transactions are required to do it.

Maintenance encapsulation also protects developers. The translation of the user's temporal transaction is done by the AVF, not by developer-written code. The management of the one or more physical transactions which implement each temporal transaction as an atomic and isolated unit of work is done by the AVF, not by developer-written code. All bi-temporal management processes are managed by code within the AVF; there is no bi-temporal management code for application developers to write.

We also note that temporal insert, update and delete transactions, by default and without any overrides to those defaults, insert, update and delete currently asserted data describing what the referenced object is currently like. This provides *temporal upward compatibility* for applications which manage conventional tables.

We conclude that Asserted Versioning *does* provide maintenance encapsulation for bi-temporal data, and also temporal upward compatibility for maintenance transactions to conventional data.

## Query Encapsulation

As we have already pointed out, production queries against Asserted Versioning databases do not have to check for TEI or TRI violations. The maintenance processes carried out by the AVF guarantee that asserted version tables will already conform to those semantic requirements. For example, when joining from a TRI child to a TRI parent, these queries do not have to check that the parent object is represented by an effective-time set of contiguous and non-overlapping rows whose end-to-end time period fully includes that of the child row. Asserted Versioning already guarantees that those parent version rows [meet] within an episode, and that they [fill$^{-1}$] the effective time period of the child row.

Ad hoc queries against Asserted Versioning databases can be written directly against asserted version tables. But as far as possible, they should be written against views in order to simplify the query-writing task of predominately non-technical query authors. So we recommend that a basic set of views be provided for each asserted version table. Additional subject-matter-specific views written against these basic views could also be created. Some basic views that we believe might prove useful for these query authors are:

(i) *The Conventional Data View*, consisting of all currently asserted current versions in the table. This is a one-row-per-object view.

(ii) *The Current Versions View*, consisting of all currently asserted versions in the table, past, present and future. This is a view that will satisfy all the requirements satisfied by any best practice versioning tables, as described in Chapter 4.

(iii) *The Episode View*, consisting of one current assertion for each episode. That is the current version for current episodes, the last version for past episodes, and the latest version for future episodes. This view is useful because it filters out the "blow-by-blow" history which version tables provide, and leaves only a "latest row" to represent each episode of an object of interest.

(iv) *The Semantic Logfile View*, consisting of all no longer asserted versions in the table. This view collects all asserted version data that we no longer claim is true, and should be of particular interest to auditors.

(v) *The Transaction File View*, consisting of all near future asserted versions. These are deferred assertions that will become currently asserted data soon enough that the business is willing to let them become current by means of the passage of time.

**(vi)** *The Staging Area View*, consisting of all far future asserted versions. These are deferred assertions that are still a work in progress. They might be incomplete data that the business fully intends to assert once they are completed. They might also be hypothetical data, created to try out various what-if scenarios.

We also note that existing queries against conventional tables will execute properly when their target tables are converted to asserted version tables. In the conversion, the tables are given new names. For example, we use the suffix "_AV" on asserted version tables and only on those tables. One of the views provided on each table, then, is one which selects exactly those columns that made up the original table, and all and only those rows that dynamically remain currently asserted and currently in effect. This dynamic view provides, as a queryable object, a set of data that is row for row and column for column identical to the original table. The view itself is given the name the original table had. Every column has the same name it originally had. This provides *temporal upward compatibility* for all queries, whether embedded in application code or free-standing.

We conclude that Asserted Versioning *does* provide query encapsulation for bi-temporal data, and also temporal upward compatibility for queries.

## The Internalization of Pipeline Datasets

Non-current data is often found in numerous nooks and crannies of conventional databases. Surrounding conventional tables whose rows have no time periods explicitly attached to them, and which represent our current beliefs about what their objects are currently like, there may be various history tables, transaction tables, staging area tables and developer-maintained logfile tables. In some cases, temporality has even infiltrated some of those tables themselves, transforming them into one or another of some variation on the four types of version tables which we described in Chapter 4.

When we began writing, we knew that deferred transactions and deferred assertions went beyond the standard bi-temporal semantics recognized in the computer science community. We knew that they corresponded to insert, update or delete transactions written but not yet submitted to the DBMS. The most familiar collections of transactions in this state, we recognized, are those called batch transaction datasets.

But as soon as we identified the nine logical categories of bi-temporal data, we realized that deferred transactions and deferred assertions dealt with only three of those nine categories—with *future* assertions about past, present or future versions. What, then, we wondered, did the three categories of *past* assertions correspond to?

The answer is that past assertions play the role of a DBMS *semantic logfile*, one specific to a particular production table. Of course, by now we understand that past assertions do not make it possible to fully recreate the physical state of a table as of any point in past time because of deferred assertions which are not, by definition, past assertions. Instead, they make it possible to recreate what we claimed, at some past point in time, was the truth about the past, present and future of the things we were interested in at the time. In this way, past assertions support a *semantic* logfile, and allow us to recreate what we once claimed was true, as of any point of time in the past. They provide the as-was semantics for bi-temporal data.

But Asserted Versioning also supports a table-specific *physical logfile*. It does so with the row create date. With this date, we can *almost* recreate everything that was physically in a table as of any past point in time, no matter where in assertion time or effective time any of those rows are located.[2]

This leaves us with only three of the nine categories—the current assertion of past, present and future versions of objects. The current assertions of current versions, of course, are the conventional data in an asserted version table. This leaves currently asserted past versions and currently asserted future versions. But these are nothing new to IT professionals. They are what IT best practice version tables have been trying to manage for several decades.

Now it all comes together. Instead of conventional physical logfiles, Asserted Versioning supports queries which make both semantic logfile data and physical logfile data available. Instead of batch transaction datasets, Asserted Versioning keeps track of what the database will look like when those transactions are applied—which, for asserted version tables, means when those future assertions pass into currency. Instead of variations on best practice version tables which support some part of the semantics of versioning, Asserted Versioning is an enterprise solution which implements versioning, in every case, with the same

---

[2]The exception is deferred assertions that have been moved backwards in assertion time. Currently, Asserted Versioning does not preserve information about the far future assertion time these assertions originally existed in.

schemas and with support for the full semantics of versioning, whether or not the specific business requirements, at the time, specify those full semantics.

With all these various physical datasets internalized within the production tables they are directed to or derived from, Asserted Versioning eliminates the cost of managing them as distinct physical data objects.

Asserted Versioning also eliminates the cost of coordinating maintenance to them. There is no latency as updates to production tables ripple out to downstream copies of that same data, such as separate history tables. On the inward-bound side, there is also no latency. As soon as a transaction is written, it becomes part of its target table. The semantics supported here is, for maintenance transactions, "submit it and forget it".

We conclude that Asserted Versioning *does* support the semantics of the internalization of pipeline datasets.

## Performance

We have provided techniques on how to index, partition, cluster and query an Asserted Versioning database. We've recommended key structures for primary keys, foreign keys and search keys, and recommended the placement of temporal columns in indexes for optimal performance. We have also shown how to improve performance with the use of currency flags. All these techniques help to provide query performance in Asserted Versioning databases which is nearly equivalent to the query performance in equivalent conventional databases.

We conclude that queries against even very large Asserted Versioning databases, especially those queries retrieving currently asserted current versions of persistent objects, will perform as well or nearly as well as the corresponding queries against a conventional database.

## Enterprise Contextualization

As temporal data has become increasingly important, much of it has migrated from being reconstructable temporal data to being queryable temporal data. But much of that queryable temporal data is still isolated in data warehouses or other historical databases, although some of it also exists in production databases as history tables, or as version tables. Often, this queryable temporal data fails to distinguish between data which reflects changes in the real world, and data which corrects mistakes in earlier data.

So business needs for a collection of temporal data against which queries can be written are often difficult to meet. Some of the needed data may be in a data warehouse; the rest of it may be contained in various history tables and version tables in the production database, and the odds of those history tables all using the same schemas and all being updated according to the same rules are not good. As for version tables, we have seen how many different kinds there are, and how difficult it can be to write queries that extract exactly the desired data from them.

We need an enterprise solution to the provision of queryable bi-temporal data. We need one consistent set of schemas, across all tables and all databases. We need one set of transactions that update bi-temporal data, and enforce the same temporal integrity constraints, across all tables and all databases. We need a standard way to ask for uni-temporal or bi-temporal data. And we need a way to remove all temporal logic from application programs, isolate it in a separate layer of code, and invoke it declaratively.

Asserted Versioning *is* that enterprise solution.

# Asserted Versioning as a Bridge and as a Destination

Asserted Versioning, either in the form of the AVF or of a home-grown implementation of its concepts, has value as both a bridge and as a destination. As a bridge to a standards-based, vendor-supported implementation of bi-temporal data management, Asserted Versioning is a way to begin migrating databases and applications right away, using the DBMSs available today and the SQL available today. As a destination, Asserted Versioning is an implementation of a more complete semantics for bi-temporality than has yet been defined in the academic literature.

## Asserted Versioning as a Bridge

Applications which manage temporal data intermingle code expressing subject-matter-specific business rules with code for managing these different forms in which temporal data is stored. Queries which access temporal data in these databases cannot be written correctly without a deep knowledge of the specific schemas used to store the data, and of both the scope and limits of the semantics of that data. Assembling data from two or more temporal tables, whether in the same or in different physical databases, is likely to require complicated logic to mediate the discrepancies between different implementations of the same semantics.

As a bridge to the new SQL standards and to DBMS support for them, Asserted Versioning standardizes temporal semantics by removing history tables, various forms of version tables, transaction datasets, staging areas and logfile data from databases. In their place, Asserted Versioning provides a standard canonical form for bi-temporal data, that form being the Asserted Versioning schema used by all asserted version tables.

By implementing Asserted Versioning, businesses can begin to remove temporal logic from their applications, and at each point where often complex temporal logic is hardcoded inside an application program, they can begin to replace that code with a simple temporal insert, update or delete statement.

Sometimes this will be difficult work. Some implementations of versioning, for example, are more convoluted than others. The code that supports those implementations will be correspondingly difficult to identify, isolate and replace. But if a business is going to avail itself of standards-based temporal SQL and commercial support for those temporal extensions—as it surely will, sooner or later—then this work will have to be done, sooner or later. With an Asserted Versioning Framework available to the business, that work can begin sooner rather than later. It can begin right now.

## Asserted Versioning as a Destination

Even if the primary motivation for using the AVF—ours or a home-grown version—is as a bridge to standards-based and vendor implemented bi-temporal functionality, that is certainly not its only value. For as soon as the AVF is installed, hundreds of person hours will typically be saved on every new project to introduce temporal data into a database. Based on our own consulting experience, which jointly spans about half a century and several dozen client engagements, we can confidently say, without exaggeration, that many large projects involving temporal data will save thousands of person hours.

Here's how. Temporal data modeling work that would otherwise have to be done, will be eliminated. Project-specific designs for history tables or version tables, likely differing in some way from the many other designs that already exist in the databases across the enterprise, will no longer proliferate. Separate code to maintain these idiosyncratically different structures will no longer have to be written. Temporal entity integrity rules and temporal referential integrity rules will no longer be overlooked, or only partially or incorrectly implemented.

Special instructions to those who will write the often complex sets of SQL transactions required to carry out what is a single insert, update or delete action from a business user perspective will no longer have to be provided and remembered each time a transaction is written. Special instructions to those who will write queries against these tables, possibly joining them with slightly different temporal tables designed and written by some other project team, will no longer have to be provided and remembered each time a query is written.

When the first set of tables is converted to asserted version tables, seamless real-time access to bi-temporal data will be immediately available for that data. This is declaratively specified access, with the procedural complexities encapsulated within the AVF. In addition, the benefits of the internalization of pipeline datasets will also be made immediately available, this being one of the principal areas in which Asserted Versioning extends bi-temporal semantics beyond the semantics of the standard model.

We conclude that Asserted Versioning has value both as a bridge and as a destination. It is a bridge to a standards-based SQL that includes support for PERIOD datatypes, Allen relationships and the declarative specification of bi-temporal semantics. It is a destination in the sense that it is a currently available solution which provides the benefits of declaratively specified, seamless real-time access to bi-temporal data, including the extended semantics of objects, episodes and internalized pipeline datasets.

# Ongoing Research and Development

Bi-temporal data is an ongoing research and development topic within the computer science and DBMS vendor communities. Most of that research will affect IT professionals only as products delivered to us, specifically in the form of enhancements to the SQL language and to relational DBMSs.

But bi-temporal data and its management by means of Asserted Versioning's conceptual and software frameworks is an ongoing research and development topic for us as well. Some of this ongoing work will appear as future releases of the Asserted Versioning AVF. Some of it will be published on our website, AssertedVersioning.com, and some of it will be made available as seminars. Following is a partial list of topics that we are working on as this book goes to press.

(i) *An Asserted Versioning Ontology.* A research topic. We have begun to formalize Asserted Versioning as an ontology by translating our Glossary into a FOPL axiomatic system. The undefined predicates of the system are being collected into a controlled vocabulary. Multiple taxonomies will be identified as KIND-OF threads running through the ontology. Theorems will be formally proved, demonstrating how automated inferencing can extract useful information from a collection of statements that are not organized as a database of tables, rows and columns.

(ii) *Asserted Versioning and the Relational Model.* A research topic. Bi-temporal extensions to the SQL language have been blocked for over 15 years, in large part because of objections that those extensions violate Codd's relational model and, in particular, his Information Principle. We will discuss those objections, especially as they apply to Asserted Versioning, and respond to them.

(iii) *Deferred Transaction Workflow Management and the AVF.* A development topic. When deferred assertion groups are moved backwards in assertion time, and when isolation cannot be maintained across the entire unit of work, violations of bi-temporal semantics may be exposed to the database user. We are developing a solution that identifies semantic components within and across deferred assertion groups, and moves those components backwards in a sequence that preserves temporal semantic integrity at each step of the process.

(iv) *Asserted Versioning and Real-Time Data Warehousing.* A methodology topic. Asserted Versioning supports bi-temporal tables in OLTP source system databases and/or Operational Data Stores. It is a better solution to the management of near-term historical data than is real-time data warehousing, for several reasons. First, much near-term historical data remains operationally relevant, and must be as accessible to OLTP systems as current data is. Thus, it must either be maintained in ad hoc structures within OLTP systems, or retrieved from the data warehouse with poorly-performing federated queries. Second, data warehouses, and indeed any collection of uni-temporal data, do not support the important as-was vs. as-is distinction. Third, real-time feeds to data warehouses change the warehousing paradigm. Data warehouses originally kept historical data about persistent objects as a time-series of periodic snapshots. Real-time updating of warehouses forces versioning into warehouses, and the mixture of snapshots and versions is conceptually confused and confusing. Asserted Versioning makes real-time data warehousing neither necessary nor desirable.

**(v)** *Temporalized Unique Indexes.* A development topic. Values which are unique to one row in a conventional table may appear on any number of rows when the table is converted to an asserted version table. So unique indexes on conventional tables are no longer unique after the conversion. To make those indexes unique, both an assertion and an effective time period must be added to them. This reflects the fact that although those values are no longer unique across all rows in the converted table, they remain unique across all rows in the table *at any one point in time*, specifically at any one combination of assertion and effective time clock ticks.

**(vi)** *Instead Of Triggers.* A development topic. Instead Of triggers function as updatable views. These updatable views make Asserted Versioning's temporal transactions look like conventional SQL. When invoked, the triggered code recognizes insert, update and delete statements as temporal transactions. As described in this book, it will translate them into multiple physical transactions, apply TEI and TRI checks, and manage the processing of those physical transactions as atomic and isolated units of work. The utilization of Instead Of triggers by the AVF is ongoing work, as we go to press.

**(vii)** *Java and Hibernate.* A research and development topic. Hibernate is an object/relational persistence and query service framework for Java. It hides the complexities of SQL, and functions as a data access layer supporting object-oriented semantics (not to be confused with the semantics of *objects*, as Asserted Versioning uses that term). Hibernate and other frameworks can be used to invoke the AVF logic to enforce TEI and TRI while maintaining an Asserted Versioning bi-temporal database.

**(viii)** *Archiving.* A methodology topic. An important archiving issue is how to archive integral semantic units, i.e. how to archive without leaving "dangling references" to archived data in the source database. Assertions, versions, episodes and objects define integral semantic units, and we are developing an archiving strategy, and AVF support for it, based on those Asserted Versioning concepts.

**(ix)** *Star Schema Temporal Data.* A methodology topic. Bi-temporal dimensions can make the "cube explosion problem" unmanageable, and bi-temporal semantics do not apply to fact tables the same way they apply to dimension tables. We are developing a methodology for supporting both versioning, and the as-was vs. as-is distinction, in both fact and dimension tables.

## Going Forward

We thank our readers who have stuck with us through an extended discussion of some very complex ideas. For those who would like to learn more about bi-temporal data, and about Asserted Versioning, we recommend that you visit our website, AssertedVersioning.com, and our webpage at Elsevier.com.

At our website, we have also created a small sample database of asserted version tables. Registered users can write both maintenance transactions and queries against that database. Because these tables contain data from all nine temporal categories, we recommend that interested readers first print out the contents of these tables before querying them. It is by comparing the full contents of those tables to query result sets that the work of each query can best be understood, and the semantic richness of the contents of Asserted Versioning databases best be appreciated.

## Glossary References

Glossary entries whose definitions form strong interdependencies are grouped together in the following list. The same glossary entries may be grouped together in different ways at the end of different chapters, each grouping reflecting the semantic perspective of each chapter. There will usually be several other, and often many other, glossary entries that are not included in the list, and we recommend that the Glossary be consulted whenever an unfamiliar term is encountered.

ad hoc query
production query

Allen relationships
time period

as-is query
as-was query

asserted version table
assertion
assertion time

Asserted Versioning
Asserted Versioning Framework (AVF)

history table

row create date

semantic logfile
transaction table

bi-temporal data
bi-temporal data management

business data

conventional data
conventional table
currently asserted current version
implicitly temporal data

deferred assertion
deferred transaction
far future assertion time
near future assertion time

design encapsulation
maintenance encapsulation
query encapsulation

effective time
version
version table
versioned data

enterprise contextualization

episode

non-current data
non-temporal data

Now()

PERIOD datatype
point in time

object

temporalized unique index

physical transaction
temporal transaction
temporal insert transaction
temporal update transaction
temporal delete transaction

pipeline dataset
internalization of pipeline datasets
production database
production table

queryable object
queryable temporal data
reconstructable temporal data
seamless access

temporal data
temporal dimension

temporal entity integrity (TEI)
temporal foreign key (TFK)
temporal referential integrity (TRI)

# APPENDIX: BIBLIOGRAPHICAL ESSAY

Except for the 1983 and 1988 articles, all the references listed here are readily accessible by IT professionals. Those two articles are listed because of their seminal importance in the field of temporal data management.

## 1983: The Allen Relationships

James F. Allen. "Maintaining Knowledge About Temporal Intervals." *Communications of the ACM* (November 1983), 26 (11), 832–843. This article defined a set of 13 positional relationships between two time periods along a common timeline. These relationships are a partitioning of all possible positional temporal relationships. They are mutually exclusive, and there are no others.

## 1988: Architecture for a Business and Information System

B. A. Devlin and P. T. Murphy. "An Architecture for a Business and Information System." *IBM Systems Journal* (1988), 27(1). To the best of our knowledge, this article is the origin of data warehousing in just as incontrovertible a sense as Dr. E. F. Codd's early articles were the origins of relational theory.

## 1996: Building the Data Warehouse

William Inmon. *Building the Data Warehouse*, 2nd ed. (John Wiley, 1996). (The first edition was apparently published in 1991, but we can find no reliable references to it.) With this book, Inmon began his work of introducing the concepts of data warehousing to the rest of the IT profession, in the process extending the concept into several iterations of his own data warehousing architecture.

## 1996: The Data Warehouse Toolkit

Ralph Kimball. *The Data Warehouse Toolkit: Practical Techniques for Building Dimensional Data Warehouses* (John Wiley, 1996). This book, and later "data warehouse toolkit" books, introduced and developed Kimball's event-centric approach to managing historical data. Concepts such as dimensional data marts, the fact vs. dimension distinction, and star schemas and snowflake schemas are all grounded in Kimball's work, as is the entire range of OLAP and business intelligence software.

## 2000: Developing Time-Oriented Database Applications in SQL

R. T. Snodgrass. *Developing Time-Oriented Database Applications in SQL* (Morgan-Kaufmann, 2000). Both this book and our own are concerned with explaining how to support bi-temporal data management using current DBMSs and current SQL.

This book is an invaluable source of SQL code fragments that illustrate the complexity of managing bi-temporal data and, in particular, that illustrate how to write temporal entity integrity and temporal referential integrity checks.

This book is available in PDF form, at no cost, at Dr. Snodgrass's website: http://www.cs.arizona.edu/people/rts/publications.html.

## 2000: Primary Key Reengineering Projects

Tom Johnston. "Primary Key Reengineering Projects: The Problem." *Information Management Magazine* (February 2000). http://www.information-management.com/issues/20000201/1866-1.html

Tom Johnston. "Primary Key Reengineering Projects: The Solution." *Information Management Magazine* (March 2000). http://www.information-management.com/issues/20000301/2004-1.html

These two articles, by one of the authors, explain why he believes that all relational tables should use surrogate keys rather than business keys. Additional material on this topic can be found at his website, MindfulData.com. For anyone contemplating the idea of an Asserted Versioning Framework of their own, in which they use business keys as primary keys instead of Asserted Versioning's object identifiers (*oids*), we recommend that you read these articles first.

# 2001: Unobvious Redundancies in Relational Data Models

Tom Johnston. "Unobvious Redundancies in Relational Data Models, Part 1." *InfoManagement Direct* (September 2001). http://www.information-management.com/infodirect/20010914/4007-1.html

Tom Johnston. "Unobvious Redundancies in Relational Data Models, Part 2." *InfoManagement Direct* (September 2001). http://www.information-management.com/infodirect/20010921/4017-1.html

Tom Johnston. "Unobvious Redundancies in Relational Data Models, Part 3." *InfoManagement Direct* (September 2001). http://www.information-management.com/infodirect/20010928/4037-1.html

Tom Johnston. "Unobvious Redundancies in Relational Data Models, Part 4." *InfoManagement Direct* (October 2001). http://www.information-management.com/infodirect/20011005/4103-1.html

Tom Johnston. "Unobvious Redundancies in Relational Data Models, Part 5." *InfoManagement Direct* (October 2001). http://www.information-management.com/infodirect/20011012/4132-1.html

These five articles, by one of the authors, show how fully normalized relational data models may still contain data redundancies. The issue of redundancies that do not violate normal forms was raised in Chapter 15, where we discussed our reasons for repeating the effective begin date of the initial version of every episode on all the non-initial versions of those same episodes.

# 2002: Temporal Data and The Relational Model

C. J. Date, Hugh Darwen, Nikos Lorentzos. *Temporal Data and the Relational Model* (Morgan-Kaufmann, 2002). While the main focus of our book and the book by Dr. Snodgrass is row-level bi-temporality, the main focus of Date, Darwen, and Lorentzos's book is column-level versioning. While the main focus of our book and Snodgrass's is on implementing temporal data management with today's DBMSs and today's SQL, the main focus of their book is on describing language extensions that contain new operators for manipulating versioned data.

## 2007: Time and Time Again

This series of some two dozen articles by the authors, succeeded by a bi-monthly column of the same name and about the same number of installments, began in the May 2007 issue of *DM Review* magazine, now *Information Management*. The entire set, amounting to some 50 articles and columns combined, ended in June of 2009. Although we had designed and built bi-temporal databases prior to writing these articles, our ideas evolved a great deal in the process of writing them. For example, although we emphasized the importance of maintenance encapsulation in the first article, we did not distinguish between temporal and physical transactions. All in all, we do not believe that these articles can usefully be consulted to gain additional insight into the topics discussed in this book. Although we intended them as instructions to other modelers and developers on how to implement bi-temporal data in today's DBMSs, we now look back on them as an on-line diary of our evolving ideas on the subject.

## 2009: Oracle 11g Workspace Manager

Oracle Database 11g Workspace Manager Overview. An Oracle White Paper (September 2009). http://www.oracle.com/technology/products/database/workspace_manager/pdf/twp_AppDev_Workspace_Manager_11g.pdf

A discussion of the Oracle 11g Workspace Manager, and in particular its key role in implementing Oracle's support for bi-temporal data management. On our website, we compare and contrast this implementation of a framework for bi-temporal data management with Asserted Versioning.

## Philosophical Concepts

The best Internet source for an introduction to philosophical concepts, including those used in this book, is the Stanford Encyclopedia of Philosophy, at http://plato.stanford.edu/. Unfortunately, while each entry is individually excellent, the choice of which concepts to include seems somewhat idiosyncratic. For example, there is no general entry for ontology. Nonetheless, we recommend the following entries there, as relevant to the concepts used in this book: assertion, change, epistemology, facts, Arthur Prior, propositional attitude reports, speech acts, temporal logic, temporal parts.

There are, of course, numerous other excellent introductions to philosophical concepts available on the Web. The problem is that there are also numerous other very poor ones, too! Philosophy is a topic that seems to lend itself to this kind of variety. We would recommend to those interested, that as a general rule, sources at dot-edu domains can be presumed reliable, while sources at other domains should be treated with caution.

## The Computer Science Literature

In this bibliography, we include no direct references to the computer science literature on temporal data management because most of that literature will not be available to many of our readers. For those who wish to access this material, we recommend getting a membership in the ACM and subscribing to the ACM Digital Library. Downloadable PDF copies of hundreds and probably thousands of articles on the management of temporal data are available from that source.

Another invaluable—and free!—source of information on temporal databases, with many links to other resources, can be found on Dr. Snodgrass's website, specifically at http://www.cs. arizona.edu/people/rts/publications.html.

# THE ASSERTED VERSIONING GLOSSARY

This Glossary contains approximately 300 definitions, nearly all of which are specific to Asserted Versioning. Most expressions have both a *Mechanics* entry and a *Semantics* entry. A Mechanics entry describes how the defined concept is implemented in the "machinery" of Asserted Versioning. A Semantics entry describes what that concept means. We can also think of a Mechanics entry as telling us what a component of Asserted Versioning is or what it does, and a Semantics entry as telling us why it is important.

In linguistics, the usual contrast to semantics is syntax. But syntax is only the bill of materials of Asserted Versioning. The Asserted Versioning Framework, or any other implementation of Asserted Versioning, has an intricately interconnected set of parts, which correspond to the syntax of a language. But when it is turned on, it is a software engine which translates metadata and data models into the database schemas it uses to do its work, transforms the data instances it manages from one state to another state, augments or diminishes the totality of the representation of the objects its data corresponds to, and facilitates the ultimate purpose of this wealth of activity, which is to provide meaningful information about the time-varying state of the world an enterprise is a part of and needs to remain cognizant of.

## Grammar

Grammatical variations of the same glossary term will not usually be distinguished. Thus both "version" and "versions" are in this book, but only the former is a Glossary entry. "Currently asserted" is listed as a component of one or more definitions, but the corresponding Glossary entry is "current assertion".

## Dates and Times

All references to points in time in this Glossary, unless otherwise noted, refer to them using the word "date". This is done for the same reason that all examples of points in time in the text, unless otherwise noted, are dates. This reason is simply convenience. Periods of time in either of the two bi-temporal dimensions are delimited by their starting point in time and ending point in time. These points in time may be timestamps, dates, or any other point in time recognizable by the DBMS. As defined in this Glossary, they are clock ticks.

## Components

Components of a definition are other Glossary entries used in the definition. Listing the components of every definition separately makes it easier to pick them out and follow cross-reference trails.

The Components sections of these definitions are also working notes towards a formal ontology of temporal data. If we assume first-order predicate logic as an initial formalization, we can think of the components of a Glossary definition, together with a set of primitive (formally undefined) terms, as the predicates with which the Mechanics and Semantics sections of those definitions can be expressed as statements in predicate logic.

Thus formalized, automated inferencing and theorem proving mechanisms can then be used to discover new theorems. And the point of that activity, of course, is that it can make us aware of the deductive implications of things we already know, of statements we already recognize as true statements. These deductive implications are other true statements. But until we are aware of them, they are not part of our knowledge about the world. These mechanisms can also be used to prove or disprove conjectures about temporal data, thus adding some of them to the totality of that knowledge, and adding, for the rest of them, the knowledge that they are wrong.

Of particular note are those few Glossary entries whose list of components is empty (indicated by "N/A"). In an ontology, the collection of undefined terms is called a controlled vocabulary, and these Glossary entries with empty component lists are part of the controlled vocabulary for a formal ontology of Asserted Versioning.

## Non-Standard Glossary Definitions

Broadly speaking, the semantics entry of a Glossary definition describes a concept, while the Mechanics entry describes its implementation. However, in some cases, there doesn't seem to be a need for both kinds of entry, and so those definitions will have just a Mechanics section, or just a Semantics section. And in other cases, it seems more appropriate to provide a general description rather than to attempt a precise definition.

But the heart of this Glossary are the definitions which have both a Semantics and a Mechanics section. Together, the collection of their semantics entries is a summary statement of Asserted Versioning as a theory of bi-temporal data management, while the collection of their mechanics entries is a summary statement of the implementation of the theory in the Asserted Versioning Framework.

# Allen Relationships

The original Allen relationships are leaf nodes in our Allen relationship taxonomy. Most of the Allen relationships, as well as our taxonomic groupings which are OR'd collections of those relationships, have an inverse. The inverse of an Allen relationship or relationship group, between two time periods which do not both begin and end on the same clock tick, is the relationship in which the two time periods are reversed. Following Allen's original notation, we use a superscript suffix $(x^{-1})$ to denote the inverse relationship. Inverse relationships exist in all cases where one of the two time periods is shorter than the other and/or begins on an earlier clock tick than the other. Consequently, all the Allen relationships except [*equals*], have an inverse.

# "Trivial" Definitions

Some Glossary definitions may appear to be "trivial", in the sense that we can reliably infer what those expressions mean from the expressions themselves. For example, "end date" is defined as "an assertion end date or an effective end date".

Definitions like these exist because the expressions they define are used in the definitions of other expressions. So they are a kind of shorthand. But in addition, our ultimate objective, with this Glossary, is to formalize it as an ontology expressed in predicate logic. For that purpose, apparently trivial entries such as "end date" are needed as predicates in the formal definitions of, for example, expressions like "assertion end date".

# Glossary Entries

**include**
See also: *Allen relationship* [<u>fills</u><sup>-1</sup>].

**"assert" cognates**
*Mechanics:* the cognate terms "accept", "agree", "assent", "believe", "claim", "know", "say" and "think".
*Semantics:* terms which, for purposes of the discussions in this book, may be taken as synonymous with "assert" as that word is defined in this book.
*Comments:*
- There are important differences among these terms, in the fields of epistemology and semantics. For example, some terms designate what philosophers call "speech acts", while others designate what philosophers call "propositional attitudes".

**12/31/9999**
*Mechanics:* the latest date which can be represented by the SQL Server DBMS.
*Semantics:* a value for an end date which means that the end of the time period it delimits is unknown but assumed to be later than Now().
*Comments:*
- For other DBMSs, the value used should similarly be the latest date which can be represented by that DBMS.
*Components:* end date, Now(), time period.

**9999**
*Mechanics:* a DBMS-agnostic representation of the latest date which can be represented by a specific DBMS.
*Semantics:* a DBMS-agnostic representation of a value for an end date which means that the end of the time period it delimits is unknown but assumed to be later than Now().
*Components:* end date, Now(), time period.

**actionable**
*Description:* data which is good enough for its intended purposes.
*Comments:*
- As a kind of shorthand, we say that the assertion time period of a row is the period of time during which we assert that it is true. And if we discover that a row is incorrect, and does not make a true statement, we do end its assertion time period.
- But some true statements are not actionable. For example, a currently effective row in a 100-column table may have 10 of its columns filled with accurate data, and the other 90 columns empty. So that row makes a true statement "as far as it goes", but because it is so incomplete, it is probably not a statement that provides enough information to act on.
- And some actionable statements are not even true. Financial forecasts, for example, may be actionable. But because they are about the future, what they describe hasn't happened yet, and so they are statements which are neither true nor false.[1]
*Components:* currently asserted.

---

[1]This, at least, is the standard interpretation of Aristotle's position on what are called "future contingents", as expressed in his work *De Interpretatione*.

**ad hoc query**
*Description:* a query which is not embedded in an application program, and which is not run as part of the IT production schedule.
*Comments:*
- These queries are usually written by business researchers and analysts, and are often run only a few times before they are discarded. Thus the cost of writing them is amortized over only a few occasions on which they are used, and so it is important to keep the query-writing costs as low as possible. This is why we recommend that, as far as possible, ad hoc queries should be written against views.

See also: *production query.*

**Allen relationship taxonomy**
*Description:* a taxonomy of Allen relationships, developed by the authors and presented in Chapter 3.
*Comments:*
- Our *Mechanics* definitions of the Allen relationships will express time periods as date pairs, using the closed-open convention. The two time periods will be designated $P_1$ and $P_2$, and the begin and end dates, respectively, eff_beg_dt$_1$ and eff_end_dt$_1$, and eff_beg_dt$_2$ and eff_end_dt$_2$. By convention, $P_1$ is the earlier of the two time periods when one is earlier than the other, and is the shorter of the two time periods otherwise.
- These definitions assume that the begin date value for a time period is less than the end date value for that time period. This assumption excludes non-sensical time periods that end before they begin. It also excludes *empty time periods.*
- Our *Semantics* definitions of the Allen relationships will be stated in terms of clock ticks contained or not contained in time periods, and so these definitions are independent of the convention chosen for using pairs of dates to delimit time periods. In particular, "begin", "end", "earlier", "later" and other terms refer to relationships in time, not to comparisons of begin and/or end dates to other begin and/or end dates.
- Boolean operators (AND, OR, NOT) are capitalized.

**Allen relationship, [aligns]**
*Mechanics:* $P_1$ and $P_2$ [align] if and only if
$((\text{eff\_beg\_dt}_1 = \text{eff\_beg\_dt}_2) \text{ AND } (\text{eff\_end\_dt}_1 < \text{eff\_end\_dt}_2))$
OR $((\text{eff\_beg\_dt}_1 > \text{eff\_beg\_dt}_2) \text{ AND } (\text{eff\_end\_dt}_1 = \text{eff\_end\_dt}_2))$
AND NOT$((\text{eff\_beg\_dt}_1 = \text{eff\_beg\_dt}_2) \text{ AND } (\text{eff\_end\_dt}_1 = \text{eff\_end\_dt}_2))$.
*Semantics:* $P_1$ and $P_2$ [align] if and only if they either start or end on the same clock tick, but not both.

**Allen relationship, [before]**
*Mechanics:* $P_1$ is [before] $P_2$ if and only if $(\text{eff\_end\_dt}_1 < \text{eff\_beg\_dt}_2)$.
*Semantics:* $P_1$ is [before] $P_2$ if and only if the next clock tick after $P_1$ is earlier than the first clock tick in $P_2$.

**Allen relationship, [before$^{-1}$]**
*Mechanics:* $P_1$ is [before$^{-1}$] $P_2$ if and only if $(\text{eff\_beg\_dt}_1 > \text{eff\_end\_dt}_2)$.
*Semantics:* $P_1$ is [before$^{-1}$] $P_2$ if and only if the first clock tick in $P_1$ is later than the next clock tick after $P_2$.

**Allen relationship, [during]**
*Mechanics:* $P_1$ is [during] $P_2$ if and only if $(\text{eff\_beg\_dt}_1 > \text{eff\_beg\_dt}_2)$ AND $(\text{eff\_end\_dt}_1 < \text{eff\_end\_dt}_2)$.

*Semantics:* $P_1$ is [during] $P_2$ if and only if the first clock tick in $P_1$ is later than the first clock tick $P_2$, and the last clock tick in $P_1$ is earlier than the last clock tick in $P_2$.

**Allen relationship, [during$^{-1}$]**

*Mechanics:* $P_1$ is [during$^{-1}$] $P_2$ if and only if (eff_beg_dt$_1$ < eff_beg_dt$_2$) AND (eff_end_dt$_1$ > eff_end_dt$_2$).

*Semantics:* $P_1$ is [during$^{-1}$] $P_2$ if and only if the first clock tick in $P_1$ is earlier than the first clock tick in $P_2$, and the last clock tick in $P_1$ is later than the last clock tick in $P_2$.

**Allen relationship, [*equals*]**

*Mechanics:* $P_1$ [*equals*] $P_2$ if and only if (eff_beg_dt$_1$ = eff_beg_dt$_2$) AND (eff_end_dt$_1$ = eff_end_dt$_2$).

*Semantics:* $P_1$ [*equals*] $P_2$ if and only if they both start and end on the same clock tick.

**Allen relationship, [excludes]**

*Mechanics:* $P_1$ [excludes] $P_2$ if and only if (eff_end_dt$_1$ <= eff_beg_dt$_2$).

*Semantics:* $P_1$ [excludes] $P_2$ if and only if the next clock tick after $P_1$ is no later than the first clock tick in $P_2$.

**Allen relationship, [excludes$^{-1}$]**

*Mechanics:* $P_1$ [excludes$^{-1}$] $P_2$ if and only if (eff_beg_dt$_1$ >= eff_end_dt$_2$).

*Semantics:* $P_1$ [excludes$^{-1}$] $P_2$ if and only if the first clock tick in $P_1$ is no earlier than the next clock tick after $P_2$.

**Allen relationship, [fills]**

*Mechanics:* $P_1$ [fills] $P_2$ if and only if (eff_beg_dt$_1$ >= eff_beg_dt$_2$) AND (eff_end_dt$_1$ <= eff_end_dt$_2$).

*Semantics:* $P_1$ [fills] $P_2$ if and only if the first clock tick in $P_1$ is no earlier than the first clock tick in $P_2$, and the last clock tick in $P_1$ is no later than the last clock tick in $P_2$.

**Allen relationship, [fills$^{-1}$]**

*Mechanics:* $P_1$ [fills$^{-1}$] $P_2$ if and only if (eff_beg_dt$_1$ <= eff_beg_dt$_2$) AND (eff_end_dt$_1$ >= eff_end_dt$_2$).

*Semantics:* $P_1$ [fills$^{-1}$] $P_2$ if and only if the first clock tick in $P_1$ is no later than the first clock tick in $P_2$, and the last clock tick in $P_1$ is no earlier than the last clock tick in $P_2$.

**Allen relationship, [finishes]**

*Mechanics:* $P_1$ [finishes] $P_2$ if and only if (eff_beg_dt$_1$ > eff_beg_dt$_2$) AND (eff_end_dt$_1$ = eff_end_dt$_2$).

*Semantics:* $P_1$ [finishes] $P_2$ if and only if the first clock tick in $P_1$ is later than the first clock tick in $P_2$, and the two time periods end on the same clock tick.

**Allen relationship, [finishes$^{-1}$]**

*Mechanics:* $P_1$ [finishes$^{-1}$] $P_2$ if and only if (eff_beg_dt$_1$ < eff_beg_dt$_2$) AND (eff_end_dt$_1$ = eff_end_dt$_2$).

*Semantics:* $P_1$ [finishes$^{-1}$] $P_2$ if and only if the first clock tick in $P_1$ is earlier than the first clock tick in $P_2$, and the two time periods end on the same clock tick.

**Allen relationship, [intersects]**

*Mechanics:* $P_1$ [intersects] $P_2$ if and only if (eff_beg_dt$_1$ <= eff_beg_dt$_2$) AND (eff_end_dt$_1$ > eff_beg_dt$_2$).

*Semantics:* $P_1$ [intersects] $P_2$ if and only if the first clock tick in $P_1$ is no later than the first clock tick in $P_2$, and the next clock tick after $P_1$ is later than the first clock tick in $P_2$.

**Allen relationship, [intersects$^{-1}$]**

*Mechanics:* $P_1$ [intersects$^{-1}$] $P_2$ if and only if (eff_beg_dt$_1$ >= eff_beg_dt$_2$) AND (eff_beg_dt$_1$ < eff_end_dt$_2$).

*Semantics:* $P_1$ [intersects$^{-1}$] $P_2$ if and only if the first clock tick in $P_1$ is no earlier than the first clock tick in $P_2$, and the first clock tick in $P_1$ is earlier than the next clock tick after $P_2$.

**Allen relationship, [meets]**

*Mechanics:* $P_1$ [meets] $P_2$ if and only if (eff_end_dt$_1$ = eff_beg_dt$_2$).

*Semantics:* $P_1$ [meets] $P_2$ if and only if the next clock tick after $P_1$ is the same as the first clock tick in $P_2$.

**Allen relationship, [meets$^{-1}$]**

*Mechanics:* $P_1$ [meets$^{-1}$] $P_2$ if and only if (eff_beg_dt$_1$ = eff_end_dt$_2$).

*Semantics:* $P_1$ [meets$^{-1}$] $P_2$ if and only if the first clock tick in $P_1$ is the same as the next clock tick after $P_2$.

**Allen relationship, [occupies]**

*Mechanics:* $P_1$ [occupies] $P_2$ if and only if
((eff_beg_dt$_1$ >= eff_beg_dt$_2$) AND (eff_end_dt$_1$ <= eff_end_dt$_2$)) AND
NOT((eff_beg_dt$_1$ = eff_beg_dt$_2$) AND (eff_end_dt$_1$ = eff_end_dt$_2$)).

*Semantics:* $P_1$ [occupies] $P_2$ if and only if the first clock tick in $P_1$ is no earlier than the first clock tick in $P_2$, and the last clock tick in $P_1$ is no later than the last clock tick in $P_2$, and $P_1$ and $P_2$ do not both begin and end on the same clock tick.

**Allen relationship, [occupies$^{-1}$]**

*Mechanics:* $P_1$ [occupies$^{-1}$] $P_2$ if and only if
((eff_beg_dt$_1$ <= eff_beg_dt$_2$) AND (eff_end_dt$_1$ >= eff_end_dt$_2$)) AND
NOT((eff_beg_dt$_1$ = eff_beg_dt$_2$) AND (eff_end_dt$_1$ = eff_end_dt$_2$)).

*Semantics:* $P_1$ [occupies$^{-1}$] $P_2$ if and only if the first clock tick in $P_1$ is no later than the first clock tick in $P_2$, and the last clock tick in $P_1$ is no earlier than the last clock tick in $P_2$, and $P_1$ and $P_2$ do not both begin and end on the same clock tick.

**Allen relationship, [overlaps]**

*Mechanics:* $P_1$ [overlaps] $P_2$ if and only if
(eff_beg_dt$_1$ < eff_beg_dt$_2$) AND
(eff_end_dt$_1$ > eff_beg_dt$_2$) AND
(eff_end_dt$_1$ < eff_end_dt$_2$).

*Semantics:* $P_1$ [overlaps] $P_2$ if and only if the first clock tick in $P_1$ is earlier than the first clock tick in $P_2$, and the next clock tick after $P_1$ is later than the first clock tick in $P_2$, and the last clock tick in $P_1$ is earlier than the last clock tick in $P_2$.

**Allen relationship, [overlaps$^{-1}$]**

*Mechanics:* $P_1$ [overlaps] $P_2$ if and only if
(eff_beg_dt$_1$ > eff_beg_dt$_2$) AND
(eff_beg_dt1 < eff_end_dt$_2$) AND

$(\text{eff\_end\_dt}_1 > \text{eff\_end\_dt}_2)$.

*Semantics:* $P_1$ [overlaps$^{-1}$] $P_2$ if and only if the first clock tick in $P_1$ is later than the first clock tick in $P_2$, and the first clock tick in $P_1$ is earlier than the next clock tick after the end of $P_2$, and the last clock tick in $P_1$ is later than the last clock tick in $P_2$.

### Allen relationship, [starts]

*Mechanics:* $P_1$ [starts] $P_2$ if and only if $(\text{eff\_beg\_dt}_1 = \text{eff\_beg\_dt}_2)$ AND $(\text{eff\_end\_dt}_1 < \text{eff\_end\_dt}_2)$.

*Semantics:* $P_1$ [starts] $P_2$ if and only if the two time periods start on the same clock tick, and the last clock tick in $P_1$ is earlier than the last clock tick in $P_2$.

### Allen relationship, [starts$^{-1}$]

*Mechanics:* $P_1$ [starts$^{-1}$] $P_2$ if and only if $(\text{eff\_beg\_dt}_1 = \text{eff\_beg\_dt}_2)$ AND $(\text{eff\_end\_dt}_1 > \text{eff\_end\_dt}_2)$.

*Semantics:* $P_1$ [starts$^{-1}$] $P_2$ if and only if the two time periods start on the same clock tick, and the last clock tick in $P_1$ is later than the last clock tick in $P_2$.

### Allen relationships

*Mechanics:* the set of 13 positional relationships between two time periods, a time period and a point in time, or two points in time, as first defined in James F. Allen's 1983 article *Maintaining Knowledge about Temporal Intervals*.

*Semantics:* the set of all possible positional relationships between two time periods, a time period and a point in time, or two points in time, defined along a common timeline.

*Comments:*
- The Allen relationships are mutually exclusive and jointly exhaustive.
- Good discussions of the Allen relationships can also be found in (Snodgrass, 2000), from Chapter 4, and (Date, Darwen and Lorentzos, 2002), from Chapter 6.

*Components:* time period, point in time.

### approval transaction

*Mechanics:* a transaction that changes the assertion begin date on the assertions in a deferred assertion group to an earlier date.

*Semantics:* a transaction that moves assertions in an deferred assertion group from far future assertion time to near future assertion time.

*Comments:*
- The transaction by which deferred assertions are moved close enough to Now() that the business is willing to let them become current by means of the passage of time. See also: *fall into currency*.

*Components:* assertion, assertion begin date, deferred assertion group, far future assertion time, near future assertion time.

### as-is

*Mechanics:* data whose assertion begin date is earlier than Now() and whose assertion end date is later than Now().

*Semantics:* data whose assertion time period is current.

*Comments:*
- See also: *as-was*. The as-is vs. as-was distinction is often confused with the distinction between current and past versions. Many best practices implementations of versioning do not distinguish between the two, and therefore introduce ambiguities into their temporal semantics.

*Components:* assertion begin date, assertion end date, assertion time period, Now().

**assert**

*Mechanics:* to place a row in an asserted version table in current assertion time.

*Semantics:* to claim that a row in an asserted version table makes a true and/or actionable statement.

*Components:* actionable, asserted version table, current assertion, statement.

**asserted version table**

*Mechanics:* a bi-temporal table in which each row can exist in past, present or future assertion time, and also in past, present or future effective time.

*Semantics:* a table each of whose rows indicates when the object it represents is as its business data describes it, and when that row is claimed to make a true and/or actionable statement about that object.

*Comments:*
- In contrast, rows in bi-temporal tables of the standard temporal model cannot exist in future assertion time.
- Also, a table whose structure conforms to the schema presented in Chapter 6. See also: *bi-temporal data canonical form.*

*Components:* actionable, assertion time, bi-temporal table, business data, effective time, object, statement, the standard temporal model.

**Asserted Versioning database**

*Mechanics:* a database that contains at least one asserted version table.

*Components:* asserted version table.

**Asserted Versioning Framework**

*Mechanics:* software which (i) generates asserted version tables from logical data models and associated metadata; (ii) enforces temporal entity integrity and temporal referential integrity constraints as asserted version tables are maintained; (iii) translates temporal insert, update and delete transactions into the physical transactions which maintain an asserted version table; and (iv) internalizes pipeline datasets.

*Comments:*
- The Asserted Versioning Framework is software developed by the authors which implements Asserted Versioning.

*Components:* asserted version table, internalization of pipeline datasets, physical transaction, temporal data management, temporal entity integrity, temporal referential integrity, temporal transaction.

**assertion**

*Mechanics:* the temporally delimited claim that a row in an asserted version table makes a true and/or actionable statement about what the object it represents is like during the time period designated by that version of that object.

*Semantics:* the claim that a statement is true and/or actionable.

*Components:* actionable, asserted version table, object, represent, statement, time period, version.

**assertion approval date**

*Mechanics:* the new assertion begin date which an approval transaction specifies for the assertions in a deferred assertion group.

*Semantics:* the near future assertion time date to which all assertions in a deferred assertion group are to be retrograde moved.

*Components:* approval transaction, assertion, assertion begin date, deferred assertion group, near future assertion time, retrograde movement.

**assertion begin date**

*Mechanics:* the begin date of the assertion time period of a row in an asserted version table.

*Semantics:* the date indicating when a version begins to be asserted as a true and/or actionable statement of what its object is like during its indicated period of effective time.

*Comments:*
- A row can never be inserted with an assertion begin date in the past, because an assertion cannot exist prior to the row whose truth it asserts. See also: *temporalized extension of the Closed World Assumption.*
- But a row can be inserted with an assertion begin date in the future because when that future date comes to pass, the row will already exist. See also: *deferred assertion.*

*Components:* actionable, assert, assertion time period, asserted version table, begin date, effective time period, object, version.

**assertion end date**

*Mechanics:* the date on which the assertion time period of a row in an asserted version table ends, or a date indicating that the end of the assertion time period is unknown but presumed to be later than Now().

*Semantics:* the date indicating when a version stops being asserted as a true and/or actionable statement of what its object is like during its indicated period of effective time, or indicating that the end of the assertion time period is unknown but presumed to be later than Now().

*Comments:*
- An assertion end date is always set to 9999 when its row is inserted. It retains that value unless and until that assertion is withdrawn.

*Components:* actionable, assertion time period, asserted version table, effective time period, end date, Now(), object, statement, version.

**assertion group**

*Mechanics:* a group of one or more deferred assertions, sharing the same assertion begin date.

*Semantics:* a group of one or more assertions sharing the same future assertion time period.

*Components:* assertion, assertion begin date, deferred assertion, future assertion time period.

**assertion group date**

*Mechanics:* the assertion begin date on a group of one or more deferred assertions.

*Semantics:* the date which indicates when a group of deferred assertions will become currently asserted.

*Comments:*
- This date is also the unique identifier of an assertion group.

*Components:* assertion begin date, currently asserted, deferred assertion.

**assertion table**

*Mechanics:* a uni-temporal table whose explicitly represented time is assertion time.

*Semantics:* a uni-temporal table each of whose rows is a temporally delimited assertion about what its object is like Now().

*Components:* uni-temporal, assertion, assertion time, Now(), object.

**assertion time**

*Mechanics:* a series of clock ticks, extending from the earliest to the latest clock ticks which the DBMS can recognize, within which assertion begin and end dates are located.

*Semantics:* the temporal dimension which interprets a time period associated with a row as indicating when that row is asserted to be true.

*Components:* assertion begin date, assertion end date, clock tick, temporal dimension, time period.

**assertion time period**

*Mechanics:* a time period in assertion time associated with a specific row in an asserted version table.

*Semantics:* the period of time during which a row in an asserted version table is claimed to make a true and/or actionable statement.

*Components:* actionable, asserted version table, assertion time, statement, time period.

**as-was**

*Mechanics:* data whose assertion end date is earlier than Now().

*Semantics:* data whose assertion time period is past.

*Comments:*
- See also: *as-is*. The as-was vs. as-is distinction is an assertion time distinction, but in supporting temporal data management in their databases, IT professionals often confuse this distinction with the effective time distinction between past and current versions.

*Components:* assertion end date, assertion time period, Now().

**atomic clock tick**

*Mechanics:* the smallest unit of time kept by a computer's clock that can be recognized by a specific DBMS.

*Semantics:* a unit of time that is indivisible for purposes of temporal data management.

*Comments:*
- See also: *clock tick*.

*Components:* N/A.

**AVF**

See *Asserted Versioning Framework*.

**basic temporal transaction**

*Mechanics:* a temporal transaction which does not specify any temporal parameters.

*Semantics:* a temporal transaction which accepts the default values for its temporal parameters, those being an effective begin date of Now(), an effective end date of 9999, an assertion begin date of Now() and an assertion end date of 9999.

*Comments:*
- Assertion end dates are the one temporal parameter that cannot be specified on temporal transactions. All temporal transactions, including basic ones, create asserted version rows with an assertion end date of 9999.

*Components:* assertion begin date, assertion end date, effective begin date, effective end date, Now(), temporal parameter, temporal transaction.

**basic versioning**

*Mechanics:* a form of versioning in which a version date is added to the primary key of an otherwise non-temporal table.

*Semantics:* a form of versioning in which all versions of the same object are contiguous.

*Comments:*
- Basic versioning is not part of Asserted Versioning. It is a form of best practices versioning. See Chapter 4.
- See also: *logical delete versioning, temporal gap versioning, effective time versioning.*

*Components:* contiguous, object, non-temporal table, version.

**begin date**

*Mechanics:* an assertion begin date or an effective begin date.

*Semantics:* a date which marks the start of an assertion or an effective time period.

*Components:* assertion begin date, assertion time period, effective begin date, effective time period.

**bi-temporal data canonical form**

*Mechanics:* the schema common to all asserted version tables.

*Semantics:* a single schema which can express the full range of bi-temporal semantics.

*Comments:*
- Any history table, logfile, or version table can be transformed into an asserted version table without loss of content.

*Components:* asserted version table, bi-temporal.

**bi-temporal database**

*Mechanics:* a database containing at least one bi-temporal table.

*Components:* bi-temporal table.

**bi-temporal envelope**

*Semantics:* a specified effective time period, included within a specified assertion time period.

*Comments:*
- The temporal scope of every temporal transaction is delimited by the bi-temporal envelope specified on the transaction.
- Every row in an asserted version table exists in a bi-temporal envelope.

*Components:* assertion time period, effective time period, include.

**bi-temporal table**

*Mechanics:* a table whose rows contain one pair of dates which define an epistemological time period, and a second pair of dates which define an ontological time period.

*Semantics:* a table whose rows contain data about both the past, the present and the future of things, and also about the past and the present of our beliefs about those things.

*Comments.*
- See also: *epistemological time, ontological time.*

*Components:* "assert" cognate (belief), epistemological time, ontological time, thing, time period.

**business data**

*Mechanics:* all columns of an asserted version table other than those columns which implement Asserted Versioning.

*Semantics:* the columns of data which record the properties or relationships of objects during one or more periods of effective time.

*Components:* asserted version table, effective time, object.

**business key**

*Mechanics:* the primary key of the entity in the logical data model from which an asserted version table is generated.

*Semantics:* the unique identifier for an object as represented in a non-temporal table.

*Comments:*
- If a surrogate key is used in the logical data model, this surrogate key is used as the business key in an asserted version table.

*Components:* asserted version table, non-temporal table, object.

**child managed object**

*Mechanics:* a version in a TRI relationship.

*Semantics:* a managed object which represents a child object in a TRI relationship.

*Components:* child object, TRI, version.

**child object**

*Semantics:* an object, represented by a managed object, which is existence-dependent on another object, also represented by a managed object.

*Components:* existence dependency, managed object, object, represent.

**child row**

*Mechanics:* a row in an asserted version table which contains a non-null temporal foreign key.

*Semantics:* a version which represents an object which is existence-dependent on some other object.

*Comments:*
- The various "parent" and "child" expressions also apply to conventional tables, of course, in which case the relationship involved is referential integrity, not temporal referential integrity. But in this Glossary, we are explicitly defining these expressions as they apply to asserted version tables.

*Components:* asserted version table, existence dependency, object, temporal foreign key.

**child table**

*Mechanics:* a table which contains at least one temporal foreign key.

*Semantics:* a table whose rows represent child objects.

*Components:* child object, temporal foreign key.

**child version**

*Mechanics:* a version in an asserted version table X is a child to an episode in asserted version table Y if and only if the version in X has a temporal foreign key whose value is identical to the value of the object identifier of that episode in Y, and the effective time period of that episode in Y [fills$^{-1}$] the effective time period of that version in X.

*Semantics:* a version in an asserted version table X is a child to an episode in asserted version table Y if and only if the object for that version in X is existence dependent on the object for that episode in Y, and the effective time period of that episode in Y [fills$^{-1}$]the effective time period of that version in X.

*Components:* Allen relationship [fills$^{-1}$], asserted version table, effective time period, episode, existence dependency, object, object identifier, temporal foreign key, version.

### chronon

*Semantics:* the term used in the computer science community for what Asserted Versioning calls an atomic clock tick.

*Comments:*
- See the 1992 entry in the bibliography for the standard computer science glossary of bi-temporal concepts.

*Components:* atomic clock tick.

### circa flag

*Mechanics:* a flag used by the Asserted Versioning Framework as a component of one or more indexes on asserted version tables, in order to improve the performance of queries which reference asserted version tables, and also of updates to those tables.

*Semantics:* a flag which distinguishes between rows which are definitely known to be in the assertion time past from all other rows. (See Chapter 15).

*Components:* Asserted Versioning Framework, asserted version table, assertion time.

### clock tick

*Mechanics:* the unit of time used for effective begin and end dates, assertion begin and end dates, episode begin dates and row create dates, in an asserted version table.

*Semantics:* the transition from one point in effective time or assertion time to the next point in effective time or assertion time, according to the chosen granularity which defines those two points in time as contiguous.

*Comments:*
- Note that chronons are atomic clock ticks, not clock ticks.
- A 1-month-per-tick clock represents a situation in which a database is updated at most once a month. By the same token, a 1-week or 1-day clock would record updates that take place at most once a week or once daily, respectively.

*Components:* asserted version table, assertion begin date, assertion end date, contiguous, effective begin date, effective end date, granularity, episode begin date, point in time, row create date.

### closed assertion

*Mechanics:* a row in an asserted version table whose assertion end date is not 9999.

*Semantics:* a row in an asserted version table with a known assertion end date.

*Components:* asserted version table, assertion end date, 9999.

### closed assertion time

*Mechanics:* an assertion time period whose end date is not 9999.

*Semantics:* an assertion time period whose end date is known.

*Components:* 9999, assertion end date, assertion time period.

### closed effective time

*Mechanics:* an effective time period whose end date is not 9999.

*Semantics:* an effective time period whose end date is known.

*Components:* 9999, effective end date, effective time period.

**closed episode**
*Mechanics:* an episode whose effective end date is not 9999.
*Semantics:* an episode whose effective end date is known.
*Components:* 9999, effective end date, episode.

**closed-closed**
*Mechanics:* a convention for using a pair of clock ticks to designate an effective or assertion time period, in which the earlier clock tick is the first clock tick in the time period, and in which the later clock tick is the last clock tick in the time period.
*Comments:*
- Using this convention, two time periods [meet] if and only if the begin date of the later one is one clock tick after the end date of the earlier one, at whatever level of granularity is used to designate the clock ticks.
*Components:* assertion time period, clock tick, effective time period.

**closed-open**
*Mechanics:* a convention for using a pair of clock ticks to designate an effective or assertion time period, in which the earlier clock tick is the first clock tick in the time period, and in which the later clock tick is the first clock tick after the last clock tick in the time period.
*Comments:*
- Using this convention, two time periods [meet] if and only if the begin date of the later one is the same clock tick as the end date of the earlier one, at whatever level of granularity is used to designate the clock ticks.
*Components:* assertion time period, clock tick, effective time period.

**contiguous**
*Mechanics:* time period or point in time X is contiguous with time period or point in time Y if and only if either X [meets] Y or X [meets$^{-1}$] Y.
*Components:* Allen relationship [meets], Allen relationship [meets$^{-1}$], point in time, time period.

**conventional data**
*Mechanics:* data in a conventional table.
*Semantics:* data which represents currently asserted current versions of persistent objects, but which lacks assertion time periods and effective time periods.
*Comments:*
- More accurately, conventional data is data which lacks *explicitly expressed* assertion and effective time periods. For in fact, conventional data is asserted, and its assertion time period is co-extensive with its physical presence in the database. And conventional data is also versioned, and the effective time of the one version of an object thus represented is always from Now() until further notice.
*Components:* assertion time period, conventional table, currently asserted current version, effective time period, persistent object.

**conventional database**
*Mechanics:* a database none of whose tables are temporal.

*Semantics:* a table whose rows describe the current state of the objects they represent.
*Comments:*
- In the early part of the book, used as synonymous with "non-temporal database". But starting in Chapter 15, a distinction is drawn in which a conventional database may contain temporal data about persistent objects, but not in the form of bi-temporal tables.

*Components:* object, represent, state.

**conventional table**

*Mechanics:* a table whose rows have no assertion or effective time periods.
*Semantics:* a table whose rows contain data describing what we currently claim things are currently like.
*Components:* assertion time period, effective time period, thing.

**conventional transaction**

*Mechanics:* an insert, update or delete against a conventional table.
*Semantics:* a request to create, modify or remove a row in a conventional table.
*Comments:*
- Conventional transactions are SQL insert, update or delete statements.

*Components:* conventional table.

**current assertion**

See also: *currently asserted.*

**current episode**

*Mechanics:* an episode whose episode begin date is earlier than Now() and whose episode end date is later than Now().
*Semantics:* an episode for an object which includes a current version of that object.
*Comments:*
- An object may have at most one current episode.
- A past episode is not a current episode because its effective time period is past.
- A no longer asserted episode is not a current episode because its assertion time period is past.
- An episode all of whose assertions are deferred is not a current episode because it is not yet asserted.
- An episode all of whose versions have an effective begin date in the future is not a current episode because it has no current version.

*Components:* episode begin date, episode end date, Now(), object, version.

**current transaction**

*Mechanics:* a temporal transaction which becomes currently effective as soon as it is applied to the database, and which also becomes currently asserted as soon as it is applied to the database.
*Semantics:* a temporal transaction which accepts the date the transaction is submitted as the begin date of the assertion period within which its transformations will be contained, and also as the begin date of the effective period within which its transformations will be contained.
*Comments:*
- See also: *deferred transaction, proactive transaction, retroactive transaction.*

*Components:* assertion time period, begin date, currently asserted, currently effective, effective time period, temporal transaction.

### current version
See *currently effective.*

### currently asserted
*Mechanics:* a row in an asserted version table whose assertion time period includes Now().
*Semantics:* a statement which we currently claim is true and/or actionable.
*Components:* actionable, asserted version table, assertion time period, include, Now(), statement.

### currently asserted current version
*Mechanics:* a row in an asserted version table whose assertion time period includes Now(), and whose effective time period includes Now().
*Semantics:* a row in an asserted version table which represents our current belief that the statement made by the business data in that row correctly describes what its object is currently like.
*Comments:*
- Rows in conventional tables are currently asserted current versions of the objects they represent.

*Components:* "assert" cognate (belief), asserted version table, assertion time period, business data, effective time period, include, Now(), object, statement.

### currently effective
*Mechanics:* a row in an asserted version table whose effective time period includes Now().
*Semantics:* a statement which describes what the object it represents is currently like.
*Components:* asserted version table, effective time period, include, Now(), object, represent, statement.

### dataset
*Mechanics:* a named collection of data that the operating system, or the DBMS, or the AVF, can recognize and manage as a single object.
*Semantics:* a managed object which represents a type, and which contains multiple managed objects each of which represent an instance of that type.
*Comments:*
- See also the Wikipedia definition.

*Components:* AVF, instance, managed object, object, type.

### de-dupped
*Mechanics:* a conventional table from which multiple rows representing the same object have been eliminated and/or consolidated, leaving at most one row to represent each object.
*Semantics:* a table from which row-level synonyms have been eliminated.
*Comments:*
- If a table needs to be de-dupped, it is because its business keys are not reliable. In a world of pure theory, rows with unreliable business keys would not be allowed into a table. But business requirements for such data, however unreliable, frequently outweigh theoretical considerations.
- See also: *dirty data, row-level homonym, row-level synonym.*

*Components:* conventional table, object, represent, row-level synonym.

**deferred assertion**
*Mechanics:* a row in an asserted version table whose assertion begin date is greater than Now().
*Semantics:* an assertion which will not be made until some future date.
*Components:* asserted version table, assertion begin date, Now().

**deferred assertion group**
*Mechanics:* a collection of one or more rows in an asserted version table which all have the same future assertion begin date.
*Components:* assertion begin date, asserted version table.

**deferred transaction**
*Mechanics:* a temporal transaction which uses a future date as its assertion begin date.
*Semantics:* a temporal transaction which creates a deferred assertion.
*Components:* assertion begin date, deferred assertion, temporal transaction.

**deMorgan's equivalences**
*Mechanics:* NOT(X OR Y) is truth-functionally equivalent to (NOT-X AND NOT-Y). (ii) (NOT-X OR NOT-Y) is truth-functionally equivalent to NOT(X AND Y).
*Semantics:* (i) if it's false that either of two statements is true, then it's true that both of them are false. (ii) If either of two statements is false, then it's false that they are both true.
*Comments:*
- Along with the truth-functional equivalence of (P IMPLIES Q) with (NOT-P OR Q), the deMorgan's equivalences allow any statement in propositional logic to be broken down into a series of ORs or a series of ANDs (including, in both cases, the NOT operand). In these simplified forms, computer software can carry out logic proofs, discovering contradictions when they exist, and presenting the logical implications of a set of assertions, many of which may turn out to be a surprise to those who accepted the original set of assertions.
- Software which does this is called an inference engine. While relational databases are the principal way that software helps us reason about instances, inference engines are the principal way that software helps us reason about types. Reasoning about types is what formal ontology is about. It is not often recognized that formal ontology and relational databases are complementary in this way, as means of reasoning about, respectively, types and instances.

*Components:* N/A.

**design encapsulation**
*Mechanics:* hiding all temporal design issues so that the design of a temporal database is a matter of (i) creating a conventional logical data model, (ii) designating those entities in the model which are to be physically generated as temporal tables, and (iii) describing all their temporal features in metadata tables.
*Semantics:* the ability to declaratively express all temporal design requirements for a data model.
*Comments:*
- Recent consulting experience by the authors has demonstrated the very significant cost savings that result from the ability to exclude all temporal design considerations from the process of creating the logical data model for a database. Discussions of how to best implement project-specific

temporal requirements are often difficult, lengthy, contentious and inconclusive—in short, costly. Those costs are incurred over and over again, for every data model in which even a single table must be given temporal capabilities. And almost every time, the result is a slightly different solution, whose maintenance and querying are never quite the same as for any other temporalized tables. Asserted Versioning's design encapsulation feature eliminates these costs, and guarantees a uniform implementation of temporal semantics across all tables in all databases in the enterprise. Moreover, firmly grounded in computer science research, Asserted Versioning guarantees that its single enterprise solution is a complete and correct implementation of bi-temporal semantics.

*Components:* temporal database.

#### directly queryable data

*Description:* data which doesn't need to be transformed before queries can be written against it.

*Comments:*
- Much of the temporal data in an enterprise is not directly queryable.
- Even if one table of temporal data is directly queryable, the needs of any specific query may require access to multiple temporal tables, and often that *combination* of tables is not directly queryable. For example, a query may need both last year's customer data from an enterprise data warehouse, and last month's customer data from an Operational Data Store (ODS) history table. But it is unlikely that the schemas in the two databases are identical, and therefore unlikely that the combination of those tables is directly queryable.
- With directly queryable data, nothing needs to be done to get the data ready to be queried, whether by native SQL or via query tools.

*Components:* N/A.

#### dirty data

*Mechanics:* a collection of data whose instances do not all have unique identifiers.

*Semantics:* a collection of data in which row-level homonyms and/or row-level synonyms may exist.

*Comments:*
- Among IT professionals, the term "dirty data" often has a broader meaning, and covers a wide range of problems with data. In this narrower sense, dirty data is the result of unreliable business keys.
- See also: *de-dupped, row-level homonym, row-level synonym.*

*Components:* row-level homonym, row-level synonym.

#### effective begin date

*Mechanics:* using the closed-open convention, the first date in an effective time period.

*Semantics:* the date indicating when an effective time period begins.

*Comments:*
- The effective begin date of an episode is the effective begin date of its earliest version.

*Components:* closed-open, effective time period.

#### effective end date

*Mechanics:* using the closed-open convention, the first date after the last date in an effective time period.

*Semantics:* the date indicating when an effective time period ends.
*Comments:*
- The effective end date of an episode is the effective end date of its latest version.

*Components:* closed-open, effective time period.

### effective time

*Mechanics:* the temporal dimension along which effective time periods are located.

*Semantics:* the temporal dimension which interprets a time period on a row as indicating when the object represented by that row existed such that the row was the unique row validly representing that object.

*Comments:*
- We do *not* say "The temporal dimension which interprets a time period on a row as indicating when that row was the unique row validly representing that object" because that suggests that this temporal dimension is a property of rows. It is not. It is a property of objects represented by rows.
- But assertion time periods *are* properties of rows or, more precisely, of the existentially quantified statements made by those rows.

*Components:* temporal dimension, effective time period, object, represent.

### effective time period

*Mechanics:* the period of time of a version or an episode starting on its effective begin date and ending one clock tick prior to its effective end date.

*Semantics:* the period of time during which an object exists, as asserted by a row in an asserted version table.

*Components:* assert, asserted version table, clock tick, effective begin date, effective end date, episode, object, time period, version.

### effective time versioning

*Mechanics:* a form of versioning similar to temporal gap versioning, but in which a row create date is added to each version, in addition to a version begin date and a version end date.

*Semantics:* a form of versioning in which versions of the same object may or may not be contiguous, in which no version is physically deleted, in which the version dates delimit an effective time period, and in which the date the row was physically created is also provided.

*Comments:*
- Effective time versioning is not part of Asserted Versioning. See Chapter 4.
- See also: *basic versioning, logical delete versioning, temporal gap versioning.*

*Components:* contiguous, effective time period, object, row create date, temporal gap versioning, version, version begin date, version end date.

### empty assertion time

*Mechanics:* an assertion time period whose begin and end dates have the same value.

*Semantics:* an assertion time period which includes no clock ticks.

*Comments:*
- Deferred assertions which are deleted before they become currently asserted are moved into empty assertion time, i.e. are given empty assertion time periods.

*Components:* assertion begin date, assertion end date, assertion time period, clock tick.

### end date
*Mechanics:* an assertion end date or an effective end date.
*Semantics:* a date which marks the end of an assertion or an effective time period.
*Components:* assertion end date, assertion time period, effective end date, effective time period.

### enterprise contextualization
*Mechanics:* the expression of the Asserted Versioning Framework in a single unit of code which is physically separate from application programs, and in a standard (canonical) schema for all bi-temporal tables.
*Semantics:* an implementation of a software framework to provide seamless access to queryable bi-temporal state data about persistent objects, consisting of: one canonical set of schemas, across all tables and all databases; one set of transactions that update bi-temporal data and enforce temporal entity integrity and temporal referential integrity across all tables and all databases; a standard way to retrieve bi-temporal data; and a way to remove all temporal logic from application programs, isolate it in a separate layer of code, and invoke it declaratively.
*Components:* Asserted Versioning Framework, persistent object, seamless access, temporal data management taxonomy (queryable temporal data) / (state temporal data) / (bi-temporal data), temporal entity integrity, temporal referential integrity.

### episode
*Mechanics:* within shared assertion time, a series or one or more rows representing the same object in which, in effective time, each non-initial row [meets] the next one, in which the initial row is [before$^{-1}$] any earlier row of the same object, and in which the latest row is [before] any later version of the same object.
*Semantics:* within one period of assertion time, a set of one or more effective-time contiguous asserted version rows representing the same object which are preceded and followed by at least one effective-time clock tick in which that object is not represented.
*Comments:*
- This is one of the most important concepts in Asserted Versioning.
- Episodes are a series of versions of the same object that are contiguous in effective time *within* a period of shared assertion time. They represent what we believe, during that period of assertion time, the life history of that object was/is/will be like, across those contiguous periods of effective time. (From Chapter 5.)

*Components:* Allen relationship [before], Allen relationship [before$^{-1}$], Allen relationship [meets], assertion time, clock tick, contiguous, effective time, object, represent, shared assertion time, version.

### episode begin date
*Mechanics:* the effective begin date of the earliest version of an episode.
*Semantics:* the date on which the episode begins to be in effect.
*Components:* effective begin date, episode, version.

**episode end date**
*Mechanics:* the effective end date of the latest version of an episode.
*Semantics:* the date on which the episode ceases to be in effect.
*Components:* effective end date, episode, version.

**epistemological time**
*Semantics:* the epistemological time of a row in a bi-temporal table is the period of time during which we claim that the statement made by that row is true and/or actionable.
*Comments:*
- A neutral term referring to either the standard temporal model's transaction time or to Asserted Versioning's assertion time.
- See also: *"assert" cognates.*
*Components:* actionable, "assert" cognates (claim), bi-temporal table, statement, time period.

**event**
*Semantics:* a point in time or a period of time during which one or more objects come into existence, change from one state to another state, or go out of existence.
*Comments:*
- Events are the occasions on which changes happen to persistent objects. As events, they have two important features: (i) they occur at a point in time, or sometimes last for a limited period of time; and (ii) in either case, they do not change. An event happens, and then it's over. Once it's over, that's it; it is frozen in time. (From Chapter 2.)
*Components:* point in time, period of time, object, persistent object, state.

**existence dependency**
*Semantics:* an object X is existence dependent on an object Y if and only if there can be no point in time at which X exists but Y does not exist.
*Comments:*
- Note the "can be". If "is" were in its place, the statements would express a correlation, but not a requirement.
*Components:* assertion time, clock tick, effective time, episode, object, occupy, version.

**explicitly temporal data**
*Mechanics:* a row of data which contains an assertion time period and/or an effective time period.
*Semantics:* a row of data whose assertion time and/or effective time is expressed by means of one or more columns of data.
*Comments:*
- See also: *implicitly temporal data.*
*Components:* assertion time, effective time.

**external pipeline dataset**
*Mechanics:* a dataset whose destination or origin is one or more production tables, and which is a distinct managed object to the operating system and/or the DBMS.
*Semantics:* a dataset whose contents are production data.
*Comments:*
- Tabular data which will become part of the production database are transactions acquired or generated by a company's OLTP systems.

They are either immediately and directly applied to the production database, or are augmented, corrected or otherwise transformed as they are moved along an "inflow data pipeline" leading into the production database.

- Tabular data which has been a part of the production database are the persisted result sets of SQL queries or equivalent processes. They are either end state result sets, i.e. immediately delivered to internal business users or exported to outside users, or are augmented as they move along an "outflow data pipeline" leading to a final state in which they are delivered to internal business users or outside users.

- The various kinds of external pipeline datasets do not form a partitioning. Most of these names are in fairly widespread usage, but no standard definition of them exists. Therefore, in this Glossary, we will provide a description of them, but cannot provide a definition.

- The distinction between inflow pipeline datasets and outflow pipeline datasets is a matter of perspective. Any physical dataset may be used to update a production table, in which case it is an inflow dataset. And any physical dataset other than those created by means of manual data entry or automated data collection from instruments, for example, contains data from production tables and so are outflow datasets.

*Components:* dataset, managed object, production data, production table.

**external pipeline dataset, batch file**
*Description:* this term is generally used to refer to a file or a table of insert, update and/or delete transactions whose target is a production table. It is a dataset that exists at the start of an inflow pipeline.

**external pipeline dataset, data extract**
*Description:* this term is generally used to refer to the results of a query which are stored as a physical dataset which will be moved to some other location before being made available to end users. It is a dataset that exists along an outflow pipeline.

**external pipeline dataset, data feed**
*Description:* this term is generally used to refer to a dataset which is being used to populate a production table. It is a dataset that exists at the end of an inflow pipeline to its target.
*Comments:*
- Of course, the same physical dataset which was an extract may, with or without going through additional modifications, also be a feed.

**external pipeline dataset, data staging area**
*Description:* this term is generally used to refer to a physical dataset of production data that is being worked on until it can be moved into its target production table.
*Comments:*
- When applied to a production table, the contents of a data staging area may or may not overlay rows already in that table.
- The contents of a data staging area may have originated as a copy of rows in a production table, or simply be a collection of transactions each of which requires data from multiple sources, and so must be built up over time. If it originated as a copy of production rows, it is both an outflow pipeline dataset and, later on, an inflow pipeline dataset.

- The purpose of a staging area is to move the row or rows representing an object into a state where they are not available to normal queries. The reason for doing this is usually to withdraw those rows into an area where a series of updates can be made to them, only after which are those rows returned to production data status.

**external pipeline dataset, history table**
*Description:* this term is generally used to refer to a table of data which contains the before-image copies of production rows which are about to be updated. It is a dataset that exists at the end of a (very short) outflow pipeline.

**external pipeline dataset, logfile table**
*Mechanics:* this term is generally used to refer to a table of data which contains the before-image copies of production rows which are about to be inserted, updated or deleted. It is a dataset that exists at the end of a (very short) outflow pipeline.

**external pipeline dataset, query result set**
*Mechanics:* this term is always used to refer to the results of an SQL query. It is a dataset that exists at the start of an outflow pipeline.

**external pipeline dataset, report**
*Description:* this term is generally used to refer to a dataset at the end of an outflow pipeline, at which point the data can be directly viewed.

**external pipeline dataset, screen**
*Mechanics:* this term is generally used to refer to a dataset at the end of an outflow pipeline, at which point the data can be directly viewed.
*Comments:*
- Aside from the difference in media (video display vs. hardcopy), screens differ from reports in that reports usually contain data representing many objects, while screens usually contain data representing one object or a few objects.

**fall into currency**
*Mechanics:* to become a current assertion and/or a current version when an assertion and/or effective begin date becomes a date in the past.
*Semantics:* to become a current assertion and/or a currently version because of the passage of time.
*Comments:*
- Once an assertion and/or a version falls into currency, it remains current until its end date becomes a date in the past.
*Components:* assertion begin date, current assertion, effective begin date, current version, passage of time.

**fall out of currency**
*Mechanics:* to become a past assertion and/or a past version when an assertion and/or effective end date becomes a date in the past.
*Semantics:* to become a past assertion and/or a past version because of the passage of time.
*Components:* assertion end date, effective end date, passage of time, past assertion, past version.

**far future assertion time**

*Mechanics:* the assertion time location of deferred assertions whose begin dates are far in the future.

*Semantics:* the assertion time location of deferred assertions that would be obsolete before the passage of time made them current.

*Comments:*
- See also: *near future assertion time.*
- A typical far future assertion begin date would be hundreds or even thousands of years in the future. In business databases, there is little risk of such assertions falling into currency by the mere passage of time.
- The intent, with far future deferred assertions, is that they exist in a "temporal sandbox" within a production table. They can be used for forecasting, for "what if" analyses, or for building up or otherwise working on one or more assertions until those assertions are ready to become visible in the production table that physically contains them. When they are ready, an approval transaction will move them to near future assertion time, where the passage of time will quickly make them current assertions.

*Components:* assertion begin date, assertion time, current assertion, deferred assertion, passage of time.

**ƒCTD function**

*Mechanics:* a function that converts an integer into that integer number of clock ticks of the correct granularity.

*Comments:*
- "CTD" stands for "clock tick duration". (From Chapter 14.)

*Components:* clock tick, granularity.

**ƒCUT function**

*Mechanics:* a function that splits a row in an asserted version table into two contiguous versions in order to [align] version boundaries in a target table to effective time boundaries on a temporal transaction.

*Comments:*
- A temporal update or delete transaction will affect only clock ticks within the effective time period specified by the transaction.
- If the first clock tick in the transaction's effective time period is a non-initial clock tick in a version of the object referenced by the transaction, then that version must be split into a contiguous pair of otherwise identical versions.
- If the last clock tick in the transaction's effective time period is a non-final clock tick in a version of the object referenced by the transaction, then that version must be split into a contiguous pair of otherwise identical versions.
- The result is that the temporal transaction can be carried out by updating or deleting complete versions.
- See also: *match.*

*Components:* Allen relationship [align], asserted version table, contiguous, effective time, target table, temporal transaction, version.

**from now on**

*Mechanics:* a time period of [Now() – 9999], where Now() is the clock tick current when the time period was created.

*Semantics:* a time period which is current from the moment it is created until further notice.

*Comments:*
- That current assertion time starts Now(), i.e. when the transaction is processed, and continues on until further notice. Every temporal transaction that accepts the default values for effective time, creates a version that describes what its object looks like *from now on*. Every non-deferred temporal transaction creates an assertion that, *from now on*, claims that its version makes a true statement. (From Chapter 9.)

*Components:* 9999, clock tick, Now(), time period, until further notice.

### *f*TRI function

*Mechanics:* a function that evaluates to True if and only if a valid TRI relationship holds between the episode and the version specified in the function.

*Components:* episode, TRI, version.

### future assertion

See *deferred assertion*.

### future version

*Mechanics:* a row in an asserted version table whose effective begin date is later than Now().

*Semantics:* a row in an asserted version table which describes what the object it represents will be like during a specified future period of time.

*Components:* asserted version table, effective begin date, Now(), object, represent, time period.

### granularity

*Mechanics:* the size of the unit of time used to delineate effective time periods and assertion time periods in an asserted version table.

*Comments:*
- More generally, the granularity of a measurement is the size of the units in which the measurement is expressed, a smaller size referred to as a "finer" granularity. For example, inches are a finer granularity of linear measurement than yards, and ounces are a finer granularity of the measurement of weight than pounds.

*Components:* asserted version table, assertion time period, effective time period.

### hand-over clock tick

*Semantics:* the point in near future assertion time to which an approval transaction sets the assertion begin date of one or more deferred assertions, and also the assertion end date of any assertions which were locked as a result of creating them.

*Components:* approval transaction, assertion begin date, assertion end date, deferred assertion, lock, near future assertion time, replace, supercede.

### historical data

*Mechanics:* rows in asserted version tables whose effective end date is earlier than Now().

*Semantics:* data which describes the past state or states of a persistent object.

*Comments:*
- Note that this term does not refer to data which is itself, historical, i.e. to no longer currently asserted data, but rather to data which is about history, i.e. about the past states of persistent objects.
- For the term which does refer to data which is itself historical, see also *as-was data*.

- Note that, in the special sense used here, historical data is data about persistent objects. Thus, fact/dimension data marts do not provide historical data because their history is a history of events, not of objects, and also because they do not make assertion time distinctions.

*Components:* asserted version table, effective end date, Now(), persistent object, state.

### implicitly temporal data

*Mechanics:* a row in a non-temporal table whose assertion time and/or effective time is co-extensive with its physical presence in its table.

*Semantics:* a row of data whose assertion time and/or effective time is not expressed by means of one or more columns of data.

*Comments:*
- Thus, rows in conventional tables are implicitly temporal data. No columns of those tables indicate assertion or effective time periods. Each row is asserted for as long as it is present in its table, and is in effect for as long as it is present in its table.

*Components:* assertion time, effective time, non-temporal table.

### incommensurable

*Mechanics:* two asserted version rows are incommensurable if and only if their assertion time periods do not [intersect].

*Semantics:* unable to be meaningfully compared.

*Comments:*
- Rows which share no clock ticks in assertion time are semantically and truth-functionally isolated from one another. They are what philosophers call *incommensurable*. (From Chapter 6.)
- Incommensurability restricts TEI and TRI relationships to managed objects in shared assertion time.

*Components:* Allen relationship [intersect], asserted version table, assertion time period.

### inflow pipeline dataset

*Mechanics:* a dataset whose destination is one or more production tables.

*Comments:*
- Inflow pipeline datasets are tabular data which will become part of the production database. They originate with transactions acquired or generated by a company's OLTP systems. They are either immediately and directly applied to the production database, or are augmented, corrected or otherwise transformed as they are moved along an "inflow data pipeline" leading into the production database.

*Components:* dataset, production table.

### instance

*Semantics:* a thing of a particular type.

*Comments:*
- See also: *type.*
- The concepts of types and instances has long history. A related distinction is that between universals and particulars.

*Components:* thing, type.

### internalized pipeline dataset, Current Data

*Mechanics:* all those rows in asserted version tables which lie in the assertion time present and also in the effective time present. (From Chapter 13.)

*Semantics:* a record of what we currently believe things are currently like.
*Components:* asserted version table, assertion time, effective time.

**internalized pipeline dataset, Current History**
*Mechanics:* all those rows in asserted version tables which lie in the assertion time present but in the effective time past. (From Chapter 13.)
*Semantics:* a record of what we currently believe things used to be like.
*Components:* asserted version table, assertion time, effective time.

**internalized pipeline dataset, Current Projections**
*Mechanics:* all those rows in asserted version tables which lie in the assertion time present but in the effective time future. (From Chapter 13.)
*Semantics:* a record of what we currently believe things may eventually be like.
*Components:* asserted version table, assertion time, effective time.

**internalized pipeline dataset, Pending History**
*Mechanics:* all those rows in asserted version tables which lie in the assertion time future but in the effective time past. (From Chapter 13.)
*Semantics:* a record of what we may come to believe things used to be like.
*Components:* asserted version table, assertion time, effective time.

**internalized pipeline dataset, Pending Projections**
*Mechanics:* all those rows in asserted version tables which lie in both the assertion time future and in the effective time future. (From Chapter 13.)
*Semantics:* a record of what we may come to believe things may eventually be like.
*Components:* asserted version table, assertion time, effective time.

**internalized pipeline dataset, Pending Updates**
*Mechanics:* all those rows in asserted version tables which lie in the assertion time future but in the effective time present. (From Chapter 13.)
*Semantics:* a record of what we may come to believe things are currently like.
*Components:* asserted version table, assertion time, effective time.

**internalized pipeline dataset, Posted History**
*Mechanics:* all those rows in asserted version tables which lie in both the assertion time past and also in the effective time past. (From Chapter 13).
*Semantics:* a record of what we used to believe things used to be like.
*Components:* asserted version table, assertion time, effective time.

**internalized pipeline dataset, Posted Projections**
*Mechanics:* all those rows in an asserted version table which lie in the assertion time past but in the effective time future. (From Chapter 13.)
*Semantics:* a record of what we used to believe things may eventually be like.
*Components:* asserted version table, assertion time, effective time.

**internalized pipeline dataset, Posted Updates**
*Mechanics:* all those rows in asserted version tables which lie in the assertion time past but in the effective time present. (From Chapter 13)
*Semantics:* a record of what we used to believe things are currently like.
*Components:* asserted version table, assertion time, effective time.

**lock**
*Mechanics:* to lock a row in an asserted version table is to set its assertion end date to a non-9999 value which is later than Now().

*Semantics:* to lock an asserted version row is to prevent it from being updated or deleted without moving it into past assertion time.

*Comments:*
- See also: *withdraw.*
- A deferred transaction locks a row by setting its assertion end date to the assertion begin date of the deferred assertion it creates. Rows that are locked by means of deferred assertions remain currently asserted until their assertion end dates fall into the past.

*Components:* 9999, asserted version table, assertion end date, Now(), past assertion.

### logical delete versioning

*Mechanics:* a form of versioning similar to basic versioning, but in which delete transactions are carried out as logical deletions, not as physical deletions.

*Semantics:* a form of versioning in which all versions of the same object are contiguous, and in which no version is physically deleted.

*Comments:*
- Logical delete versioning is not part of Asserted Versioning. See Chapter 4.
- See also: *basic versioning, temporal gap versioning, effective time versioning.*

*Components:* basic versioning, contiguous, object, version.

### maintenance encapsulation

*Mechanics:* hiding the complexity of temporal insert, update and delete transactions so that a temporal transaction needs, in addition to the data supplied in a corresponding conventional transaction, either no additional data, or else one, two or three dates representing, respectively, the effective begin date of a version, the effective end date of a version or the assertion begin date of an assertion.

*Semantics:* the ability to express all temporal parameters on temporal transactions declaratively.

*Comments:*
- Maintenance encapsulation means that inserts, updates and deletes to bi-temporal tables, and queries against them, are simple enough that anyone who could write them against non-temporal tables could also write them against these tables. (From the Preface.)

*Components:* assertion, assertion begin date, conventional transaction, effective begin date, effective end date, temporal transaction, version.

### managed object

*Semantics:* a named data item or collection of data that is manipulable by the operating system, the DBMS or the AVF, and which references persistent objects.

*Comments:*
- For example, tables, rows, columns, versions and episodes are all managed objects. Individual customers, clients or policies, while examples of objects, are not examples of managed objects.
- In the phrase "managed object", the word "object", by itself, has no meaning. In particular, it has no connection with the technical term "object".
- Managed objects are data which transformations and constraints treat as a single unit. (From Chapter 5.)

*Components:* reference, persistent object.

**match**

*Mechanics:* to apply the *f*CUT function to any non-locked version in the target table of a temporal update or delete transaction whose effective time period [overlaps] that specified on the transaction.

*Semantics:* to modify the target table for a temporal update or delete transaction so that there is no non-locked version for the object specified on the transaction whose effective time period [overlaps] the effective time period specified on the transaction.

*Components:* Allen relationship [overlaps], effective time period, *f*CUT, lock, object, target table, temporal delete transaction, temporal update transaction, version.

**near future assertion time**

*Mechanics:* the assertion time location of deferred assertions which are about to fall into currency.

*Semantics:* the assertion time location of deferred assertions that the passage of time will make current soon enough to satisfy business requirements.

*Comments:*

- See also: *far future assertion time.*
- Deferred assertions located in the near future will become current assertions as soon as enough time has passed. In a real-time update situation, a near future deferred assertion might be one with an assertion begin date just a few seconds from now. In a batch update situation, a near future deferred assertion might be one that does not become currently asserted until midnight, or perhaps even for another several days. What near future deferred assertions have in common is that, in all cases, the business is willing to wait for these assertions to fall into currency, i.e. to become current not because of some explicit action, but rather when the passage of time reaches their assertion begin dates. (From Chapter 12.)

*Components:* assertion begin date, assertion time, current assertion, deferred assertion, fall into currency, passage of time.

**non-contiguous**

*Mechanics:* time period or point in time X is non-contiguous with time period or point in time Y if and only if either X is [before] Y or X is [before$^{-1}$] Y.

*Components:* Allen relationship [before], Allen relationship [before$^{-1}$], point in time, time period.

**non-temporal data**

See *conventional data.*

**non-temporal database**

See *conventional database.*

**non-temporal table**

See *conventional table.*

**Now()**

*Mechanics:* a DBMS-agnostic representation of a function which always returns the current clock tick.

*Semantics:* a variable representing the current point in time.

*Comments:*

- SQL Server may use *getdate()*, and DB2 may use *Current Timestamp* or *Current Date.* (From Chapter 3.)

- Now() stands for a function, not a value. However, we will often use *Now()* to designate a specific point in time. For example, we may say that a time period starts at Now() and continues on until 9999. This is a shorthand way of emphasizing that, whenever that time period was created, it was given as its begin date the value returned by Now() at that moment. (From Chapter 3.)

*Components:* clock tick, point in time.

## object

*Mechanics:* what is represented by the object identifier (oid) in an asserted version table.

*Semantics:* an instance of a type of thing which exists over time, has properties and relationships, and can change over time.

*Comments:*
- See also: *events*. Events, whether points in time or durations in time, are not objects, because events, by definition, do not change.
- Examples of objects include vendors, customers, employees, regulatory agencies, products, services, bills of material, invoices, purchase orders, claims, certifications, etc.

*Components:* asserted version table, instance, object identifier, oid, represent, type, thing.

## object identifier

*Mechanics:* the unique identifier of the persistent object represented by a row in an asserted version table, used as part of the primary key of that row.

*Comments:*
- The unique identifier of a row in an asserted version table is the concatenation of an object identifier, an effective begin date, and an assertion begin date.

*Components:* asserted version table, persistent object.

## occupied

*Mechanics:* a series of one or more clock ticks is occupied by an object if and only if those clock ticks are all included within the effective time period of a version of that object.

*Semantics:* a time period is occupied by an object if and only if the object is represented in every clock tick in that time period.

*Components:* clock tick, effective time period, include, object, represent, version.

## oid

See *object identifier.*

## ontological time

*Semantics:* the ontological time of a row in a bi-temporal table is the period of time during which its referenced object exists.

*Comments:*
- A neutral term referring to either the standard temporal model's valid time or to Asserted Versioning's effective time.

*Components:* bi-temporal table, object, referent, time period.

## open episode

*Mechanics:* An episode whose effective end date is 9999.

*Semantics:* an episode whose effective end date is not known.

*Comments:*
- The effective end date of an episode is the effective end date of its latest version.

*Components:* 9999, effective end date, episode.

**open version**
*Mechanics:* a version whose effective end date is 9999.
*Semantics:* a version whose effective end date is unknown.
*Components:* 9999, effective end date, version.

**open-closed**
*Mechanics:* a convention for using a pair of clock ticks to designate an effective or assertion time period, in which the earlier clock tick is the last clock tick before the first clock tick in the time period, and in which the later clock tick is the last clock tick in the time period.
*Comments:*
- Using this convention, two time periods [meet] if and only if the begin date of the later one is the same clock tick as the end date of the earlier one, at whatever level of granularity is used to designate the clock ticks.

*Components:* assertion time period, clock tick, effective time period.

**open-open**
*Mechanics:* a convention for using a pair of clock ticks to designate an effective or assertion time period, in which the earlier clock tick is the last clock tick before the first clock tick in the time period, and in which the later clock tick is the first clock tick after the last clock tick in the time period.
*Comments:*
- Using this convention, two time periods [meet] if and only if the begin date of the later one is one clock tick before the end date of the earlier one, at whatever level of granularity is used to designate the clock ticks.

*Components:* assertion time period, clock tick, effective time period.

**outflow pipeline dataset**
*Mechanics:* a dataset whose origin is one or more production tables.
*Comments:*
- Outflow pipeline datasets are tabular data which has been a part of the production database; they are the persisted result sets of SQL queries or equivalent processes. They are either end state result sets, i.e. immediately delivered to internal business users or exported to outside users, or are augmented as they move along an "outflow data pipeline" leading to a final state in which they are delivered to internal business users or outside users.
- The termination points of outflow pipelines may be either internal to the organization, or external to it; and we may think of the data that flows along these pipelines to be the result sets of queries applied to those production tables. (From Chapter 12.)

*Components:* dataset, production table.

**override**
*Mechanics:* to set the assertion end date of a row to the same value as its assertion begin date.

*Semantics:* to withdraw a row into empty assertion time.
*Comments:*
- An assertion is overridden only when an approval transaction retrograde moves a matching version to an earlier assertion period than the assertion period of the assertion being overridden.

*Components:* assertion begin date, assertion end date, empty assertion time.

## parent episode

*Mechanics:* an episode in an asserted version table X is a parent to a version in asserted version table Y if and only if the version in Y has a temporal foreign key whose value is identical to the value of the object identifier of that episode in X, and the effective time period of that episode in X includes ($[fills^{-1}]$) the effective time period of that version in Y.

*Semantics:* an episode in an asserted version table X is a parent to a version in asserted version table Y if and only if the object for that version in Y is existence dependent on the object for that episode in X, and the effective time period of that episode in X includes ($[fills^{-1}]$) the effective time period of that version in Y.

*Components:* Allen relationship $[fills^{-1}]$, asserted version table, effective time period, episode, existence dependency, include, object, object identifier, temporal foreign key, version.

## parent managed object

*Mechanics:* an episode in a TRI relationship.
*Semantics:* a managed object which represents a parent object.
*Components:* episode, parent object, TRI.

## parent object

*Semantics:* an object, represented by a managed object, on which another object, also represented by a managed object, is existence dependent.
*Components:* existence dependency, managed object, object.

## parent table

*Mechanics:* X is a parent table if and only if there is a table, not necessarily distinct, which contains a foreign key or a temporal foreign key which references X.
*Semantics:* X is a parent table if and only if its rows represent parent objects.
*Components:* temporal foreign key, parent object.

## passage of time

*Semantics:* the means by which asserted versions may move from future to current, and from current to past time, in either or both temporal dimensions.
*Comments:*
- Creating future versions and/or deferred assertions is a way of managing a large volume of transactions so that the result of those transactions will all become current on exactly the same clock tick. An example would be a corporate acquisition in which the entire set of customers, policies, accounts and other objects managed by the acquired company need to become part of the acquiring company's production databases—and thus available to the maintenance processes, queries and reporting processes of the acquiring company—all at the same time, on precisely the same clock tick.

*Components:* asserted version, temporal dimension.

**past assertion**

*Mechanics:* a row whose assertion end date is earlier than Now().

*Semantics:* a row which represents a statement we are no longer willing to claim is true and/or actionable.

*Components:* actionable, assertion end date, Now(), represent, statement.

**past episode**

*Mechanics:* an episode of an object whose latest version has an effective end date which is earlier than Now().

*Semantics:* the representation of an object in a period of past effective time which is either [before] or [before-$^1$] all other representations of the same object.

*Components:* Allen relationship [before], Allen relationship [before$^{-1}$], episode, effective end date, effective time, Now(), object, represent, version.

**past version**

*Mechanics:* a version of an object whose effective end date is earlier than Now().

*Semantics:* the representation of an object in a period of past effective time which [*excludes*] all other representations of the same object, in shared assertion time.

*Components:* Allen relationship [*excludes*], effective end date, effective time, Now(), object, represent, version.

**pending transaction**

*Description:* an insert, update or delete statement that has been written but not yet submitted to the applications that maintain the production database. Sometimes pending transactions are collected outside the target database, in batch transaction files. More commonly, they are collected inside the target database, in batch transaction tables. (From the Preface.)

*Comments:*
- Pending transactions are collected in batch transaction files. See also *external pipeline dataset, batch transaction file.*
- As internalized by Asserted Versioning, they are those semantic collections of asserted version rows called Pending History, Pending Updates and Pending Projections.

**PERIOD datatype**

*Mechanics:* the representation of a time period as a datatype.

*Semantics:* the representation of a time period by a single column of data, a well-defined set or range of values, and a well-defined set of operations on those values.

*Comments:*
- Several DBMS vendors, including Oracle and Teradata, have defined PERIOD datatypes, but we do not know whether or not their definitions are equivalent.
- We would regard any PERIOD datatype as inadequate unless it could express a time period with an unknown starting point or an unknown ending point. We would regard DBMS support for any PERIOD datatype as inadequate unless a unique index could be defined on any column with a PERIOD datatype that would treat any two time periods as duplicates if they shared even a single clock tick.

*Components:* N/A.

**persistent object**

See *object.*

**physical logfile**
*Mechanics:* the ability of the AVF to recreate the state of an asserted version table as of any past point in time, using the row create date.
*Comments:*
- See also *semantic logfile*.
- Deferred assertions which have been retrograde moved from far future to near future assertion time are the one exception to this ability to recreate any past physical state of an asserted version table. Currently, Asserted Versioning does not preserve information about the far future assertion time these assertions originally existed in. (From Chapter 16.)
*Components:* asserted version table, AVF, row create date.

**physical transaction**
*Description:* a SQL insert, update or delete transaction submitted to the DBMS.
*Comments:*
- The AVF translates each temporal transaction into the one or more physical transactions that, when processed, carry out the intentions expressed by the user who submitted the temporal transaction.

**pipeline dataset**
*Mechanics:* a dataset whose destination or origin is one or more production tables.
*Comments:*
- Pipeline production datasets (*pipeline datasets*, for short) are points at which data comes to rest along the inflow pipelines whose termination points are production tables, or along the outflow pipelines whose points of origin are those same tables. (From Chapter 12.)

*Components:* dataset, production table.

**pipeline dataset, internalization of**
*Mechanics:* the representation of the contents of external pipeline datasets as rows in asserted version production tables which exist in non-current assertion time and/or non-current effective time.
*Components:* asserted version table, assertion time, current assertion, current version, effective time, external pipeline dataset, production table, represent.

**pipeline dataset, re-presentation of**
*Mechanics:* the ability to recreate the contents of any external pipeline dataset from internal pipeline datasets by means of a query.
*Components:* external pipeline dataset, internalized pipeline dataset.

**point in time**
*Mechanics:* a time period whose begin date value, using the closed-open representation of time periods, is one clock tick before its end date value.
*Semantics:* a time period consisting of a single clock tick.
*Comments:*
- For purposes of temporal data management, a point in time is considered indivisible.
- Note that in this book, in which we use a month as our level of temporal granularity, that one month is considered indivisible. For example, if a transaction is applied, it is assumed that its results will remain unchanged until the next month.
*Components:* begin date, clock tick, closed-open, end date, time period.

**posted transaction**

*Description:* copies of data about to be inserted, and before-images of data about to be updated or deleted. The contents of various forms of logfiles. (From the Preface.)

*Comments:*
- Posted transactions are collected in logfiles. See also *external pipeline dataset, logfile table.*
- As internalized by Asserted Versioning, they are those semantic collections of asserted version rows called Posted History, Posted Updates and Posted Projections.

**proactive delete**

*Mechanics:* a temporal delete transaction that removes the representation of an object from one or more clock ticks in future effective time.

*Components:* clock tick, effective time, object, represent, temporal transaction.

**proactive insert**

*Mechanics:* a temporal insert transaction that adds the representation of an object to one or more clock ticks in future effective time.

*Components:* clock tick, effective time, object, represent, temporal transaction.

**proactive transaction**

*Mechanics:* a temporal transaction that specifies an effective begin date that is later than Now().

*Semantics:* a temporal transaction which anticipates the effective-time future.

*Comments:*
- See also: *retroactive transaction.*

*Components:* temporal transaction, effective begin date.

**proactive update**

*Mechanics:* a temporal update transaction that changes the business data representing an object in one or more clock ticks in future effective time.

*Components:* business data, clock tick, effective time, object, represent, temporal transaction.

**production data**

*Semantics:* business data that describes the objects and events of interest to the business.

*Components:* business data, object, event.

**production database**

*Mechanics:* a database that contains production data.

*Semantics:* the logical collection of databases whose currently asserted contents are the company's official statements describing the objects and events represented by those statements.

*Comments:*
- Production databases are the collections of production datasets which the business recognizes as the official repositories of that data. Production databases consist of production tables. (From Chapter 12.)

*Components:* currently asserted, event, object, production data, represent, statement.

**production dataset**

*Description:* a dataset that contains production data.

**production query**
*Description:* a query which is usually embedded in an application program, and
which is run as part of the IT production schedule.
*Comments:*
- See also: *ad hoc query.* (From Chapter 5.)

**production row**
*Mechanics:* a row in a production table.
*Semantics:* a row which describes an object or event of interest to the business.
*Components:* event, object, production table.

**production table**
*Mechanics:* a table in a production database.
*Semantics:* a table whose rows describe an object or event of interest to the
business.
*Comments:*
- The term "production" indicates that these tables are in use by business
processes, and contain "real" data. Regularly scheduled processes are
being carried out to maintain these tables, and to keep their contents as
accurate, secure and current as possible. Regularly scheduled processes,
as well as non-scheduled ones, are being carried out to access this data to
obtain needed information. So production tables are the tables that the
business tries to keep accurate, current and secure, and from which it
draws the information it needs to carry out its mission and meet its
objectives. (From Chapter 3.)
- Production tables are production datasets whose data is designated as
always reliable and always available for use. (From Chapter 12.)
*Components:* event, object, production database.

**query encapsulation**
*Mechanics:* hiding the complexity of many temporal queries so that (i) a query as of
a past or future point in either or both of the data's two temporal dimensions
can be written as if it were a query against a conventional table with the
addition or one or two predicates to the WHERE clause of the query; and (ii) a
query for data current in both its temporal dimensions can be written as a
conventional query against a view generated from a temporal table.
*Semantics:* the ability to express most temporal query criteria with simple
predicates added to the WHERE clause of an otherwise conventional query.
*Comments:*
- Query encapsulation means that queries against asserted version tables are
simple enough that anyone who could write them against non-temporal
tables could also write them against these tables. (From the Preface.)
*Components:* conventional table, temporal dimension, temporal table.

**queryable object**
*Semantics:* a managed object that can be named in a SQL query.
*Components:* managed object.

**referent**
*Mechanics:* the persistent object identified by the object identifier of a row in an
asserted version table.
*Semantics:* whatever is referred to and described by a managed object.
*Components:* asserted version table, managed object, object identifier, persistent
object.

**reliable business key**

*Mechanics:* a business key which can be used to match data on a temporal transaction to one or more rows in the target table for that transaction.

*Semantics:* a business key which represents one and only one object.

*Components:* business key, object, represent, target table, temporal transaction.

**replace**

*Mechanics:* a row X replaces a row Y if and only if X and Y both represent the same object, X's effective time period [*equals*] Y's effective time period, X's business data is identical to Y's business data, and X's assertion time period [*finishes*] Y's assertion time period.

*Semantics:* a row X replaces a row Y if and only if X and Y both represent the same object, and X is a business-data identical assertion about what Y is like during the effective time period specified by Y.

*Comments:*

- See also: *withdraw, supercede.*
- A row X replaces a row Y if and only if X says the same thing about what the object Y represents is like, during the effective time period specified by Y.
- If a superceding version was also created as part of the temporal update transaction which created a replacement version, then this replacement version will [meet] that superceding version in effective time, while having an [*equal*] assertion time.
- A temporal update transaction whose effective time period [*intersects*] that of a target version, but does not [*equal*] it, requires the AVF to withdraw the target version and then to split that target version into one version that matches the transaction, and one (or two) versions that do not. This is done with the *f*CUT function. The resulting version or versions that do not match the transaction are replacements, with identical business data. The one version that does match the transaction is updated with the new business data, and supercedes the corresponding effective timespan of the withdrawn version.

*Components:* version, assertion, effective time, match, withdraw, supercede, temporal.

**represent**

*Mechanics:* a managed object represents an object in a series of one or more clock ticks if and only if those clock ticks are all included within the time period of that managed object.

*Comments:*

- See also: *occupy.*

*Components:* managed object, clock tick, object, time period.

**re-present**

*Description:* we use the hyphenated form "re-present" advisedly. We do mean that we will show how to *represent* those internalized datasets as queryable objects, in the ordinary sense of the word "represent". But we also wish to emphasize that we are re-presenting, i.e. presenting again, things whose presence we have removed.[2] Those things are the external pipeline datasets

---

[2]We also wish to avoid confusion with our technical term *represent*, in which business data, we say, is represented in an effective time clock tick within an assertion time clock tick just in case that business data exists on an asserted version row whose assertion and effective time periods contain those clock tick pairs.

which, in Chapter 12, we showed how to *internalize* within the production tables which are their destinations or points of origin. (From Chapter 13.)

## retroactive delete

*Mechanics:* a temporal delete transaction that specifies an effective begin date that is earlier than Now().

*Semantics:* a temporal delete transaction that removes the representation of an object from one or more clock ticks in past effective time.

*Comments:*

- In a conventional table, the only mistake in data that can be corrected is a mistake in data values, and the correction is done "destructively", by overwriting the old data.
- But in an asserted version table, there are two other mistakes in data. One is to mistakenly claim that an object was represented during a past effective time period. The other is to mistakenly claim that an object was not represented during a past effective time period. A retroactive delete transaction is the means by which the former mistake is corrected. A retroactive insert transaction is the means by which the latter mistake is corrected.

*Components:* clock tick, effective begin date, Now(), object, represent, past version, temporal transaction.

## retroactive insert

*Mechanics:* a temporal insert transaction that specifies an effective begin date that is earlier than Now().

*Semantics:* a temporal insert transaction that adds the representation of an object to one or more clock ticks in past effective time.

*Comments:*

- See also: *retroactive delete.*

*Components:* clock tick, effective begin date, Now(), object, represent, past version, temporal transaction.

## retroactive transaction

*Mechanics:* a temporal transaction that specifies an effective begin date that is earlier than Now().

*Semantics:* a temporal transaction which alters the effective-time past.

*Comments:*

- See also: *proactive transaction.*

*Components:* temporal transaction, effective begin date.

## retroactive update

*Mechanics:* a temporal update transaction that specifies an effective begin date that is earlier than Now().

*Semantics:* a temporal update transaction that changes the business data representing an object in one or more clock ticks in past effective time.

*Components:* business data, clock tick, effective time, object, represent, temporal transaction.

## retrograde movement

*Mechanics:* changing the assertion begin date on a deferred assertion to an earlier date.

*Semantics:* the movement of a deferred assertion from far future to near future assertion time.

*Components:* assertion begin date, deferred assertion, far future assertion time, near future assertion time.

**row create date**
*Mechanics:* the date on which a row in an asserted version table is physically inserted into that table.
*Comments:*
- The means by which a physical logfile can be re-presented as a queryable object.

**row-level homonym**
*Mechanics:* a row whose business key identifies two or more different objects.
*Semantics:* a row which represents two or more different objects.
*Comments:*
- A row-level homonym is eliminated by replacing it with multiple rows, one for each object represented by the row. For example, a row in a Client table which has been updated with data representing two or more different clients, is a homonym.
- See also: *de-dupped, dirty data, row-level synonym.*

*Components:* business key, object.

**row-level synonym**
*Mechanics:* two or more rows which cannot be distinguished by means of their business keys.
*Semantics:* two or more rows which represent the same object or, in a temporal context, represent the same object in at least one clock tick.
*Comments:*
- Row-level synonyms are eliminated by replacing them with one row that represents the one object that each of the synonym's references. For example, multiple rows in a Client table which are discovered to represent the same client, are synonyms.
- See also: *de-dupped, dirty data, row-level homonym.*

*Components:* business key, clock tick, object.

**seamless access**
*Description:* the ability, in a query, to assemble result sets containing rows which exist in past, present or future time, in either or both of the two temporal dimensions, from the same set of tables that would be specified if the query were to retrieve current data only.

**seamless access, performance aspect**
*Description:* query performance against asserted version tables whose rows represent both non-current and current states of persistent objects must be nearly as good as query performance against non-temporal tables with an equivalent number of rows.
*Comments:*
- Queries which return temporal data, or a mix of temporal and current data, must return equivalent-sized results in an equivalent amount of elapsed time. Chapter 15 discusses the performance issues involved in using asserted version tables.
- Differences in maintenance performance will be greater than differences in query performance because one logical unit of work—the insertion, update or deletion of business data about one object—will affect only one row in a conventional table, but one update or deletion to an asserted version table will usually physically insert several rows.

**seamless access, usability aspect**
*Description:* access to both current and non-current states of persistent objects which is just as easy for the data consumer to obtain as is access to only current states.

*Comments:*
- Increasingly, temporal data must be available on-line, just as current data is. Transactions to maintain temporal data must be as easy to write as are transactions to maintain current data. Queries to retrieve temporal data, or a combination of temporal and current data, must be as easy to write as are queries to retrieve current data only. (From Chapter 1.)

## semantic logfile
*Semantics:* the set of all past assertions and empty assertions in an asserted version table.
*Comments:*
- See also: *physical logfile.*
- The contents of a physical logfile of a particular table, as of point in time X, are all those rows physically present in the table as of that point in time. The contents of a semantic logfile of that table, as of that point in time, are all those rows asserted on or prior to that point in time. The difference is the set of all assertions which are deferred assertions as of that point in time.
*Components:* asserted version table, assertion, empty assertion.

## shared assertion time
*Mechanics:* the shared assertion time of two or more versions are all those assertion time clock ticks that include both their assertion time periods.
*Semantics:* the shared assertion time of two or more versions is the assertion time period within which they are commensurable.
*Components:* assertion time, assertion time period, clock tick, (in) commensurable, version.

## state
*Semantics:* the set of values in the business data columns of a row in an asserted version table which describes the properties and/or relationships which the object represented by that row has at a point in time or over a period of time.
*Components:* asserted version table, business data, object, point in time, represent, time period.

## statement
*Mechanics:* what is said to be the case by a currently asserted row in an asserted version table.
*Semantics:* what is asserted, during a specified period of current assertion time, is true of a referenced object during a specified period of effective time.
*Comments:*
- In Asserted Versioning, a row in past assertion time is a record of a statement we once made, and a row in future assertion time is a record of a statement that we may make at some point in the future. Neither are statements because neither have truth values.
*Components:* asserted version table, assertion, assertion time period, currently asserted, effective time period, object, referent.

## successor
*Mechanics:* a row in an asserted version table that supercedes all or part of another row.

## supercede
*Mechanics:* a row X supercedes a row Y if and only if X and Y both represent the same object, X's effective time period [*intersects*] Y's effective time period, X's

business data is not identical to Y's business data, and X's assertion time period [finishes] Y's assertion time period.

*Semantics:* a row X supercedes a row Y if and only if X and Y both represent the same object, and X is a business-data different assertion about what Y is like during all of part of the effective time period specified by Y.

*Comments:*
- See also: *withdraw, replace.*
- A row X supercedes a row Y if and only if X says something new about what the object Y represents is like, during all or part of the effective time period specified by Y.
- If either one or two replacement versions were also created as part of the temporal update transaction which created this superceding version, then this superceding version will [meet] the earlier replacement version, and [meet$^{-1}$] the later replacement version in effective time.

*Components:* Allen relationship [intersect], Allen relationship [meets, meets$^{-1}$], assertion time period, business data, effective time period, object, represent.

### tabular data

*Mechanics:* a collection of data structured as rows and columns.

*Semantics:* a collection of data in which the collection itself represents a type of object, and whose contents represent one or more properties and/or relationships of one or more instances of that type.

*Comments:*
- Besides DBMS tables, files and their records are tabular data, as are the rows and columns in spreadsheets.

*Components:* instance, object, type.

### target episode

*Mechanics:* an episode that a temporal transaction will create, delete or modify.

*Comments:*
- There can be more than one target episode for a temporal update or delete. A temporal insert can insert only one episode.

*Components:* episode, temporal transaction.

### target row

*Mechanics:* a row in an asserted version table that a temporal transaction will create, delete or modify.

*Comments:*
- There can be more than one target row for a temporal update or delete. A temporal insert can insert only one row.

*Components:* asserted version table, temporal transaction.

### target span

*Mechanics:* the effective time period specified on a temporal transaction.

*Semantics:* the time period into which a temporal insert transaction will place a representation of an object, within which a temporal update transaction will modify existing representations of an object, or from which a temporal delete transaction will remove the representation of an object.

*Components:* effective time period, object, represent, time period, temporal delete transaction, temporal insert transaction, temporal transaction, temporal update transaction.

### target table

*Mechanics:* the table specified on a temporal transaction.

*Comments:*
- Temporal transactions have one and only one target table, even though temporal delete transactions can modify multiple tables.

*Components:* temporal transaction.

## taxonomy

*Mechanics:* an acyclic hierarchy, in which each child node is a KIND-OF its parent node, and in which the collection of child nodes under a common parent are jointly exhaustive and mutually exclusive. (From Chapter 2.)

*Semantics:* a partitioned semantic hierarchy.

*Comments:*
- We leave KIND-OF as formally undefined, i.e. as part of our controlled vocabulary of primitive terms. When X is a KIND-OF Y, it follows that every instance of X is also an instance of Y, and that this is so because of what "X" and "Y" mean.

*Components:* N/A.

## TEI

See *temporal entity integrity.*

## temporal container

*Description:* a spatial metaphor for the relationship of data to a time period, or for the relationship of assertion time to effective time.

## temporal data

*Semantics:* data about the past, present and future states of objects, and/or about our past, present and future assertions that what that data says is true.

*Comments:*
- See also: *explicitly temporal data, implicitly temporal data.*

*Components:* assertion, object, state.

## temporal data management taxonomy

*Description:* a taxonomy of methods for managing temporal data, developed by the authors and presented in Chapter 2.

## temporal data management taxonomy, (bi-temporal data)

*Description:* any method of managing state temporal data in two temporal dimensions.

*Components:* temporal data management taxonomy (state temporal data), temporal dimension.

## temporal data management taxonomy, (event temporal data)

*Description:* any method of managing queryable temporal data that keeps track of changes to an object by recording the initial state of an object, and then by keeping a history of the events in which the object changed. (From Chapter 2.)

*Comments:*
- An event, once completed, cannot change. If data describing an event needs to be altered, it is because the data is incorrect, not because the event changed.

*Components:* event, object, state, temporal data management taxonomy (queryable temporal data), temporal dimension.

**temporal data management taxonomy, (queryable temporal data)**
*Mechanics:* any method of managing temporal data that does not require manipulation of the data before it can be queried. (From Chapter 2.)
*Components:* temporal data.

**temporal data management taxonomy, (reconstructable temporal data)**
*Description:* any method of managing temporal data that requires manipulation of the data before it can be queried. (From Chapter 2.)
*Components:* temporal data.

**temporal data management taxonomy, (state temporal data)**
*Description:* any method of managing queryable temporal data that keeps track of the states of things as they change over time.
*Comments:*
  • As an object changes from one state to the next, we store the before-image of the current state, and update a copy of that state, not the original. The update becomes the new current state of the object.
  • When managing time using state data, what we record are not transactions, but rather the *results* of transactions, the rows resulting from inserts and (logical) deletes, and the rows representing both a before- and an after-image of every update. (From Chapter 2.)
*Components:* state, temporal data management taxonomy (queryable temporal data).

**temporal data management taxonomy, (temporal data best practices)**
*Description:* as described in Chapter 4, best practices in managing temporal data concern themselves with versioning, i.e. with keeping track of the changes to objects of interest by recording the states which those objects pass through as they change.
*Components:* object, state, temporal data, versioning.

**temporal data management taxonomy, (temporal data management)**
*Description:* any method of managing temporal data, at the table and row level, by means of explicit temporal schemas and constraints on the instances of those schemas.
*Comments:*
  • Thus, for example, data warehouses and data marts are not part of this taxonomy because they are methods of managing temporal data at the database level.
*Components:* temporal data.

**temporal data management taxonomy, (the alternative temporal model)**
*Description:* a method of managing uni-temporal versioned tables at the column as well as at the row level, using transformations not specifiable with current SQL, that are based on various composition and decomposition operations defined in other publications by Dr. Nikos Lorentzos.
*Comments:*
  • The temporal model described by C. J. Date, Hugh Darwen and Nikos Lorentzos in their book *Temporal Data and the Relational Model*. (Morgan-Kaufmann, 2002).
*Components:* uni-temporal, versioned table.

**temporal data management taxonomy, (the Asserted Versioning temporal model)**

*Description:* a method of managing bi-temporal data, using transformations specifiable with current SQL, that manages each row in a temporal table as the assertion of a version of an episode of an object.

*Comments:*
- The temporal model described in this book.
- Distinguished from the alternative temporal model in particular (i) in all the ways it is distinguished from the standard temporal model, and also (ii) by its recognition and treatment of assertion tables and bi-temporal tables and (iii) its decision to not manage temporal data at the column level.
- Distinguished from the standard temporal model in particular by providing design and maintenance encapsulation, managing data located in future assertion time, its reliance on episodes as managed objects, and its internalization of adjunct datasets.

*Components:* assertion, episode, object, temporal data management taxonomy (bi-temporal data), temporal table, version.

**temporal data management taxonomy, (the standard temporal model)**

*Description:* a method of managing bi-temporal data, using transformations specifiable with SQL available in 2000, that manages each row in a temporal table as a row in a conventional table which has been assigned a transaction time period, a valid time period, or both.

*Comments:*
- The temporal model described by Dr. Rick Snodgrass in his book *Developing Time-Oriented Database Applications in SQL* (Morgan-Kaufmann, 2000).

*Components:* conventional table, temporal data management taxonomy (bi-temporal data), temporal table, transaction time, valid time.

**temporal data management taxonomy, (uni-temporal data)**

*Description:* any method of managing state temporal data in a single temporal dimension.

*Comments:*
- Thus versioning, in any of its forms, is a method of managing uni-temporal data.

*Components:* temporal data management taxonomy (state temporal data), temporal dimension.

**temporal database**

*Mechanics:* a database that contains at least one table whose rows include one or more columns representing an assertion and/or effective time period.

*Semantics:* a database at least one of whose tables is explicitly temporal.

*Components:* assertion time period, effective time period.

**temporal date**

*Mechanics:* a date which is either a begin date or an end date.

*Semantics:* a date which delimits a bi-temporal time period.

*Components:* begin date, end date, temporal, time period.

**temporal default values**

*Mechanics:* the values for the assertion time period and effective time period which the AVF assigns to a temporal transaction unless those values are specified on the transaction itself.

*Comments:*
- Those values are Now() for the assertion and effective begin dates, and 9999 for the assertion and effective end dates.

*Components:* assertion time period, AVF, effective time period, temporal transaction.

### temporal delete cascade

*Mechanics:* a temporal delete transaction which removes all dependent child data from the transaction timespan specified on the temporal delete transaction.

*Comments:*
- a temporal delete cascade will attempt to remove both the parent managed object, and all its dependent children, from the clock ticks specified in the transaction. (From Chapter 11.)

*Components:* temporal delete transaction, transaction timespan.

### temporal delete transaction

*Mechanics:* a temporal transaction against an asserted version table which removes business data representing an object from one or more contiguous or non-contiguous effective-time clock ticks.

*Comments:*
- A temporal delete is like a temporal update except that it specifies that every version or part of a version of the designated managed object that falls, wholly or partially, within that target span will be, in current assertion time, removed from that target effective timespan. (From Chapter 9.)
- A temporal delete withdraws its target object from one or more effective time clock ticks. In the process, it may {withdraw} an entire version from current assertion time, or {split} a version in two, or {shorten} a version either forwards or backwards, or do several of these things to one or more versions with one and the same transaction.

*Components:* asserted version table, business data, effective time, object, represent, temporal transaction.

### temporal dimension

*Semantics:* a type of time within which points in time and/or periods of time are ordered.

*Components:* type, point in time, time period.

### temporal entity integrity

*Mechanics:* (i) for episodes, the constraint that no two episodes of the same object, in the same period of assertion time, either [meet] or [intersect]; (ii) for versions within an episode, the constraint that each effective-time adjacent pair of versions [meet] but do not [intersect].

*Semantics:* the constraint that, in any clock tick of assertion time, no clock tick of effective time is occupied by more than one representation of an object.

*Comments:*
- One of the two constraints by means of which Asserted Versioning expresses the semantics of bi-temporal data.

*Components:* Allen relationship [meet], Allen relationship [*intersect*], assertion time, episode, object, temporally adjacent, version.

### temporal extent

*Semantics:* the number of clock ticks in a time period.

*Components:* clock tick, time period.

**temporal extent state transformation**

*Mechanics:* a transformation to an asserted version table in which, within a given period of assertion time, the number of effective-time clock ticks which a given episode occupies is increased or decreased.

*Semantics:* a transformation altering the temporal extent of an episode's effective time period, within a given period of assertion time.

*Comments:*

- In the definitions of the temporal extent state transformations, the phrase "in a given period of assertion time" will be present implicitly.

*Components:* asserted version table, assertion time, clock tick, effective time, episode, occupied.

**temporal extent state transformation taxonomy**

*Description:* a taxonomy of additions to or deletions from the set of clock ticks which contain a representation of an object in an asserted version table, developed by the authors and presented in Chapter 9.

**temporal extent state transformation taxonomy, {create}**

*Mechanics:* the temporal extent state transformation that adds the representation of an object to an effective time period that is either [before] or [before$^{-1}$] the effective time period of any episode of that object already present in the table.

*Semantics:* the temporal extent state transformation that adds a new episode to an asserted version table.

*Components:* asserted version table, effective time, episode, object, represent.

**temporal extent state transformation taxonomy, {delete}**

*Mechanics:* the temporal extent state transformation that, in a given period of assertion time, removes the representation of an object from an effective time period that is either [before] or [before$^{-1}$] all other representations of that same object.

*Semantics:* the temporal extent state transformation that removes an entire episode from current assertion time.

*Components:* Allen relationship taxonomy [before], Allen relationship taxonomy [before$^{-1}$], assertion time, effective time, object, represent.

**temporal extent state transformation taxonomy, {lengthen backwards}**

*Mechanics:* the temporal extent state transformation that adds the representation of an object to an effective time period that [meets] the effective time period of an episode of that object already present in the table.

*Semantics:* the temporal extent state transformation that expands the effective time period of an episode into a contiguous, earlier time period.

*Components:* Allen relationship [meets], effective time period, episode, object, representation.

**temporal extent state transformation taxonomy, {lengthen forwards}**

*Mechanics:* the temporal extent state transformation that adds the representation of an object to an effective time period that [meets$^{-1}$] the effective time period of an episode of that object already present in the table.

*Semantics:* the temporal extent state transformation that expands the effective time period of an episode into a contiguous, later time period.

*Components:* Allen relationship [meets$^{-1}$], effective time period, episode, object, representation.

**temporal extent state transformation taxonomy, {lengthen}**
*Mechanics:* those temporal extent state transformations that increase the number of clock ticks within the effective time period of an episode.
*Semantics:* the temporal extent state transformation that enlarges the effective time period of an episode.
*Components:* clock tick, effective time period, episode, object.

**temporal extent state transformation taxonomy, {merge}**
*Mechanics:* the temporal extent state transformation that adds the representation of an object to an effective time period that [meets$^{-1}$] the effective time period of an earlier episode of that object, and that also [meets] the effective time period of a later episode of that object.
*Semantics:* the temporal extent state transformation that transforms two adjacent episodes of the same object into one episode.
*Components:* effective time period, episode, Allen relationship [meets], Allen relationship [meets$^{-1}$], object, representation, temporally adjacent.

**temporal extent state transformation taxonomy, {modify}**
*Mechanics:* those temporal extent state transformations that increase or decrease the number of clock ticks occupied by an object, but that neither increase nor decrease the number of episodes that represent that object.
*Semantics:* those temporal extent state transformations that add or remove clock ticks from one or more episodes.
*Components:* clock tick, episode, object, represent.

**temporal extent state transformation taxonomy, {shorten backwards}**
*Mechanics:* the temporal extent state transformation that removes the representation of an object from one or more contiguous clock ticks that were the latest clock ticks of an episode of that object.
*Semantics:* the temporal extent state transformation that removes the effective time period of an episode from a later time period.
*Components:* clock tick, contiguous, effective time, episode, object, representation.

**temporal extent state transformation taxonomy, {shorten forwards}**
*Mechanics:* the temporal extent state transformation that removes the representation of an object from one or more contiguous clock ticks that were the earliest clock ticks of an episode of that object.
*Semantics:* the temporal extent state transformation that removes the effective time period of an episode from an earlier time period.
*Components:* clock tick, effective time, episode, object, representation.

**temporal extent state transformation taxonomy, {shorten}**
*Mechanics:* those temporal extent state transformations that reduce the number of clock ticks within the effective time period of an episode of that object.
*Semantics:* the temporal extent state transformation that reduces the effective time period of an episode.
*Components:* clock tick, effective time period, episode, object.

**temporal extent state transformation taxonomy, {split}**
*Mechanics:* the temporal extent state transformation that removes the representation of an object from one or more contiguous clock ticks that were neither the earliest nor the latest clock ticks of an episode of that object already present in the table.
*Semantics:* the temporal extent state transformation that transforms one episode into two adjacent episodes of the same object.
*Components:* clock tick, contiguous, episode, object, representation, temporally adjacent.

**temporal foreign key**
*Mechanics:* a non-primary key column of an asserted version table which contains the unique identifier of the object on which the object represented by each of its own rows in an asserted version table is existence dependent.
*Semantics:* a column which designates an object on which the object represented by the row which contains it is existence dependent.
*Comments:*
- At the schema level, a temporal foreign key points from one table to a table it is dependent on. But at the row level, it points from one row, which is a version, to a group of one or more rows which make up an episode of the object whose *oid* matches the oid value in that temporal foreign key.
- At the instance level, temporal referential integrity guarantees that, for every temporal foreign key, there is an episode of the designated object in the referenced table, and that the effective time period of that episode in the referenced table includes ([fills$^{-1}$]) the effective time period of the version which contains the referring temporal foreign key. (From Chapter 6.)
- Temporal foreign keys, like conventional foreign keys, are the managed object construct which represents the existence dependency of a child object on a parent object.
*Components:* asserted version table, existence dependency, object, object identifier, represent.

**temporal gap**
*Mechanics:* the existence of at least one unoccupied effective-time clock tick between two time periods for the same object.
*Components:* clock tick, effective time, object, occupy, time period.

**temporal gap versioning**
*Mechanics:* a form of versioning similar to logical delete versioning, but in which both a version begin date and a version end date are used to delimit the time period of the version.
*Semantics:* a form of versioning in which versions of the same object may or may not be contiguous, and in which no version is physically deleted.
*Comments:*
- Temporal gap versioning is not part of Asserted Versioning. See Chapter 4.
- See also: *basic versioning, logical delete versioning, effective time versioning.*
*Components:* contiguous, logical delete versioning, object, time period, version, version begin date, version end date.

**temporal insert**
*Mechanics:* a temporal transaction against an asserted version table which creates a single-row episode of the object specified in the transaction.

*Semantics:* a temporal transaction against an asserted version table which places business data representing an object into an effective time period that is not contiguous with any other clock ticks in which the same object is represented.

*Comments:*

- A temporal insert adds a representation of its specified object to a series of one or more contiguous effective time clock ticks. In the process, it may {create} an entire single-episode version, or {merge} two adjacent episodes, or {lengthen} an episode either forwards or backwards.

*Components:* asserted version table, business data, clock tick, contiguous, effective time period, episode, object, represent, temporal transaction, temporally adjacent.

**temporal parameter**

*Mechanics:* one of the three asserted versioning dates that can be specified on a temporal transaction, those being the effective begin date, the effective end date and the assertion begin date.

*Semantics:* the means by which an assertion time period and an effective time period are defined on a temporal transaction.

*Components:* assertion begin date, assertion time period, effective begin date, effective end date, temporal transaction.

**temporal primary key**

*Mechanics:* the unique identifier of a row in an asserted version table, made up of (i) an object identifier (oid), (ii) an effective begin date, and (iii) an assertion begin date.

*Semantics:* the unique identifier of a row in a bi-temporal table, made up of (i) the unique identifier of a persistent object, (ii) a unique designation of an effective time period, and (iii) a unique designation of an assertion time period.

*Components:* asserted version table, bi-temporal, effective begin date, effective time period, assertion begin date, assertion time period, object identifier, oid, persistent object.

**temporal referential integrity**

*Mechanics:* the constraint that for every version which contains a temporal foreign key, there is an episode of the object which that temporal foreign key references such that, within shared assertion time, the effective time period of that episode includes ([fills$^{-1}$]) the effective time period of that version.

*Semantics:* the constraint that, in any clock tick of assertion time, every clock tick that is occupied by a representation of a child object is also occupied by one representation of each of its parent objects.

*Comments:*

- A temporal referential integrity relationship between a child managed object and a parent managed object is based on an existence dependency between the objects which those managed objects represent. (From Chapter 11.)

*Components:* Allen relationship [fills$^{-1}$], asserted version table, assertion time, child object, clock tick, effective time period, episode, include, object, occupy, parent object, reference, shared assertion time, temporal foreign key.

**temporal tag**

*Description:* a metaphor for the association of a row of data with a time period. The time period is a temporal tag applied to the row.

**temporal transaction**

*Mechanics:* an insert, update or delete transaction whose target is an asserted version table.

*Semantics:* an insertion, update or deletion of a temporally delimited assertion of a statement describing an object as it exists during a specified period of effective time.

*Components:* asserted version table, assertion, effective time period, object, statement, target table.

**temporal update**

*Mechanics:* a temporal transaction against an asserted version table which modifies business data representing an object in one or more contiguous or non-contiguous effective-time clock ticks.

*Semantics:* a temporal transaction against an asserted version table which changes one or more business data items describing that object in one or more clock ticks included in the transaction's specified period of effective time.

*Comments:*

- Note that a temporal update will change the business data for an object in occupied clock ticks, and will ignore unoccupied clock ticks. Thus the clock ticks that a temporal update affects are not necessarily contiguous clock ticks. And consequently, to be valid, it is not necessary that all clock ticks in the effective-time range of a temporal update be occupied by the specified object. It is only necessary that at least one of them be occupied.

*Components:* asserted version table, business data, clock tick, contiguous, effective time period, object, represent, temporal transaction.

**temporalize**

*Mechanics:* to temporalize a managed object is to associate an explicit assertion time period and/or an explicit effective time period with it.

*Components:* assertion time period, effective time period, managed object.

**temporalized extension of the Closed World Assumption**

*Mechanics:* the constraint that a temporal transaction cannot insert data into past assertion time, update data in past assertion time, or delete data from past assertion time.

*Semantics:* the assumption that if a statement was not represented in the database at time $T_1$, then at time $T_1$ we did not make that statement.

*Comments:*

- Note, by contrast, that a temporal transaction can insert data into past effective time, update data in past effective time, and delete data from past effective time.
- In Chapter 12, we explained the reason that we can modify the statement content of past effective time but not of past assertion time. We said: ". . . . . a belief is expressed by the presence of a row in a table. No row, no belief. So if we write a transaction today that creates a row stating that we believed something yesterday, we are creating a row that states that we believed something at a time when there was no row to represent that

belief. . . . . . (But) it would be a logical contradiction to state that we had such a belief at a point or period in time during which there was no row to represent that belief."

*Components:* past assertion time, statement, temporal transaction.

### temporally adjacent

*Mechanics:* two rows in an asserted version table are temporally adjacent if and only if they have the same object identifier and, in shared assertion time, have no other rows with the same object identifier whose effective time period is later than that of the earlier row and earlier than that of the later row.

*Semantics:* temporally adjacent rows are rows representing the same object that, in shared assertion time, have no rows representing that same object between them in effective time.

*Comments:*
- If two rows in an asserted version table are adjacent, then either one is [before] the other, or one [meets] the other. This is because they would otherwise violate the temporal entity integrity constraint, which the AVF prevents.
- If one row in an asserted version table is adjacent to and [before] the other, then they belong to different episodes.
- If one row in an asserted version is adjacent to and [meets] the other, then they belong to the same episode.

*Components:* asserted version table, effective time period, object, object identifier, represent, shared assertion time.

### temporally contiguous

*Mechanics:* two time periods occupied by the same object are temporally contiguous just in case they [meet], i.e. they share no clock ticks and there are no clock ticks between them.

*Components:* Allen Relationship [meet], clock tick, object, occupy, time period.

### temporally delimited

*Semantics:* to be restricted to a time period.

*Comments:*
- A temporal transaction is temporally delimited to its effective time period within its assertion time period.
- Note that these time periods can, and often do, remain current until further notice, i.e. that they can, and often do, end in 9999.

*Components:* time period.

### terminate

*Mechanics:* to withdraw the latest version of an episode and replace it with a version identical to it except that it has as an effective end date the date specified on a temporal delete transaction.

*Semantics:* to set an effective end date for an episode.

*Comments:*
- The termination of an episode {withdraws} that episode from some but not all of the effective-time clock ticks which it occupies.
- The termination of an episode should be thought of as the by-product of a temporal delete transaction, not as that transaction's semantic objective. The semantic objective of a temporal delete transaction is to remove the representation of an object from all clock ticks within the effective timespan specified on the transaction. If that effective timespan

on the delete transaction includes the entire episode, then we say that the episode has been deleted, not that it has been terminated.

*Components:* effective end date, episode, replace, temporal delete transaction, version, withdraw.

**TFK**

See *temporal foreign key.*

**thing**

*Semantics:* things are what exist through time, and can change over time. (From Chapter 2.)

*Comments:*
- See also: *object, event.*

**time period**

*Mechanics:* a continuous length of either effective or assertion time, with a known begin date.

*Semantics:* a series of one or more contiguous clock ticks in either effective or assertion time, whose initial clock tick has a known value.

*Comments:*
- If the end date of a time period is not known, 9999 is used as the end date. Because of its interpretation as a valid date by the DBMS, the effective semantics is "until further notice".

*Components:* assertion time, begin date, contiguous, clock tick, effective time.

**timeslice**

*Mechanics:* an object as it exists during a specified closed effective time period.

*Semantics:* a closed effective period of time of an object.

*Comments:*
- A timeslice of an object represented in an asserted version table does not have to align on episode or version boundaries. It is just a continuous period of time in the life history of an object (or in the projection of that life history into the future).

*Components:* closed effective time, object.

**timespan**

*Mechanics:* the period of time specified on a temporal transaction.

**transaction**

*Mechanics:* (i) a row in a transaction table; or (ii) an insert, update or delete to a database.

*Semantics:* (i) data which is the record of an event; or (ii) the transformation of database.

*Comments:*
- The first sense designates a row of data that represents an event. For example, a customer purchase is an event, represented by a row in a sales table; the receipt of a shipment is an event, represented by a row in a receipts table. In this sense, transactions are what are collected in the fact tables of fact-dimension data marts.
- The second sense designates any insert, update or delete applied to a database. For example, it is an insert transaction that creates a new customer record, an update transaction that changes a customer's name, and a delete transaction that removes a customer from the database. (From Chapter 2.)

- (In any formalization of this Glossary, of course, this homonym would have to be resolved. In this book, we rely on context to do so.)

*Components:* event.

### transaction begin date

*Mechanics:* in the standard temporal model, the date a row is physically inserted into a table.

*Semantics:* in the standard temporal model, the date which designates the start of the transaction time period of a row, using the closed-open convention.

*Comments:*
- Another one of the several homonyms of "transaction".

*Components:* closed-open, temporal data management taxonomy {the standard temporal model}, transaction time period.

### transaction table

*Semantics:* a table whose rows represent events.

*Comments:*
- Transaction tables record the *events* that change the states of objects and, in particular, the relationships among them. (From Chapter 1.)
- Transaction tables are often used as the fact tables in fact-dimension data marts.
- There can be only one version of an event, since events do not persist and change over time. Multiple rows for the same event can only be multiple assertions about that event, presumably a series of corrections to the data.

*Components:* events.

### transaction time

*Description:* "A database fact is stored in a database at some point in time, and after it is stored, it may be retrieved. The transaction time of a database fact is the time when the fact is stored in the database. Transaction times are consistent with the serialization order of the transactions. Transaction time values cannot be after the current time. Also, as it is impossible to change the past, transaction times cannot be changed. Transaction times may be implemented using transaction commit times." From [Jensen, 1992].

*Comments:*
- As defined by Jensen, the computer science term "transaction time" may be treated as co-extensive with our term "row creation date". But the two terms cannot be said to be *synonymous* because they are defined by means of two vocabularies between which semantic correlations have not been established. Also, while Jensen's definition, given here, indicates that transaction time is a point in time, Snodgrass's use of the term, in [Snodgrass, 2000] has it referring to a period of time, usually open-ended, but not necessarily so. In this second sense, the term is co-extensive with a proper subset of our term "assertion time period".

### transaction time period

*Mechanics:* the assertion and effective time periods specified on a temporal transaction.

*Semantics:* the set of assertion time and effective time clock ticks outside of which a temporal transaction will have no effect on the database.

*Comments:*
- In this entry, "transaction" refers to "temporal transaction", not to any of the other homonyms of "transaction".

*Components:* assertion time period, clock tick, effective time period, temporal transaction.

**transaction timespan**

See *transaction time period.*

**TRI**

See *temporal referential integrity.*

**TSQL2**

*Description:* a temporal extension to the SQL-92 language standard, by Dr. Rick Snodgrass and others, first published in March 1994 in the *ACM SIGMOD Record.* A final version was published the following September.

*Comments:*
- This standard has not been adopted by the SQL standards committee.

**type**

*Semantics:* a kind of thing.

*Comments:*
- See also: *instance.*
- In a database, tables represent types of things, and rows represent instances of those types.

*Components:* thing.

**uni-temporal data**

*Mechanics:* data which has either an assertion time period or an effective time period, but not both.

*Semantics:* data which has one and only one explicitly expressed time period.

*Comments:*
- We say "explicitly expressed" to emphasize that all data is bi-temporal. In a conventional table, in which no assertion and/or effective time period columns are included, each row is nonetheless bi-temporal. Each row is a current assertion about what the object it represents is currently like. As a claim that its object exists, each row's assertion and effective time periods are co-extensive with the row's physical presence in its table.

*Components:* assertion time period, effective time period, time period.

**uni-temporal table**

*Mechanics:* a uni-temporal assertion table or a uni-temporal version table.

*Semantics:* a table with a single explicitly expressed temporal dimension.

*Comments:*
- Uni-temporal version tables are common in business databases; Chapter 4 describes their major variants. But see *update in place* for a common misuse of this kind of table.
- Uni-temporal assertion tables are single-table logfiles. They are usually described as the history table companions to conventional tables. However, history tables are often designed with a primary key which is the same as the primary key of the table whose changes they track, but with the addition of a low-order date (or timestamp) to that primary key. In general, history tables like this are not semantically complete uni-temporal assertion tables, being unable, for example, to distinguish entries which represent a delete from those which represent an update.

*Components:* assertion, uni-temporal, temporal dimension, version.

**unreliable business key**

*Mechanics:* a business key which cannot be used to match data on a temporal transaction to one or more rows in the target table for that transaction.

*Semantics:* a business key which may represent more than one object.

*Comments:*

- The distinction between reliable and unreliable business keys can be seen at work in the description of the match logic for Asserted Versioning's temporal transactions, in Chapter 9.

*Components:* business key, object, represent, target table, temporal transaction.

**until further notice**

*Mechanics:* an assertion time period or an effective time period whose end date is 9999 (the highest temporal value the DBMS can represent).

*Semantics:* an assertion time period or an effective time period whose end date is unknown, but which is interpreted to be in the future.

*Comments:*

- In general, this term means "unknown but presumed valid". In a SQL Server asserted version table, a row is asserted until further notice if and only if its assertion end date is 12/31/9999, and is in effect until further notice if and only if its effective end date is 12/31/9999.
- Mechanically, a time period with a begin date in the past, and that is presumed to be current until further notice, will be interpreted by the DBMS in that way because in any query, Now() will *always* be greater than that begin date and less than that end date.
- Neither 12/31/9999, nor any other DBMS representation of 9999, is valid as an assertion begin date or effective begin date.
- If 12/31/9999 (or any other DBMS representation of 9999) is used in a business data column, of course, it has whatever semantics the business chooses to give to it.

*Components:* 9999, assertion time period, effective time period, end date.

**update in place**

*Mechanics:* to update data on a row by overwriting it.

*Comments:*

- In a conventional table, all updates are updates in place, and therefore all updates destroy historical information. An update which reflects a change in the object represented by a row of data has the effect of replacing a current version with a new current version, thus destroying effective-time history. An update which reflects a correction to a mistake made in the data has the effect of replacing a current assertion with a new current assertion, thus destroying assertion-time history.
- And so, in a uni-temporal table, either one or the other of those two types of updates must be done as an update in place, thus destroying one or the other of those two kinds of history, or else the two kinds of updates are not distinguished and both result in the creation of a new row of data. But this second way of managing uni-temporal tables makes it impossible to distinguish true versions, i.e. rows which are part of the effective-time history of an object, from corrections to bad data. All too frequently, in business databases, this second way of managing uni-temporal tables is called versioning, and the rows in those tables are called versions. Interpreted in this way, these tables are themselves mistaken data, and provide incorrect information to their business consumers.

*Components:* N/A.

**valid time**

*Description:* the computer science term "valid time" may be treated as co-extensive with our term "effective time".

*Comments:*
- "The valid time of a fact is the time when the fact is true in the modeled reality. A fact may have associated any number of events and intervals, with single events and intervals being important special cases." From [Jensen, 1992].

**version**

*Mechanics:* a row in an asserted version table which makes a statement about what the object it represents is like during a specified effective time period.

*Semantics:* a row in a table which represents the state of an object during a specified period of time.

*Comments:*
- Every row in an asserted version table is either a past, present or future version representing an object.

*Components:* asserted version table, effective time period, object, represent, statement.

**version begin date**

*Description:* the date on which a row in a best practices version table begins.

*Comments:*
- This expression does *not* apply to a row in an asserted version table. A row in an asserted version table is a version, and the begin date associated with that row, as a version, is its effective begin date. The version begin date of a row in any other kind of version table might represent either the physical date on which the row was created, or a logical date on which the version becomes effective.

**version end date**

*Description:* the date on which a row in a best practices version table ends.

*Comments:*
- This expression does *not* apply to a row in an asserted version table. A row in an asserted version table is a version, and the end date associated with that row, as a version, is its effective end date. The version end date of a row in any other kind of version table might represent either the physical date on which a delete transaction was applied to the row, or a logical date on which the version ceased to be in effect.

**version split**

*Mechanics:* a process in which the representation of an object is removed from one or more effective-time clock ticks that [fill] the effective time period of a version.

*Semantics:* a process in which one version is withdrawn, and replaced by two versions.

*Comments:*
- When a version is split, the earlier half becomes a new version which is located [before] the latter half. Because the two versions are not contiguous, the result of splitting a version is always to split an episode. See also: *temporal extent state transformation {split}.*

- Although a version split always results in an episode split, an episode may be split without splitting any of its versions.

*Components:* clock tick, effective time, Allen relationship [fill], object, represent, version, withdraw.

**version table**

*Mechanics:* a uni-temporal table whose explicitly represented time is effective time.

*Semantics:* a uni-temporal table each of whose rows is a current assertion about what its object was, is or will be like during the specified period of effective time.

*Comments:*

- To be semantically valid, a uni-temporal version table *must* correct errors in data by overwriting those errors. Frequently, businesses have uni-temporal tables which they think are version tables, but in which every update results in a new row in the table. But this means that the begin, or begin and end dates, of those rows are not true version dates. They are just dates of physical database activity. If the update reflects a change in the object being represented, then the version date or dates have the semantics of effective dates. But if the update reflects a correction to bad data, then the version date or dates have the semantics of assertion dates. By mixing both kinds of updates, the semantics are destroyed, and we don't know what any row in the table is really telling us.
- An asserted version table is one kind of version table. IT best practices have given rise to many other kinds of version tables, which we grouped into four main types in Chapter 4. What the standard temporal model calls a *valid-time table* is another kind of version table.

*Components:* effective time, object, uni-temporal.

**version(ed) data**

*Description:* data that describes what its object is like during a stated period of time.

*Comments:*

- What kind of period of time is involved depends on the kind of version table. In many best practice implementations of versioned tables, unfortunately, effective time and assertion time are not distinguished. An update that reflects a change to the object represented in the table results in a new version, but an update that reflects a correction to erroneous data also results in a new version. And in both cases, the version begin date is simply the date the new row was physically created. Nearly all best practice support for versioned data is semantically incomplete. But when effective time changes are not clearly distinguished from error correction changes, those implementations are semantically *flawed*, and the data thus supported is semantically ambiguous.

**withdraw**

*Mechanics:* to set the assertion end date of a row in an asserted version table to Now().

*Semantics:* to move an asserted version row into past assertion time.

*Comments:*

- See also: *replace, supercede.*
- See also: *lock.*
- Non-deferred update and delete transactions set the end date of versions they will then replace and/or supercede to Now() which, upon the

conclusion of the temporal transaction, immediately becomes a past date. This is a "clearing the decks" transformation which removes the representation of the object affected by the transaction from current assertion time.

- A temporal transaction cannot set a row's assertion end date to a past date because, if it did, it would create a contradiction. During the time period from that past date to the time the transaction took place, the database asserted that row. But after Now(), the record of that assertion is erased from the database. Just as we cannot retroactively begin an assertion, we cannot retroactively end one, either. This is another manifestation of the temporalized extension of the Closed World Assumption.

- If a temporal transaction sets a row's assertion end date to a future date, it locks that row, making it a closed version. Only deferred transactions can set a row's assertion end date to a future date.

- Thus, no temporal transaction can set a row's assertion end date to a past date. Deferred transactions set that date to a future date. Non-deferred transactions set that date to Now(), and then as soon as the transaction is complete, that row is in past assertion time.

*Components:* 9999, assertion end date, asserted version table, past assertion time.

# INDEX

Note: Page numbers followed by *f* indicate figures.

Printed and bound by CPI Group (UK) Ltd, Croydon, CR0 4YY

03/10/2024

01040317-0005